MEDIATION AND LOVE

BRILL'S STUDIES IN INTELLECTUAL HISTORY

VOLUME 93

TUTA SUB AEGIDE PALLAS · 1683 ·

MEDIATION AND LOVE

A Study of the Medieval Go-Between in Key Romance and Near-Eastern Texts

BY

LEYLA ROUHI

BRILL
LEIDEN · BOSTON · KÖLN
1999

This book is printed on acid-free paper.

Library of Congress Cataloging-in-Publication Data

Rouhi, Leyla.
Mediation and love : a study of the medieval go-between in key Romance and Near Eastern texts / by Leyla Rouhi.
p. cm. — (Brill's studies in intellectual history, ISSN 0920-8607 ; v. 93)
Includes bibliographical references (p.) and index.
ISBN 9004112685 (cloth : alk. paper)
1. Literature, Medieval—History and criticism. 2. Go-betweens in literature. 3. Seduction in literature. 4. Love in literature.
I. Title. II. Series.
PN682.G64R68 1999
809'.933538—dc21 98–53963
CIP

Die Deutsche Bibliothek - CIP-Einheitsaufnahme

Rouhi, Leyla:
Mediation and love : a study of the medieval go between in key romance and Near Eastern texts / by Leyla Rouhi. – Leiden ; Boston ; Köln : Brill, 1999
(Brill's studies in intellectual history ; Vol. 93)
ISBN 90–04–11268–5

ISSN 0920-8607
ISBN 90 04 11268 5

PRINTED IN THE NETHERLANDS

TABLE OF CONTENTS

ACKNOWLEDGMENTS

The present study has benefited from the instructive and indispensable attention of Francisco Márquez Villanueva from the very moment in which it began. From him I have learned invaluable lessons on the *adab* of teaching and learning, and I shall never be able to express adequately my gratitude for his generosity, interest, and guidance at every stage of this project.

I owe very special thanks to Professor Jan Ziolkowski for his attentive and knowledgeable reading, and for his much-needed advice and direction.

Many thanks go to Mr. Theo Joppe and Mr. Job Lisman, and Ms. Gera van Bedaf at Brill for their valuable help.

Throughout the development of this project I have had the privilege of receiving the support and kindness of numerous friends and colleagues. I should like to thank in particular Gene Bell-Villada, Antonio Giménez, and Jorge Pedraza at Williams College, for taking an interest in my work and encouraging me with sound advice. I thank, from the bottom of my heart, Laura McKeon at Williams College for her continual support.

To Bettina Brandt, Virginie Guiraudon, Johanna Liander (Harvard University), Benjamin Liu (University of Connecticut at Storrs), Irene Mizrahi (Boston College), Rahim Shayegan (Harvard University), Joseph Snow (University of Michigan), Hossein Ziai (UCLA), I am grateful for the inestimable help that they have offered me time and again. I thank Mariam Wozniak, Afarin Assadian, and Mariame Clément for their loving encouragement.

The World Fellowship at Williams College and a grant from the Oakley Center for the Humanities and Social Sciences at Williams College, as well as Division One research funds at Williams, enabled me to carry out the last stages of research for this book. My gratitude also to the Dean of the Faculty's Office at Williams for their generous help. I would like to express my thanks also to the Fellows at the Departamento de Estudios Árabes at the Consejo Superior de Investigaciones Científicas in Madrid, for generously offering me space and facilities that contributed to the completion of the final stages of this project.

Finally, I dedicate this book to the following, whom I have had the privilege to count as my friends and family and without whom I would have little – if any – direction in my intellectual pursuits. To Francisco Márquez Villanueva, teacher and friend; to Julie Cassiday for her love as well as her ability to clarify many enigmas of my inquiry with her typical clarity and insight; to Michael Cooperson for teaching me a new language and enlightening me with some of his countless astute observations on medieval and modern life; to Mani Haghighi for sharing with me the difference between Anxiety and anxiety as well as between Fashandak and Manhattan; to Gail Newman for infusing every single conversation with an exemplary blend of intelligence and humanity; and to Amir-Hossein, Safieh, Safi-Ali and Hossein-Ali Rouhi, for everything.

INTRODUCTION

The Medieval Go-Between: A Problem for Comparative Literature

The topic of illicit carnal love in urban society provides an inspiration behind countless literary works in the Middle Ages, and very often implicates in addition to the lovers a third character involved in the amorous relationship at some or all stages of the evolution of the love affair. The nature and functions of this figure undergo notable changes according to each text and genre. She or he is designated in texts as go-between, third party, intermediary, bawd, procuress, confidante, friend, family member, servant, or messenger, each label implying a different shade of meaning and helping to construct a discourse of mediation for the text. The present study employs the most comprehensive designations for the figure ('third party,' 'intermediary,' 'mediator,' and 'go-between,') in the discussion of the character, while other terms are used and evaluated according to the particulars of each text considered.

The third party in Latin, Romance, and Near-Eastern literatures possesses a number of core features which help her or his initial identification in every work as a figure privy to a nonmarital and illicit sexual relationship. This character's interference in the affair can help or hinder the relationship, depending on the direction of the plotline. Frequently represented as female, the character often has a professional or personal reason to aid or impede the progress of a love affair. She might appear, for example, as an old woman operating strictly within the realm of prostitution, or as a young maidservant motivated by loyalty or duty. Certain texts emphasize her access to the occult while others stress her clever manipulation of language. In some cases she inspires the profound wrath and disdain of one of the lovers, and in others she is hailed as the savior of both. In a few instances the role is fulfilled by a man, warranting a close look at the ways in which gender differences determine the portrayal of the go-between. In all cases the character engages in mediation, or at least a performance of that act, and advances the dynamics of illicit love into the realm of three players instead of two. The variations are diverse and numerous, shaping in significant ways the notion of mediation in each text.

The present study considers the role of the go-between in a wide range of medieval literary traditions to assess the nature and function of mediation in the portrayal of illicit love, both within the individual works and in terms of intertextual links. Such a consideration is motivated by a twofold aim: to offer a dynamic comparative typology of the figure and to signal the numerous meanings of mediation in medieval texts. The comparative approach is required by the recurrence of the third party in a broad range of texts and genres: the continual reappearance of the figure in so many guises and with such varying degrees of influence warrants its analysis within a comparative framework that would throw light on differences in the treatment of mediation by each genre.

This approach does not imply an arbitrary nor a fully comprehensive selection of works. In each cluster of texts considered in the chapters that follow, works have been chosen on the basis of the significant treatment of the go-between as well as conceivable intertextual links. Key texts from Antiquity, Old French, medieval Spanish as well as English and Italian form the core of investigation alongside pertinent texts from the literature of the Islamic empire between the ninth and the fifteenth centuries. Each selected work presents a conception of the go-between that at once engages intertextuality and the text's own thought-provoking approach to mediation in illicit love. The present study is therefore neither a catalog of all texts in which go-betweens have appeared nor a survey of every third party in every medieval text. Rather, it turns to works whose representation of the topic involves significant poetic choices and figures, and that show some type of intertextual dialogue with other genres and texts. It is important to note that the third party's lack of impact, especially in cases where great power is attributed to her by the narrative only to prove tenuous upon close readings, is also addressed in detail by this work. That is to say, the failure of an assigned mediator to carry out her or his task impinges upon the language and poetics of profane love in a given text, and this failure must be taken into consideration as a necessary parameter for the study of mediation.

The old woman is one of the most common manifestations of third-party activity in medieval texts dealing with illicit love, and this fact calls for special focus on her characterization. A substantial number of the texts studied here make use of the old woman as go-between, and at first sight it might appear that all the old women acting as intermediaries possess identical features and therefore fulfill identical tasks. Many show a predilection for chatter and wine, make no secret of their financial greed, boast familiarity with male and female sexual behavior, assume the guise of another profession (such as seamstress or midwife) to gain access to unsuspecting parties, and hint at their knowledge of the occult. These features appear to constitute the principal attributes of the procuress in numerous Latin, French, Italian, Spanish – as well as Arabic and Persian – texts that mention her either in passing or as a character of some consequence. Based on these shared features, several critics have conceived of a general intermediary type with essentially similar functions.

According to the perspective of such critics the medieval Spanish *alcahueta* (go-between) is no different from the character often hailed as her predecessor, the Latin *lena* (old bawd), nor from her counterparts in the French *fabliaux* or Italian prose narrative, to name but a few genres in which she appears. Thus Bonilla y San Martín considers the Spanish Celestina – the famous bawd of Fernando de Rojas' eponymous play – a descendant of the Latin type,[1] while Puyol y Alonso cites bawds from Ovid's *Amores* and the *Ars amatoria* in addition to the twelfth-century Latin comedy *Pamphilus de amore* and the later *Roman de la Rose* as embryonic versions of creations that reach their full vigor in later Spanish works.[2] Similarly, Castro Guisasola relates the Iberian bawd to classical paradigms,[3] and Joseph de Morawski in his introduction to *Pamphile et Galatée* offers several descriptive categories of "vieille" and perceives a direct link between late medieval bawds and the elegiac model provided by the *Pamphilus de amore*.[4] According to such a perspective, all procuresses represent a direct and essentially unchanged bond with "servants and old ladies

[1] Adolfo Bonilla y San Martín, "Antecedentes del tipo celestinesco en la literatura latina," *Revue Hispanique* 15 (1906) 372-386.

[2] Julio Puyol y Alonso, *El Arcipreste de Hita* (Madrid: Sucesora de M. Minuesa de los Ríos, 1906) 281-286.

[3] F. Castro Guisasola, *Observaciones sobre las fuentes literarias de* La Celestina (Madrid: Instituto de Miguel de Cervantes, 1973).

[4] Joseph de Morawski, *Pamphile et Galatée par Jehan Bras-de-Fer de Dammartin-en-Goële, poème français inédit du XIVe siècle* (Paris: Champion, 1915). Under the headings "L'imitation espagnole de Jean Ruiz" and "La Celestina," Morawski concludes that both Trotaconventos and Celestina represent a logical development of the character of the old bawd in *Pamphilus*. See in particular 51-56 and 90-155 in "La Vieille," where the procuress/bawd of medieval – in particular French – literature is categorized according to her profession and according to the means she uses to carry out the task of *entremetteuse*.

[who] act as go-betweens and bawds" in medieval Latin comedy.[5] For his part Francisco Rico links the thirteenth-century pseudo-Ovidian *De Vetula* to Juan Ruiz's fourteenth-century *Libro de buen amor*, one of the connecting elements being the old bawd in the former who, in Rico's view, fulfills the function of intermediary and shows direct intertextual links with Juan Ruiz's bawd, named Trotaconventos.[6] The scholar William Matthews views the medieval bawd as an essentially non-changing, universal figure from Antiquity to Chaucer; beginning with a *lena* (an old bawd) in Ovid's *Amores*, Matthews goes on to *De Vetula* and the *Pamphilus*, mentions the old nurse/confidante Thessala in Chrétien's *Cligès*, the meddlesome old women in the *fabliaux*, the allegorical "Vieille" of the *Roman de la Rose*, Trotaconventos and Celestina, all as direct inspirations in the creation of Chaucer's Wife of Bath. He therefore perceives a single medieval "literary tradition of the randy old woman."[7] More recently Tomás González Rolán lists a number of bawds from Latin comedy and elegiac poetry of Antiquity, pointing out that these – due to the traits of old age, affinity for chatter, and financial greed – represent prototypes for the medieval Spanish *alcahueta*.[8] Charles Platter, in an otherwise highly useful study of George Buchanan's *Apologia pro Lena*, prefaces his remarks with a series of generalizations on the power of the Latin bawd over the lovers which, as we will show in the next chapter, are quite prone to reconsideration and critique.[9]

As descriptive surveys, general categorizations of the go-between in terms of visible characteristics highlight many useful sources of study for the comparatist. However, two significant critical shortcomings mar a panoramic process of cataloguing in which all bawds are considered to fulfill essentially the same tasks. The first concerns a

[5] Marc Wolterbeek, *Comic Tales of the Middle Ages, an Anthology and Commentary*, Contributions to the Study of World Literature, Number 39, (Connecticut: Greenwood Press, 1991) 107.

[6] Francisco Rico, "Sobre el origen de la autobiografía en el *Libro de buen amor*," *Anuario de estudios medievales* 4 (1967) 301-325.

[7] William Matthews, "The Wife of Bath and All of her Sect," *Viator* 5 (1974) 413-443.

[8] Tomás González Rolán, "Rasgos de la alcahuetería amorosa en la literatura latina," in *La Celestina y su contorno social: Actas del I Congreso Internacional sobre* La Celestina, dirección Manuel Criado de Val (Barcelona: Borras, 1977) 276-289.

[9] Charles Platter, "The Artificial Whore: George Buchanan's *Apologia pro Lena*," in *Sex and Gender in Medieval and Renaissance Texts: The Latin Tradition*, edited by Barbara K. Gold, Paul Allen Miller, and Charles Platter (Albany: State University of New York, 1997) 207-222.

reluctance to interpret the very notion of mediation in and of itself, and a consideration of what third-party activity might mean in the language of seduction and profane love; the evaluation of mediation requires the study of the old woman's views of seduction, the actual impact of her deeds on the love affair, and the nature of her dialogic relation with other characters. In the catalogues of medieval or Classical bawds these considerations are subordinated to the enumeration of features such as age, wine-drinking, or assumed guise. The second shortcoming in a descriptive survey consists of the risk of a reductive and simple interpretation of the mechanisms of intertextual rapport. Given, for example, that all old women acting as third parties chatter a great deal, seem aware of sexual matters, and show a willingness to participate in the development of a clandestine relationship, the critics mentioned above appear convinced that the medieval manifestations of the figure hark back directly to the Classical model of the Latin bawd, often called *anus* and *lena*, and that even the more complex representations of the type are logical replicas of earlier medieval and Classical prototypes.[10] This assertion has been and continues to be made in spite of the marked differences between so-called origin and copy. For example, Juan Ruiz's bawd Trotaconventos and her elegiac predecessor, the bawd in *Pamphilus*, differ in remarkable ways and this has not escaped the notice of critics. Yet for the most part critics continue to perceive the two figures as linked in fundamental ways.[11]

---

[10] For example, drawing on previous research by Morawski, as well as the work of Theodore Lee Neff, *La satire des femmes dans la poésie lyrique française au moyen âge* (Paris: Giard et Brière, 1900) and Blanche H. Dow, *The Varying Attitudes towards Women in French Literature of the Fifteeenth Century* (New York: Publications of the Institute of French Studies, 1936) in addition to his own readings of medieval texts, Matthews views "La Celestina, Regnard's Macette, (...) Juliet's nurse (...), Trotaconventos, La Vieille, Auberée, La Belle Heaulmière" all as representing the "traditional" and "amusing" old woman whose "individuality" is apparent in the case of the livelier specimens but does not represent any substantial differences for each case (443).

[11] The differences between that model and Trotaconventos are also signaled by Félix Lecoy, *Recherches sur* El libro de buen amor (Paris: Droz, 1938) (henceforth *Recherches*) chapter XIV. In addition, Menéndez y Pelayo notes the discrepancies in *Orígenes de la novela* (Santander: Ardus, 1943) vol 3, 304-311; also, Gail Phillips, *The Imagery of* El libro de buen amor (Madison: Hispanic Seminary of Medieval Studies, 1983) shows that the supposed similarities of Trotaconventos and the bawd in *Pamphilus* do not always hold. Yet, most recently, the significant reliance of Juan Ruiz on *Pamphilus* as a source is assumed by Richard Burkard in "Courtly Love and Hideous Love: Gentility Followed by Rape in *El libro de buen amor*," *The Journal of the Association for the Interdisciplinary Study of the Arts*, 1996 (1:2) 21-31. The conviction that the Arch-

An inspiring and cautionary remark regarding the risks of such panoramic views comes in Américo Castro's *España en su historia* where he posits that the Islamic tradition constitutes a meaningful intertextual link with the figure in Spanish literature, and that Latin *lenae* may not be an inspiration for the *alcahueta* (Spanish bawd) no matter what the visible evidence suggests.[12] More recently, in the study *Orígenes y sociología del tema celestinesco* by Francisco Márquez Villanueva, the problem of the Peninsular *alcahueta* finally receives a much-needed inquiry into the question of literary traditions from non-Western sources.[13] Such strategies of inquiry are much more useful than cataloguing and assuming that all old bawds are basically similar. Close attention needs to be given to the subtle shifts that occur as traditions and texts continue to interact. This is not to say that the Western-European, Latin, and Spanish bawds have nothing at all to do with one another; quite on the contrary, it alerts the reader to the fact that the characterization of the bawd in these literatures does indeed involve strong intertextual links, but that such links are dynamic and are brought forth somewhat differently in each case, compelling the reader to ask questions on the very meaning of intermediary activity for each work.

An investigation of intertextual factors, questions of poetics, and the currents that inform intermediary activity in each text are in order for third-party activity in all Romance and Near-Eastern texts. The investigation of Near-Eastern sources is an increasingly significant task for comparative medievalists working with Romance languages in particular. For a character as recurrent as the go-between, across so many traditions with conceivable links to one another, the

---

priest's work is firmly rooted in the Western tradition, and a famous episode of his book on the *Pamphilus*, also governs the argument made by Richard Kinkade, "A Thirteenth-century precursor of *El libro de buen amor:* The *Art d'Amors,*" *La Corónica* 1996 (24:2) 123-39. While Juan Ruiz clearly commands Ovidian and Western sources, the non-Christian elements of his work are as important as the Christian ones, a fact to which few scholars lend adequate attention. We will turn to this point in Chapter 4.

[12] Américo Castro, *España en su historia: cristianos, moros y judíos* (Barcelona: Editorial Crítica, 1983) 434-445.

[13] Francisco Márquez Villanueva, *Orígenes y sociología del tema celestinesco* (Barcelona: Antropos, 1993) (henceforth *Orígenes y sociología*). See also Francisco Márquez Villanueva, "Para el encuadre del tema celestinesco: el tratado de alcahuetería de Nafzāwī," in *Proyección histórica de España en sus tres culturas: Castilla y León, América y el Mediterráneo* II, Eufemio Lorenzo Sanz (Coordinador), (Junta de Castilla y León: Consejería de Cultura y Turismo, 1993) 445-459.

consideration of intertextual dynamics must lead to scrutiny of the issue of mediation in illicit love in a wide variety of related texts, and the ways in which discourse affects (and is affected by) the triangular formation of lovers and go-between. In the texts studied below, parameters have been expanded to include a range of currents from Western and non-Western sources that inform the conception of third-party activity, with special attention to each author's different treatment of the poetics of mediation as well as the areas that he chooses simply to replicate. That is to say, the point of departure has not been the staunch conviction that all intermediaries are different or similar: rather, it has consisted of inquiry into the reasons for which a recurrent and seemingly predictable motif continues to emerge across the ages and genres in various forms.

The focus of this study consists of Romance and Near-Eastern texts as the title indicates; however, the rigorous consideration of intertextuality for Romance texts would be impossible without the study of important Classical works, hence the content of chapter 1, which examines the Latin heritage of medieval Romance texts. The Classical works considered there include texts by Plautus, the elegiac poets, Ovid, and Apuleius, followed in chapter 2 by the medieval European works that engage these sources dynamically: Chrétien de Troyes, Boccaccio, Chaucer, as well as medieval Latin comedy and texts in the spirit of courtly and non-courtly love. Outside Romance languages, Chaucer receives attention in chapter 2 due to his significant engagement of Romance and Ovidian traits, an engagement that in turn derives material from and throws light on French and Italian treatments of intermediary activity.

The imaginative literature of the medieval Near East, in Persian and Arabic, provides ample opportunity for the study of the figure and for the creation of an indispensable point of reference for the typology of medieval European cases. Chapter 3 includes the study of selected Persian and Arabic works from the ninth to the fifteenth centuries, each of which is chosen for the special contribution that it makes to the representation of the figure. As with Western texts, the portion of this study dealing with Near-Eastern material does not center upon a fully comprehensive categorization of all go-betweens in Arabic and Persian literature. With the awareness that many sources remain to be considered, focus is placed on the representation of intermediary activity in a number of texts that create in the form of tales and anecdotes a discourse of mediation in the world of illicit love. Intermediary activity appears for the most part in anecdotes from erotological treatises and love-tales from popular and courtly literature; the choice of specific texts from these bodies has been based upon each work's approach to mediation as affecting discourse, as well the work's conception of the poetics of illicit love. The literature of the medieval Islamic world abounds in love tales in which an *ʿajūz* – old woman – facilitates communication between two secret lovers. She appears either in a professional capacity, for example as a visible member of the community known for her skill in organizing secret meetings, or as a resident of a harem or court, involved specifically with the affairs of one person. Special attention has been paid to portrayal of the *ʿajūz* whose characterization offers the reader a fertile premise for the study of third-party discourse and activity.

Continuing with the critique of mediation and its actors, analysis is made in the last chapter of the literary manifestation of the third party in medieval Spanish literature. The *alcahueta* intervenes in the love affairs of others in numerous medieval Spanish texts. She appears in strikingly diverse genres throughout the Spanish Middle Ages with different degrees of impact. In the two works already mentioned – the fourteenth-century *Libro de buen amor,* by Juan Ruiz (the Archpriest of Hita), and *La Celestina,* by Fernando de Rojas, published in 1499 – the figure becomes a full-fledged literary character while making use of many intertextual currents from Romance and Near-Eastern literature. Her status as such warrants her inclusion as a highly important frame of reference for the literary history and typology of the medieval go-between, for she involves a remarkable variety of traditions in her makeup and brings forth a dynamic representation of medieval intertextuality and cross-cultural impact.

The chapters which follow take into account not just obvious bawds and old women, but also the mothers, friends, servants, relatives, and acquaintances whose relationships with the lovers translate into intermediary activity. In those cases where professional go-betweens such as bawds or panderers take on the task of intervening in the love affair, more often than not the texts considered here appear to infuse the figure's identity with visible moral judgment hailing from the narrator as well as an extra-textual presupposition on the evils of prostitution. The professional go-between in medieval literature has a known counterpart in medieval society, and this societal analogue has almost always inspired contempt from legal and ethical standpoints because of her or his links with the brothel. Much of medieval literature also posits a morally driven conception of the go-between by relying on the 'realities' available to readers on the figure's counterpart outside the literary text. By extension, and as we shall see, even those who fulfill the task of go-between without professional or mercenary motivations can potentially come under moral attack.

An inherent idea thus exists in the Middle Ages that third-party interference contains by nature a strong negative connotation. Of great relevance to our work here is the relentless presence of value judgments, presuppositions, and attributed evils found frequently in any portrayal of third-party activity in relation to nonmarital love. The presupposed and almost automatic disdain often attached to the figure obfuscates to some extent the nature of each text's poetics of mediation as well as the representation of the interdependent triangle formed by the three characters. One of the tasks of the following chapters is to analyze the relationship between extra-literary presuppositions and textual strategies for the portrayal of intermediary activity in a comparative light. As Claudio Guillén argues:

> Comparativism is not limited to an immanent criticism of literature. The categories that we have glossed here, such as genres, formalizations, thematizations, translations, all presuppose some classes of past and future historical activity. This activity occupies the space of an aesthetic distance – no longer between reader and work, but between work and society(...)[14]

Georges Duby demonstrates the necessity for this type of contextualization by explaining the link between the history of feudalism and the works of fiction associated with it in terms that are applicable to the literary history of the go-between also:

> To be listened to, these works must obviously have had some link with that which concerned those for whom they were produced, in real life(...). This gives the historian the right to consider the content of these [literary] works against that which he can come to know through

[14] Claudio Guillén, *The Challenge of Comparative Literature*, translated by Cola Franzen (Cambridge: Harvard University Press, 1993) 318. The recourse to certain basic historical relations with the texts is partially prompted by his notion that "[o]nce we identify a genre, form, or theme that seems to be a supranational diachronic structure, we must of necessity investigate those options, relations, semantic and formal spaces that encompass or link different periods or places (...)" (323).

> other accounts of the structures and the development of Feudal society. [15]

The study of extra-literary sources (namely anthropological, social and historical factors related to a literary phenomenon) must of course be carried out with the realization that "such interweavings and superpositions are complex and cannot be simplified."[16] With regards to the go-between, evidently the most useful data comes to us from sources dealing with patterns of sexual behavior in urban society: prostitution, courtship rituals, and evidence of subversive amorous contact between the sexes. Taking into account society's preconceived (if sometimes latent) attitudes towards sexual behavior will help identify some of the factors which have gone into the shaping of go-between activity in literature. The study of mediation in literature requires an awareness of how each environment outlines the boundaries which define illicit sexual activity, where tolerance appears low and where it indicates great flexibility towards illicit behavior, and to whom or what do legal and moral authorities attribute the principal agency for such behavior.[17] Also, knowledge of each society's legal and ethical concepts of illicit sexuality offers clues to the tensions and conflicts inherent in the moral standpoint of a given community regarding specific types of behavior such as premarital intimacy, adultery, or recourse to prostitution.

Another constituent that greatly affects the function of the third party is her or his involvement with the task of seduction in each text. After all, even on the most basic level of the plotline, the effort to set up the right context for an illicit love affair requires that the go-between first prove a degree of skill with a seductive language or posture. Interestingly, the basic dictionary definition of the term "to

---

[15] "Pour être écoutées, il fallait bien que ces oeuvres fussent de quelque manière en rapport avec ce qui préoccupait les gens pour qui elles étaient produites, avec leurs situations réelles. (...) Ceci autorise l'historien à confronter le contenu de ces ouvrages [littéraires] à ce qu'il peut connaître par d'autres témoignages des structures et de l'évolution de la société féodale" (Georges Duby, *Mâle Moyen Age, de l'amour et autres essais* [Paris: Flammarion, 1988] 74). (My translation. NB: hereafter, all translations into English are mine unless otherwise noted).

[16] Guillén, *The Challenge of Comparative Literature*, 288.

[17] These parameters are often recorded as anthropological and legal information in both medieval Islamic and Western European societies. Several studies have facilitated access to such information in this study, the references to which will be given in the proceeding chapters.

seduce" implies an inextricable link with deceit: "lead astray (...) persuade (person) into abandonment of principles, esp. chastity and allegiance; persuade by temptingness or attractiveness."[18] Jean Baudrillard states: "Seduction has nothing to do with a natural order, but rather with the order of artifice – never with the order of energy, but with that of sign and ritual."[19] Baudrillard demonstrates that the power to seduce connotes a turning away from the expected and understandable order of things in favor of a venture into a dark world of artificial structures designed to entrap the victim of seduction. A basic value judgment, apparently comfortable with clear notions of good and evil, underlies the very definition of seduction: "For all orthodox ways, seduction continues to be evil and artifice, a black magic that twists all truths, an invocation of signs, an exaltation of signs in their evil currency."[20] Femininity maintains a close, organic link with this notion of evil:

> That is where seduction and femininity blend, where they have always blended. Masculinity in all its forms has always been haunted by this sudden reversibility in that which is female. Seduction and femininity are as inevitable as the failure of sex, meaning, power. [21]

The significance of the intermediary's impact is closely intertwined with the extent of her or his involvement in this artificial, feminine order. That is to say, all those traditions and genres in which the figure exerts some sort of substantial impact underscore the character's involvement with the artifice of seduction, however this artifice may be realized. In the readings that follow attention is paid to the third party's access to a discourse of seduction and to the ways in which the figure's dialogic relationship with others is inscribed within a poetics of desire, artifice, and mediation.

As specified earlier, one axis of our comparative study involves

---

[18] *The Concise Oxford Dictionary of Current English*, s.v. "seduce."

[19] "Or la séduction n'est jamais de l'ordre de la nature, mais celui de l'artifice – jamais de l'ordre de l'énergie, mais de celui du signe et du rituel" (Jean Beaudrillard, *De la séduction* [Paris: Folio, 1979] 9).

[20] "Pour toutes les orthodoxies elle continue d'être le maléfice et l'artifice, une magie noire de détournement de toutes les vérités, une conjuration de signes, une exaltation des signes dans leur usage maléfique" (Baudrillard, *De la séduction*, 10).

[21] "C'est là où séduction et féminité se confondent, se sont toujours confondues. Toute masculinité a toujours été hantée par cette soudaine réversibilité dans le féminin. Séduction et féminité sont inéluctables comme le revers même du sexe, du sens, du pouvoir" (Baudrillard, *De la séduction*, 10-11).

Romance texts from the European Middle Ages and the various types of intermediary activity encountered therein. This requires a preliminary study of the Latin heritage that provided much of the inspiration for the medieval Western-European intermediaries portrayed as old women. The study of the Latin type will include a close look at her paradigmatic features and will lead to the investigation of any significant changes undergone by the subsequent medieval literary types. In the following chapter then, we will consider the intermediary in representative cases from the lyric, narrative poetry, and comedy of Antiquity, before embarking on the interpretation of works from medieval France, Italy, and England.

CHAPTER ONE

THE GO-BETWEEN IN CLASSICAL LATIN TEXTS

I. Carnal Love in Latin Literature: A Definition of Parameters

The topic of carnal love appears in many forms in elegiac poetry, comic drama, and prose narrative by Latin authors, reflecting Hellenistic themes as well as Roman attitudes to illicit love in urban society. The poets and writers under consideration here – Plautus, Propertius, Tibullus, Ovid, and Apuleius[1] – thematize love in varied ways, using comic, ironic or tragic tones, creating a poetic discourse on love which invites study from several angles.

The literary frameworks chosen by these writers involve certain *a priori* assumptions about the identity and social rank of the characters who play out specific roles in the progress of each love affair. That is to say, the themes of seduction and sexual desire follow a culturally determined order and develop in relation to points of reference whose understanding facilitates the appreciation of each role in the poetics of love. For instance, the character of the principal female love interest appears in elegiac poetry and Plautine comedy as either a courtesan or a woman inclined of her own volition to the pursuit of illicit love. This aspect of her identity, in turn, exerts a significant impact on the nature and function of the go-between – the *anus* (old woman) or *lena* (procuress, bawd) – who frequently interacts with her.

As is well-known, the elegiac poets direct their amorous attention

[1] The following editions have been used: *Plautus in Five Volumes*, (*Cistellaria* and *Curculio*, vol II; *Asinaria*, vol. I), edited by Paul Nixon (London: The Loeb Classical Library, 1928 and 1932); Titi Macci Plauti, *Mostellaria*, edited by Frank R. Merrill (London: Macmillan, 1972); Max Ponchont, *Tibulle et les auteurs du Corpus Tibulliamnum* (Paris: Les Belles-Lettres, 1924) (henceforth *Tibulle*); Propertius, *Elegies I-IV*, edited by W. A. Camps (Cambridge: Cambridge University Press, 1965); Ovid, *Heroides and Amores*, edited by E. H. Warmington (Cambridge: Harvard University Press, 1914); P. Ovidia Nasonis, *Ars amatoria*, edited by F. W. Lenz (Torino: Corpus Scriptorum Latinorum Paravianum, 1969); Ovid, *Metamorphoses (Vol. IV)*, edited by Frank Justus Miller (Cambridge: Harvard University Press, 1976); Apuleius, *Metamorphoses*, edited by J. Arthur Hanson (Cambridge: Harvard University Press, 1989). The works have been studied in chronological order of composition. Henceforth, references will be to the title of each work, except in the case of Apuleius' *Metamorphoses* in whose case the author's name is used.

for the most part to a specific mistress; thus Propertius suffers from the inconsistencies of Cynthia, Tibullus shares the pains and joys of love with Delia and Nemesis, and Ovid oscillates between celebration or complaint with Corinna. The internal evidence of the poems leaves little doubt as to the social status of these women, albeit in a subtle form; in the elegies of Propertius, for instance, the references to Cynthia's greed (II, 16: 1-2) and the frequent mention of her rivals (II, 8:8; II, 9:1-2; II, 24: 11-16; III, 8: 33-4, among others) have led critics to perceive them unequivocally as courtesans.[2] Another firm indication of this lifestyle derives from the references to her dress: Tibullus, for example, speaks on two occasions of a garment worn by Nemesis (II, 3:53 and II, 4:29) known for its exclusive connection to courtesans in his period.[3] Outside the elegiac genre, to his manual on seduction called *Ars amatoria* Ovid brings a number of hypothetical female characters who remain unnamed, but whose particular social identity is nonetheless clear. This amusing and lively work – which deals with the very topic of seduction using the format of a 'how to' manual – deals only with *hetairae*, staying well away from respectable or inexperienced women and girls. As Gordon Williams points out, Ovid's own introduction clarifies this matter right away: "Stay away, you head-bands, signs of pudor, and the long skirts which hide the feet: we celebrate secret love which is allowed, and in my song there will be no misdemeanor." [4]

The procuress's typological features maintain a direct relationship with the attributes of the female love interest, for it is according to the disposition of the love interest that the intermediary must develop strategies of communication. The Classical Latin *lenae* represent

[2] J. P. Sullivan, *Propertius: A Critical Introduction* (Cambridge: Cambridge University Press, 1976) 95.

[3] Saara Lilja, *The Roman Elegists' Attitude to Women* (New York: Garland, 1978) 38.

[4] "este procul, vittae tenues, insigne pudoris,/quaeque tegis medios instita longa pedes:/nos Venerem tutam concessaque furta canemus/inque meo nullum carmine crimen erit." *Ars amatoria*, vv. 31-34, cited in Gordon Williams, *Change and Decline: Roman Literature in the Early Empire* (Berkeley: University of California Press, 1978) 70. Williams cites the passage to show that Ovid is clearly warning off "slender head-dresses, the mark of chastity, and the long dress that stretches to the ankles," for he is only interested in singing of a love which is "permitted by law" and will thereby spare him the pain of accusation. The very spaces explored in Book I of Ovid's *Ars amatoria*, for instance – vv. 67-262 of Book I – temples, banquets, the games, the theater, among others, are known to have been frequented by people interested in nonmarital encounters. By distancing himself from married women, and emphasizing his interest in *hetairae*, Ovid defends himself against any allegations of immorality.

agents and advisors of more or less professional courtesans.[5] This aspect plays an important part in the determination of the significant typological features of the *lenae* and other third parties in Latin literature, since their mode of operation responds to the special attributes of a world inhabited by women who need no initiation or guidance for entry into the realm of carnal love.[6] A clear picture of this context emerges both from the social backdrop to the texts and the evidence of the works themselves.

Naturally, these mistresses represent literary creations and not exact replicas of real life.[7] Duncan F. Kennedy argues that an inherent limitation exists in the historical reading of elegy, for such a reading assumes the existence of hard facts such as "flesh-and-blood women" or "the past as it really was," all of which are ultimately "signifiers never identical with themselves."[8] Informed by the often

---

[5] *Orígenes y sociología del tema celestinesco*, 66. It must be noted that the mistress of the *Amores* is not exactly far from the world of prostitution herself.

[6] Gordon Williams, in "Some Aspects of Roman Marriage Ceremonies and Ideals," *Journal of Roman Studies* 48 (1958) 16-30 (henceforth "Some Aspects") shows the prevalence of the idea of incompatibility of marriage with true love as "typical of the misogynistic attitude of comedy. The other genre of Roman poetry where this attitude is common is erotic elegy: there the married state is the antithesis and frustration of true love." 28. Also in *Games of Venus: An Anthology of Greek and Roman Erotic Verse from Sappho to Ovid*, introduced, translated, and annotated by Peter Bing and Rip Cohen (New York: Routledge, 1991) the pursuit of women with citizenship status is underlined as an unpopular activity in the Classical period, a fact borne out in literary texts and society. The punishment for this form of adultery is known to have been severe, and segregation a definite obstacle, so that "men were not encouraged to feel sexual desire for women of citizen status" (2).

[7] The question of real experience and its role in Latin poetry is naturally open to debate; useful perspectives are offered by A. W. Allen, "Sincerity and the Roman Elegists," *Classical Philology* 45 (1950) 145-160, and Sullivan, chapter 4. Responding to the earlier trend of recognizing in elegy a revelation of real life, Allen argues convincingly that in Latin elegy sincerity is ultimately a function of style, and one need not concern oneself with whether or not the poet actually lived through the events he describes. For his part Sullivan points out that "We no longer apply a *simpliste* criterion of 'sincerity,' that of correspondence with fact[,]" but rather that we must, in our appreciation of the experiences recounted in the elegy, observe the "relation between technique and style." 107-108. Also, Robert Maltby, in *Latin Love Elegy* (Bristol: Bristol Classical Press, 1980), notes: "Despite the impression given by Propertius and Ovid that their books trace the development of an affair from initial enchantment to final disillusionment, there is no attempt by any of the elegists to chronicle (...) the actual progress of a real love affair" (9). The important step to be taken, then, concerns understanding the beloved's identity as constructed by the text and in light of relevant information on the status of such women in the surrounding conditions of the work.

[8] Duncan F. Kennedy, *The Arts of Love: Five Studies in the Discourse of Roman Love Elegy* (Cambridge: Cambridge University Press, 1993) 7.

legitimate doubts and challenges of deconstruction, arguments such as Kennedy's against a hard fact-seeking historical reading raise important and relevant issues. Kennedy is right in pointing out that a reader who looks for a specific historical woman in elegy invariably "occludes the textuality of that which [he] posits as [his] object."[9] However, some caution must be exercised when voicing one's skepticism of historical readings. To take the caveat that historical readings are risky to its logical extreme would undermine the relevance of those factors which, in a given type of inquiry, do play a substantial part in guiding interpretation.

The assertion that the mistress of elegy corresponds to a social courtesan is not intended here as a straightforward parallelism that would solve all problems of representation, nor does it seek to solve the problem of the *lena*'s representation by looking for the real identities of Cynthia or Delia, thereby reading the go-between as a replica of her social counterpart also. Rather, the reference to the social status of the mistress is concerned profoundly with the issues of textual discourse and poetics: that the mistress of elegy corresponds to the figure of the courtesan is a fact which helps direct our interpretation of the nature of her interaction with her go-between, given that being a courtesan impinges directly on the way a character handles sexuality and seduction. This parameter must be specified to ensure a plausible reading of the poetics of carnal love and intermediary activity in the texts, otherwise, one risks missing an important frame of reference for the interpretation of mediation in Classical texts. Were the reader unaware of the relevant parameters of a courtesan's existence – even at the level of literary representation, obviously open to multiple tensions and conflicts – he or she might attribute meanings to the go-between's role which, in light of the mistress's textual projection as a courtesan, would find themselves entirely redundant or inapplicable. Corinna, Cynthia, and Delia each interact with a *lena* who inspires the wrath of the poet, since he places the blame for their indifference on the old woman's bad influence, among other factors. This triangular configuration, expressed entirely by the poet, centers above all upon a perception of the go-between and the courtesan whose social contours direct poetics to a certain extent. The location of the mistress in terms of her social context is

[9] Kennedy, *The Arts of Love*, 87.

needed for some basic orientation regarding the type of discourse that she would logically hold with the *lena*. Such an identification would also clarify some of the limits which one might expect in such a relationship. Given especially that the *lena* is a minor character in Latin literature, the literal fact of her material relationship with the mistress is the most useful point of departure for her discourse analysis.

The frequent references in elegy to infidelity, the mistress's liberty to travel, the fear of rivals, and stress on the beloved's sophistication, leave no doubt that that the female love interests are "either freedwomen courtesans of the higher class, unmarried or living in *concubinatus*, or freeborn Roman matrons who had conformed to freedwomen's manner of living."[10] The world of 'virtuous' young women and their private homes rarely comes into contact with the realm of seduction and amorous adventure in the works of the poets discussed here. The poetics of love encountered in elegy and comedy revolves around the representation of women as sophisticated, initiated figures who do not require the seductive process used for an innocent or inexperienced party. The *meretrix*, actress, concubine, or freed slave who are the objects of desire in the genres considered here are "not bound by the constraints of citizenship."[11] In this setting, Romans pursuing amorous relationships came into contact with "the cultivated *meretrix* and the life of pleasure,"[12] while poetry and comedy continued to be generated "almost exclusively by men and reflect upper-class values."[13] These men choose to portray the elegiac mis-

[10] Lilja, *Roman Elegists' Attitudes to Women*, 41. See also Ponchont *Tibulle et les auteurs*, 9, who observes that the results of investigation into Delia's "real" identity can at best be arbitrary. The main point is that Delia emerges as a figure open to financial compensation in exchange for amorous attentions, in spite of the assertion in Book I of Tibullus' elegies that she has a husband; also, she is potentially interested in other men. For information on the status of courtesans, see Jasper Griffin, "Augustan Poetry and the Life of Luxury," *Journal of Roman Studies* 66 (1976) 87-104.

[11] *Games of Venus*, 4.

[12] Griffin, "Augustan Poetry and the Life of Luxury," 98.

[13] *Games of Venus*, 11. The prevalence of recourse to *hetairae* and *meretrices* in Roman society and its literary texts is borne out in numerous studies, for example *Women in the Ancient World: The Arethusa Papers*, edited by J. Peradotto and J. P. Sullivan (Albany: State Univeristy of New York Press, 1984), under the heading "The Role of Women in Roman Elegy," by J. P. Hallet, who views the aversion to marriage as an act of political protest: "the 'new, monied' aristocracy, the equestrian rank, opposed Augustus' marriage and moral legislation. We have, in addition, a far more eloquent and extensive protest against the sanctimonious moral assumptions and abusive social conventions of the late Republic and early Empire(...) I refer to Latin love

tress as a sophisticated, willful, and experienced woman of the *demi-monde* whose whims cause the poets to suffer on a regular basis. Such a perception plays a significant role in the portrayal of the mistress and her role in the love affair with the narrating poet.

One exception to the generally known courtesan status of the female character occurs in Apuleius' *Metamorphoses*. In the section of his tale where mention is made of a go-between, the author does not enter the world of courtesans and *hetairae* but rather takes the narrative into the household of a baker, showing how sexual intrigue occurs within the spatial limits of a married couple's hearth.[14] Nonetheless, the narrator undermines the respectability of the household by mentioning the debauched behavior of the wife who uses the service of a go-between. In other words, illicit love and seduction appear in conjunction with a wanton female: "Cruel and evil, lustful and drunk, single-minded and stubborn, extravagant in her thievery and stingy in her contemptible spending, enemy to loyalty and enemy to chastity."[15] This ethical judgment parallels the mistrust of, and fascination with, sexual experience and whimsicality attributed to the courtesan in elegy, and attributes a large portion of the agency for guilt, misbehavior, or unpredictability to the female whose only representation occurs from the point of view of the male poet, her identity, in the words of Duncan Kennedy, grounded in a male taxonomy.[16]

The elegiac mistress and the courtesans of Plautus clearly express the parameters of their love lives according to an established model which underscores – again, from the point of view of the males who portray them – the women's ample experience in matters related to sexual love, be it mercenary or not. This experience imposes certain limitations on the figure of the procuress, for the poets' and dramatists' perceptions of the mistress as such endow the latter with a sophisticated vocabulary on love, as well as a great talent for the construction of the artifice of seduction. Contrary to the claims of the poets, the role of the go-between is defined according to the power of the mistress.

---

elegy, a form of self-revelation and indirect social criticism created and developed by members of the dissident equestrian class" (246). T. P. Wiseman, in *Catullus and His World* (Cambridge: Cambridge University Press, 1985) also demonstrates that adulterous or illicit relationships were by and large pursued only with courtesans (10-14).

[14] Apuleius, Book IX.

[15] "saeva scaeva, virosa ebriosa, pervicax pertinax, in rapinis turpibus avara, in sumptibus foedis profusa, inimica fidei, hostis pudicitae" (Apuleius, 150).

[16] Kennedy, *The Arts of Love*, 75.

II. The Comedies of Plautus

(i) *The Social Background to Intermediary Activity*

Plautus situates a great number of his plays in brothels and the homes of courtesans, building comic momentum using the dilemmas of characters associated with these worlds. The old *lena* or *anus* attached to the principal courtesan is a fixture of such a lifestyle. Documented social versions of the counterpart of this figure do exist: in Ancient Greek and Roman societies, procuresses and panderers indulged in a highly institutionalized activity. Pimps and proxenets took specific charge of the managerial and financial aspects of prostitution, and supervised financial transactions with the clients, in addition to purchasing young orphans or abandoned children whom they trained for prostitution.[17]

Proxenetism, that is, pandering, concerned above all the acts of buying and selling.[18] The process began with the purchase or collection of an unwanted child, and then followed the course that would seem most profitable financially to the agent in charge. Thus in addition to running brothels that might vary greatly in price range, female pimps on occasion trained young women for high-class prostitution and prepared them for eventual marriage with wealthy older men.[19] Having often lived as prostitutes themselves at a younger age, the agents perpetuated a system that derived its staying power from mercenary sexuality. With regards to details such as dress and make-up, and techniques of luring and seduction, evidence suggests that prostitutes themselves played as active a role as any, creating many of the marketing strategies of their profession. That is, ultimately the main emphasis for proxenets fell on the financial aspect of the profession.[20]

In Rome, evidence points to the existence of a paradigm that since

---

[17] The nature and scope of the procuress's or pimp's activities are outlined by Catherine Salles, "Les prostituées de Rome," in *Amour et sexualité en Occident*, introduction de Georges Duby (Paris: Éditions du Seuil, 1991) 79-92.

[18] Violaine Vanoyeke, *La prostitution en Grèce et à Rome* (Paris: Les Belles Lettres, 1990). Vanoyeke's study shows that pimps were not involved in the cases of ritual prostitution in temples (linked to religious belief).

[19] Vanoyeke, *La prostitution*, 35.

[20] Vanoyeke, *La prostitution*, 33-41, where the specifics of bought and sold young girls are discussed, explaining the role of the brothel-owners and agents who took over their upbringing.

has become well known in many urban societies: on the one hand, the city housed low-life street prostitution with poverty-stricken girls living off overcrowded, popular areas, and on the other, a more luxurious courtesan lifestyle flourished, inspired and transmitted by the Greeks.[21] Governed by the maxim which also prevailed in Hellenic society, the Romans considered "prostitution a necessity, a key to the security of their wives. Romans support an institution which they believe to be one of the best guarantors of honor and family."[22] This would explain the abundance of the literature set in the world of prostitutes, for the institution and its stock characters evoked familiar elements for the reading public and were a familiar part of upper-class male life.

Proxenetism in Rome followed the Hellenic model closely, concerning itself systematically with preserving the profession and facilitating financial transactions. The tremendous preoccupation with money and the adherence to the boundaries of the world of prostitution constitute the trademarks of the Greco-Roman go-between and appear as such in the comedies of Plautus. Set against a Greek background, the Plautine *lena* remains forever concerned with financial questions. However, the similarity with her counterpart in society stops there: Plautus replicates the obsession with money as a distinguishing mark of the procuress and then goes on to problematize the position of the *lena* within the poetics of desire and seduction in the brothel.

(ii) *Intermediary Activity in the Comedies:* Asinaria, Aulularia, Cistellaria, Mostellaria *and* Curculio

A basic paradigm in Plautus' comedies shows the separation of lovers, one of whom (female) pertains to the less acceptable milieu of prostitution and the other (male) to a respectable household. Separation occurs as a result of a particular obstacle and ends with the reunion of the lovers once the hurdle is passed; usually, this obstacle relates to financial or status conflicts, undergoing variations with

[21] Historical information on sexual mores in Roman society is collected in many volumes; in addition to Vanoyeke's book, those utilized in the present study are J. N. Robert, *Les plaisirs à Rome* (Paris: Belles Lettres, 1983); *Histoire mondiale de la femme*, vol. I: *Préhistoire et Antiquité* (Paris: Nouvelle Librairie de France, 1974).

[22] "la prostitution comme une nécessité, un remède pour la sécurité de leurs épouses. Les Romains encouragent une institution dont ils pensent qu'elle est l'un des meilleurs garants de l'honneur et de la famille" (Vanoyeke, *La prostitution*, 77).

regards to specific details. Scholars agree in general that in the typology of comic plots such conflicts form a significant aspect of the fundamental storylines expounded by Roman comedy.[23] The recurrent setting of one street leading to both public and private houses permits regular depictions of stock characters with specific functions towards the resolution of the class or economy-related problems, creating plots that "at the most general level of abstraction, (...) may perhaps be regarded as versions of a single type."[24]

As David Konstan observes:

> The meanings of the plays, however, are not reducible to a function of the blocking character. Plot forms are combined or varied in extraordinary ways, and the dramatic issues and conflicts are correspondingly transformed. To identify the obstacle or blocking figure in such cases (...) is itself an interpretation.[25]

Each comedy provides a set of obstacles and resources that guides the trajectory of the lovers and upon which the reader must base further interpretation as to any significant underlying critique or irony offered by the play. Beyond comic and entertainment purposes, the works of Plautus touch on issues of "loyalty (*fides*), dutifulness (*pietas*), consistency of behavior (*constantia*) and a sense of obligation for benefits received (*gratia*)[,]" allowing us to examine "a variety of boundary problems."[26] The boundaries concern sexual codes, rights of citizens versus aliens, or class structure in city-state society. As Konstan notes:

> Old motifs are subjected to ironic inversions (...) Taken together, the dramas of ancient comedy map out the ideology of city-state society and reveal to us the sensitive areas where the borders were vague, weak, or changing under the pressure of new historical circumstances.[27]

For the study of the *lena* in this useful light, one must also establish the proper literary context for the old woman. The reader should

---

[23] David Konstan, *Roman Comedy* (Ithaca: Cornell University Press, 1983). The information in Konstan's book is used here for the general background on Roman comedy, as it effectively synthesizes the prevalent themes in the more recent scholarship on the topic.

[24] Konstan, *Roman Comedy*, 27. He draws this conclusion on the basis of comments by several scholars.

[25] Konstan, *Roman Comedy*, 32.

[26] Konstan, *Roman Comedy*, 17, 20.

[27] Konstan, *Roman Comedy*, 21.

remain aware of the extent of Greek influence – particularly of New Comedy – on Roman works and of the numerous situations, figures and motifs that have been transmitted from the former to the latter. The consideration of this influence is indispensable to understanding the trajectory of several topics in Roman comedy, among them the figure of the *lena* who, while appearing recurrently in Roman comedy and therefore establishing a literary identity as such, nonetheless maintains significant links with the Greek heritage.[28] In the specific realm of love literature and related topics, Arthur Leslie Wheeler provides useful information regarding the influences of Greek motifs.

As Wheeler has observed, the figure of third party harks back to Greek Comedy, subsequently followed up in romance and the love epistle. In these genres, an experienced older man or woman, and sometimes a youth, provides different kinds of "erotic teaching" from a position of authority for a novice who is about to embark on a love affair and needs advice on how to go about securing the beloved's attention.[29] The role of erotic teacher "is assigned to the *lena* and the *meretrix*, to the old man and the youth – in all cases to one who is *peritus* (or *perita*)."[30] This kind of teaching deals with such issues as the nature of passion, the effects of love, the ways of punishing an ungrateful lover, or the symptoms of desire. On occasion, the experienced party establishes contact with the younger one's lover, usually in epistolary form, to object to mistreatment or neglect, thereby undertaking the role of a protective intermediary.[31] Filled with *sententiae* and *praeceptae* on amorous questions, the instruction provided by the older *magister* allows the younger and less experienced party to

[28] The bibliography on Greek influences on Latin literature is naturally extensive in range and focus. In the specific case of comedy, the following studies provide ample information on the trajectory of numerous motifs from Greek (especially New Comedy) to Latin: L. D. Reynolds, *Scribes and Scholars: A Guide to the Transmission of Greek and Latin Literature* (New York: Oxford University Press, 1991); Arthur Leslie Wheeler, "Erotic Teaching in Roman Elegy and the Greek Sources, Part I," *Classical Philology* 5 (1910) 440-450; Arthur Leslie Wheeler, "Part II" *Classical Philology* 6 (1911) 57-77. For the educating role of an older person, albeit from a marginal point of view, see the very useful study by Helen King, "Sowing the Field: Greek and Roman Sexology," in *Sexual Knowledge, Sexual Science: The History of Attitudes to Sexuality*, edited by Roy Porter and Mikulas Teich (Cambridge: Cambridge University Press, 1994) 29-47.

[29] Wheeler, "Part II," 58.

[30] Wheeler, "Part I," 446-447.

[31] Thus in the *Epistolae* of Alciphron, and of Aristaenetus, letters are sent out by the teacher figure on behalf of the mistreated lover. (See Wheeler, "Part II," 57).

become familiar with the anticipated tribulations of love.[32] As Wheeler shows, an added feature in conducting amorous situations has to do with financial greed, not recurrent but nonetheless present: in the *Epistolae* of Aristaenetus for example, the experienced *meretrix* clarifies that the lover's stratagems, music, and song "are of no avail without money[.]"[33]

In the comedies of Plautus – set against the Hellenic background – the *lena* attempts to retain few of the traits seen in Greek predecessors in positions of mediation and teaching. The *lenae* of Plautus appear on the whole extremely partial to wine and money, hail from a past in prostitution, and encourage multiple, wealthy partners for the girl with whom they interact. Thus Syra from *Cistellaria*, Leaena from *Curculio*, Scapha from *Mostellaria*, and Cleareta from *Asinaria* display these essential characteristics. González Rolán sees the *lenae* of Plautus in two interrelated capacities: as those who add new layers to the figure's identity within the Latin tradition itself and also as obvious precursors to the Spanish *alcahueta*.[34]

To recall briefly the plotlines: in *Mostellaria*, the old Scapha is maid to Philatelum, encouraging the latter to discard the idea of a single lover in favor of several so that financial reward will come of amorous escapades; in this respect, she attempts to replicate the "erotic teaching" highlighted by Wheeler. Her advice, however, falls on deaf ears. She accepts this predicament, transforming the contents of her advice into suggestions on dress and perfume towards the gratification of Philatelum's only lover. *Cistellaria* presents Syra, an old and perpetually inebriated bawd who claims to be the mother of the courtesan Gymnasium. As the owner of the brothel, she spills out drunken thoughts on the benefits of her profession. In *Curculio*, the

[32] See Wheeler, "Part I," where extensive examples of this kind of teaching are cited throughout the article, as found in the works of Longus, Moschus, and Aristaenetus. In "Part II" he provides further examples from Lucian, Heliodorus and Alciphron.

[33] Wheeler, "Part II," 66.

[34] For the case of the *alcahueta* in Spain, the place of these old women in the literary tradition leading to the works of Rojas and Juan Ruiz has been discussed by Menéndez y Pelayo and Bonilla, who consider their impact a direct one, and by María Rosa Lida and Castro Guisasola (he specifically rejects Plautus as a model), who have shown a reluctance to acknowledge a direct debt. See Menéndez y Pelayo, *Orígenes de la novela*, 294; Castro Guisasola, *Observaciones sobre las fuentes literarias de* La Celestina, 50; María Rosa Lida, *La originalidad artística de La Celestina* (Buenos Aires: Editorial universitaria, 1962) 534-542.

intoxicated old woman Leaena, who works for the *leno* Cappadox, is one of many resources used by an enamored Phaedromus to gain access to his beloved. Her function consists of bringing the latter out of the house so that Phaedromus may speak with her. Summarizing the attributes of each old woman in the above plays, González Rolán concludes that Leaena in *Curculio* fulfills the function of intermediary or *alcahueta* as carrier of messages, adding that she is an intermediary ("medianera").[35] The critic also considers Scapha in *Mostellaria* as an *alcahueta;* similarly, the term "intermediary" denotes Syra's function in *Cistellaria.*[36]

It is important to note at this point that our critique addresses above all the question of definitions. "Intermediary" and "go-between" imply some type of an active participation in the act of seduction. Close textual reading of the plays of Plautus incites a redefinition of the *lena* as a legitimate and skillful go-between. The *lena* is indeed located in the position of mediator and overloaded with designations that suggest intermediary activity. In fact, as we shall see, the plays of Plautus undermine her actual impact as mediator to a severe degree, while seemingly and curiously insisting on defining her in terms of her physical and predetermined position as a third party. The aim, therefore, is not simply to refute one scholar's views but rather to challenge a widely held notion that his study confirms, which is that the Plautine *lena* fulfills the tasks of a go-between. More importantly, this enables us to build a dynamic pre-history of the medieval go-between based on a much closer reading of her role in the poetics of love and mediation. The commonly held view, articulated in González Rolán's essay, states that the *lena* in Plautus' texts is a powerful mediating agent. Yet as will be shown, she enters the stage identified as bawd or confidante to the female character and continues to exist only in terms of a series of stock characteristics: a predilection for drink and/or an obstinate, rhetorical reiteration of the benefits of her profession. Furthermore, in every play the decisive change in the lovers' fate has to do with other sources, for example a fortuitous revelation of identity or the presentation of a large sum of money that solves all problems, and not with the interference of the *lena*. These factors beg several questions: how does the text under-

[35] González Rolán, "Rasgos de la alcahuetería," 281 (henceforth "González Rolán").

[36] González Rolán, 281-282.

mine the mediatory power of the bawd? What exactly does her function become, as a result of this? And why is there an insistence on locating her as go-between when in fact, her position enacts other functions? These questions constitute not just the basis of our study of the Plautine *lena*, but also the others who appear in this chapter. The occasional references to the Spanish bawd in the process of this inquiry have to do with the fact that the *lena* is seen as a predecessor to the Spanish *alcahueta*, and that this perception in fact obscures the significant qualities inherent to both literary figures.

In *Curculio*, Leaena's sole contribution to the lover's plight consists of literally opening a door and letting out the girl for a meeting with him, disappearing from the scene with no other influence on the relationship whatsoever. Her one and only effective gesture in the play is marked by a comical shade as she ascertains that by facilitating the girl's exit she will be rewarded with wine. The audience catches a brief glimpse of her drunken incoherence prior to the gate scene, and the slapstick quality of her near stupor frames her entire representation. In *Cistellaria*, Syra reveals no traits to this effect, for she, too, enters and exits the play in a drunken haze, her role consisting of providing the audience with clues on Gymnasium the courtesan's familial background.[37] Her qualification as a "great talker"[38] must in all fairness take into account the fact that her speech comes across as rambling and drunken, neither focused nor aimed at establishing a specific point, especially regarding the question of her own walk of life.[39] Her discourse is blatantly comic in nature due to her drunkenness and provides no serious reflection because of its incoherent character. Here again one leaves the *anus* with the unequivocal impression of slapstick and comic overtones, enhanced by the fact that her speech gives rise to a considerable degree of embarrassment for Gymnasium, who attempts in vain to extract some focus from it in the initial scene of the play. These factors debunk the notion of her power as mediator and bring forth instead Plautus' thematic

[37] *Cistellaria*, vv. 120-147.

[38] González Rolán, 281.

[39] *Cistellaria*, vv. 23-42: Syra attempts to explain her profession, but is sidetracked by peripheral thoughts on prejudices against her class, momentarily forgetting her age and speaking as though she were concubine to a highborn gentleman. Furthermore, her speech produces a comical effect due to its misplaced character: her two interlocutors, the courtesans Gymnasium and Selenium, make efforts to quiet her for she is not addressing the issues brought up by them.

interest in using the figure as a source of comedy and an antithesis to the strong courtesan.

Turning to Scapha in *Mostellaria*, we face a textual problem with significant implications for her representation. The dialogue between Scapha and Philematium occurs in the third scene of Act 1, between lines 157 and 312. The latter part of it comes under the subtitle "toilet scene" since it takes place at the young woman's dressing table and contains a long discussion of the dress, makeup, and jewelry that will bring satisfaction to the lover. The beginning of the conversation consists of old Scapha's suggestion that Philematium, a recently freed slave, take on several wealthy lovers as opposed to dedicating herself solely to Philolaches (who eavesdrops on the entire dialogue). The latter delivers frequent, angry, but nonetheless comical asides directed at the old woman. Scapha's advice falls on deaf ears since Philatelium expresses ardent interest in Philolaches only, whereupon Scapha changes her focus and proceeds to exchange ideas on makeup and dress for the young girl. Her effect on the course of the love affair amounts to nil, for her traditional plea for financial gain goes unnoticed and even ignored, and she fades into Philematium's own monogamous scheme by assisting her with decorative details.

This weak impact relates to findings on the passage itself; scholars have noticed that there is a forced element in the dialogue between Scapha and Philematium, for it suffers from incoherencies: the old woman's questions have little relevance and no point of reference in context.[40] In addition, the passage has been considered excessively lengthy.[41] This concerns in particular lines 208-223 where Scapha, pointing out the dangers of keeping oneself for one lover only, urges Philematium to devote her attentions to many rich pursuers. The lines containing this advice (208-223) appear to be a later composition intended as a substitute for the preceding twenty-one lines on Philematium's dress and her foolishness in devoting herself to one man.[42] Williams elaborates further on this observation, suggesting that "the forced dialogue between Scapha and Philematium is only intended to give an opportunity for the amusing asides of Philolach-

[40] Williams, "Some Aspects," 22, 26, 27.

[41] "The scene is certainly too long, and this has been felt by most critics" (Williams, "Some Aspects," 22).

[42] Cited from Ladewig's 1861 *Philologus* XVII, 466 in Williams, "Some Aspects," 22.

es[.]"[43] The principal focus of the passage lies elsewhere, using the interference of the *anus* as a platform to showcase the wit of the central character. More importantly though, in this toilet scene the situation between Philematium and her lover is likened to marriage, a fact viewed disapprovingly by Scapha.[44] Bearing in mind a similar mention of eventual marriage in *Cistellaria* where the young woman Selenium effectively ends up marrying her lover, Williams notes:

> [in *Cistellaria*] the mention of marriage arouses the anticipation of the audience and gives them a clue as to what will happen. But in *Mostellaria* Philematium simply disappears from the play (...) there is not the slightest suggestion of [Philolaches'] marrying the girl nor is there the faintest shred of evidence that Plautus has left out a recognition-scene. [45]

The incoherencies in Scapha's dialogue with Philematium and the irrelevance of marriage as a topic of conversation lead Williams to conclude that Plautus is inspired by a Greek play with a similar toilet scene about dress, makeup and jewelry, here broken in unity by Philolaches' jokes, and by the discussion of marriage "remembering some such scene in *Cistellaria* I, I [.]" But in so doing Plautus "overburdens the scene." It appears more than likely that a later producer, seeking to reduce artistic proportions, felt compelled to write the very lines in which Scapha criticizes the idea of marriage and advocates the pursuit of several rich lovers as a substitute for the previous lengthy scene between Scapha and Philatelium. [46] In the present form of the play, his substitution does not quite achieve its purpose, and both Plautus' lengthy scene and the later producer's insertion appear in the text; however, the convincing argument that the very lines which portray Scapha in terms of greed and mercenary promiscuity are not by Plautus and that they exist for the reason of artistic reduction confirms and justifies the relative weakness of Scapha's presence and the insubstantial nature of her argument. It confirms that the figure is unimportant enough to have been the obvious target of rigorous editing, since her impact on the play was deemed negligible.

[43] "Some Aspects, "27.

[44] "This is a version of the familiar theme that a *meretrix* who devotes herself to one man denies her vocation and dooms herself to poverty. Here Scapha provides the cautionary example of herself (200 ff.) and uses the language of marriage (*uni gessi morem*)" ("Some Aspects," 23).

[45] Williams, "Some Aspects," 27.

[46] Williams, "Some Aspects," 27.

Asinaria places greater structural importance on the bawd: here Cleareta, who runs the brothel, refuses to allow access to the penniless lover. Her businesslike attitude and unequivocal interest in financial compensation overwhelm her discourse with references to profit and money, constantly evoking transactions, bargaining, deals, and prices; she discusses access to the girl purely in terms of an exchange, waiting for the lover to pay up.[47] The urgency of financial recompense constitutes her sole guiding principle, shaping every facet of her discourse. The description of her profession, the ultimatums and conditions placed upon the penniless Argyrippus, all revolve around that single, unequivocal concern: "I work for money" ("opera pro pecunia").

For Cleareta, these preoccupations are a known aspect of her profession, familiar not only to herself but also to her clients and readers. She cautions Argyrippus that her position replicates a collective and routine stance against poverty-stricken lovers: "Why do you accuse me, when all I do is my work? Nowhere is it shown in stone, or paintings, or poems that a woman such as myself would treat a lover well."[48] Her idea of a generic *lena* as inscribed in stone, in poetry and painting, and to whose paradigm she refers for confirmation, betrays the preexistence of a fixed image upon which she has no intention of elaborating, for in its static form it serves perfectly the sole purpose she has in mind. Thus she repeats and reconfirms the precepts laid out by her own predecessors, who by now occupy immobile positions etched in stone. Not only does she possess a very clear notion of her role, but also she insists on keeping it unchanged.

Cleareta's exact, meticulous description of her profession excludes any mention of movement between male and female parties, nor does it include the coercion of either into an amorous situation. In her own words, Cleareta defines herself as a fundamentally stationary figure unconcerned with seductive mediation and the nature of the relationship between men and women. Her kind of mediation concerns the opening or closing of a space between the lovers purely in terms of money. Like the predecessors she mentions, having set up an official place of meeting for those who fully comprehend its oper-

---

[47] *Asinaria*, 147 and vv. 241-243, 141.

[48] "Quid me accusas, si facio officium meum?/nam neque fictum usquamst neque pictum neque scriptum in poematis/ubi lena bene agat cum quiquam amante, quae frugi esse volt" (*Asinaria*, 142).

ative conditions, Cleareta now stands guard and protects a well-defined system of transactions. In this regard she fulfills the functions of an intermediary insofar as she supervises the two parties who interact in a space to which she has full access, and insofar as she facilitates or impedes sexual union therein. The role of money in mediation is simplified by Cleareta into a clear-cut equation that permits no ambiguity or problematization. Either a man has money and can therefore enter, or he does not. The literature of the Middle Ages, and of Spain in particular, will derive significant momentum from the presence of money in mediatory tasks; Cleareta, however, chooses to present this *topos* in its most simplified form to the lovers.

For the lovers money transforms into an obstacle awaiting removal. It represents a means as opposed to an end, while the *lena*'s concern with money constitutes an end in itself, as attested by its overwhelming presence in her language and imagination. This inverse relationship brings about the collapse of any common ground between the *lena* and the lovers, for each side's concerns differ radically from the other's. It also annuls any possibility of meaningful communication between the two sides in terms that would resound mutually. As a result, the *lena* turns into a static figure whose function has clear limits, and who calls for her perception as a function of her stance as an obstacle. Her exaggerated obsession with finances also adds a comic slant to her portrayal, for in her steadfast pursuit of money she employs images of outdoor hunting and preying that offer a stark contrast to her own position, that of an old woman inhabiting closed, indoor spaces.

In his study of Roman comedy Konstan observes that old motifs undergo ironic inversions towards demonstrating the areas where the "borders were vague, weak, or changing under the pressure of new historical circumstances." The *lenae* of Plautine comedy provide a marked contrast with their Greek predecessors because of the extent to which their impact as erotic teachers has transformed into an essentially comic or stock effect. These old women voice their concerns in repetitive terms, in turn ignored or overridden by principal characters: "Matronae, non meretricium est, unum inseruire amantem" or "multisque damno et mihi lucro sine meo saepe eris sumptu."[49] Little or no internal development occurs in their characteriza-

[49] *Mostellaria*, vv. 189-190; *Cistellaria*, vv. 49-50.

tion, nor does their conflict with the external world generate momentous tensions in the text. Their portrayal indicates the disappearance of a particular triangular configuration, present in Greek sources but no longer relevant for Roman comedy. The configuration has to do with the very meaning of *eros* which Anne Carson, in her study of ancient Greek literature, explains as a force tied up inextricably with lack, want, and absence.[50] For *eros* to survive, a space must be maintained between the lovers so that the tension and longing so necessary for erotic feeling can continue to exist: "The lover wants what he does not have. It is by definition impossible for him to have what he wants if, as soon as it is had, it is no longer wanting."[51] Separation and the promise of distance – in whatever shape – ensure the survival of erotic feeling. The erotic teacher of Greek sources is one embodiment of this distance: a significant mediator between lover and beloved, this character serves to point out the tribulations associated with love and to teach lessons on the sentiment, as mentioned earlier. This very act perpetuates the existence of a space between the lovers, given the continual presence of the third party in their interaction and the need for a reference to this figure before any communication can take place. By mediating, the teacher creates a distance between the lovers, bringing them closer only insofar as the protocol of love is concerned: this appears, at first sight, to bring the lovers closer, but in fact it places an authoritative third party between the two and compels them to make contact across its distance. A dynamic "tactic of triangulation"[52] therefore takes place, obliging the lovers to take a third person into account in their erotic journey and to assimilate the teachings of this third person at once into their experience of love, of absence, and of want.

The *lena* of Plautus' comedies exerts little or no impact in that regard, given the boundaries of the space which she attempts to create between the lovers. The space in which she shows interest cannot maintain any structural integrity in the experience of the lovers, for it concerns elements that they know how to surpass or ignore. Her position vis-à-vis the lovers does not ensure the survival of *eros:* rather, the *lena* provides a comic touch of local color in the depiction

---

[50] Anne Carson, *Eros the Bittersweet* (Princeton: Princeton University Press, 1986) 10.

[51] Carson, *Eros the Bittersweet*, 10.

[52] Carson, *Eros the Bittersweet*, 79.

of the world of the brothel. Her drunkenness, her rambling conversation, and her abrupt entrance and departure signify the burned-out end of the profession, and she fades away into the general decor of the place as a standard identifying feature. Moreover, the courtesans who surround her eventually resolve their status conflict and end up with one lover, showing that the somewhat pathetic end of the *lena* does not await them: in addition to a comical figure, then, she represents failure in matters related to love. The *lena* serves to highlight that which the young courtesan must not become and thus acts as a foil for the lead female character. These factors all point to the disappearance of the procuress as a dynamic element for the poetics of triangulation and her reemergence as a stock figure with a much clearer and more limited scope. In this respect she metamorphoses into a flat character described by E. M. Forster;[53] the critic David Galef observes:

> (...)most stories of any substantial length involve not just several major characters but also a whole supporting cast. These minor characters have their uses: they take down the pistol from over the mantel; they become a confidant for the protagonist; (...) The essence of a flat character is in its limitations (...) Flat characters not only have their appropriate functions – as stock characters, humorous butts, pawns in the game (...) They may even appear full of life, though such life represents a circumscribed view.(...) The point is that flat characters tend toward the allegorical and thus express equivalencies, whereas more problematic creations partake more of the confusion of reality and hence are more symbolic.[54]

Naturally, the novel constitutes a genre quite different from Latin works of antiquity and operates under different sets of literary rules. Yet the *lena* fits the contours outlined above and derives her dramatic justification from the foil created with the principal female character as well as the comic touch she provides. As for the reasons behind her disappearance from the realm of *eros* and the poetics associated with it, these can only be assessed fully in the contexts of elegy.

---

[53] See E. M. Forster, *Aspects of the Novel and Related Writings* (London: Edward Arnold, 1974).

[54] David Galef, *The Supporting Cast: A Study of Flat and Minor Characters* (Pennsylvania: The Pennsylvania State University Press, 1993)1-2.

III. The Case of Roman Elegy

(i) *The Bawds of Tibullus*

The elegiac genre contains a number of features that are repeated in the works of Tibullus, Propertius, and Ovid. In general, as regards a plotline, the elegiac poet follows an observable pattern of joy and pain with his mistress, with some variation, so that in Ovid's case, for example, "Book One portrays the happy first stages of the affair (...) Book Two introduces tensions and disloyalty and the first mention of parting, and Book Three brings a series of complaints and the attempt for a final severance."[55] This basic structure recurs in the elegies of the three poets considered here and involves the mention of an old woman who acts as confidante to the mistress. Referred to as the *lena*, the old woman appears to aggravate the poet's situation at a given point by encouraging the mistress to look elsewhere for profitable love.[56]

It was mentioned that in earlier genres the older figure of *praeceptor* – *peritus* or *perita* – took on the assignment of erotic teacher for the younger character and that with Plautus this phenomenon underwent a shift towards the comic, with two elements surviving as the bawd's essential role: the prevalence of financial greed and ultimate failure. Roman elegy brings about yet another significant change in the role of the erotic teacher:

> the leading *praeceptor* is the poet himself, whereas a character appears in the rôle of *praeceptor* much less frequently. This change is due to difference of genre. In elegy, erotic teaching is connected with the subjective attitude – the poet's personal experience and feeling. The poet is, therefore, naturally the *praeceptor*. [57]

The shift of emphasis in elegy radically affects the function of the *lena:* She associates with a woman whose lover articulates in full the lessons of Cupid, from the pleasures of consummation to the bitterness brought about by rivals or jealousy. The poet has absolute control in chronicling the love affair, the ideas on eroticism, and the nature of male-female relationships. The poetic voice displays considerable discomfort with this power and makes consistent attempts to undermine the impression

[55] John Barsby, *Ovid: Amores, Book One* (Oxford: Oxford University Press, 1973) 18.
[56] These references are found in *Tibulle*, Book I, 5; Book II, 6, vv. 47ff., 44ff.
[57] Wheeler, "Part I," 447.

of control. The bawd serves as one element among many to enhance the sense of the poet's instability as a figure of authority.

Tibullus brings the bawd into his poetry in capacities that have been read as those of a full-fledged go-between, with a genetic relationship with the Spanish *alcahueta:*

> the go-between who ceases to be the impassive guardian, such as we have seen in comedy, in Propertius and Ovid, and becomes instead the modern type of Celestina [go-between], that is to say, the person who, called upon by the lover and financially rewarded, attempts to conquer the beloved for carnal purposes, using in her art of seduction those spells about which she knows a great deal.[58]

The passage suggests that Tibullus changes a paradigm created by Ovid and Propertius. It is fitting to mention that Tibullus, in fact, wrote before both poets.

A meaningful step taken by Tibullus, according to the above assertion, consists of the added element of sorcery and black magic in her repertoire.[59] Furthermore, it is remarked, Tibullus offers the first instance of the old bawd "as intermediary, and not as an obstacle between lover and beloved."[60] Another development mentioned in this evaluation concerns the fact that the intermediary in Tibullus, in addition to keeping a public house for prostitution, "now can approach free women, even married ones."[61] The critic then concludes that Tibullus adds the elements of sorcery and the sinister caricature of the *lena*, and above all gives the go-between an air of modernity, placing her as an intermediary and not as an obstacle between lover and beloved.[62] Once again, the following response to these assertions is not intended as anything other than a substantiat-

[58] "la alcahueta [que] deja de ser la guardiana inflexiva, tal como hemos visto en la comedia, en Propercio y Ovidio, para convertirse en el tipo moderno de celestina, es decir, aquella persona que solicitada por un amante, previo pago, trata de conquistar a la amada para usos lascivos, sirviéndose, en su arte de seducción, de hechizos en los que es diestra" (González Rolán, 286).

[59] González Rolán, 287.

[60] "como intermediaria y no como obstáculo entre amante y amada" (González Rolán, 287).

[61] "ya puede abordar a mujeres de condición libre, incluso casadas" (González Rolán, 287).

[62] "por su parte, añade los rasgos de la hechicería y de la caricatura siniestra de la lena (...) pero sobre todo le da a la alcahueta un aire de modernidad, poniéndola como intermediaria y no como obstáculo entre amante y amada" (González Rolán, 287).

ed warning against a type of cursory reading of this recurrent motif that tends to attribute power where there is none. The function of the *lena* lies in her presence on the comic or ethical levels of the text, warranting a rigorous redefinition of her tasks as go-between. The repercussions of her role as bawd are enormous for some medieval Romance texts which draw so extensively on her for their own portrayals of the go-between.

Interestingly, at no time in any of Tibullus' elegies does the *lena* actually appear. The poet evokes her, either retrospectively or in a mention to the mistress. He mentions the sorceress in Book I as one of the potential tools at his disposal to coerce Delia into continuing her liaison with him: threatening his mistress with recourse to methods that will affect her opinion of him, the poet first evokes the power of Venus. Directly afterwards, faced with the prospect of a jealous husband, he boasts access to a sorceress.[63]

The poet goes on to emphasize the magical powers of this woman whose resources consist of herbs, incantations, and witchcraft, devices that will blind Delia's husband to any illicit activity. She does not operate as a manipulator of words nor a messenger between man and woman: this is a facet of mediation that must be taken into account, for it adorns the representation of the thrid party with a commonly found feature, that of access to the occult. In this particular case, however, this feature stands alone and no recourse is made to dialogue, thus locating the sorceress's potential mediation purely in the realm of the occult and calling into question her designation as go-between.

The conclusion that she can approach free women, including married ones, is also problematic. Delia's married status – if indeed that is the case, for it has provided much debate – represents a precarious one, as the text makes it plainly clear that she does not shy away from offering her favors to several lovers. In fact, the poet feels compelled to warn her against cavorting with others.[64] Thus her official status does not present an obstacle for the pursuit of intrigue.

That the sorceress is simply recalled by Tibullus and never shown in action raises perhaps the most important question, taking our inquiry away from practical concerns and directing it at the very

[63] *Tibulle*, 19, vv. 41-42.
[64] *Tibulle*, 20, v. 57.

question of discourse: does she actually exist in the world of Tibullus, or does she represent a device used in desperation, in his attempts to threaten his mistress with the powers at his disposal? As he pleads with her in a variety of ways, several trump cards such as his summons of Venus, his undying adoration, the flowers he has sent, are listed one after another, among them his claim of access to a sorceress. Leaving her description somewhat abruptly and moving on to other reasons for which Delia should love him (I, 2, vv. 64-65) the poet accumulates a series of last-minute entreaties rather than project a sense of utter confidence in one particular resource. Within the general scheme of his argument, the sorceress appears as a figure in his coercive discourse, not an external reality in his life, and this is emphasized by the fact that she never does appear. It does seem, therefore, that González Rolán's conclusions on her impact as a "medianera," one who can accost free women and one who approximates the celestinesque type using an art of seduction, are completely undermined by a text which only mentions her in a very specific rhetorical capacity, that of one desperate trope among many. In this case, a more useful conclusion to draw would concern the poet's formulation of mediation; not only does he perceive mediation as a coercive and desperate measure, but also he allows it to exist only at the level of his own depiction of it, not producing the real sorceress at any point. For the elegiac poet, recourse to the third party represents the insertion of threat into his own discourse, an attempt to maintain his seductive stance by infusing it with a hint of intimidation, using the trope of a sorceress. His idea of mediation, then, borders on aggression and the introduction of the occult, as though he were steadfastly preserving the right to discourse for himself and none other. This perception of mediation is an important feature of his poetics of seduction and will play a significant part in the writings of European medieval authors.

In addition to this probably non-existent sorceress, evoked solely as a threat, the poet mentions old women on two other occasions, blaming them for his misfortune.[65] In one instance, he cannot gain access to his beloved since she has settled with a richer lover on the advice of a *lena* (Book I, 5). In the other, he cannot enter the house of Nemesis on account of the reported stratagems and lies elaborated

[65] *Tibulle*, I-5, vv. 49-60, and II-6, vv. 43-55.

by a *lena* named Phryne. Both old women, again absent and simply recalled by the poet in a flashback, inspire his violent diatribe and cursing. González Rolán does not elaborate on the significance of these two figures in detail, only remarking on Phryne from Book II: "But Phryne not only carries messages, but also regulates the comings and goings of the lovers into and from the house (perhaps she runs a brothel?)"[66] Concerning the other, from Book I, González Rolán states "But it is above all significant that for the first time, (...) this *lena* is a greedy sorceress."[67]

The use of sorcery and black magic does not represent an innovation on the part of Tibullus; the greedy old woman as sorceress – either in reality or by accusation – is a motif found in Greek literature, and even used by Plautus. Wheeler offers an exhaustive list of Greek and Roman comedies with older female characters who provide erotic teaching for younger *meretrices* in terms of *avaritia* and financial gain.[68] As for the use of sorcery in the making and unmaking of amorous desire, that is, in the capacity of *lena*, Lefkowitz and Fant have demonstrated that this is a known theme in Greek and earlier Roman literature, for its dramatic representation can be seen in detail in the second *Idyll* of Theocritus.[69]

More importantly, close reading of the verses in question shows that the mention of the *lena* constitutes a preface to the main focus of the passage, that is, the poet's anger. Thus the one-line reference to the richer lover paves the way for a twelve-line diatribe against the *lena* who has caused the poet's downfall. The diatribe, a particularly fiery *accusatio* which goes on to list the punishments deemed appropriate for the *lena*, takes precedence over the figure's role in the plot; instead the poet focuses on his own desperate anger. The reference to her as a sorceress – "sagae praecepta" ("sly witch")[70] – marks the final mention of her, with no elaboration on her technique, influence, or method. These twelve lines in Book I ultimately offer negligible information on the figure of the *lena* herself, for they do not

---

[66] "Pero Friné no sólo se encarga de llevar mensajes, sino también de regular las entradas y salidas de los amantes (¿mantiene casa pública?)" (González Rolán, 285).

[67] "Pero es sobre todo significativo el que por primera vez (...) esta lena sea una codiciosa hechicera" (González Rolán, 286).

[68] See in particular Wheeler, "Part II," almost all of which is structured around the parallels to such elegiac motifs in Greek and Roman Comedy.

[69] Lefkowitz and Fant, *Women's Life in Greece and Rome*, 125.

[70] *Tibulle*, I (v), v. 59.

elaborate in any manner other than "diues amator" and "sagae praecepta" on the old hag, remembered in line 49 and left behind in line 60. The focus remains clearly on the poet's fury, and this incident inscribes itself as one of the many vicissitudes of his affair, such as his poverty, the threat of rivals, and the mistress' own fickle attitude.

As for Phryne (most probably named after a courtesan in Horace's *Epodes*)[71] in Book II, she first enters the poem in terms of an activity and a shift of blame away from the mistress: "The bawd causes our break-up; this girl [herself] is good. The bawd Phryne shuts me out, as she moves around craftily, carrying secret messages in her heart."[72] Subsequent mention has to do with two obstacles she has raised for the poet: he attempts to visit his mistress, and according to the poet, the old woman tells him that Nemesis is absent or that she is ill.[73] Significantly, these obstacles appear in the last elegy composed for Nemesis, chronicling the death of the poet's love affair with her. Here Nemesis herself emerges as a cold and whimsical courtesan, no longer interested in pursuing the relationship.[74] As Max Ponchont has remarked, throwing the blame on the *lena* represents no more than an illusory effort by the poet to deceive himself.[75] Nemesis has at this point already displayed her lack of enthusiasm, and the knowledge of this wider context clearly affects our perception of the degree of Phryne's influence. The poet's accusation of the *lena* translates into no more than a self-deceiving act of transferring responsibilities, a last-minute effort to give his cruel mistress some benefit of doubt. This has to do, in part, with what Lilja has labeled the overall gentleness of Tibullus' tone towards his mistresses:

> Tibullus' gentleness is seen (...) in his general tendency to avoid attacking his beloved directly. In the case of Delia he lays it on Amor – *renuente deo* (I, 5, 20); in the case of Nemesis he lays it on Venus – *illa malum facinus suadet* (II, 4, 25). Or else it is the procuress who is held to be responsible for the beloved's unfaithfulness.[76]

[71] *Tibulle*, 116, n. 1.

[72] "lena nocet nobis; ipsa puella bona est./ Lena uetat miserum Phryne furtimque tabellas/occulto portans itque reditque sinu;" (*Tibulle*, II [vi], vv. 44-46).

[73] *Tibulle*, II (vi), vv. 45-50.

[74] *Tibulle*, II (vi), vv. 11-28.

[75] *Tibulle*, 113.

[76] Lilja, *Roman Elegists' Attitudes to Women*, 157.

It also concerns the poet's relentless creation of spaces between himself and the beloved in the attempt to sustain a tension that is dying: aware that triangulation is a necessary component of the type of passion celebrated by elegy, Tibullus appears to latch on to anything that might keep open the gap that separates him from his mistress, so that he can verbalize the lament of distance. The third parties at whom he lashes out are none other than tropes for such an expression.

Thus terms such as "sorceress" or "evil" used in reference to the procuress appear as tired epithets for the description of these old women. For Tibullus, the old women serve as rhetorical tools, and this best explains the absence of most of those whom he mentions. Moreover, from a quantitative point of view, the *lena* occupies a visibly small place in the elegies of Tibullus and, similar to the bawds of Plautus, enters and exits the narrative in an abrupt fashion; in this respect the assertion that the elegies give us a "varied and rich range of *lenae*"[77] does appear exaggerated, as they offer three examples, each of which takes up relatively few lines constructed around the poet's innermost feelings of frustration, and one of which provides sufficient room for doubt as to her very existence.

(ii) *Propertius' Acanthis*

The four books of elegies by Propertius follow much the same pattern as those of Tibullus, chronicling for the most part the stormy trajectory of the poet's love affair with Cynthia. An old bawd named Acanthis appears in Book IV (v); the appreciation of her input requires a brief overview of the four books.[78] Briefly, Book I describes the initial stages of the affair, and Book II expands on the range of themes while venting some of the poet's emotions on the difficulties of the affair, mentioning Cynthia in only one-half of the poems. In Book III, the love poems diminish in number and Cynthia is named in only two bitter poems in which rejection is the main topic; the

---

[77] González Rolán, 284.

[78] The name in itself does not appear to be of particular significance; according to Leverett's *Latin Lexicon* (Philadelphia: The Peter Reilly Company, 1931), "'Acanthis' probably means 'goldfinch,' and is also definitively known to be the name of an herb otherwise known as 'senecio.'" "Senecio" is additionally referred to as "same as senex" meaning old. Here, in reference to old age, may lie an indirect definition of the term.

love affair thus comes to a close.[79] As the critic Maltby notes, in the fourth book "Propertius seeks to widen the range of his elegy by turning to aetiological themes," and while the "theme of love is still important (...) when Cynthia herself reappears there is a new poise and greater realism in the poet's approach to the subject."[80]

Acanthis the bawd enters at this stage as the object of vehement insult by the poet because of the instructions she has imparted to the mistress. The insults occur as the old hag lies dying a horrific death described with relish (some scholars consider her already dead at this stage).[81] A description of the bawd's magical powers follows the curses, then in retrospect, the poet recalls the avalanche of advice given by the *lena* to a pupil concerning the pursuit of rich lovers.[82] The passage draws to a close in a vivid description of Acanthis' illness – a blend of consumption and the plague – and the cursing of her funeral and tombstone.

The critic W. Camps perceives this fragment as

> a genre piece depicting a strongly characterized type, in this case the bawd or procuress (...) The piece has all the appearance of an essay in imagination. There is no ground for supposing that the *lena* is a real person or that the *amica* of line 63 is Cynthia.[83]

Furthermore, the exact place of the passage in the poet's love life is unclear. This uncertainty derives primarily from the actual location of the piece: it appears after the love affair with Cynthia has come to an end, with no mention of the latter's name in the condemnation of the *lena.* The sudden entrance of the old hag is external to the situation of the principal lovers, given that their affair has by now run its course. Additionally, a pattern already perceived in Plautus repeats itself more forcefully here: the poet describes the bawd in terms of one set of terms and activities, that is, witchcraft and the use of potions, as

---

[79] Maltby, *Latin Love Elegy*, 8.

[80] Maltby, *Latin Love Elegy*, 8-9.

[81] This has to do with the choice between the verbs "fuerant" or "fuerint" in line 72, each of which would imply a different state. The typographical problem is explained by D. R. Shackleton Bailey, *Propertiana* (Cambridge: Cambridge University Press, 1956) 244. Bailey opts for the form "fuerint" and concludes that the *lena* is alive, but acknowledges that many scholars assume part v of Book IV to be a cursing epitaph for an already dead *lena.*

[82] *Propertius' Elegies, Book s I-IV*, edited by W. A. Camps (Cambridge: Cambridge University Press, 19 65) *Book* IV, 26, vv. 53-54.

[83] Camps, *Propertius' Elegies, Book IV*, 96-97.

well as a tremendous power to twist fate with such instruments, and then shows her using an altogether different set of tools, mainly a succession of rapid hints on the benefits of seeking numerous, wealthy lovers. The difference gives rise to considerable incongruity, since the hag in action turns out to be concerned with issues visibly outside the range of supernatural and occult elements, turning her attention (according to the poet) completely to a worldly question. The effect of her words is not chronicled, and once she conveys her advice, the passage moves directly to her illness and funeral. The poet elaborates two specific stylistic devices by using Acanthis: the first concerns his development of realist description, [84] and the second has to do with Propertius' handling of tactics already used by Tibullus.

In the verses on the *lena*, Propertius draws on several traits seen in Tibullus and contributes to the solidification of the *lena* as a standard motif for the projection of anger and disgust, feelings that also relate to the recurrent theme of self-deception in elegy. In the case of Tibullus we saw that the poetic voice shifted the blame for the mistress's cruelty to factors such as poverty, Venus or the *lena*. Self-deception regarding to the infidelity of the beloved is not an uncommon theme, as seen for instance in Book II (xx), where Propertius claims to disregard the rumors on Cynthia's misbehavior. For the *lena*'s portrayal, where a great deal of initial description by Propertius harks back to Tibullus,[85] a similar dynamic of last-minute self-deception exists which uses the bawd as an excuse to find some way of accounting for infidelity.

The overall evidence for the elegiac *amica*'s disinterest in monogamy is overwhelming and not limited to instances spent with the *lena*. A great cause for complaint across the four Books of Propertius (as well as those of Tibullus) has to do precisely with the constant threat, and reality, of divided attention, such that the ensuing jealousy and anger become commonplace motifs. Sullivan observes correctly that the poet worries lest someone should assault Cynthia in her sleep, or that she might find herself tempted by "the opportunities offered by the games and temples of Rome[,]" or that, as shown

[84] Theodore D. Papanghelis, *Propertius: A Hellenistic poet on Love and Death* (Cambridge: Cambridge University Press, 1987) 167.

[85] W. A. Camps offers a detailed list of these parallelisms and demonstrates that many attributes of Acanthis are drawn almost exactly from those portrayed by Tibullus for his *lenae*. *Propertius, Book IV,* 96.

[86] Sullivan, *Propertius*, 98-99.

in I (v) and II (xxxiv), several other rivals might be waiting to receive her favors.[86] Set against this context, once old Acanthis appears in IV (v), she represents yet another excuse for the poet to sense the threat of infidelity. In this capacity, the poetic voice projects a sense of fragmentation and disorientation as it describes the bawd: on the surface the voice directs much blame at her, yet in light of the existence of infidelity as an integral part of the elegiac *amica*'s life, the blame assumes a self-deceiving tone, enhanced by the fact that no evidence supports the corrupting effect of Acanthis.

Propertius confirms that the kind of mediation carried out by the *lena* exists primarily in the poetic imagination and erects a consciously self-deceiving obstacle so that the fickle nature of the mistress may be traced back to another agency. Even if the *lena* does not truly exert an impact, her representation contains many negative undertones and inscribes her among the targets of poetic ire. It is only after the discussion of Ovid's handling of the bawd's mediation that we can draw conclusions on why the *lena* occupies the Classical texts under discussion in such a way.

(iii) *The Transformation of Elegy: Ovid's Dipsas in the* Amores

Ovid follows many of the poetic conventions explored by Tibullus and Propertius, reproducing similar configurations in his elegies. The basic structure remains the same, and Ovid chronicles the tale of his loves with Corinna in adherence to the structural requirements of the genre. The poet recalls the joys and pains of love alongside reflections on broader Augustan themes, continuously exploring the potential of elegy to expose one of the most significant timbres of his voice, which is wit.[87]

Ovid's wit has much to do with his chronological position; as the last of the great poets writing elegiac material, in this capacity he must make substantial innovations.[88] Scholars agree by and large

[87] "The greatest characteristic of all Ovid's work is wit – wit of a special kind, unknown in Rome before him (...) it is a highly conceptual and verbal wit. (...) at its most characteristic[,] the familiar is suddenly transfixed by a line of thought from an unexpected direction" (Barsby, *Amores, Book One*, 16). See also Williams, *Change and Decline*, 62-63.

[88] Maltby, 13.

that Ovid's greatest contribution to the last chapter of the genre has to do with the humorous tone that allows for the application of the unexpected to well-known motifs.[89] Thus throughout the poems, while he chronicles trouble and joy, the persona of the poet creates an ironic slant: "Whereas the earlier elegists had adopted a brooding introspective attitude towards love, Ovid projects a more detached, highly civilized, predatory *persona*. Love for him is a game, but a game which has its serious side."[90]

Ovid devotes one passage (Book I, viii) to the description of a bawd named Dipsas who attempts to talk the mistress into taking wealthier lovers. The poet brings about a transformation in the treatment of this motif by relating more vividly the actual words of the bawd as he eavesdrops, in theatrical fashion, stating that the door was open and that he overheard the *lena*'s corrupting words. [91] Both Tibullus and Propertius invariably depicted the *lena*'s acts in retrospect, after supposed completion, distancing her further from the forefront of the narrative. Ovid situates the episode with Dipsas at a location which, compared with previous elegists, makes more sense thematically: the preceding episode (Book I [vii]) relates an encounter between the poet and Corinna during which he batters his mistress, only to express deep regret and a desire for immediate punishment. No corollary remarks appear at the beginning of Book I (viii) for the introduction of Dipsas, but the poet's self-reprehensive tone from the previous episode does carry into the next passage. A thematic link between the two episodes may thus be discerned in light of Dipsas' negative influence on the poet's emotional stability, leading to his punishment of sorts. This stands in contrast with the treatment of the motif by Tibullus and Propertius, who introduce and retrieve the *lena* in a strikingly abrupt manner and who appear concerned with her concrete impact at a given moment, setting her on the periphery of the overall narrative structure of the elegies.

Essentially, Dipsas' words to Corinna do not differ in content from

---

[89] Maltby observes for instance that the very opening lines of the *Amores* "burlesque the traditional *recusatio* theme of e.g. Propertius," given that for Ovid, the playful Cupid inspires the verses, rather than the more serious figures of Apollo and the Muses who did so for the previous poets. "The reader of the *Amores* should thus be prepared to be amused rather than moved by the poems which follow" (Maltby, *Latin Love Elegy*, 133).

[90] Maltby, *Latin Love Elegy*, 13.

[91] *Amores* I (viii) vv. 19-22.

the words of other *lenae* in elegy, nor from those of Cleareta in Plautus' comedy. A fierce advocate of mercenary love and the pursuit of multiple, wealthy lovers, Dipsas reconfirms the disposition of the elegiac mistress by dropping hints as to the latter's success with rivals ("So, my sweet, you pleased that rich young man so much. He could not look at anyone but you.") [92] and further encourages a life of prostitution that will guarantee financial security. The change brought about by Ovid in this recurrent motif has to do with the liveliness with which he conveys the words of Dipsas, showing step by step the instruction and justification for her suggested path. The elaboration of detail in Dipsas' speech allows Ovid to provide a number of humorous and witty reflections on Roman life, subjecting the very notion of love in an urban climate to ironic twists by filtering it through the greedy perceptions of Dipsas.[93] Gordon Williams has noticed that, taken out of context, one part of this speech has a shocking quality: vv. 39-42 suggest that the men in Rome happily pursue soldiers' wives now that the army is away pursuing patriotic aims.[94] This could be a scandalous assertion, and Williams points out: "But the sentiments are spoken by the wicked old *lena* Dipsas and we wittily view Rome through her opportunistic eyes. Ovid loves this sort of surprise."[95] Ovid thus sets up a clear context for the expressed view, maintaining all the while his witty and playful tone. Old Dipsas' advice to Corinna offers other such examples; for instance, the extent to which all love comes intermingled with mercenary inclinations is revealed casually by Dipsas when she recommends that Corinna always ask a handsome young lover for money; should he prove unable to provide it, Corinna must order him, in turn, to procure finances from his own male lovers.[96] From Dipsas' standpoint, every kind of amorous situation revolves around both parties' financial limits and demands, showing this system to be perfectly operational even if two members of the courtesan class wish to

[92] "scis here te, mea lux, iuveni placuisse beato?/ haesit et in vultu constitit usque tuo" (*Amores* I [viii] vv. 23-24).

[93] The very name he chooses for the bawd highlights an attribute that affects her perspective on life; "Dipsas" means "thirsty. So a serpent is called, which having stung a man puts him into a great thirst" (Leverett's *Latin Lexicon.* s.v. "dipsas.") This is a thinly-veiled reference to her thirst for wine and her corrupting approach to relationships.

[94] Williams *Change and Decline*, 62.

[95] Williams, *Change and Decline*, 62.

[96] *Amores* I (viii) vv. 68-69.

embark on an affair, as long as a source for money exists. The exposition of this possibility by the bawd places a humorously ironic twist on the idea of love in an urban climate, since the pursuit of love turns into a fast-paced game in which players can trade places at any time upon payment. The ever-present subject of money, so intrinsic to the *lena*'s discourse, now assumes an added humorous layer, while becoming further and further established as a part of mediation technique.

The game-like quality is enhanced as Dipsas rapidly checks items on her list of instructions, going from the uses of feigned emotions to the different methods of inspiring jealousy. The abundance of suggested tricks, almost all of which have to do with ways to obtain presents or cash, and the lively delivery make for an amusing list that undermines any serious idea of wickedness; again, the *lena*'s worldly and material-oriented advice stunts her initial presentation as a sorceress. The details of everyday life and the playfully mischievous nature of the tricks distance the old Dipsas from the darker, more abstract portrayals by Tibullus and Propertius, who used the bawd as a platform for cursing and lament. Ovid's anger comes across as less acute, and he bids farewell to the figure in two lines of considerably lighter tone: "May she have no place to live, be poor in her old age, with long winters, and an unquenchable thirst!"[97]

For Ovid, distant and retrospective evocations of the figure that seek to shift the blame are replaced by an immediate, somewhat offended but nonetheless amused portrayal mingled with observations on the absurdities of mercenary love. Blame no longer appears in terms of serious frustration as it did for Ovid's predecessors; if anything, bearing in mind the previous episode, the poet of the *Amores* has realized that this sort of punishment is part of the game of love. Ovid's touch has rendered the *lena* less abstract, more visible and entertaining, contributing a few lines to the poet's witty treatment of established themes.

The change transforms the *lena* into a more integrated figure within the elegy and drives home the idea that for some, love constitutes a game whose ultimate objective concerns arrival at a life of luxury in favor of the exhaustion caused by intense emotions of jealousy or

[97] "di tibi dent nullusque lares inopemque senectam/et longas hiemes perpetuamque sitim" (*Amores* I, [viii] vv. 92-93).

guilt. This transformation takes place within certain bounds, however: while the *lena* finds her way into the narrative in a more coherent manner by voicing ideas in line with the general tone of the work, she does not exceed the essential barriers of the elegiac world as regards the idea of third-party activity. Her interference, like that of her predecessors, has to do with the further coercion of the *amica* into the realm of prostitution, and her effect on the principal love affair emerges as negligible for it leaves no trace in subsequent events. Her basic scope continues to conform to the boundaries set by Tibullus and Propertius; in terms of actual function, Dipsas is as concerned with financial gain as her predecessors, and equally powerless in the development of the plotline.[98]

Having analyzed the selected cases in detail and against an appropriately wider context, we can assert that the very advice offered by the *lena* to the semiprofessional *meretrix* operates on tenuous ground. For in reporting this evil advice, the ultimate focus of the poet lies elsewhere: a shift of blame, an excuse to voice anger, a platform for the playing out of rhetorical devices, or the chance to place twists on conventional themes. The basic attributes of the elegiac third party and her ostensibly corrupting words are a small part of the anxiety evident in the poet's laments of insecurity, infidelity, anger, and corruption.

To express these, and therefore to construct a poetics of love, elegists resort to several figures and tropes which help the many aspects of articulate erotic and amorous feelings. Duncan F. Kennedy analyzes some of these tropes in his study on elegy, showing how phenomena such as war, or journeys, or enslavement, represent a given aspect of amorous feeling.[99] In this light, the *lena* helps maintain that space needed for the survival of *eros*, mentioned by Anne Carson, and in this respect turns into a trope for the expression of love and the anxiety attached to it. The close study of each instance in which she appears has shown that as far as her literal impact is concerned, her claim to any power or authority remains unjustified. Thus, as with the comedies of Plautus, one has to search for her *raison d'être* and her effects on the poetry elsewhere, and not in the spaces where impact is measured in terms of actual effect on the plot. In the case of elegy, the

[98] *Orígenes y sociología*, 67.
[99] Kennedy, *The Arts of Love*, 46-63.

lena operates in the realm of poetic expression and the creation of tropes and figures towards the development of a discourse on love. The textual presence of the *lena* does not create a meaningful parallelism with any possible social counterpart: that is to say, elegy does not conceive of the *lena* in terms of her functions within the community. Instead, in addition to creating a small portion of the absence needed for the perpetuation of *eros*, the genre explores the special dynamic brought about by the *lena* as an essentially ineffectual or absent character in the context of lyric expression.

Her invalidity as a guilty element to be blamed for the poet's misery endows the poet's diatribes against her with a strongly ironic twist; the barrage of insult and the associations of evil that accompany her portrayal resound in a discordant fashion in light of her implausibility as a target. Unwarranted and unjustified as such, the diatribes and negative images place the subject which utters them under an ironic light: this irony – resulting from the essential disjuncture between utterance and its object – indicates the collapse of the go-between as a crucial tenet of the world of *eros*, yet points also at the poet's refusal to let go of the old woman as an object of address and blame. These two contrasting forces unveil each poet's own hidden acknowledgment of one of the most significant elements in elegy, which is its failure to produce a uniformly triumphant scenario for love in which seduction and happiness emerge as victors. This failure, of course, is thoroughly planned, for it ensures the survival of *eros* and forms a part of the lover's "shifty logic." As Carson argues with respect to the ancient Greek lyric:

> The shifty logic of the lover unfolds naturally from his ruses of desire. We have seen how lovers (...) recognize Eros as a sweetness made of absence and pain. The recognition calls into play various tactics of triangulation, various ways of keeping the space of desire open and electric. To think about one's own tactics is always a tricky business. The exegesis measures out three angles: the lover himself, the beloved, the lover redefined as incomplete without the beloved. But this trigonometry is a trick. The lover's next move is to collapse the triangle into a two-sided figure and treat the two sides as one circle. 'Seeing my hole, I know my whole,' he says to himself. His own reasoning process suspends him between the two terms of this pun. [100]

[100] Carson, *Eros the Bittersweet*, 33.

The lover's simultaneous undermining and validating of the *lena* is precisely such a procedure: he refuses to look too closely at the flaws inherent in shifting the blame to the old bawd, yet prepares the ground for diminishing her contribution to the triangle made up of lover/beloved/distance. Consequently, he reaffirms the dominance of his own presence over all other obstacles, and reiterates his status as the supreme *magister* in the poetics of love.

Ovid's *Ars amatoria* provides another perspective for the study of the go-between by writing in seemingly literal terms on the limits of the character's influence on the love affair. The conception of the figure along the terms offered by the *Ars* complements her portrayal in comedy and elegy in several meaningful ways.

IV. Towards a Theory of Intermediary Activity: Ovid's *Ars amatoria*

Ovid's manual of advice on how to encounter and seduce an object of desire, maintain the relationship, and dissolve it when necessary, has given rise to divergent analyses by critics from numerous perspectives. Yet almost all recent interpretations of the work acknowledge the witty tone with which he infuses the frame of a seduction handbook for city-dwelling men and women.[101]

The poet claims to explore the world of transitory flirtation rather than serious, committed love. The very fact that he provides advice on everyday details such as dress, food, and financial arrangements,

---

[101] Williams, *Change and Decline*, 79. See 52-101, "Ovid: The Poet and Politics," which draws a detailed picture of Augustus' Rome and the backdrop to Ovid's political condition. Williams argues that the poet remained at all times adamant about staying away from mainstream politics and conflict, choosing for this purpose techniques involving refuge in antiquarianism, extensive use of Greek mythology, and flattery of the emperor. His *Ars* does not represent a politically critical stance against Augustus; his dilemma concerns, above all, such questions as the adaptation of unlikely poetic forms to his topic; in the case of one passage (vv. 205-222) viewed by some critics as ironic, Williams points out:

> [picking up girls] is what Ovid's poem is about, and it can be said at once that there is no irony here: not only are no criteria of irony satisfied, but Augustus would have to be reckoned with both as a discerning reader and also as the prime (indeed, the only) victim of it. (...) The problem that Ovid has solved was not how to make fun of Augustus, but how to accommodate panegyric artistically to the context of his poem without painful disruption (79).

See also Kennedy, *The Arts of Love*, 67-68; Ralph Hexter, *Ovid and Medieval Schooling* (Munich: Bei der Arbeo-Gesellschaft, 1986) 21.

and that he shows how to discontinue a relationship once it has become tedious, mark a downplaying of the grave emotional implications of love in favor of indulgence in its lighter aspects. In this way he constructs a setting much like that of a game; his stance as the ultimate authority on the subject of seduction requires that his voice in the first person dominate chief areas in the work, supervising the conduct of his players. In the course of the elaboration of this game, Ovid pays close attention to different tactics that will facilitate the love affair both for the man and the woman, introducing intermediary figures as aids in those strategies.

For Ovid, the entire process derives its strength from an uplifting and optimistic attitude based on the notion that all women can be won.[102] With this confident point of departure, the task as laid out by the principal narrative authority consists of exploring of every possible triumphant scenario, never entertaining the possibility of failure for long. Thus seduction becomes a process of drawing out trump cards at appropriate moments, as opposed to an uncertain challenge fraught with the tremor of possible defeat. Books I and II address the male lover, offering numerous ploys and schemes that will guarantee success over the woman of his choice. The wide variety includes dress, perfume, well-timed suggestive gestures, letters, presents, and above all, eloquent speech and the arts of rhetoric, which enjoy special emphasis, for therein lies the key to victory: "Do not take the learning of the arts too lightly, nor neglect to learn the two languages well."[103]

The game of seduction requires an alert and sharp lover who must perform the right tasks at appropriate moments. One of the many devices that he must employ with precision and care is a third party, for example the mistress's maidservant, who, under his guidance, will facilitate part of his endeavor. The beloved's maid requires instruction by the lover as to the time and place of her task; for instance, when combing her mistress's hair, she might mention his name in a favorable light, the context of which will have been determined by the lover.[104] In Book II, Ovid relegates the role of third party to a group of characters: porters, slaves, and the chambermaid. The lover bribes these characters

---

[102] *Ars Amatoria* I, vv. 248-349, where several stories are told, followed by a general conclusion, to confirm the point.

[103] "Nec levis ingenuas pectus coluisse per artes/Cura sit et linguas edidicisse duas" (*Ars Amatoria* II, vv. 121-122).

[104] *Ars Amatoria* I, vv. 351-358.

to gain better access to the woman's residence.[105] Book III, which provides advice for women, categorizes potential messengers or aids in similar ways; the woman must write eloquent letters, which are carried to their destination by a trusted maid and not a foolish messenger. Now and again she must create a feigned sense of danger in her room with the help of her maid so as to emphasize her own inaccessibility.[106]

The art of carnal love according to Ovid, therefore, requires some recourse to third-party assistance. For Ovid, this assistance operates purely under the direction of either of the two lovers. The intermediary must contribute to the cumulative effect of all devices, opening otherwise closed doors in his or her capacity as doorkeeper, slave, or maid, or providing a necessary mention when instructed. Ovid designates a specific space for intermediaries as secondary aids who help overcome individual obstacles of the strategic kind, involving doors, gates, discreet delivery of letters, or fortuitous mentions of the lover's name. In this scheme intermediaries are instruments used by either lover to fulfill a purpose. The game of seduction requires two principal players, male and female, considered skillful enough to undertake it on their own. Careful control over all the devices used in this game, including any third party, shows clearly the subordination of messenger to lovers' designs. The messenger pertains to the fabric of artifice, sign, and ritual mentioned by Baudrillard.[107] The limited circle of the *lena*'s scope of action expands in the *Ars* to include the go-between as a useful albeit small element in the grand artifice of seduction: from the object of diatribe to a controlled asset. The assignation of this role to her can be understood in light of the manual's focus, which, unlike elegy and comedy, has to do with the union and not the separation of lovers. The triumphant tone that guides the discourse of the *Ars* contrasts with the despondent moments of elegy during which the poet struggles to catch a glimpse of the *amica*. The *Ars* proposes a theory of seduction which it then substantiates with concrete examples: within this scheme the third party must be transformed into an element in favor of the erotic project but kept at all times under the strict supervision of the lovers. This specification points implicitly at the acknowledgment that her presence is potentially threatening if it is not kept under rigid control.

---

[105] *Ars Amatoria* II, vv. 251-260.
[106] *Ars* III, vv. 470-472, 485, 605-610.
[107] Baudrillard, *De la séduction*, 29.

One element which, albeit in cursory fashion, endows the go-between with a hint of danger is brought up by Ovid and requires inclusion in the typology of the figure, in spite of its minimal development. In the case where the mistress's young maid plays the role of assistant, the poet refers to the possibility of erotic association with the maid.[108] This added feature, though mentioned very briefly, removes the maid from the realm of pure auxiliary capacity and tinges her portrayal with a color that connotes a streak of threat to the mistress and the source of some pleasure for the pursuer. But the manual leaves the threat in its very initial stages, and exploits the erotic dimension of the maid as yet another indication of the lively inconstancy advocated by the poet on behalf of the lover, enhancing all the more the playful, false nature of his sentiments for his beloved.[109] The comment on sexual association with the maid does not so much affect the portrayal of the latter as it confirms the non-committal character of carnal love as seen in the *Ars amatoria.* In a typical gesture of unreliability, the lover can choose to invalidate any truth attached to his sentiment by pursuing his mistress's maid, an act which is in line with his general insincerity.

The suggestion of an erotic aspect to the messenger might have influenced her representation substantially in the *Ars* if pursued a little further; Ovid chooses not to do so, organizing his topic in such a way that the said feature serves to reveal another insincere side of the lover, as opposed to developing a facet of the messenger's own character. Due to her brief appearance, which is so intertwined with other devices such as letters, wine, other doorkeepers or slaves, she does not encourage any serious contemplation regarding the significance of the added trait of possible erotic interest. The stress falls unequivocally on the lighthearted nature of the pursuer. However slight its impact on the portrayal of herself though, the messenger in Ovid's *Ars* has been sexualized, and this must now be included as one of her features in the typology of the third party.

Money governs Ovid's game throughout. Constant reminders pervade the text to show that financial power holds the key to the entire

---

[108] *Ars Amatoria* I, vv. 375-399. The poet specifies that he, on the whole, is against such a measure, for the maid's indiscretion may backfire later thus damaging the main objective which is to gain the mistress. At the same time he does not categorically oppose it, stating that, ultimately, the wisest solution is to enjoy the maid after the mistress.

[109] *Ars* II, vv. 311-314, where the sentiment's falsehood is confirmed.

process, allowing for the construction of the artificial scenery needed to lure the pursued.[110] Third-party assistants such as maids or doormen who solve minor logistical problems are manifestations of the pursuer's economic status. Money's vital role endows it with manipulative qualities that surpass the scope of all other individual devices, for it remains omnipresent in the *Ars amatoria;* furthermore, coupled with the idea that no woman will resist a lover's advances, the basic recourse to money as the support behind every stratagem emphasizes the arbitrary nature of the techniques employed for success. Money, used for such preparations as the purchase of presents, bribery, or the creation of a luxurious setting for intimate conversation, equalizes these techniques, creating a panoramic rather than individual vision of their impact, for it brings them all under the same heading as cumulatively effective accessories to the plan.

The *Ars amatoria* does introduce and develop a full-fledged go-between: one who takes initiative, imparts advice, and penetrates both the masculine and the feminine spheres of urban life. This is none other than the poet himself. Speaking as a witty authority to both sides, spicing his suggestions with anecdotes, and paying attention to every detail, Ovid fulfills the role of an experienced go-between and teacher effectively, recalling the Greek model that telescoped the two roles into one. By assigning the role of an indispensable third party to the poet's voice, Ovid constructs a triangle in which teaching becomes the essential task of the figure situated between the two lovers. As one who describes and teaches the procedures of seduction, this figure gains the most prominent place in the poetics of love, taking upon himself the agency for the creation of the artifice of seduction, as well as communicating with both parties, and helping them seduce one another. He shows that a pedagogical stance, however playful and ironic, elevates the third party to the position of *magister,* for it divulges necessary knowledge associated with love, the awareness of which will lead to conquest. The convergence of pedagogy and intermediary activity is *Ars amatoria*'s principal contribution to the typology of the go-between; yet, as far as messengers or confidantes are concerned, Ovid remains clear that their place in the scheme of seduction is quite limited.

---

[110] As mentioned earlier, the regular purchase of presents, the preparation of a comfortable and luxurious setting, and bribery so as to avoid outside interruptions are the basic factors considered by Ovid as indispensable.

V. Outside the Realm of Courtesans: The Intermediary in Ovid's *Metamorphoses*

With the *Metamorphoses,* Ovid creates an artistic form that defies strict categorization. As the scholar Peter E. Knox has observed, the fifteen books of hexameter narrative by the poet of *Ars amatoria* and the *Amores* have given rise to much discussion by critics as to their place within genres such as "epic" or "counter-epic," and the work's genre seems to have concerned readers excessively.[111] In fact, here Ovid has combined various elements from diverse areas and included motifs from several sources.[112] Regarding the figure of the go-between, in one tale Ovid brings in an old woman as third party to an illicit affair and for her portrayal draws on Greek sources, elegiac traits, and features uncommon to both. The dialogue of genres and sources contributes to the construction of an identity subsequently encountered frequently in the European texts of the Middle Ages, since the figure in question operates within the confines of a private home as opposed to a public house.

This old woman appears in Book X (vv. 298-502) of the *Metamorphoses* as the faithful nurse to Myrrha, a young woman consumed by sexual passion for her father, but unwilling to admit this to the nurse even at the moment of her attempted suicide. Faced with the young girl's silent torment, the nurse invitingly suggests a number of reasons that may lie behind Myrrha's despair and proposes immediately to eliminate any trouble using sorcery and then religious ritual; the occult, then, represents the first weapon exposed to the reader in shape of a potential remedy: "'Tell me,' she asks, 'let me offer you help: my old age is not feeble. If it is madness, I have incantations and herbs; if someone has cast a spell on you, magic can save you; if the gods are angry with you, sacrifice will calm their anger.'" [113]

Next, realizing that love has brought about the young woman's distress, the nurse abandons any vocabulary related to sorcery and

---

[111] Peter E. Knox, *Ovid's* Metamorphoses *and the Traditions of Augustan Poetry* (Cambridge: The Cambridge Philological Society, 1986) 1.

[112] Knox, *Ovid's* Metamorphoses, 1.

[113] 'dic,' inquit, 'opemque
me sine ferre tibi: non est mea pigra senectus.
seu furor est, habeo, quae carmine sanet et herbis;
sive aliquis nocuit, magico lustrabere ritu
ira deum sive est, sacris placabilis ira. (...)' (*Metamorphoses X,* vv. 395-399).

proposes her service in terms no longer related to the occult: '"You are in love! in this situation I will do everything for you[.]"'[114] demonstrating her alertness vis-à-vis the father's possible wrath should Myrrha wish to embark on a secret affair with a young man. The last stage of her dialogue with Myrrha leads to the revelation of the scandalous secret, whereupon the nurse, though horrified, assumes the role of intermediary and arranges the consummation of the forbidden love with King Cinyras, Myrrha's father, by conveying to him that a young girl unknown to him feels passion for him. The encounter happens relatively easily, and without much need for the nurse's eloquence, thanks to Cinyras' own willing disposition. The mention of the young girl arouses the King's interest. The arrangements take up no more than ten lines of verse, with the nurse's direct speech to Cinyras conveyed in three words. In the buildup to a disastrous end, the tale gains a tense momentum, and thus little time is spent describing the preliminary stages of the affair.

Under such narratological circumstances, the elaboration of a critical discourse for the intermediary cannot occur fully; we have seen that similar to the elegiac bawd, her initial references to sorcery assume a static, redundant quality. As for her words to Myrrha's father, an efficient simplicity stands out due to the specific objectives and the limited time frame within which they must occur so that the tale may proceed. Her portrayal is burdened, in addition, by the fact that in spite of her attachment to a household totally unassociated with the brothel, the nurse in this episode displays some of the characteristics witnessed in the elegiac bawd, mixed with the specific, limited utility of the messenger in the *Ars*. Her initial projection occurs in terms of sorcery as a cure or antidote to a perceived problem, and, as has been the case of elegy, these otherworldly skills do not find any projection in the narrative. Her brief words produce effective results, only because the King's disposition favors such an outcome.

But Myrrha's nurse makes a contribution to the typology of the go-between in a direction opposite to elegy and Plautine drama. She demonstrates briefly some of the ways in which discourse supports the facilitation of an illicit task by producing words of consolation and comfort. The tone of her utterances poses a contrast with the

[114] "amas! et in hoc mea (pone timorem)/sedulitas erit apta tibi" (*Metamorphoses X*, vv. 408-409).

disturbing connotations that haunt the representation of an old woman in the position of intermediary. The principal difference with elegy lies in the intermediary's posture in relation to the "lovers": she no longer threatens one of the parties, nor does she attempt to exert influence on the woman's will. Intense emotions of pity and loyalty drive the third party to action, and this path foreshadows that of third parties in several texts of the Middle Ages. Financial gain, a crucial aspect of the third party's concerns, disappears here in favor of emotional motivation. After her initial horror, the nurse displays great enthusiasm for the realization of the secret desire, allowing her fervor to overshadow any moral difficulty, in contrast to the perspective of the narrator who continuously expresses dread at the nature of Myrrha's passion. Affection and loyalty override moral concern, and Myrrha's nurse acts as the prototype of medieval go-betweens who elaborate strategies of mediation around this conviction.

For the union to occur, the plot requires a point of transition. Similar to the concepts explained in the *Ars amatoria*, third-party activity in the *Metamorphoses* centers upon this specific moment of transition and implies above all the fulfillment of two obligatory gestures: the revelation of the secret desire and the subsequent accompaniment of the girl into the meeting place. The narrative proceeds, thanks to the nurse, from one set of complex events (the tale of Myrrha's desire) into the other (realization and punishment). The common thread running through the narrative concerns Myrrha's psychological dilemma, maintained at all times in the forefront, and enhancing all the more the sense that her nurse must ultimately carry out a specific logistical task, acting as an instrument of change at a particular instant.[115] The absence of moral anxiety on the nurse's part further emphasizes this position, for it accelerates the process at the level of the plot and distances her from a contribution to aspects of the psychological dilemma. Her profile recalls elegy while her acts bring to mind the *Ars amatoria*. The dialogue of genres that occurs in the *Metamorphoses* brings in recognizable traits from the two works and intro-

[115] The tale of Myrrha's incestuous passion for her father is evidently not Ovid's original creation. It is indebted to the *Zmyrna* of Helvius Cinna. Knox points out that the general mythographical tradition, plus what is left of *Zmyrna*, allow us to gauge Ovid's adjustments to the tale, among them the poet's interest – contrary to his predecessors – in "portraying Myrrha's passion as a psychological problem without external narrative [so that] it is her character that is the center of the narrative" (Knox, *Ovid's* Metamorphoses, 55).

duces the new elements of loyalty and emotion. Both on the level of the plot and in terms of a conceptualization of intermediary activity, the mixture of factors creates a figure who stands at the crossroads of two familiar realms explored by Ovid and his predecessors in elegy and the *Ars amatoria*, advancing mediation into the realm of paradox, where morality and loyalty struggle briefly.

VI. Narrative Prose: The Old Bawd in Apuleius' *Metamorphoses*

Descended from a Greek source, the *Metamorphoses* of Apuleius trace the many adventures of the young man Lucius from his transformation into an ass to the eventual restoration of human form and religious redemption by the Goddess Isis.[116] Scholars acknowledge the entertaining quality of the episodes of the novel but recognize also that the adventures of Lucius happen according to a moral vision that leads to didactic conclusions regarding the human condition, a view confirmed by Lucian's retransformation in the last Book. Here the priest of the Goddess Isis interprets Lucius' journey by providing a meaning for the steps the latter has had to take in his path towards becoming a servant of Isis: "Every word uttered by the priest is of the utmost import. He is, in effect, providing the novel's (Apuleius') interpretation of Lucius' experiences."[117] The reader must approach the novel with this moralist vision in mind, for its force establishes meaning for each separate episode in relation to the whole novel.

The topic of carnal love, relevant for its moral implications to the fate of Lucius, adds entertaining and colorful elements to the *Metamorphoses* but generates a despondent and sometimes violent image:

> In the *Met*, the experience of sexual pleasure, *veneria voluptas*, is evocatively described, but is presented as rare, brief and precarious, subject not only to the whims of *saeva Fortuna* but to human malevolence. Erotic desire is repeatedly shown turning to hate, cruelty and revenge. The uncontrolled passions which dominate the ten books of adventures stand in contrast to the ascetic devotion of the redeemed Lucius.

[116] The sources and genre of Apuleius' work are discussed in H. J. Mason, "Fabula Graecanica: Apuleius and his Greek Sources," in *Aspects of Apuleius'* Golden Ass, edited by B. L. Hijmans Jr. and R. Th. van der Paardt (Groningen: Bouma's Boekhuis, 1978) 1-17.

[117] James Tatum, *Apuleius and* The Golden Ass (Ithaca: Cornell University Press, 1979) 82.

> This moral vision, consonant with the Platonism which Apuleius so proudly professed, is basic to the serious meaning of the work.[118]

The episodes that deal with desire and carnal love do not, therefore, stand alone but require the acknowledgment of a broad moralist context.[119] Of great significance in this broad assessment is Apuleuis' treatment of witchcraft as inextricably linked with sexual desire. Carl C. Schlam notes that from the very outset of Lucius' adventures, Thessalian witchcraft goes hand in hand with erotic goals,[120] as seen in the initial violent carnal encounters with witches from the opening tale of the novel: "The first woman we meet in the *Met.* is the witch, Meroe (...) The account establishes an intimate connection between magic and both sex and religion."[121] Subsequently other witches (Circe, Pamphile and Byrrhena) enter the narrative, each of whom punishes indifferent or unfaithful lovers in horrendous ways, using magic towards erotic purposes.[122] The predatory tendencies of these excessively lustful witches underscore the link between carnal desire and the occult: women's sexual activity engages otherworldly, evil elements which ultimately bring about men's downfall. This link finds itself revitalized in Book Nine in the context of a hateful, adulterous wife's illicit activities. Here an old bawd attempts to assist the wife in her sinful pursuits, and with her enter the unequivocally immoral connotations of mediation linked with witchcraft and evil.[123]

The bawd makes an entrance into the narrative in a somewhat unclear manner; Lucian presents her prefaced by the word "Sed" as a conjunction, implying that the *anus* stands for an obstacle in his attempt to betray the wife: "However an old woman who knew of her

---

[118] C.C. Schlam, "Sex and Sanctity: the Relationship of Male and Female in the *Metamorphoses*," in *Aspects of Apuleius'* Golden Ass, 95-105 (95).

[119] Schlam, "Sex and Sanctity," 98.

[120] Carl C. Schlam, *The* Metamorphoses *of Apuleius* (Chapel Hill: The University of North Carolina Press, 1992) 67.

[121] Schlam, "Sex and Sanctity," 96.

[122] Schlam, "Sex and Sanctity," 96.

[123] Schlam, *The* Metamorphoses *of Apuleius*, 80. González Rolán lists this old woman as an inspiration for medieval Peninsular writers in their conceptualization of the Spanish *alcahueta*, based on the unproven assumption that the work was known in the Spanish Middle Ages; the critic refers to this *anus* as "un preciosísimo ejemplo de alcahueta" ("a superb example of the go-between") (287) and expresses surprise that she has remained unnoticed by previous scholars such as Bonilla or Menéndez y Pelayo.

misdemeanors and was her mediator in adulterous affairs, was inseparable from her, everyday."[124] He goes on to describe briefly the activities of the wife and *anus*, that is, the fact that they would start drinking wine together starting in the morning, and that the old woman would think up various plans for bringing about the downfall of the baker.[125] The reader's first encounter with the old woman compels the expectation that she will somehow impede the ass from revealing the wife's sinfulness and also that she will prepare for the financial ruin of the baker. Interestingly, neither of these introductory remarks finds realization in the plot: the bawd goes on to tell a story about a desirable young man named Philesitherus and his successful exploits in pursuing an adulterous relationship. Upon hearing of Philesitherus' many talents, the wife, already involved in another affair, decides to change lovers and so the old bawd brings the young man to her and disappears from the narrative. Nowhere does she impede Lucius from betraying the wife, nor does she bring about the husband's financial ruin, as is suggested by the prefatory remarks about her.

The depiction of the third-party figure in Apuleius follows a pattern similar to such an exposition in the elegiac poets and in Plautus, and confirms this pattern as paradigmatic for the Roman writers: the figure enters the text in terms of a set of activities and adjectives that fade away as soon as the tale moves towards a principal episode. Thus no indication is given of how the old woman might have stopped Lucius from betraying the wife's intentions to the husband, nor does the financial downfall of the husband provide any further interest for the plot. Instead, the old woman serves as the teller of an inserted story and as the instrument for bringing the story's protagonist to the wife.

The wife's disposition affects the role of mediation considerably, if not fully. After hearing the tale, the wife takes control, reiterating the negative associations of carnal love and recalling the evils represented by the witches in the first books of the novel. The delivery of the lover by the old woman represents a moment in the background in light of the grandiose preparation of the baker's wife for his arrival; the narrative conveys the bawd's contribution thus: "and the dauntless lover appeared, closely accompanying the dis-

[124] "Sed anus quaedam stuprorum sequestra et adulterorum internuntia de die cotidie inseparabilis aderat" (Apuleius, 152).

[125] Apuleius, 152.

gusting old woman."[126] Afterwards, the old woman disappears completely.

Intermediary activity, given the three stages of the bawd's presence, has here reached a formal and almost ritualistic stage: it involves the fulfillment of certain appropriate gestures such as displaying further options for an already experienced woman whose needs remain very clear to herself. After all, the fragment begins with the news that the wife has procured a lover for herself without the bawd.[127] The latter adds more color to the plot with the insertion of her tale and contributes to some degree of suspense by virtue of her storytelling skills. But the true intrigue begins once she has left, upon the return of the baker, for at this point the wife confronts the principal conflict in the tale on her own.

Later, when the baker's wife has been shunned by her husband, she seeks the aid of an enchantress so that her husband may forgive her; the enchantress has been perceived as a go-between in criticism, but misleadingly so.[128] The witch's words do not appear in the text as a dialogue with the baker, but rather an attempt to soften his heart using the supernatural and her evil science. Upon its failure she feels infuriated with the spirits and proceeds with witchcraft in condemnation of the husband, using instruments of the occult. [129] The text gives no indication of a personal confrontation using words. As her activity shows, her single identifying factor and impact on the narrative derive from her recourse to the supernatural. It cannot be denied that she has tremendous impact on the plot, since this part of the tale finally reaches a definitive end because of her acts, but the witch's methods place her in a realm of pure sorcery with the end-result of murder. As regards the poetics of mediation, her role is limited to the occult, a feature that does not fit into the realm of verbal discourse in the text. That is to say, Apuleius portrays triangulation in terms of a power that exists outside speech and which, therefore, establishes no contact

---

[126] "et ecce nequissime anus adhaerens lateri temerarius adulter adventat" (Apuleius, 168).

[127] The bawd expresses disgust with this lover who was found "sine meo consilio[.]" ("without my advice") (Apuleius, 154). He may not be ideal, but the fact remains that his attentions were secured independently.

[128] González Rolán, 288. The critic's summary of the events with this enchantress contains an error, as he states that the witch attempts first to soften the wife with words.

[129]Apuleius, 180.

of import with the characters who have recourse to it. This fundamental lack of dialogic communication pushes the witch's impact into an essentially inferior sphere, away from language, and serves to reinforce the link between sexuality and evil witchcraft. The witch is not a practitioner of the black magic of seduction such as Baudrillard qualifies it, since her tasks are entirely categorizable.

Scholars have noted that the final book of the *Metamorphoses*, the so-called "Isis-book," fits adequately in the novel given that the redemption of Lucius maintains a close link with the specific adventures he witnesses in the previous ten books. This relationship holds the key to the proper thematic localization of every episode and applies equally to the figure of the bawd. Apuleius has constructed a novel in which

> Serious themes, expressed through the juxtaposition of stories and patterns of motifs and symbols, relate the Isis-book to the previous course of adventure. Examination of these reveals how the comic adventures of a man transformed into an ass has been reshaped into an aetiology of Isis.[130]

In this last Book, a moral sense finally emerges for the entire tale. Lucius turns into a man and becomes devoted to Isis; this is made possible only by intervention: "The conversion of Lucius, like his retransformation to his human form, is due to Isis and to no one else."[131] This conversion by the intervention of a higher being happens elsewhere in the book also, in the tale of Cupid and Psyche: "Like Psyche, he [Lucius] has required the intervention of a high being, a *mesites* or *daimon*, to save him from his natural state."[132] In the symmetrical scheme of the novel, the old bawd who accompanies the baker's wife also represents intervention on a much less significant but evil plane; her intervention – providing a new option and delivering the goods – takes place for a party already disposed towards it and reflects, in the context of the entire novel, an incident in which interference by a lower being can lead to the exact opposite of redemption. In this episode we have one of the many patterns of motifs and symbols that endow the novel with a strongly didactic meaning as seen from the final perspective of the Isis episode.

---

[130] Schlam, "Sex and Sanctity," 95.
[131] Tatum, *Apuleius and* The Golden Ass, 88.
[132] Tatum, *Apuleius and* The Golden Ass, 88.

The strong moralizing tone guides the conceptualization of the figures of the old woman and enchantress and better illustrates the necessity of their characterization in terms of mechanical and stylized gestures, since the ultimate purpose of their role must serve a didactic aim. This excludes ironic or ambiguous exploitation of the character, for such a treatment would jeopardize the didactic aim by opening up multiple possibilities of interpretation: it confirms, instead, the easy potential of the figure of the go-between to act as a screen for the projection of moral concerns. Indeed, this is one of the most prominent features of figures who act in positions – albeit minor, or even negligible – of mediation: they help articulate the text's didactic disapproval with little or no difficulty.

VII. Conclusion

The old women considered above have entered each literary work under the qualification *lena* or *anus*, and this qualification has presupposed a set of characteristics. These have constituted the basis for the construction of her identity: greed, inebriation, and a continuing predilection for the pursuit of carnal desire, which the old woman attempts to act out through a younger party. The conclusion can now be drawn that the *lena* in antiquity is not concerned with two of the most transgressive and dangerous elements related to illicit love: the artifice of seduction, and the mediation or teaching of that artifice. The evils attributed to her invariably exceed the scope of her actual impact.

Seduction, as Ovid points out in his guide to the art of love, intertwines with eloquent speech on the one hand, and financial power on the other. The two factors help construct the most appropriate artifice for the successful expression of desire and hence for conquest. Similarly, while the plots in other genres recount the literal unfolding of events and the importance of successful seduction to the central characters, the language of each text elaborates a poetics of carnal love for the description of and gloss on the events. We have seen that on the level of the plot, the overwhelmingly strong presence of the lovers has stunted the go-between's ability for a type of mediation which would exert significant impact on the lovers. Sullivan observes, for example, that the poets' mistresses "are their equals, if not (...) their superiors. They are valuable not simply as beauties, but as possible friends and intellectual companions."[133] Within such a context, the *lena* attempts to construct another triangle by calling for new affairs between the mistress and a rival, crediting herself as the instigator. The destructive implication of this gesture soon gives way to irony and even slapstick in the obvious absence of any proof of the *lena*'s success. The effect of this projection for Plautus emerges in the contrast provided by her pathetic or rigid interference against the transitions explored by Comedy. For Tibullus she represents one of the many addressees who inspire the poet's exploration of his own voice in despair or anger.[134] For Ovid in the *Ars*, the maid as intermediary reinforces an already prevalent idea of lighthearted insincerity, which is enhanced by her own erotic potential. The *Metamorphoses* of Apuleius uses the figure for the reiteration of a moral stance.[135] In all cases, that which is underscored is the facility with which the old woman's attempts at mediation – against or for the lovers – draws moral reproach. The definition of mediation lies not in the *lena* but elsewhere.

The *magister* status of the writers contains one of the explanations for the role of the old go-between. Elegy showcases the status of the poet and its impingement upon the go-between; the genre cannot allow for the existence of another *magister* figure, for this would bring about an essential and dangerous conflict as regards mastery over the artifice of seduction. Even if Baudrillard refers to the artifice as an inherently feminine construct, no doubt remains – in elegy particularly – as to the poet's domination over the discourse that expresses

[133] Sullivan, *Propertius*, 90.

[134] It will be recalled that what the *lena* aims to inspire in the mistress has already been realized by the latter, based on the frequent mentions of the mistress's love of gold and her pursuit of rivals throughout the elegies.

[135] In the *Metamorphoses* by Apuleius, the tone of the *anus* as she recounts the story of Philesitherus is worthy of attention. The bawd's introduction to the desirable young man through this tale is marked by a surprisingly moralist and misogynist perspective; the married woman whom she describes as enjoying Philesitherus' attentions is labeled as typically weak when confronted with gold (Apuleius, 160). In the same tale, the slave Myrmex, who in the tale facilitates the reunion, is portrayed by the old woman in terms of the destruction of his loyalty. The build-up to the affair is recounted as a function of disgrace and greed, thereby creating a reprehensive tone. This judgmental account of the affair does not so much reveal a moralist awareness in the old woman as it converges her voice with that of the principal narrator Lucius. His discourse is at all times governed by identical qualifications of right and wrong. This merger with the moral preoccupation of the principal narrator overshadows to a large degree the evil connotations represented by the term "sequestra" ("mediator") upon her entrance into the novel.

the artifice. An older woman with significant access to the knowledge on seduction would present a substantial threat to the poet's status as the teacher and builder of the artifice. The same applies to Ovid's stance in the *Ars* and to the independent-minded lovers of Plautine comedy. The writers make a bold distinction between bawd (the *lena*) and pedagogue (themselves or the young lovers), as though fully aware of the potential for the convergence of the two roles into one which would therefore exert a fundamental influence over the construction of the artifice of seduction.

The old woman thus occupies a position without bringing to fruition the tasks attributed to that spot. Her discourse encompasses certain areas that highlight the extent to which she represents an antithesis of the haughty courtesan or any other female lover. That is to say, rather than complete the triangle composed of male, female, and go-between, she completes a configuration in which the young female axis faces a diametrically opposed version of herself while the male lover (or narrator) encounters a site into which he can place misplaced declarations of ire, guilt, or frustration. Where mediation does enter the picture, texts tend to charge her enactment of it with moral reprehension so as to undermine any substantial authority that her intermediary activity might entail. The *lena* is a convenient trope for a limited type of mediation: a logistical act with clearly designated boundaries, conceived as the type of interference that provokes mockery and disdain. In the worst cases, its prostibulary and slapstick connotations annul all possibility of the articulation of a complex language of mediation. Witchcraft, evil powers, and an obsession with money represent elements that never reach fruition, yet occupy the poetic imagination as permanent features of the old woman. Of special importance is the fact that these elements reside within a type of dialogic encounter that places the old woman in a clearly inferior position. Her supposed witchcraft and her real greed do not endow her with authority, but rather render her vulnerable to particularly aggressive forms of address. The discourse that forms in relation to her appears to throw the negative sentiments associated with seduction (frustration, anger, and unresolved moral preoccupations) onto a screen that she forms as she stands between pursuer and pursued.

The insistence that the old woman reside within such a sphere indicates a certain anxiety born of the knowledge that mediation can produce a powerful dialogic relationship with the object of desire, and in so doing, exert substantial impact on poetic language. Given the dominant nature of the poet's voice in elegy and that of the lovers' presence in Plautine comedy, the serious (that is, on the level of poetic language) mediation of a third party would threaten the distribution of power and result in a type of triangulation that would have to be taken into account when elaborating the artifice of seduction for the object of desire. The stereotypical portrayal of mediation in the form of an essentially weak old woman diminishes that threat and restores the hierarchically dialogic structure of the poet's relationship with his beloved and with the go-between. It is only upon close reading that the unresolved nature of the *lena*'s portrayal – excessive, directionless power attributed to a flat character – comes to light. The *lena* provides an impression of a safe and manageable space for mediation, for the narrators and poets discussed above appear all too aware of the potentially invasive power of this act if left unleashed.

Mediation, then, is a perturbing act, especially if peformed by older women, as the Latin writers show by downplaying and repressing the influence that such figures might exert. The reasons behind the old woman's marginal status in this literature create the premise for the evaluation of the figure's role in the European Middle Ages which, in addition to its specific elaborations of the character, draws heavily on Latin literature in its conception of the go-between. In the next chapter we will continue to explore the figure by scrutinizing the nature and functions of the descendants of the *lena* – and her variations – in medieval texts from medieval Latin, French, English and Italian.

CHAPTER TWO

THE MEDIEVAL EUROPEAN GO-BETWEEN

I. (i) *The Social Background: Christian Doctrine and Profane Love*

Concerning the figure of the go-between, the discussion of illicit love as represented in medieval literary texts requires an understanding of her roots in Antiquity as well as the notions expressed on profane love by the Church Fathers and subsequent doctrinal, religious writers in the Middle Ages. It is a well-known fact that literature does not simply replicate or record facts found in history and society. Yet, in light of the presence of procuresses and pimps in the legal and religious documents of the Middle Ages, it is fitting to outline how the character was perceived in extra-literary sources and to broaden the context for close textual readings. We must begin, therefore, with the common opinions expressed in medieval Christian doctrine on the question of illicit love, paying specific attention to the declarations on the type of intermediary activity used for the purpose of facilitating nonmarital relations, which at times show a continuity from the Classical period.[1]

In his study of the sixth- to twelfth-century penitentials, Pierre J. Payer notes that with such influential writers as Jovinian, Jerome, and Augustine, early in the Middle Ages "there emerged a standard for evaluating the various kinds of sexual behavior, a standard that set a higher priority on asexual ways of life and realized itself in the exhortation to virginal chastity."[2] This standard could only derive

---

[1] For an enlightening collection of views on medieval attitudes towards sexuality, see *Handbook of Medieval Sexuality*, edited by Vern L. Bullough and James A. Brundage (New York: Garland Publishers, 1996). Alongside the moral conceptions of love, the condition was also considered a sickness and therefore doubly subjected to critique as an unreasonable state. For medieval Western medicine and lovesickness, especially as relates to women, see Joan Cadden, *Meanings of Sex Difference in the Middle Ages: Medicine, Science, and Culture* (Cambridge: Cambridge University Press, 1993); Mary Frances Wack, "The *Liber de heros morbo* of Johannes Afflacius and Its Implications for Medieval Love Conventions," *Speculum* 62/2 (1987) 324-344, and *Lovesickness in the Middle Ages* (Philadelphia: University of Pennsylvania Press, 1990).

[2] Pierre J. Payer, *Sex and the Penitentials: The Development of a Sexual Code 550-1150* (Toronto: University of Toronto Press, 1984) 4.

from a rigorously judgmental attitude towards any type of nonmarital amorous relationship. Such an attitude appears time and again in canonistic and doctrinal writings, and as James Brundage explains, leads to the strong impression that medieval Christian doctrine often associates virtue with abstinence and sexuality with "something intrinsically evil or as the central element in morality."[3]

Indeed, the view articulated by Augustine, that "the good Christian (...) must lead a chaste life, even in marriage,"[4] is reiterated with frequency throughout the Middle Ages. Brundage's extensive study traces the prevalent attitudes from the early patristic writers and exegetes through to the Reformation, highlighting the abundance of material produced by the Church in its condemnation of sexual misbehavior. At the same time, he shows that instances of tolerance and leniency can be discerned in discussions of generally condemnable issues. Thus, for example, certain early decretists consider concubinage acceptable if occurring with marital affection, which would equate it with a secret marriage.[5] Elsewhere, for Justinian prostitution comes to signify the victimization of women, calling for society's protection of females rather than their relentless persecution.[6] The sources convey that while the Church articulated ideas on sexuality as the "prototype of all offenses,"[7] many a canonist or writer contributed to the generation of debate on several issues such as clerical celibacy, prostitution, and concubinage, now and then softening or problematizing the notions of guilt and acceptability. Shifts and changes in perception therefore occurred in the degrees of gravity attached to certain nonmarital offenses, especially with regards to the extent of evil attached to prostitution.[8] Brundage explains:

> The moral ambivalence that canonists and other legal experts showed towards prostitution was emblematic of the difficulties that medieval

[3] James A. Brundage, *Law, Sex, and Christian Society in Medieval Europe* (University of Chicago Press: 1987) 8-9 (hereafter "Brundage"). See also James A. Brundage, "Sex and Canon Law," in *Handbook of Medieval Sexuality*, 33-51.

[4] Brundage, 82.

[5] Brundage, 297.

[6] Brundage, 120.

[7] Brundage, 62.

[8] Brundage, 301. For example, in the twelfth century the decretists postulated that the gravity of the sex offense must be calculated according to "the place of the offense in the scale of sexual sins and the circumstances of the offender." This stands in marked contrast with the much more rigid view taken by the exegetes of any type of extramarital sexual offense.

> societies experienced in confronting the realities of human sexuality. Committed in principle to restricting sexual activity as narrowly as possible, canonists nonetheless had to take account professionally of the fact that systematic enforcement of the limits they wished to impose was difficult, if not impossible.[9]

One fact remains certain, however. The attitude of medieval Christian society towards go-betweens who facilitated nonmarital encounters was unanimously and overwhelmingly negative. Identified with pimping and pandering, the activity left no room for tolerance. For example, while Justinian displayed relative lenience towards prostitutes by pointing out their plight, he remained fierce in his judgment of pimps: "In an enactment of 535, he described in graphic detail the panderers who crawl through the provinces in quest of young girls who live in poverty and the wiles with which procurers deceive their victims by enticing them with shoes and clothes to come to the capital city."[10] For the early decretists, prostitution appeared acceptable in some cases, yet "Pimps and panderers were an altogether different matter. They incurred infamy by their very occupation, Rufinus asserted, and the faithful must shun them at all costs."[11] Likewise, from the time of Pope Alexander III (1159-81) through the mid-thirteenth century, general opinion held that the pimp was "*ipso iure* infamous[.]"[12] In the thirteenth and fourteenth centuries, from both ecclesiastical and royal authorities, "legal action was usually directed against bawds, not their clients."[13] In fact, the occupation was so well-defined in the minds of legal authorities that it labeled as pimp or bawd anyone who facilitated prostitution in any way at all.[14] So, while prostitution went on to represent a public utility by the fourteenth century – so much so that regulation turned it into tax revenue by the municipality in many cases – throughout the Middle Ages the acts of procuring and pandering maintained an intrinsic link in legal and didactic opinion with sinful and evil disposition.

Knowledge of third-party operation in medieval European society

[9] Brundage, "Sex and Canon Law," 45.
[10] Brundage, 120.
[11] Brundage, 310.
[12] Brundage, 394.
[13] Brundage, 463. The author goes on to provide several examples of the application of this legal stance in France, Italy, and England.
[14] Brundage, 467. Thus, for example, a man who made no rigorous effort towards the termination of his wife's adulterous behavior would be considered a pimp.

comes to us on the one hand from facts available on prostitution. Literary texts, on the other hand, portray go-betweens in situations outside the context of prostitution as well, so that the designation of pimp or panderer would not represent an altogether correct label for the person carrying out the task. However, as Brundage clarifies, the definition of the figure in legal and religious discussions suggests that the very act of procuring denotes sinful behavior, warranting reproach and condemnation. This strong resonance finds its way into medieval literature to varying degrees and is further complicated by the webs of intertextuality and literary influence in the medieval period.

(ii) *The Question of Intertextuality*

The literary texts considered here treat the topic of nonmarital love in remarkably diverse ways. Every text offers a unique dialogue with themes from the past and from contemporary sources, engaging the dynamics of intertextuality in a significant manner. As Claudio Guillén has suggested, generally speaking, the "genetic substrata of intertextuality" resist simplification. Guillén chooses to concentrate on specific examples to illustrate the mechanisms of intertextuality for particular writers and texts. His method helps demonstrate the unique characteristics of the dialogue of texts in individual cases as opposed to an overall formula that might apply to all and calls for a further sketching of coordinates according to period and genre.[15]

In the particular context of medieval European literature, Michael Riffaterre defines intertextuality as a phenomenon that guides the interpretation of the text in light of previous modes of representation known to the reader. The words in the text acquire meaning in terms of this preexisting representation, be it from a known work, a fragment, or a descriptive system.[16] Reading, therefore, is guided by an understanding of the nature of the presuppositions underlying the words in the text:

> Since each pertinent word of the literary text, that is each word with stylistic import, has a meaning insofar as it *presupposes a text.* The text that we read (...) is only literary insofar as it combines also the texts to

---

[15] Guillén, *The Challenge of Comparative Literature*, 258.

[16] Michael Riffaterre, "L'intertexte inconnu," *Littérature* 41 (1981) 5-7.

> which the original words belonged, and the texts whose syntagms are only partial citations.[17]

In the case of the figure playing out the specific role of third party in an amorous situation, the reader must remain aware of any presuppositions carried over from the past as well as from influential contemporary trends. For instance, the common designation of *lena* produces certain consistent results in Latin literature with regards to the nature and function of the figure. As mentioned in chapter one, she inspires comic effect, stands to represent immutability and rigidity, and evokes, albeit barely, the insecurities associated with mercenary sexuality. On the surface, the Latin *lena* projects much threat and potential for impact, yet upon close analysis it is found that she does not require a particularly complex or powerful discourse for seduction or providing aid, since in fact, she exists in the texts as a function of acts and gestures for a specific structural purpose. Any discourse elaborated by the figure revolves rigidly around pecuniary concerns, leading to an ultimately comic effect due to excessive repetition and general failure. The recurrence of these elements in the bawd's representation helps construct the body of presuppositions which carry across into the medieval works. This transmission of motif from Antiquity to the Middle Ages offers a challenge for interpretation, for it continues to generate the often false impression of the bawd's evil power.

Intertextuality for medieval works does not limit itself, naturally, to Antiquity, and exists in relation to medieval sources also. Paul Zumthor notes that intertextuality in the literature of the Middle Ages can take several forms: significant variants in manuscripts of the same work; intentional mixtures of different types of discourse and register within the same work so as to create a new effect such as parody; evidence that entire fragments have been "copied" from another source in ways which today would be considered plagiarism.[18] These constituents and their numerous variations contribute to the shaping of the phenomenon designated by Zumthor as the movement of texts within a network of close relations, each text

---

[17] "Car chaque mot pertinent du texte littéraire, c'est-à-dire chaque mot stylistiquement marqué, signifie dans la mesure où il *présuppose un texte*. Le texte que nous lisons (...) n'est littéraire que dans la mesure où il combine aussi les textes auxquels appartiennent originairement [l]es lexèmes, et les textes dont [l]es syntagmes ne sont que des citations partielles" (Riffaterre, 6).

[18] Paul Zumthor, "Intertextualité et mouvance," *Littérature* 41 (1981) 8-16, 14.

maintaining a stable identity while deriving many thematic currents from contact with other texts.[19] The figure of the go-between engages the notions of movement and contact between texts continually, for it relies as much on inherent, invisible presuppositions from outside each text as on the actual poetics employed within the work.

The variety of genres ranging from courtly romance through comedy and prose narrative, therefore, offer intertwined conceptions of third-party activity, relying for their portrayal of the act and its (supposed or real) agents on notions that are assumed to be already present vis-à-vis the Classical heritage of the go-between and contemporary moral implications of the task. Even when texts assign the task to a male figure or otherwise leave the space occupied by the professional bawd, the go-between by definition remains inextricably linked with the world of nonmarital love and sexuality and, as such, labors under the weight of moral anxiety, however imperceptible.

One of the most important areas for the study of nonmarital love in literature is that of "courtly love," a designation ever subject to debate as any glance at the relevant bibliography will reveal. Given that this concept reigns over much of the written literature of the twelfth century and onwards, it is fitting to begin with an analysis of the ways in which third-party implication inscribes itself into the thematics of this particular concept.

II. The Twelfth Century: The Spirit of Courtly Love

Some scholars feel that the notion identified as courtly love has been cursorily subject to a "monolithic evaluation of the nature and meaning of love in medieval literary texts."[20] The editors of *Poetics of Love in the Middle Ages* argue:

> The various modes of love illustrated in medieval literature, from the twelfth century on, have often been reduced to a single concept and term: *amour courtois*, courtly love. This term, used only once in Provençal love songs (*cortez' amor*, from a poem by Peire d'Alvernhe), and coined quite independently by Gaston Paris in his essay on Chrétien de Troyes' *Lancelot*, has since served to describe a variety of dis-

[19] Zumthor, "Intertextualité et mouvance," 9.

[20] *Poetics of Love in the Middle Ages: Texts and Contexts*, edited by Moshe Lazar and Norris J. Lacy (Virginia: George Mason University Press, 1989) vii.

> tinct and sometimes contradictory notions of love. (...) It is thus essential that we progress beyond the point of using terms such as "courtliness" or "courtly love" as catch-all categories comprising *fin'amors*, passionate love, and conjugal relationships. (...) we should now direct our efforts (...) toward a recognition of the diversity and complexity of medieval notions of love[.][21]

The editors, correctly, do not suggest the abandonment of the term courtly love; rather, they call for an appreciation of "the remarkable variety of means, modes, and expressions of love" that would account for the complexity of the phenomenon instead of reducing it to a single notion.[22] As Barbara Nolan suggests in her study of Chaucer, the mere naming of a tradition need not limit one's critical frame of reference:

> I do not mean to imply that by naming a tradition we can fully account for the specific formal or ethical dynamics of each text. I use the notion of a tradition as a pragmatic, heuristic tool always focusing on the reciprocal relation between the supposed tradition and the particular contours of each text in the group. [23]

The notion that each work contains individual contours responding to a set of thematic priorities applies also to the work of writers associated with courtly love. The compositions of Chrétien, Andreas Capellanus and the troubadours lead us in multiple interpretative directions, yet they contain certain elements of setting and characterization that betray a strong affiliation with a broad definition of courtly love. The treatise by Andreas offers an adequate point of departure for the appreciation of the contours of this term:

> By and large, we are dealing with commonplaces attributable to the entire courtly tradition. Among the courtly themes repeatedly developed by Andreas we find: the ennobling power of love, the necessity for fidelity and for concealment, the haughtiness of the lady, the danger of slanderers, the importance of sight and beauty in the generation of love, the passion of the lover, the beloved as object of dreams and meditation, and love as a cause of suffering and death. [24]

---

[21] *Poetics of Love*, vii-viii.

[22] *Poetics of Love*, ix.

[23] Barbara Nolan, *Chaucer and the Tradition of the 'Roman Antique'* (Cambridge: Cambridge University Press, 1992) 2.

[24] Donald A. Monson, "*Auctoritas* and Intertextuality in Andreas Capellanus' *De Amore*," in *Poetics of Love*, 69-79, 74.

These are the constants in the courtly tradition, which lead in turn to the individual preferences in focus and treatment by each writer.

In the broad realm of the literature which engages courtly love, relatively few texts provide substantial depictions of the go-between. Naturally, the portrayal enhances narrative quality by allowing for the elaboration of another interesting character in the tale and is absent from lyric poetry, for example, due to the more confined narrative premise of the genre. Other important reasons for the relative absence and silence of the figure come to light in the cumulative study of a number of pertinent texts, the first of which are the *Romans d'antiquités* in which the old woman and the mother fulfill the function of go-between according to a special set of parameters.

(i) *The Twelfth-Century French* Romans d'antiquité

These twelfth-century *estoires* depict incidents from ancient history and problematize contemporary moral values using narrative structure.[25] As Barbara Nolan suggests, the tales stand for epistemological exercises that offer a paradigm for public and private moral values, in addition to the entertaining aspect made up of the "*solaz* of *bon dits* and *merveilles*."[26] These romances also create a significant intertextual relation with Chrétien's work, as well as with the literary creations of Boccaccio and Chaucer, which we will be analyzing later.

Numerous scholars have helped discern the principal features of the *Romans d'antiquité;* full of motifs and narrative techniques reminiscent of Ovid, the tales deal with secular moral conduct and are known to have been composed largely for a small elite audience of aristocrats.[27] Love is by no means the only theme of the *Romans;* however, it does play a significant part in the narrative, and the tales pay close attention to romantic and erotic gender relations. In the words of Nolan, the works "pose urgent, practical questions about the place of sexual love in a highly structured, politically ambitious aristocracy."[28]

---

[25] Paul Zumthor, *Langue, texte, énigme* (Paris: Éditions du Seuil, 1975) 242. According to the scholar, the re-questioning has to do with the transition from the ethics imposed by the epic genre.

[26] Nolan, *Chaucer and the Tradition,* 10-11.

[27] Nolan, *Chaucer and the Tradition,* 14. Acknowledging the work of previous scholars, the writer draws in her synthesis on such critics as Faral, Frappier and Huchet.

[28] Nolan, *Chaucer and the Tradition,* 75.

In two of the romances, Benoît de Sainte-Maure's *Roman de Troie* and the anonymous *Roman d'Éneas*, the central love affair draws at some point on third-party help provided by older women.[29] In Benoît's tale, Medea has an old governess who enters the scene after the preliminaries for the love affair – the most important of which is Medea's tryst with Jason – have been established. As the young woman awaits the hour of her tryst with Jason, she summons her old nurse and tells her to accelerate the events and bring Jason to her without making any noise.[30] Nolan's close commentary on the passage attributes the introduction of a go-between to a clear source, to which she refers as an Ovidian pattern.[31] It must be specified that Ovid offers a number of options for the role of go-between: from the despised elegiac *lena* to the pretty maidservant of the *Ars* in addition to the frightened yet experienced nurse of the *Metamorphoses*. Above all, the "vieille" corresponds to the latter; she gives the young girl advice, a gesture unheard of in the *Ars* and largely ignored as well as disdained in the elegies: she tells her to lie down and await her lover in bed, for that would be a more elegant and decorous way of conducting the tryst.[32] The words imply reflection and experience in matters related to the protocol of love, and in that regard do not replicate the Ovidian model. The "vieille"'s concern here has to do with decorum, politeness, and all avoidance of "vilenie." She thereby serves, in her limited appearance, to remind the reader and Medea of an element of protocol which matters in sexual behavior. The detail to which she draws attention – that Medea must await Jason in bed – represents attention to formality, in the shape of a sign expressed by the young woman's posture at the moment of encounter.

Subsequently the governess leads Jason to the bed in complete silence and disappears.[33] Like Myrrha's nurse in Ovids' poem, she brings about a necessary transition under instruction, then leaves the scene. The great difference lies in the fact that her experience and initiative have nothing to do with financial gain.[34] Instead, the figure

---

[29] *Éneas, roman du XIIe siècle*, edited by J. J. Salverda de Grave (Paris: Champion, 1925-1929); Benoît de Ste-Maure, *Le roman de Troie* (Paris: Firmin-Didot, 1904-1912).

[30] *Le roman de Troie*, I, 1539-1542.

[31] Nolan, *Chaucer and the Tradition*, 35.

[32] *Le roman de Troie*, I, 1543-1548.

[33] *Le roman de Troie*, I, 1599-1600.

[34] It will be recalled that Myrrha's wet nurse facilitates the girl's intimacy with her father, a fact reported by the poem in a tone of great sorrow and horror.

now contributes to the perpetuation of "courtoisie" favored by the text. An attempt has been made, therefore, to discard any negative presuppositions of sorcery or unethical inclination. This change of direction has not required a radical departure from the Ovidian norm, and the slight variation (infusing logistical help with some small advice) has sufficed; for Benoît, the basic Ovidian model of specific help at a given instance appears sufficient.

The *Roman d'Éneas* makes more use of the figure of the third party in its treatment of one of the principal love affairs. Here, Lavine's mother takes on the role of confidante to her daughter, thus learning of her feelings for Eneas. Critics have pointed out that in the encounter between mother and daughter the composer of the *Éneas* shows a move away from Virgil and a closer reproduction of Ovidian traits.[35] In the episode, the queen attempts at once to dissuade her daughter from her love for Eneas and to describe to the young girl the exact nature of love itself. The stress falls on the third party's role as confidante and teacher rather than go-between, a trait more in line with the introspective concerns of the genre. John Yunck observes that this motif constitutes one of many that "were apparently enormously successful and popular with the poet's audience, and quickly became the staples of romance."[36] The queen does make some active effort to undo the Eneas-Lavine relation, yet she stands out above all as instructor to her daughter and, by extension, comes through as a confidante: this dynamic is a significant component of a go-between's character, for it promotes dialogue and discussion with much attention to the inner workings of the sentiment.

In stressing the teaching role of the confidante, *Éneas* reinforces the genre's concern with the communication of the rules of proper conduct by an experienced party to a younger character. In the *Roman de Troie* the third party's role consisted of the conveyance of one point of detail; the *Éneas* expands on that role as well as on that of the Ovidian

---

[35] In Virgil's version, the reader only sees Lavinia twice and is not made witness to any mother-daughter conversation. See *Eneas: A Twelfth Century French Romance* translated by John A. Yunck (New York: Columbia University Press, 1974) 210, n. 132. The Ovidian treatment of love's symptoms is addressed in detail in Edmond Faral, *Recherches sur les sources latines des contes et romans courtois du moyen âge* (Paris: Champion, 1913). The scholar notes that in the entire Lavine episode, the author follows Ovid step by step (126). Numerous examples of Ovid's influence are provided in Faral's study, from the symptoms of love to the characteristics of interior dialogue and various side-effects of the amorous sentiment.

[36] Yunck, *Eneas,* 211, n. 133.

confidante to provide a more authoritative voice which is able to articulate ideas and raise issues in further detail. The third party in this romance verbalizes the symptoms of love as a brief commentary on Lavine's situation, offering generalized answers, references to past experience, and warnings about the future. Her focus falls on interior sentiments rather than external, logistical problems.[37] The mother's undertaking of this role expands the sphere of activity for the intermediary's role and infuses the discourse of the third party with a more visible didacto-pedagogical preoccupation. This infusion subordinates the act of mediation to the cautionary shades of discourse, setting up a dichotomy whereby the will to fulfill desire presents a conflict with the experience of the third party, subjecting mediation to a reversal of meaning, as it now signifies a mediation away from the object of desire. This is not a reproduction of the *lena*'s task, for the purpose of caution has nothing to do with financial gain. Rather, it concerns the notion of past experience and potential mistakes in the present, drawing emotion and filial bonds into the third party's discourse. Lavine confirms the tension between lover and third party by showing great independence of movement, establishing contact with Eneas according to her own will and, as such, dismissing the need for productive mediation. The boundary referred to briefly in Ovid's work – that is, the boundary between the two distinct roles of confidante/advisor and of messenger – reaffirms itself in a new manner in the portrayal of the queen. It inscribes itself into the poetics of courtly love in terms of the identification of advice as good, and logistic help as inferior, though not necessarily bad.

In the *Romans d'antiquité* a conscious effort is made to discard the unethical presuppositions attached to the go-between; in this way the works attempt to maintain the ennobling character of love and keep it away from indications of mercenary or financial concern. The mention of money would militate strongly against the guiding tone of courtly love, concerned with the spirit reserved for characters of high birth. The *Roman de Troie* and the *Éneas* suggest that mediation, as long as it is kept to a minimum, can substitute loyalty and affection for financial greed and can move into the realm of helpful advice for the young lovers. Loyalty and teaching in third-party activity have to do with the shift in focus from external difficulty to internal senti-

[37] For example, avoiding precise answers, the queen tells Lavine of her own experiences in love, and of the pain it caused her. *Le roman d'Éneas*, 7902-7906.

ment, subordinating the go-between to the confidante. Chrétien de Troyes and Andreas Capellanus, in *Cligès* and the *De amore* respectively, elaborate significantly on the tensions between the two roles, highlighting the problems that arise in the incorporation of the go-between within the context of courtly love.

(ii) *Chrétien de Troyes and the Arthurian World*

The subject matter of Chrétien's *Cligès* represents an amalgam from many European traditions incorporating Celtic motifs, troubadour rhetoric, and the *Roman d'Éneas.*[38] A Byzantine ambiance informs the romance; Jean Frappier has noted that with *Cligès* "Chrétien leaves the *matière de Bretagne*, or, more exactly, it is fused with a tale of Greco-Oriental character (...). The Arthurian coloring is thus tinged with hues of Byzantium."[39] As noted by Alexandre Micha, one of the ele-

[38] Extensive work has been done on Chrétien's use of sources in his treatment of courtly love. See Douglas Kelly, *Chrétien de Troyes: An Analytic Bibliography* (London: Grant and Cutler, 1976); Claudia Seebass-Linggi, *Lecture d'Érec: traces epiques et troubadouresques dans le conte de Chrétien de Troyes* (New York: Peter Lang, 1996); *Amour et chevalerie dans les romans de Chrétien de Troyes: actes du colloque de Troyes (27-29 Mars 1992)* edited by Danielle Queruel (Paris: Diffusion Les Belles lettres, 1995).

[39] Jean Frappier, *Chrétien de Troyes, the Man and His Work*, translated by Raymond J. Cormier (Ohio: Ohio University Press, 1982). Other studies pinpoint elements which further confirm this identification; Henry and Renée Kahane suggest that the name Cligès is of Turkish origin (Kilidj) and support their view with historical evidence from the time Chrétien composed the story (Henry and Renée Kahane, "L'énigme du nom de Cligès," *Romania* 82 [1961] 113-21). Lucie Polak, noting the uncanny resemblances between the 11th-century Persian romance *Vīs and Ramin* and*Tristan et Iseut* argues that the Persian tale may have also been known to Chrétien (Lucie Polak, "*Tristan* and *Vīs and Rāmīn*," *Romania* 95 [1974] 216-34). Ruth H. Cline, "Heart and Eyes," *Romance Philology* 25 (1971-2) 263-297, takes Chrétien's *Cligès* as a powerful example of the diffusion of Arab ideas on the role of the heart and the eyes in the process of falling in love. Cline writes on the Aristotelian (via Averroes) influence on the theory of the operation of the eyes. She concludes her detailed textual study with the suggestion that: "In both *Cligès* and *Eneas* the heart pursues and dwells in the eyes in true Arabic fashion. Since Arabic erotic literature seems to be the only source for all the motifs in this seemingly original passage in the *Eneas*, it must be concluded that the author's source was that literature. That Chrétien borrowed from the *Eneas* is certain, but it is most likely that both Chrétien and Bernard [of Venatadorn] had some acquaintance with the same general body of literature that influenced the author of *Le roman d'Eneas.* (...) though the earliest Christian writers may have been influenced slightly by Greek sources, it is the Hebraic conception [of the heart/eye strife] that was taken up and developed by the Christian philosophers and preachers. The Arabic presentation of this strife suggests either an Hebraic origin or a source common to the Arabs and Hebrews" (296).

ments in this Greco-Oriental character is Thessala, the old nurse to Fénice.[40] The character is thus infused with a presupposition of exoticism and, more importantly, identified with "Oriental" traits so as to disengage itself from any serious moral objections. That is to say, her association with a world separated from Western and Christian morality implies an attempt by Chrétien to alleviate the weight of anxiety normally associated with pandering.

Chrétien makes some other decisions in such a direction in the effort to protect Thessala, partially, from moral judgments. At the same time he weaves elements from the anxious presuppositions surrounding the third party into her character, thereby creating an irresolvable tension between the two currents which inform the old woman's makeup. The old woman offers practical solutions to some of the many problems which daunt Cligès and Fénice; yet Chrétien insists on presenting the character first and foremost as a sorceress. This choice brings about the problematization of the notion of sorcery in third-party activity, for it posits a hovering definition of the term. The sorcery available to the old woman has, for once, a true scope of application in a favorable direction and yet continues to evoke sinister signs as she explains her skills: "And if I may say so, I know more true spells and charms, all of them tried out, than Medea herself."[41] Prior to this self-portrait, the reader has learned that Thessala had been Fénice's nurse and that she knew a great deal about the occult. The narrator attributes this to the old woman's being from Thessaly: "Her governess was called Thessala, and had nursed her in childhood, and she knew a great deal about magic. She was called Thessala because she was born in Thessaly, where diabolical charms are taught and practised. The women of that country make charms and enchantments."[42]

Thessala perceives her own practical skills as a fundamental aspect of her ability to help; she approaches Fénice at the moment of the

---

[40] Alexandre Micha, *Les romans de Chrétien de Troyes, II: Cligès* (Paris: Librairie Honoré Champion, 1982) (henceforth *Cligès*; references to the text are to verse numbers) viii-ix.

[41] "Et sai, se je l'osoie dire,/ D'anchantement et de charaies/ Bien esprovees et veraies/ Plus c'onques Medea n'an sot" (*Cligès*, 2988-91).

[42] "Sa mestre avoit non Thessala,/ Qui l'avoit norrie en enfance,/ Si savoit molt de nigromance./ Por ce fut Thessala clamee/ fu de Tessalle nee,/ Ou sont feites les diablies,/ Anseigniees et establies./ Les fames qui el païs sont/ Et charmes et charaies font" (*Cligès*, 2962-70).

latter's distress by iterating the medical cures that she can offer.[43] This facet recalls Myrrha's nurse in the *Metamorphoses* (even if there, no magic was used) but has no equal in comedy or elegy and is clearly discouraged in the *Ars amatoria*, interestingly, with an explicit reference to Thessaly as a source of the magic arts.[44] A twofold effect is achieved: the intertextual resonance with Ovid and his strict disapproval of magic places a mistrustful twist on the representation of Thessala; at the same time, from Chrétien's point of view, Thessala's access to science and experience elevates the status of the nurse and provides a contrast with the *lena* whose supposed dabbling in magic went against the lover, and never reached fruition anyway. Now attached to the household of a young woman of high birth, and equipped with knowledge – note the verbs "savrai" and "sai," forms of "to know" – the intermediary has moved into a more privileged space, where her effect on the plot is clearly visible in favor of the lovers. At the same time, the vocabulary utilized in her description is not entirely devoid of negative connotations for it still engages the sceptical perspective of Antiquity.

The tension between these two modes of representation is partly resolved when the Arthurian concern with the *merveilleux* is taken into account. Arthurian characters often find solutions in otherworldly phenomena such as potions, incantations, and talismans. Thessala contributes to the construction of one of the fundamentals of the Arthurian tradition, the use of magic and sorcery towards the hero's success in his amorous quest, bringing about a new adventure for him.[45] Discourse plays a negligible part in this context, and the old woman is ever removed from the realm of seduction; she facilitates elopement on a level which requires no verbal eloquence, except for some perfunctory words of comfort.

Less visible is her identity as confidante: the impact of her consolatory words is overshadowed by her actual help, and the words of

[43] "I can restore your health to you./ I know how to cure the dropsy,/ I know how to cure gout,/ quinsy, and asthma;/ I know so much about urine and pulse/that you do not need another doctor;" ("Car bien vos savrai santé rendre./ Je sai bien garir d'itropique,/Si sai garir de l'arcetique,/De quinancie et de cuerpous;/Tant sai d'orines et de pous/Que ja mar avroiz autre mire;") (*Cligès*, 2982-2987).

[44] Ovid briefly discusses magic, and considers it useless if not counterproductive in the art of seduction. According to him, philtres and magic do not advance the cause of love at all. See *Ars amatoria*, Book II, 99- 103.

[45] Jean Batany, *Approches du* Roman de la rose (Paris: Bordas, 1973) 21.

comfort simply set the scene for more significant action. The basic utterances of help equal a pledge of allegiance and a desire to serve, and they are visibly reminiscent of the words of a vassal to his liege. Thessala's comforting words to Fénice involve the notions of loyalty and service set within a feudal context, where the interaction of the confidante with the lady parallels that of the vassal and his liege, continually reassuring the young woman that she can place all her trust in the able Thessala: "You can trust me with it [your trouble]" ("A moi vos en poez atandre[.]")[46]

These words recall the type of aid offered by ladies-in-waiting or confidantes in contemporary and later Arthurian romances. For example, in the thirteenth-century romance of *Fergus*, the lady-in-waiting Arondele, upon seeing her mistress Galiene's despair, consoles the maiden and vows that she will help the latter with loyalty; she assures her mistress that she will not stop until the problem has been resolved and that she will resort to any means necessary. In addition, she asks that her mistress have faith in God, enhancing the chivalric tone of her discourse with her superior.[47]

Similarly, in Chrétien's *Yvain*, the young Lunete displays strong allegiance to her mistress by initiating a conversation with Yvain, having specified that her devotion to her lady inspires her to do so.[48] In the thirteenth-century romance of *Gliglois* this goes one step further, and the knight Gliglois fulfills the function of intermediary to catch the attention of the fair Beauté on behalf of his friend Gauvin. In so doing, he pledges complete fealty, and once he finds himself enamored of the maiden, his greatest source of distress concerns the violation of loyalty that he has caused.[49] A similar notion to that of servitude to one's liege governs the words of these confidantes and intermediary figures.[50]

---

46 *Cligès*, 3011.

47 Guillaume le Clerc, *The Romance of Fergus*, edited by Wilson Frescoln (Philadelphia: W. H. Allen, 1983) 5341-5359.

48 *Yvain: (Le Chevalier au Lion)* the critical text of Wendelin Foerster with introduction, notes and glossary by T. B. W. Reid (Manchester: Manchester University Press, 1967) 1740-1790.

49 *Gliglois: A French Arthurian Romance of the Thirteenth Century*, edited by Charles H. Livingstone (Cambridge: Harvard University Press, 1932).

50 Not every Arthurian romance depicts such a figure; in *Ille et Galeron*, *Yder*, and *Floire et Blancheflor*, for example, no recourse is made to a third party for the attainment of the love object. In *Claris et Laris* (thirteenth century) the lady-in-waiting offers her loyal help at one point.

Thessala appears more frequently than other intermediaries in romances of the genre and brings about several important transitions in the romance. The more prolonged appearance allows Chrétien to continue the work initiated by the *Romans d'antiquité* and to attempt to undo a number of negative connotations otherwise discernible in an old woman acting as third party. This attempt is concentrated in the figure's loyalty and the total absence of financial motivation. It leads to a certain degree of success, insofar as it adds to the typology of the old woman as go-between the rare elements of fidelity and compassion, expanding the field of mediation to include the bonds of allegiance.

It was mentioned above that the tension between Thessala as sorceress and Thessala as aid remains partly unresolved: this has to do with the charged quality of the words used to describe the old woman, portraying her as one who is able to manipulate medicine and magic. As such, she creates the scope for the types of diatribes brought against the *lenae* of Antiquity. The sincerity of the lovers and the loyalty of Thessala allow sorcery to emerge as a tool over which sympathetic characters have some control. Sorcery advances the cause of the hero, and in the depiction of its productive use a number of intertextual threads are brought together and partially deprived of their previous connotations of immorality. With *Cligès*, the reader witnesses that rare moment of the subtle transformation of a recurrent motif towards new uses. The failure to bring about a total absence of anxiety and scruple in the portrayal of the old woman resides in the facts that, first, she is allowed little time in the narrative and, second, she operates within a referential field which is simply too loaded with stock, overdetermined epithets to allow for a complete regeneration of the motif.

Still, it is fitting to note that *Cligès* offers by far the most detailed portrayal of the character in question in Arthurian literature; the go-between used in a secret love affair is not otherwise a well-elaborated figure in Arthurian romance, emphasizing the secretive nature of the relationship between lovers in the genre. The tribulations of love test the resilience of the lovers with considerable focus on their process of development: an overly visible third party would diminish the strength of that focus. Thessala only acts as a beneficial and significant go-between within the parameters of the genre: a sorceress whose appearance poses no visible threat to the secret nature of the love, nor to the development of the lovers insofar as their discourse on love is concerned.

(iii) *The* De Amore *of Andreas Capellanus*

Paul Zumthor adequately describes the main function of the *De Amore* of Andreas as a text that problematizes courtly love as a doctrine.[51] Through a unified conceptual form, Andreas' carefully argued discussion and examples construct a theory of love which perceives this irrational sentiment as a discipline and an art.[52] Though it is an illogical sensation dwelling outside the realm of reason, love relies on the laws of reason for its definition and requires efficiency and discipline for the successful conquest of the beloved.[53] The same rigor in reasoning applies to the specific role of the third party in this quest.

The work brings together Ovidian material, vernacular fiction, and poetry alongside philosophical reasoning, and does not lend itself to a simple interpretation as to its purpose or meaning.[54] However, it is evident that the treatise, written from an authoritative standpoint and addressed to an inexperienced lover, is concerned above all with the qualities of discourse in the love affair. Andreas draws on an impressive variety of sources that resist reduction to a single point of view, yet the notion of eloquence in speech (*sermonis facondia*) occupies at all times a prominent place within the work, a fact borne out by the choice of dialogue as the main expository vehicle of the work.[55] This feature relates to the influence of poetic tradition on Andreas:

> The extraordinary extension given this subject [language] in the *De Amore* is due to the existence and tremendous popularity of a vernacular poetic genre entirely devoted to the winning of love through eloquence of speech, the love songs of the troubadours and trouvères.

---

[51] Paul Zumthor, "Notes en marge du traité de l'amour de André le Chapelain," *Zeitschrift für Romanische Philologie* 63 (1943) 178-191 (179).

[52] That love is a fundamentally irrational and even foolish emotion is a position adopted by Andreas from the very beginning; describing the causes and effects of love at the outset, Andreas repeatedly mentions the painful and unpredictable vicissitudes brought about by the indulgence of amorous feeling.

[53] Zumthor, "Notes en marge," 183.

[54] André le Chapelain, *Traité de l'amour courtois*, trad., intro. et notes par Claude Buridant (Paris: Klincksieck, 1974) 19.

[55] Donald A. Monson, "*Auctoritas* and Intertextuality," 74. Monson shows that there are at least six different types of reference in the *De amore*, each of which adds a distinct level of intertextuality to the work. Andreas brings together several authorities – Ovid, the Bible, vernacular poetry, in addition to a social intertext involving his lady patrons – making his treatise an "assembling [of] all the pertinent opinions (...) a kind of summa on love, in the tradition of Abelard's *Sic et non* or Peter Lombard's *Sentences*" (77).

> Indeed, the words of the lovers in the Dialogues appear often to be modeled on those of the poet-lover in the *chanson*.[56]

The overwhelming attention to speech constitutes a significant variation on the Ovidian norms of *Ars amatoria* which, while highly aware of the power of words, created considerable space for other stratagems as well. These schemes required financial manipulation, and Andreas eliminates them from his focus in order to pay full attention to language, shifting the power of seduction from money to commanding linguistic manipulation. In addition he restricts the narrative scope of seduction, for the most part reducing the number of characters and concentrating on dialectical speech. The author creates a game played by three participants: man, woman, and voice of authority. As the man attempts to seduce, the woman evaluates or resists his intentions while the author provides a running commentary.

In the *sic et non* of love and seduction, a number of hypothetical scenarios which might approximate narrative structure appear which address details or matters of protocol in the male-female interaction. Mention of third-party implication occurs only in these instances. Young Walter, the addressee of the treatise, learns initially of the many symptoms of love that lead to action on the part of the smitten lover; at this point, the very first act mentioned by Andreas concerns the securing of an intermediary: "he goes straight to action; he works hard to get assistance, and to have an intermediary."[57] Curiously, the idea is left at that point, and the text moves immediately to other matters related to the lover's sentiments. No indication is given of the identity or function of this go-between.

In the fifth chapter of Book II, the matter is taken up again somewhat abruptly and without any introductory remarks; in fact, no nexus can be located which links this mention of third-party activity to the brief lines in Book I. Here, the woman's avoidance of the man's messenger or her reluctance to send her go-between to the lover are interpreted as signs of diminishing interest in the love affair:

> If she attempts to hide from your loyal messenger, undoubtedly she is leaving you to drift in waves, and her love for you is faked. Also, if you

---

[56] Monson, "*Auctoritas* and Intertextuality," 74.

[57] "Sed statim procedit ad actum; statim enim iuvamen habere laborat et internuntium invenire" (*De amore: Andreas Capellanus on Love*, edited with an English translation by P. G. Walsh [London: Duckworth, 1982] 34) (henceforth *De amore*).

> see that she no longer sends you regular messages, or that her messenger does not visit you as much as before, and that he is now a stranger to you, you can recognize that love is now against you.[58]

In this context messengership is a dramatization of the beloved's moods, and the messenger serves as a screen on which some sentiments and symptoms may be discerned. He does not describe the person fulfilling this function but rather evokes the figure matter-of-factly as an instrument. In his or her capacity as a tool for the conveyance of selected words or implicit gestures, the go-between bears an essential similarity to his/her counterpart in Ovid's *Ars amatoria*. The figure acts as a simple messenger of specific words (dictated by the lover). The shift which has occurred from Ovid concerns the figure's failure to sustain a structure of narrative interest and its utter integration into the lovers' codes of behavior. This sets a substantial limit on the figure's scope of activity, further emphasized by the stress placed throughout the work on secrecy and privacy. It confirms the notion that the dialogical world constructed by the two lovers is sacred and inhabitable only by them.[59]

In the sixth chapter of Book II Andreas expands on the identity of the intermediary in one of his explorations of the issue of infidelity. He states that three people can know of the secret love affair in addition to the lovers themselves:

> We say that love can be known by three people other than the lovers, since the lover has the right to find a confidante who will give him secret consolation in his love and who will give him solace under adverse conditions. The woman has the right to have a similar sort of confidante. In addition to these, the lovers can have one faithful messenger upon whom they agree, through whom secret love can be conducted always in the right way.[60]

---

58 "Sed et si studeat internuntio se celare fideli, te sine dubio valida relinquit in unda et te subterfugit amare. Praeterea, si perpenderis coamantem a solitis per nuntium visitationibus abstinere, vel eius fidelem internuntium et specialem in eo, quod referre solebat, cognoveris esse remissum vel tibi quasi alienum, eam tibi subversam credere debes [amantem]" (*De amore*, 234).

59 Various passages in Book II specify that love survives as a result of the lovers' guarantee of secrecy.

60 "Dicimus enim quod coamantium personis exceptis tribus aliis potest amor licite propalari personis. Nam permittitur amatori sui amoris secretarium invenire idoneum, cum quo secrete valeat de suo solatiari amore, et qui ei, si contigerit, in amoris compatiatur adversis. Sed et amatrici similem conceditur secretariam postulare. Praeter istos internuntium fidelem de communi possunt habere consensu, per quem amor occulte et recte semper valeat gubernari" (*De amore*, 246).

For the most part, Ovid and other Roman poets consider intermediary activity as an evidently inferior, purely logistical function, and the overall impression created by texts from Antiquity is that of some slapstick humor mingled with devious advice. Like the *Romans d'antiquités* and Chrétien, here Andreas attempts to elevate the status of the figure by endowing it with a degree of trust, attempting to erase the negative presuppositions of pandering or indiscretion. The general designations of messenger and confidant as opposed to, say, bawd or maidservant, form a part of this endeavor. Donald Monson has remarked that the *De Amore* contains many "narrative passages with strong links to vernacular poetry" and mentions two examples of this dialogue of the genres.[61] The conception of go-betweens and confidants represents another element in this link: figures acting in third-party capacity without the comical touch of Ovid appear in Arthurian adventure and the *Romans d'antiquités* as well as in the treatise of Andreas. Like Chrétien, Andreas attempts to overcome any unfavorable resonance by stressing the notion of fidelity and omitting entirely the preoccupation with financial reward. He moves even further away from Chrétien by excluding the familiar old woman from the system altogether. He designates a figure who operates on the basis of servitude and allegiance, but who does not enter the realm of seduction or linguistic manipulation. In the paragraph quoted above, Andreas devotes only some attention to the separation of confidante from messenger: similar to the Ovidian scheme, messengership implies an outlined physical duty subordinated to the wishes of the lover. The one who will on occasion speak with the lover and who will represent him to the ladies of the court telescopes mediation and companionship into one task (and a limited one, at that), further distancing the task from dubious connotations by not being, clearly, an old woman. The figure occupies a minor space in the privileged location where useful speech is possible.[62]

But the elimination of old women from the scheme presents a problem. The confidante and mediator's discourse must remain limited in scope since Andreas fears the third party's potential seductive power. Thus the sixth chapter of Book II strictly forbids the active procuring of an object of desire on another's behalf because of such a

[61] Monson, "*Auctoritas* and Intertextuality," 73.

[62] *De amore*, 248.

fear. In the cautionary tale of the seventh chapter of Book II, the go-between who betrays the friend by courting the lady reinforces the idea of the risks involved in soliciting the help of another.[63] Andreas minimizes the risk factor by suggesting that each lover choose a same-sex familiar, thereby proposing gender segregation as one remedy against the dangers of third parties. He separates the silent go-between from the speaking confidante, yet advises that even the latter's discourse deal briefly with consolation and defense as facets of mediation. Clearly, in his poetics of courtly love, mediation also poses the threat of seduction with direct benefits for the third party, since the task of mediation makes use of the language, which by acknowledgment of the text is the most potent tool for success. The rigid limits set by Andreas Capellanus for the third party drive home a latent anxiety seen in the words of Roman poets as well as in those of Chrétien and the writers of the *Romans d'antiquité*. If the go-between were to leave the realm of comic, negligible, or purely logistical impact, his or her mediation would then absorb language as a resource and gain substantial powers of manipulation, as lovers and poets know too well. Additionally, in the realm of courtly love, speech would be suggestive of the garrulous bawd and would recall the mercenary and popular shades of physical love.

The courtly spirit, therefore, implicitly acknowledges the potential power of intermediary activity in much the same way as Antiquity had and comes up with various strategies to curtail that potential as much as possible. The courtly tradition displays a latent anxiety regarding the distribution of power in the discourse of love, and therefore modifies the third party's scope to control the access available to various characters in matters of language and manipulation. Non-courtly and popular literature offer an altogether different angle on carnal love and the characters engaged therein, for their discourse is governed by a different set of concerns and aims, and they provide a distinct perspective for the conception of the figure.

---

[63] The episode is modeled on Ovid's *Ars amatoria*, I, 739-40.

III. The Non-courtly Spirit

(i) *The Go-Between in Medieval Latin Comedy*

Twelfth-century elegiac comedy stands out as a contrast to courtly love and a vehicle that mingles comic and satiric intentions at once.[64] Influenced by ancient Latin and classical satire, the plays from this genre present figures from decidedly non-courtly ranks, whose primary concerns have to do with financial gain and sexual fulfillment. The subject-matter explored in many of these regards the comic potential of characters' quest to fulfill basic sensations in everyday life: hunger, poverty, sexual desire, and financial ambition.[65] These topics reappear subsequently in the *fabliaux*, whose plotlines often concern the use of tricks for financial advancement.[66]

Four Latin plays lend themselves particularly well to the study of the genre's treatment of intermediary activity, for the character enjoys substantial development within their central amorous and financial intrigues. The plays in question are the *Pamphilus*, William of Blois' *Alda*, the anonymous *Baucis et Traso*, and *De Nuncio Sagaci*.[67] *Pamphilus* presents the old bawd who deceitfully convinces Galatea that a meeting with Pamphilus would not lead to scandal. In *Alda* the function of go-between falls initially to the slave Spurius, who achieves no success, and then to an old nurse; in *Baucis et Traso* the bawd Baucis cons male clients into paying for the services of an old courtesan, while in *De Nuncio Sagaci* a valet, Davus, takes on the task of coercing a young woman on behalf of his master.

In matters related to love, physical conquest remains the center of gravity for the plot in every play, requiring a central deceit to con

---

[64] Giovanni Orlandi, "Classical Latin Satire and the Medieval Elegiac Comedy," in *Latin Poetry and the Classical Tradition: Essays in Medieval and Renaissance Literature*, edited by Peter Godman and Oswyn Murray (Oxford: Clarendon Press, 1990) 97-115 (100).

[65] All citations are from *La "comédie latine en France" au XIIe siècle: I & II*, textes publiés sous la direction de Gustave Cohen (Paris: Les Belles Lettres, 1931). The references are to line numbers.

[66] Maurice Hélin, *A History of Medieval Latin Literature*, translated by Jean Chapman Snow (New York: W. Salloch, 1949) 98-101 where the hybrid nature of these plays is discussed, as well as some of the traits they share with the *fabliaux* among other genres.

[67] *Alda* is anterior to 1170; *De Nuncio sagaci* and *Baucis et Traso* are dated between 1150 and 1180; the *Pamphilus* belongs to the very end of the eleventh century.

one or more characters into a sexual or financial trap. Several male and female figures act in the capacity of third party to help construct the central deceit: this increase in numbers, taken in contrast to the courtly spirit, solidifies the link between mediation and an essentially unrefined or immoral kind of love. In spite of differences in age or gender, the intermediaries in the plays mentioned above share a number of features. Since the quest of the object of desire (be it a person, or money) relies on the deception of an innocent party, the talkative go-betweens in all comedies show a talent for prevarication from the very outset. This talent is accompanied by a marked absence of loyalty towards client or master and a requirement for material compensation in exchange for services. The go-betweens of elegiac comedy, therefore, fuse mediation with financial aims and a necessity for lying. (A possible exception is the nurse in *Alda*, who does not actively demonstrate disloyalty to her master).

The central deceit fabricated by the characters working on behalf of others involves some linguistic manipulation in addition to logistical details. These third parties use language with more frequency and force than the *lenae* of Antiquity. Discourse emerges as one of their important identifying features, contributing to the accumulation of comic momentum and the coercion of unsuspecting parties. In all cases, the reader shares with the go-between knowledge of a deception unknown to other characters and is thus "in the know," not forced to second-guess the intermediary's acts. Such an awareness strips the third party of any mysterious qualities, compelling the reader to focus on the comical nature of the third party's existence. The third party's discourse consists of the presentation of a lie to an unsuspecting character, with numerous false reassurances, and the subsequent construction of as many untruths as possible around the central lie; thus Baucis enumerates the virginal qualities of the old and ugly Glycerium so as to lure more pursuers, while the messenger in *De Nuncio Sagaci* paints an exaggeratedly ideal, chivalric portrait of his master so that the girl will shed any doubts regarding the master's motives.[68] Spurius in *Alda*, having at first designed one lie which fails,

[68] Praising the "virgin" Glycerium, Baucis declares: "If you need a virgin, I have one at home. A virgin, a blossom, a flower, a fruit of love, she has the shine of a virgin, she has all the elements of beauty." ("Virgine si sit opus, est mihi uirgo domi./Virgo, set uirga, set flos, set fluctus amoris,/Lumen uirgineum, forma decore nitens") (*Baucis et Traso*, 36-38). False assertions of the blatant type are made in many plays.

shows presence of mind and invents a greater one in order to explain his failure to his master.[69] The manipulation of lies is a standard feature of the intermediary's language. Since this manipulation often takes the shape of a debate with either a disbelieving or gullible character, it permits some development of devices such as rhetorical questions, feigned offense, quick replies to unexpected objections, and allows for a much wider verbal scope for this go-between than courtly or ancient counterparts.[70]

As mentioned, the obsession with physical conquest expressed by the male protagonist runs through every play. Accordingly, the third party's discourse responds to that obsession to build the main deceit. The go-betweens' tricks with language and action inspire much laughter, yet ultimately they serve the realization of a single purpose: physical union. The structural organization of *Alda*, for example, adequately demonstrates this fact: here, the first intermediary, Spurius, disappears from the comedy once he fails to bring about physical union. The nurse who replaces him does not require the space for direct speech enjoyed by Spurius, concocts a plan, and the lover Pyrrhus takes center stage to carry out the plan.[71] In so doing he inevitably shifts the focus to the emphasis on physical consummation.

The go-between exists to perpetuate the central trick, fading once the deceit has ended or reached some purpose. His or her manipulation of language has to do with the basic fraud that lures the victim. As such, a decipherable fraud takes the place of the incomprehensible seduction described by Baudrillard. In Latin comedy, the coercion of men and women occurs because of a lie whose beginning, middle, and end are engineered in visible and clear terms. The lie is neither evasive nor incomprehensible, for its ingredients are known to the reader who also has access to the truth. What occurs in Latin comedy therefore is not an evil art premised on the manipulation of language and residing outside the grasp of every concep-

---

69 *Alda*, 360-366.

70 For example, from *Alda*, Spurius' speech on the importance of material goods towards seduction (212-260); or the false teaching on love by Baucis, 290-300.

71 *Alda*, 385-409. In fact, the nurse does not speak in the play. The extent of her instruction is shown by a brief illustration of her trick – dressing Pyrrhus in women's clothing – and a cryptic reference to her teaching: "What he should do, what he should say, when he should speak, the how and why of it, the old woman shows him [all this]" ("Qualiter et quare, quid agat, cur, quando loquator/Quoue modo, puero sedula monstrat anus") (407-408).

tual system known to man, otherwise known as seduction; rather, it is the deceitful luring of one party towards another, thanks to the falsification of facts such as age, motivation, or end result. For instance, Baucis enters the play falsely guaranteeing the virginity of the courtesan.[72] From this initial point onwards, her speech is dedicated to the defense of this lie, be it in her diatribes against those who accuse her of lying or in the fake lesson she gives Glycerium in front of an ardent lover.[73] The messenger in *De Nuncio Sagaci*, who in fact ends up as the girl's lover, begins by promising to protect the girl by not leaving her alone with his master: "Listen to what I say: my job is to look after you. If you believe me, only pleasing things will happen to you."[74] Having broken this vow blatantly, he continues to deny his culpability stating that he has not engaged in any wrongdoing.[75] The girl ends up experiencing physical intimacy with the poet and the messenger; nonetheless, the latter continues to claim that he is protecting her virtue and even her life: "As long as you live, it is your task to show me your gratitude, since it is thanks to me that your daughter is alive."[76] Essentially, he repeats the same assertion time and again in an effort to facilitate or cover up the act of physical intimacy, observed by the reader who knows the truth. Consequently, the figure's ability for linguistic manipulation does not betray a talent for the elusive and slippery tactics of seduction, but rather a skill for the construction of a clear deceit and stubborn insistence on its validity even when it has crumbled upon the revelation of true motives. A key element in the comedies concerns the fact that the task of these intermediaries consists of luring (by way of a lie) to bring about physical intimacy, not seducing, by way of complex reasoning, to inspire amorous feeling. Their discourse concentrates on upholding the structural integrity of the lie that they have presented. Nonetheless, a step further from Antiquity has been taken since the character now possesses a particular discourse of mediation and has transcended the world of empty comments or brief physical acts of assistance. With the medieval Latin go-between, the

---

[72] *Baucis et Traso*, 37-38.

[73] See for example, *Baucis et Traso*, 290.

[74] "Audi quid dicam: cupio te uiuere saluam./Et michi si credis, fit quod placuisse uidebis" (*De Nuncio sagaci*, 136-137).

[75] *De Nuncio sagaci*, 200-201.

[76] "Et, dum uiuatis, mihi grates ut referatis /Est uestrum facere, per quia uita puelle /Est prolungata" (*De Nuncio sagaci*, 305-306).

recurrent designation of talkative receives a new definition since it now succeeds in forwarding the cause of he or she who has turned to third-party assistance.

When seen together, the intermediaries' attributes also recall the image of the panderer in society, for they have to do with greed, excessively deceitful verbal manipulation, and absence of loyal allegiance. Non-literary sources such as Justinian's vehement criticism represent the panderer as possessing just such attributes in his or her attempt to lure a potential client. In the comedies, the go-between's emphasis on monetary gain reinforces this image, but a clear victim/oppressor division such as the one construed in legal writings does not occur with clarity in the plays, and the impossibility of total guilt attribution to the figure once again calls into question the established presuppositions attached to it.

The resistance of the comedies to the creation of a clear victim/oppressor division has to do with the disposition of the characters who interact with the go-betweens in all four plays. In these, the intermediary provides a great part of the initiative towards the realization of the affair, yet the task is greatly facilitated by the comedies' revelation of a latent willingness in the lured party. Thus, faced with the bawd's enticing description of the pursuer, Galatea in *Pamphilus* states clearly that she would go ahead and indulge were it not for her fear of scandal: "I would grant you what you wish, were it not for my fear of what people might say, since they in this type of affair make more noise than ever."[77] In *Alda*, the young girl experiences great joy in the fulfillment of the trick elaborated by Pyrrhus and his nurse and shows marked enthusiasm for a continuation of the "lesson" given to her, having enjoyed it at length.[78] In *De Nuncio Sagaci*, the seduced young girl is quick to turn the tables and announce her satisfaction with her lot, going on to convey her own plans for further deceit.[79]

Similarly, the duped male party defies the label of victim. In *Baucis et Traso*, the young man is fooled by the go-between into believing that he will have access to a young and pretty virgin. Upon receiving adequate payment, the bawd Baucis creates that illusion so success-

---

[77] "Quod petis annuerem, fame nisi uerba timerem, /Que magis in tali crimine lumen habent" (*Pamphilus*, 419-420).

[78] *Alda*, 470-482.

[79] *De Nuncio sagaci*, 267-268.

fully that Traso has no cause for complaint, especially since the courtesan's virginity is restored by Baucis with an elaborate potion: "Having made these preparations, from the courtesan she makes a young girl. The night arrives. Traso arrives happily. He has with him that which he promised, and gives it to Baucis. He enjoys Glycerium and having possessed her, he takes his leave."[80] As far as Traso is concerned, he has achieved his aim, even if the virginity that he has enjoyed is not genuine. The deceit constructed by Baucis, unlike Baudrillard's notion of seduction as a phenomenon which defies any conceptual framework, is entirely accessible to the audience, defining this instance of mediation as relying completely on one identifiable lie. The weight of this lie is lessened by the duped party's ultimate enjoyment of the deceit.

All plays show their initial "victims," therefore, as individuals who either end up enjoying the sexual trap set for them or at least put up little resistance at the crucial stages. The absence of clear divisions between corrupter and corrupted is a significant aspect of the go-between's typology in Latin comedy, for it lessens the weight of responsibility or guilt on the figure, distinguishing it from its assumed social counterpart. The comedies do not end on an overwhelmingly reproachful moral note vis-à-vis the go-between, since the ruse creates pleasure and satisfaction for all parties by the end. Also, the intermediary does not exert an all-encompassing influence on the turn of events: the fickle disposition of the targeted men and women facilitates the task of luring and distances the go-between from any centrally important position as sole seducer. The comedies leave the reader with the distinct impression that all parties are more or less responsible for the success of the central trick, and that agency is too diffuse to be identified with one character. One reason for this is that the plays produce fast-paced and lively events, and excessive resistance or influence by any one character would impede the rapid flow of episodes.

One opportunity offered by this genre concerns the study of differences between male and female intermediaries. In the case of the female go-between, the obvious intertextual references and presuppositions attached to the figure create a sense of predictability, espe-

[80] "His sibi confectis facit ex meretrice puellam. Noxque sequens aderat./En Traso letus adest/Secum promissa gerit hic et dans ea Bauci/Glicerio fruitur atque potitus abit" (*Baucis et Traso*, 321-324).

cially regarding the bawd who boasts past experience and imparts reassurances as part of her strategy. In *Pamphilus* and *Alda*, the old women formulate universally acknowledged concepts on sexuality: "The old woman gathers herself in deep thought, and a thousand plans circle in her head. Old women are crafty: there is light in these fertile means, and she knows what to do."[81] The bawd in *Pamphilus* hints at a past life which may well have been that of a courtesan, projecting this experience in ways which will coerce Galatea.[82] In *Baucis et Traso*, the older woman in charge of Baucis adds the weight of experience to her words precisely because she, too, is a courtesan.

Clearly, these old women have much to do with the world of mercenary love, and reap the familiar benefits of the lifestyle while suffering equally familiar consequences. They inspire vituperative comments by other characters in moments of threat and recall the profanities directed at the elegiac *lena* from Antiquity. The evils of the profession are viewed as an essential part of the old woman's makeup. A dramatic case of this occurs in *Baucis et Traso*, where the valet Davus bombards the old bawd with insults on her falsehood, old age, and corrupt disposition.[83] He regards her profession as intrinsically evil and incorporates her old age into his diatribe as he lists some of the accusations also mentioned in non-literary sources against procuresses.[84] Galatea voices similar ideas about luring against the bawd: "How able is your craftiness in hiding itself! Your art and your sly acts have succeeded: the hare has landed in your trap!"[85]

In a fashion similar to the texts in Antiquity, this anger represents a shift of blame (for example, Galatea's refusal to assume responsibility) also denoting a preconceived and established image, found extensively in satirical sources, of the evils of womanhood and old age brought together. The outbursts against the old woman form the basis for the perception of her identity by others, yet they add nothing new to the commonplace notions of misogyny. The bases for

---

[81] "Mentis ad archanum fugit atque recolligit intus/Se totam et secum multa uolutat anus./ Dum bene fecundum sollertia pectus anilis/Discutit, occurrit quid sibi posset agi" (*Alda*, 389-392).

[82] *Pamphilus*, 322-326

[83] *Baucis et Traso*, 141-143.

[84] *Baucis et Traso*, 151-155.

[85] "Quam bene uestra suas ars tegit insidias!/Impleuere suos ars et fallacia cursus: /In laqueum fugiens decidit ecce lupus!" (*Pamphilus*, 738-740).

these notions are found in the diatribes against the elegiac *lenae* of Antiquity, the sarcastic portraits of Juvenal and Horace, the more zealous assertions of the Church Fathers, and the wide range of insults covered by the writers of satire. The transposition of these vituperative ideas into the plays conforms to Zumthor's third category of intertextuality, in which an idea maintains its essential contours from text to text without substantial transformation.[86] In the particular case of mediation, the contempt for old age and womanhood identifies third-party activity with a branch of women's deceits, to be regarded in a satirical light.

This impression provides a significant contrast with the male go-between, who does not bring with him such a bundle of presuppositions from literature. In *De Nuncio Sagaci*, the male messenger does not betray an established professional identity such as panderer. He assumes the role of protector for the young girl, guaranteeing that he will not leave her alone with his master, the poet. When he breaks his promise, the seduced girl attacks him verbally but does not base her diatribe on a known presupposition. She points to a general mistrust of valets without highlighting a particular vice in detail, contrary to the case of old bawds, whose vices are catalogued in more specific terms.[87] Nothing identifies the valet with the professional role of pimp, and he quickly undergoes a shift from go-between to lover: the young girl falls in love with him and plots against the first lover in order to reward the go-between.[88] It will be recalled that courtly texts had expressed the fear of the male go-between's seductive powers, and this anxiety goes back to Ovid's warning against male messengers. Both courtly and non-courtly genres elaborate

[86] As Ronald E. Pepin notes, the tradition of misogyny in Western texts "is so well documented that one need not trace again its glum development." *Literature of Satire in the Twelfth Century* (New York: Mellen House, Studies in Medieval Literature, vol. 2, 1988) 12.

[87] *De Nuncio sagaci*, 225.

[88] Alphonse Dain, the editor of *De Nuncio sagaci* in Cohen's volume, complains that the transition from go-between to lover is not shown adequately in the play: "Why does the beauty, who has just offered herself to the young man, fall in love with the valet and have him take the money of his master through this ruse?" ("Pourquoi la belle, qui vient de se donner au jeune homme, devient-elle amoureuse du valet et lui fait emporter par ce subterfuge la bourse de son maître?") (160, n. 1). He partially answers his own question by pointing out the girl's contradictory character. To this one might add that the pace of the comedy cannot permit detailed psychological development, requiring instead a concentration on visible plot twists with a marked emphasis on the characters' sexual behavior.

briefly on Ovid's notion without adding any substantial changes of their own in this matter.[89]

The principal difference brought about by the use of a male intermediary is the fruition of the third party's erotic potential. Andreas Capellanus and the Arthurian tradition view this as a clearly unacceptable path: in the *De Amore*, it constitutes the violation of the code of knights, and if committed by the woman, it shows lack of respect for the constraint expected of the lady.[90] However, since the *De Nuncio Sagaci* does not take place in the realm of knightly codes of honor, this turn of events adds yet another humorous plot twist and contributes to the lively pace of the play. It also reconfirms the text's underlying convictions on woman's fickle nature and man's quick investment in that inclination, satirizing both. The male go-between's shift from third party to lover intensifies the atmosphere of rapid change that dominates the comedies. This shift parallels the equally inconstant nature of all other characters who can change heart whenever financial or physical gain demand it. As events unravel and old priorities fade away, the go-between's transformation into lover enhances the cumulative impression of instability and hypocrisy in the fast-paced world of comedy.

To sum up, the intermediary brings about the complete subversion of the laws of courtly love and violates the sacred codes of discretion, honesty, and loyalty. The character also transgresses against Christian morality: the focus on financial reward and lack of scruples regarding sexuality provide ample proof of this. The third party does not stand alone as the unethical force behind sexual intrigue; rather, he or she contributes to the general atmosphere of immorality alongside several others. Be that as it may, the character perpetuates the notion that her or his role is intrinsically linked with deceit. In the context of the go-between's literary history, the most significant contribution of the non-courtly figure has to do with the foil it sets up with the courtly counterpart: both now occupy the space of mediation between lovers, with markedly different implications. The coex-

---

[89] *Ars amatoria*, I, 739-740; and *De amore*, Book II, chapter vii, sixteenth anecdote, where a knight's confidant and go-between betrays him by becoming the lady's suitor and lover. The thirteenth-century Arthurian romance *Gliglois* also presents a similar situation, but with more stress on the issues of loyalty and betrayal presented by this complication. It will be recalled that Andreas had warned against this danger also.

[90] *De amore*, 264.

istence of both types in twelfth-century literature brings about a continual tension within the space of mediation which they occupy together, and is problematized in the literature of subsequent centuries, to which we will turn after analyzing one more twelfth-century genre.

(ii) *Goliardic Verse*

This body of verse, which extols physical love and excessive drinking, shows much thematic affinity with medieval Latin comedy in its focus on the pursuit of carnal pleasure. The poems make few references to intermediary activity, however, since in terms of actual characterization they allow for little aside from the physical description of the beloved and minimal flirtatious conversation.

One exception is the poem "Si Linguis Angelicis," attributed to Abelard.[91] Here the poet expands the dialogue with the beloved to a considerable degree, giving it the form of a debate. Prior to the conversation, the poet mentions his beloved – the Rose – as guarded in the grip of an old crone:

> Well I might despair indeed
> There is no denying
> Since an old crone kept the rose
> Sacred from all prying,
> Neither loving nor beloved,
> Thanks to this duenna –
> Such a flower as Pluto snatched
> Midst the fields of Enna. [92]

The poet does not describe the old woman in any detail. Rather she personifies an impediment, inspiring the poet's momentary anger.[93] Abelard projects the old woman as even more of a static image than

---

[91] *The Goliard Poets: Medieval Latin Songs and Satires*, introduced and translated by George F. Whicher (Cambridge: Cambridge University Press, 1949) 50-62. Note that I have used the translations from this edition.

[92] "Si despero merito,/nullus admiretur,/nam per quandam vetulam/rosa prohebitur,/ut non amet aliquem,/atque non ametur,/quam Pluto subripere/flagito dignetur" ("Si Linguis Angelicis," 25-31).

[93] "How I hoped the hag would leave/ If I bade her pray go/ Or that sudden lightning would/ Smite the old virago." ("Cumque meo animo/verterem predicta,/optans, anum raperet/fulminis sagitta") ("Si Linguis Angelicis," 32-35).

the elegiac poets of Antiquity, so much so that he ignores her part in his tale, and continues to convey his conversation with the Rose without any further mention of the "vetula."[94] He thereby invalidates the old woman's literal function as guardian in retrospect.

Although of an essentially non-courtly spirit, goliardic poetry resembles the lyric of the troubadours insofar as it traces the development of amorous feeling in the lovers only. In both cases, the poets concentrate on the two players in the game of love, stressing the notions of complicity or privacy. Abelard's laconic mention of an old woman as impediment reiterates an elegiac idea, but stylizes the "vetula" even further so that she comes to symbolize any type of hindrance, adding a minimum of dramatic spice to the narrative aspect of his poem and enhancing the elements of tension and conflict.

The poem's simultaneous erasure and inscription of the old woman creates the distinct impression of anxiety as regards triangulation involving just such a figure. The weight of tradition requires that the poet include this recurrent motif of separation in his lyrics: his refusal to bring the introduction of the figure to any development and closure indicates at first sight the insignificance of the old woman; on closer inspection, it points to the poet's inability to confront this motif as simply a recurrent feature of poetry and in a more intense confirmation of Latin elegists, compels him to leave her suspended, with a beginning but no end. The old woman resembles a task which may be small, but to which one is reluctant to return, for it may or may not generate serious anxiety if addressed fully. The suspension of the old woman in the poem is an important poetic decision and strengthens the impression that her type of mediation, be it for or against the lover, generates a type of anguish that occupies an uncertain space. It defies exact formulation, for such an act would acknowledge the anxiety and undermine the poet's flamboyant contempt for the old woman. Yet it also resists complete erasure, and thus stays on. Texts from subsequent centuries help shed some light on this resistance to both absence and presence.

---

[94] "Let me, looking back, forget/ That old woman's strictures, But describe the sight which yet/ Recollection pictures." ("Ecce retrospiciens,/vetula post relicta,/ audias quid viderim,/dum moraret icta.") ("Si Linguis Angelicis," 36-39).

IV. The Thirteenth Century

(i) *The Pseudo-Ovidian* De Vetula

The long narrative poem sometimes attributed to Richard de Fournival offers a thought-provoking problem for the typology of the medieval bawd.[95] An autobiographical piece attributed to "Ovid," the poem contains all the necessary elements for the display of skills by an old bawd, yet deals with her presence in thought-provoking ways. In Book II of the narrative, the poet seeks the attention of a well-guarded young girl and subsequently procures the help of his sister's former nursemaid to achieve his purpose.

Curiously, the "vetula" is not a bawd by definition, nor does she volunteer such services. To begin with, the poet comes to her as a last resort, thinking of her almost accidentally.[96] This may suggest that he remains implicitly aware that a professional bawd connotes a close association with prostitution and will therefore prove inadequate for the seduction of a virtuous young woman. The "vetula" shows much reluctance in assisting in the project and concedes only after threats by the poet.[97] As noted in *Orígenes y sociología del tema celestinesco*, the old woman's eloquence comes into full view with the expression of her fear; her speech has nothing to do with the art of seduction.[98] Fear, then, emerges as a component of mediation, placing an important twist on the notion of the go-between's confidence.

Significantly, once the old woman goes about seducing the girl, she does not even fulfill the assigned task. She subjects the narrator to a series of lies about her activities and in the end leads him into a farcical trap. A number of scholars have viewed her as a typical bawd in the tradition of the old *lena*, whereas the content of the poem clearly problematizes such a designation both in attitude and in function.[99] The "vetula" has found herself forced to fit the mold of

---

[95] D. M. Robathan, *The Pseudo-Ovidian* De Vetula (Amsterdam: A. M. Hakkert, 1968) (henceforth *De Vetula*).

[96] *De Vetula*, II, vv. 350-355.

[97] *De Vetula*, II, v. 365.

[98] *Orígenes y sociología*, 69.

[99] Francisco Rico, "Sobre el origen de la autobiografía en el *Libro de buen amor*," *Anuario de estudios medievales* 4 (1967) 301-325. The scholar qualifies the "vetula" as an *alcahueta*; the same view, that she is a bawd similar in nature and function to the *lenae* and the entire parade of old female go-betweens, is also held by William Matthews, mentioned earlier.

a go-between by a somewhat aggressive and desperate narrator: such a pre-history draws attention to the extent to which the power of the client determines the discourse of the third party. Throughout the poem, the reader witnesses a tense narrator in a position of struggle rather than cooperation with his go-between; the relationship suffers many blows: retrospective instructions by the poet, moments of doubt as to the credibility of his "vetula."[100] The bawd's familiar traits such as greed and promises of success create a comic effect once her overwhelming failure becomes clear.

The pseudo-Ovidian "vetula" represents in essence a parody of the known stock character, and this highlights implicitly the weaknesses of the original model. Her portrayal bears a close resemblance to a *lena*, in light of her old age and the issue of financial reward, but key distortions point to the dangers of attributing to her the skills that she does not possess. The most blatant distortion consists of her lack of experience and her reluctance to assist; the text enhances the comic factor by adding various other touches: for instance, the poet's promise of a reward consists of an unusually long list of objects and comestibles, while the traditional *lena* usually simply asks for wine or a garment.[101] Elsewhere, the anguished exchanges between the poet and his mediator confuse the distribution of authority and reduce any remaining impressions of efficiency as the two communicate in a mixture of mistrust and prevarication.[102] This deliberate confusion of roles achieves the parodic effect signaled by Zumthor in his outline of intertextual dynamics.

The parodic representation of the "vetula" creates a humorous effect which culminates in the narrator's failure to achieve his aim; at the same time, the portrayal offers a critique of mediation in demonstrating the extent to which misguided third-party manipulation can lead to undesirable ends. The key concept in this critique consists of the narrator's lack of guidance for the go-between; we have seen, from Antiquity through to the twelfth century, that the success of the bawd has to do with the favorable disposition of her intended target or with the careful guidance under which she must fulfill a specific task. *De Vetula* unravels the disastrous yet funny consequences of the absence of these elements, thus singling out mediation as a potential-

[100] *De Vetula*, II, 409-415.
[101] *De Vetula*, II, 390-393
[102] *De Vetula* II, 407-410.

ly dangerous activity. Both the courtly and the non-courtly spirits advocate clear guidance for the bawd, and in the pseudo-Ovidian poem the absence of clear instruction results in a haywire turn of events. In its unique way, *De Vetula* confirms once again that, contrary to first impressions, the bawd requires management and favorable disposition in order to succeed. The narrator's failure to give guidance also points to his ineptitude regarding the reading of signs: just because a woman is old, has financial needs, and has once been a nursemaid, does not qualify her as an experienced bawd. The same cautionary remark may be aimed at the readers who invariably have read old women in so many texts as dangerous procuresses: as *De Vetula* shows only too well, not all talkative old women with a background in nursing make efficient bawds.

(ii) *The Bawd in the* Fabliaux

A well-established genre of the early thirteenth century with roots in oral storytelling, the *fabliaux* deal for the most part with the types of transgression that "go counter to medieval notions of purity in matters of personal conduct, of money, and especially of sex."[103] They demonstrate an affinity with Latin comedy of the twelfth century, for they derive comic momentum from the depiction of graphic or unethical situations involving a variety of stock characters such as priests, peasants, or jealous husbands.[104]

The *fabliaux* demonstrate shifting social structures and chronicle a certain mobility, often involving the emerging urban classes with some reference to rural life. Mary Jane Stears Schenk points out that they "present a world view which is not so much bound to a particular social class as it is common to those individuals for whom class structure is an obstacle to be overcome."[105] The scholar points out

---

[103] Charles Muscatine, *The Old French Fabliaux* (New Haven: Yale University Press, 1986) 2-3.

[104] Willem Noomen and Nico Van Boogaard, *Nouveau recueil complet des fabliaux* (henceforth *NRCF*) nine volumes, (Pays Bas: Van Gorcum, 1983-1993). See also Joseph Bédier, *Les Fabliaux: Études de littérature populaire et d'histoire littéraire du moyen âge* (Paris: Champion, 1925); Per Nykrog, *Les Fabliaux: Étude d'histoire littéraire et de stylistique médiévale* (Copenhagen: E. Munksgaard, 1957).

[105] Mary Jane Stearns Schenk, *The Fabliaux: Tales of Wit and Deception* (Indiana: Purdue University Monographs in Romance Languages 24, 1987) 109.

that the regions of Picardy and Flanders which constitute the setting for the tales saw much mobility in social classes in that period. There, the multi-faceted ascent of the peasantry led to development and change, creating an urgent sensitivity to money for inhabitants of small towns or large villages. [106]

Alexander Murray identifies social mobility as a feature of thirteenth-century society, a period marked by the challenge to the doctrine of the three estates.[107] A new mentality emerged which, according to Murray, favored the importance of practical wisdom and even shrewdness.[108] Following up on this idea, Stearns Schenk notes:

> although the characters of the fabliaux do not aspire to power in any broad or lasting sense, these tales are all permeated by the ethic of practicality, ambition and celebration of quick-wittedness (...) [they] reflect the fusion of a peasant mentality with the ethos of the money economy.[109]

The tales often link sexual behavior with financial advancement, and the lascivious priests and resourceful spouses engineer their escapades using a "practical wisdom" which highlights monetary gain as the jewel in the crown of benefits. Promises of gifts and plans to improve financial status abound in the collection as the necessary background to sexual involvement. The characters' desire for upward mobility can even make partners out of husband and wife in the fake seduction of a wanton priest or "chevalier" who will pay up.[110]

The representation of third parties in the genre is affected by the urgency of mobility and by the strong initiative and imagination of those who turn to intermediaries. The practical wisdom at the disposal of so many characters overshadows the third party to some extent; this is logical, since in a context where an urgent financial motivation on the part of husbands, wives and rivals goes hand in hand with sexual stratagems, the presence of a go-between would require a further division of wealth and would not be desirable.

---

[106] Stearns Schenk, 111-112.

[107] Alexander Murray, *Reason and Society in the Middle Ages* (Oxford: Oxford University Press, 1978) 98.

[108] Murray, *Reason and Society*, 122.

[109] Stearns Schenk, *The Fabliaux*, 119-120.

[110] Examples of this type of stratagem are seen, among others, in "Le sacristain," "Le meunier et les deus clercs," "Le bouchier d'Abbeville," "Constant du Hamel," and "Estormi."

Moreover, the *fabliaux* pay little attention to the world of prostitution and turn instead to the home and the institution of marriage, where the presence of a procuress seems superfluous. The few old go-betweens in the tales exert their skill or power only at the outer limits of transgression. Thus Galestrot fulfills the function of simple maidservant and messenger in "Constant du Hamel," while it is left to the clever wife Ysabeau to find an ingenious way out of her predicament; old Hersent in "Aloul" provides a physical shield for a priest escaping the cronies of a jealous husband. The most prominent portrayal occurs in "Auberée," a tale of Eastern origin, where the old woman plants the central decoy.

Asked to arrange the meeting of a "borjois" with a young married woman, Auberée first names her fee; rewards such as food or clothing no longer interest the third party who now has a rate, confirming the centrality of money economy. Subsequently, the ruse she employs serves to bring the completely unsuspecting wife to her house away from the jealous husband; as of that moment, the power of verbal coercion seems not to interest the old woman. The "borjois" asks the bawd how he might overcome the young woman's probable unwillingness, to which the old woman simply replies that he ought to ignore her resistance and use force.[111] Interestingly, he does not implement the suggestion of the bawd but coerces the young woman by presenting a convincing argument: either way, she has lost her honor now that she finds herself alone with him in a strange house, so she may as well give in. Sexual conquest therefore takes place as a result of the manipulation of sensitivities by the man. Auberée's contribution to the affair has had only to do with the preamble, that of bringing the wife over to the house, using a complex trick. Auberée, then, emerges as a go-between whose advice is not foolproof, and whose suggestion for the use of physical force has required modification by the pursuer. The difference of opinion creates a space of significant distance between the old woman and the "borjois:" the former perceives physical consummation as a straightforward display of power, requiring no ruse. The latter believes in conquest as a result of dialectical battle, here parodying Andreas Capellanus' belief in eloquent speech. The gap presents the old woman as one who has lit-

[111] "Auberee," *NRCF*, vol. I, 305. 354-360.

tle or no interest in the intellectual dimension of seduction, that is, the power of speech and reasoning. She stands on the margins of the seductive space, showing once again that her reputation exceeds her ability. With the *fabliaux*, the impression that projection plays a crucial part in the representation of the old woman is solidified; she acts as a screen upon which presuppositions on womanhood, old age, and poverty create an exaggerated conviction of crafty and sly behavior. A certain moral blame is thus implicitly placed on poverty, womanhood, and old age, only to find itself vulnerable to contradiction upon analysis.

Other examples confirm the indispensable and misleading role of projection in the old woman's portrayal. The old maidservant Hersent in "Aloul" has been called a go-between of the type encountered in the works of Ovid.[112] First, one must always clarify the type of bawd to whom one refers, for as we have shown, Ovid presents a relatively broad spectrum of go-between activity. Second, the function of Hersent does not have to do with mediation: she is asked by a wanton priest to protect him from an angry mob and agrees to do so.[113] The entire scene contains a slapstick quality, and emphasis falls clearly on the farcical confusion caused by the chase and the hiding. Hersent demonstrates no desire or talent to mediate. That a critic would refer to her as a go-between demonstrates how her surface attributes (old age, willingness to provide one stepping-stone for an adulterous situation) suddenly render her prone to a moral and thematic designation which, in all fairness, is not hers.

Yet, an old woman described as "sage" ("wise"), also named Hersent, appears in "Le prestre teint" in the clear capacity of go-between, this time making an important contribution to the typology of the figure.[114] Asked by a priest named Gerbaus to talk a married woman into having an affair with him, Hersent enters the former's home. Perhaps oddly, Hersent employs no lie whatsoever in her attempt to convince the married woman. She walks into the house and expresses the purpose of her visit in unequivocally truthful terms, using the word "verité" ("truth") with legitimacy: "You must not wonder why I have come to see you. The gentleman sends you his regards (...) and wants you to know the truth. – And who is he? –

[112] William Matthews, "The Wife of Bath," 424.
[113] "Aloul," *NRCF*, vol. III, 28-31.
[114] "Le prestre teint,"*NRCF*, vol. VII, 31.

Sire Gerbaus, (...) who through me sends you an amorous message, and asks that you be his lover."[115]

This honest and almost laconic approach, free of any dissimulation, results in utter failure. The young woman slaps Hersent in the face and throws her out, inspiring the priest to search for other methods. In spite of Hersent's brief appearance, the *fabliau* contains a meaningful implication with respect to the definition of mediation in illicit love: a go-between causes the collapse of the mediatory space when she offers a direct expression of the truth. To state the purpose of her client, she must create an artifice that would dispel the threatening or immoral aspects of his objective. Or, she must venture into a territory rarely if ever explored by the go-betweens studied so far: she must present his true intention in a compelling manner. She does neither and instead communicates his purpose without using a consciously seductive or coercive framework. Her failure emphasizes the indispensability of artifice in mediation and shows the futility of the unimaginative expression of simple truth in the realm of seduction.

In their portrayal of the go-between, the *fabliaux* strengthen the idea that the medieval European bawd operates at the periphery of trangression, in this case due to the wealth of initiative available in the practical independence of mind shown by those who surround her. The tales further reduce the character to a stock figure, yet the intrinsic conviction regarding her role as evil procuress continues to haunt the tales; the stories rely almost exclusively on the effect of presuppositions in her portrayal. The heavy burden of presuppositions from social and other literary sources is intensified within the body of the *fabliaux* with occasional references to old women in capacities other than basic mediation which, nonetheless, enhance the impression of stereotypical vice. In "La vieille truande," a handsome young squire is harassed by the aggressive sexual advances of an old woman who resorts to several low tricks to engage in lovemaking with him.[116] Her appetite for the young man, and her frenzied elaboration of tricks, cumber the character of the old woman with blatant flaws, all of which revolve around unfulfilled and misplaced sexual desire. Thus the signifier "vieille" triggers off a set of associations which can

[115] "Si ne vos devez merveillier/Por quoi je sui a vos venue:/Li mieusdres sire vos salue/(...)/ – Et qui est ce? – Sire Gerbaus,/Qui (...) par moi vos mande druerie,/Prie vos que soiez amis" ("Le prestre teint," 141-149).

[116] "La vieille truande," *NRCF*, vol. IV, 339-344.

only evoke greed, chatter, and predilection for sexual intrigue. The attempts at mediation point at the flaws of old women rather than the task itself, reaffirming the function of the "vieille" as a convenient trope for the expression of mockery.

The bawd receives detailed treatment in the hands of Jean de Meun, redefining some of the stock features attributed to her in several other medieval traditions. We shall now consider the Vieille of the *Roman de la Rose*, a figure who occupies a special place in the history and typology of the medieval go-between.

(iii) *The Old Woman of* Le Roman de la Rose

The *Roman de la Rose* engages many genres such as the *Romans d'antiquité*, Arthurian literature, the poetry of the troubadours and Ovidian themes in its treatment of love. Several voices argue on the topic of love using a polemical form, and, as such, the *Roman* brings to mind the *De Amore* of Andreas as well as the entire debating tradition of the twelfth century.[117] The part elaborated by Jean de Meun delves with more attention than his predecessor into the physical and erotic aspects of love, aligning the text more closely with Ovid than with the solemn and analytical Chrétien. This does not imply a distancing from the courtly spirit;[118] rather, the author provides more deliberation on the nature of erotic love as he follows the narrator in the actual quest for the Rose. He provides a questioning and reflective attitude towards physical love through a narrative scheme whose allegorical figures enjoy considerable characterization.[119]

---

[117] See Charles Oulmont, *Les débats du clerc et du chevalier dans la littérature du Moyen Age* (Paris: Champion, 1911).

[118] Batany, *Approches du* Roman de la Rose, 19.

[119] As Batany states: "With Jean de Meun, the tendency for scholarly writing is back, but each abstraction presents things in such a personal light which would make one draw the conclusion that – paradoxically – the long speeches in the *Roman de la Rose* are closer to a work of drama than the rather impersonal dialogues of Andreas Capellanus." ("Chez Jean de Meun, on tend de nouveau à l'exposé scolaire, mais chaque abstraction présente les choses sous un jour si personnel qu'on pourrait dire, paradoxalement, que les longs discours du *Roman de la Rose* sont plus proches d'une oeuvre dram)atique vivante que les dialogues bien impersonnels d'André le Chapelain") (17). The idea of an intellectual premise based on narrative strength is also explained by Per Nykrog, *L'amour et la rose: le grand dessein de Jean de Meun* (Harvard Studies in Romance Languages 41, 1984) 25.

In one sense, all the allegorical figures surrounding the narrator act as third parties, since each one plays a part in the quest for the Rose, be it to dissuade or encourage the lover in the task. Clearly, the Vieille corresponds to the figure of the bawd and occupies a space already designated for third-party activity.[120] Her profession entitles her to speak with Bel Accueil on behalf of the narrator and to attempt to coerce the former into letting the lover further inside the Rose's domain.

For his portrayal of the narrator and the Rose, Jean de Meun devotes no time to social hierarchization.[121] Clearly, though, the Rose does not betray the traits of a courtesan, but rather those of an inexperienced girl facing the prospect of deflowerment. In relation to the Rose, the Vieille corresponds to a surprising social identity: she makes it clear that she has been a prostitute and has been affected by intense cynicism with the cruel passage of time; her identity as such marks one of several contradictions at work in the Old Woman's portrayal.

The primary discrepancy in the Vieille's depiction has to do with the very nature of her representation. She stands guard to the allegorical Bel Accueil, a young man whose conquest would finally guarantee access to the Rose. At the same time, she transcends the realm of allegorical representation and outlines a social and personal history by speaking of her trip to "this country" and of taking up service with the Rose.[122] Upon securing Bel Accueil's agreement to a meeting, she asks the lover for the very corporeal reward of a pair of gloves, which indicates yet again her concrete association with the physical world. As an allegory, the Vieille occupies tenuous ground. The next discrepancy involves the nature of her task: why, of all people, would such a woman guard Bel Accueil's virtue? The presuppositions attached to the motif of the old woman with past amorous and mercenary experience strongly question such a choice, for her background does not render her compatible with the world

---

[120] Initially, as the guardian of Bel Acueil, she is asked by Courtoisie and Largesse to deliver a present to him. Guillaume de Lorris et Jean de Meun, *Le Roman de la Rose* III, edited by Ernest Langlois (Paris: Société des Anciens Textes Français, 1912) 12200 ff. The references will be to line numbers from this edition, henceforth referred to as *Le Roman de la Rose.*

[121] Attention to social status, according to Batany, marks the *Roman*'s main distinction with the *De amore.* Batany, *Approches du* Roman de la Rose, 17.

[122] *Le Roman de la Rose* III, 12949-12952.

of virtue.[123] One explanation for this would lie in the issue of intertextual continuity and her links with the Goliardic "Si Linguis Angelicis."

These contradictions never achieve full resolution. The poem does not attempt to problematize these in their own right: rather, it makes use of the Old Woman to offer one perspective among many on love as part of the ongoing debate on the matter. The Vieille, whose beauty and erotic potential have long since disappeared, expresses great bitterness about the passage of time and advocates for young women the *carpe diem* approach to sexual love. Her significant contribution to the history of the go-between has to do with the text's inclusion of a motive for her world vision. The motive is couched in standard rhetorical terms and includes the well-known lament on the passage of time and the warnings on the transitory nature of beauty.

In her own words, revenge has guided the Old Woman looking back with bitterness at her treatment in the hands of her lovers. First cheated due to her own ingenuity and ultimately abandoned by male lovers on account of her old age, the bawd sets herself up as a cautionary example, intermingling advice with a marked personal bitterness: "I cannot have my vengeance in any other way than to teach my doctrine."[124] Consequently, she offers dissimulation as the best lesson in love, adding that lying and falsehood constitute the best methods for success in love.

The actual lesson offers an expanded version of the advice given by the *lenae* of comedy and elegy. In essence, she adds nothing new to the adages of those old bawds: her predecessors have all rooted for multiple lovers, provocative attire, or simulated fidelity; the Vieille offers many details on every topic and echoes the *Ars amatoria* in some of the advice she gives.[125] Her type of mediation, then, draws on the

[123] Note Bel Acueil's own distinctly negative impression of the Vieille: he has no confidence in her and cannot bring himself to trust her (*Le Roman de la Rose* III, 12563-12565).

[124] "Ne m'en puis autrement venchier/Que par aprendre ma doctrine" (*Le Roman de la Rose* III, 12878-12879).

[125] For example, in her suggestion that maids and nurses be used as assistants in the woman's task to plunder the lover (*Le Roman de la Rose* III, 13709-13712). That her advice pertains clearly to the Ovidian heritage is illustrated in detail by Alan M. F. Gunn, *The Mirror of Love: A Reinterpretation of the "Romance of the Rose"* (Texas: Texas Tech Press, 1952). See also Peter L. Allen, *The Art of Love: Amatory Fiction from Ovid to the* Romance of the Rose (Philadelphia: University of Pennsylvania Press, 1992). This

construction of the status of instructor for herself. But the constant references to her own anger and present predicament undermine the consistency of her lesson, since the exposure of her own fragility dominates her discourse and diverts attention from the lesson, raising questions on the validity of her posture, rather than the content of her lesson.[126]

Another undermining factor has to do with the tone used in the portrayal of the Vieille. With regards to her contribution to the debate on love, the critic Alan Gunn points out:

> (...) the poet intended us to place it [the debate of the Vieille] beside the discourse of Amors, Raison, and Amis; and to regard it as structurally, if not ethically, equal in value to these earlier examples of *enseignement*. It also is a distinct and coordinate part of the *symposium* that runs through the poem; an additional contribution to the poet's exposition of the varied and often contradictory meanings and aspects of love.[127]

However, unlike Amors and Amis, the Old Woman's perspective is projected from an angle which invalidates her arguments considerably. Bel Accueil chooses to answer courteously that he does not experience the same bitterness and greed as the Vieille, announcing his decision to admit the lover for reasons of courtesy and not out of revenge. The bulk of her advice, then, has fallen on deaf ears, and its impact on the plot limits itself to characterizing the speaker, with no further influence on others. In short, the Old Woman fails as a mediator. The referential quality of her discourse, that is, her construction of self through the relation of specific memories, fails to make a meaningful connection to the task of amorous mediation. Her status reveals the impossibility of mediation when driven only by personal vengeance, for such an attitude impedes the making of a dialogic encounter with her interlocutors; rather, it restrains the Old Woman in an isolated space in which the well-known *topoi* of time and van-

---

is a valuable study of the fictional frame used for expounding theories on love and on Ovid's profound influence on medieval French writers. The scholar focuses on the importance of the consciousness that this love is fiction and strictly textual in conception.

[126] For example, rather than ending her lesson in a strong encouraging note for Bel Acueil, she chooses to recall once again her sorry state as possessor of a withered Rose, lamenting her lot in life (*Le Roman de la Rose* IV, 14544-14546).

[127] In addition, the type of advice given by the figure is studied in detail by Gunn, with the conclusion that she pertains unequivocally to an Ovidian heritage (Gunn, *The Mirror of Love*, 385).

ished beauty are repeated. This failure is important for the typology of medieval amorous mediation: it draws attention to the reiteration of personal experience as a potentially useful tool for the go-between, and simultaneously invalidates the tool when it is shown to possess no seductive – that is, dialogic – qualities of vital communication.

The short, formulaic reply by Bel Accueil to the Old Woman's drawn-out discourse creates a humorous scene much like a double act in which the "straight man" nullifies the comic's bombastic discourse with a flat reply. The gesture slows down the momentum of her speech. Additionally, the conflict of registers in the content of her utterances causes a comic effect which mars the validity of her lesson on love. She boasts her access to science and announces her eligibility to deliver her lectures from a professional academic chair. Her passion in delivery stands in amusing contrast with the places and the means she suggests for the teaching of her doctrine, for she announces that she can teach love as well as any academic, in any place. She proceeds to name these locations, creating a distinct quality of slapstick as they all suggest the acts of hiding and quick, indiscriminate pairing off: thickets, curtains, stables, and pantries.[128] Her advice on dress or eating habits creates an equally comical effect: for instance, women sitting at the dinner table must not fall asleep or else they will fall backward, forward, or sideways, breaking ribs and elbows.[129] These touches diminish the gravity of her status in comparison with Amis and Amors.

The *Roman de la Rose* confirms the comic potential of the bawd as a stock literary figure by explaining some of the reasons for which the bawd has no choice but to inspire laughter and contempt. In terms of her final impact on the text, Jean de Meun situates his go-between well within the traditions of Ovid, the *fabliaux*, and medieval comedy. He expands her territory by allowing her space for the elaboration of personal history, as well as reminding the reader of her potential (though unfulfilled) status as erotic instructor. Significantly, the autobiographical portrait contextualizes the identity of the bawd according to a number of familiar principles. It does not surprise the reader nor problematize the immoral nature of the go-between's intentions: the history of the bawd as a young woman contains the same preexisting moral assumptions as that of the panderer in legal texts. The

[128] *Le Roman de la Rose* IV, 13506-13514.
[129] *Le Roman de la Rose* IV, 13457-13470.

Roman documents the path of the bawd and attempts to validate the assumption that she has little or no redeeming features. In other words, a history is provided for the bawd – in her own words, to increase validity – which explains the reasons behind her present moral turpitude. The go-between displays bawd-like features even in the courtly world of the Lover, implying the universality of her attributes regardless of the context in which she finds herself.

As regards her capacity of teaching lessons on love, the parodic touches of Jean de Meun emphasize her lack of access to the intellectual realm of dialectical reasoning on love. She has retained the forms of pedagogy, but lost contact with the content and the places which would equate her lessons with those offered by other allegorical figures. It is quite possible that in addition to comic potential, the invalidity of her lesson reflects a mistrust of any type of popular philosophy, especially if offered by a non-academic character on the margins of mainstream learning (i.e., an old woman). The literate and intellectual nature of the debate on love in written sources would not, logically, attribute much importance to the opinions voiced by a marginal figure, and represent them primarily as comic and ultimately inconsequential, as we have seen in the case of *Le Roman de la Rose.* Indeed, it is known that mainstream medical authorities complained throughout the Middle Ages of the foolish trust placed by people in non-certified, non-Establishment figures of scientific authority, and to some extent the Vieille constitutes the dramatization of such an authority as seen through the eyes of mainstream intellectual activity.[130]

[130] For disdainful views taken of any non-academic, non-certified scientific activity, that is, by women or religious minorities, see See Jon Arrizabalaga, "The Ideal Medical Practitioner in Counter-Reformation Castile: The Perception of the Converso Physician Henrique Jorge Henriques (c. 1555-1622)" in *Medicine and Medical Ethics in Medieval and Early Modern Spain: An Intercultural Approach*, edited by Samuel S. Kottek and Luis García Ballester (Jerusalem: The Magnes Press, 1996) 61-91; Michael R. McVaugh, "Royal Surgeons and the Value of Medical Learning: The Crown of Aragon, 1300-1350," in *Practical Medicine from Salerno to the Black Death*, edited by Luis García Ballester, (Cambridge: Cambridge University Press, 1994) 211-236; R.I. Moore, *The Formation of a Persecuting Society: Power and Deviance in Western Europe, 950-1250* (Oxford: Blackwell, 1987).

V. The Fourteenth Century

(i) *The Go-Between in Boccaccio's* Decameron

Giovanni Boccaccio's collection of tales, a bold venture into the exploration of original style and language, also "imitates and sometimes parodies the full range of medieval genres, from courtly lyric and *chansons de geste* to saint's life and fabliau."[131] Boccaccio situates these tales in an urban middle-class atmosphere and offers a panoply of a society known well to him. Alongside current literary themes and motifs he provides vivid depictions of everyday life: "The *Decameron* is the representation, or rather the consecration, artistic and, in a sense, metaphysical, of the history of every man and the daily reality of that very human world."[132] The collection, impressive in thematic scope, uses love as one of its unifying themes.[133] The tales on love often hail from a specific source from Antiquity or the Middle Ages; characterization filters through the context of fourteenth-century urban and middle-class life. In the treatment of adulterous or illicit love, Boccaccio pays particular attention to the figure of the go-between in two of his tales by bringing the old and new contexts together against the urban background.[134]

Book IX of the *Metamorphoses* of Apuleius inspires the tenth story of the fifth day by Dioneo, known as the tale of Pietro di Vinciolo.[135] In the Latin text the baker's wife took the significant steps towards adultery at the bawd's suggestion that she try a new lover. Boccaccio's narrative transfers the choice entirely to the young wife. Frustrated with her dull marriage, the young woman decides to take a lover and chooses an assistant to help her

---

[131] David Wallace, *Giovanni Boccaccio: Decameron* (Cambridge: Cambridge University Press, 1991) 2.

[132] Vittore Branca, *Boccaccio: the Man and His Works,* translated by Richard Monges (New York: New York University Press, 1976) 216.

[133] Critics have noted "the forward progression of the tales as they move towards the illustration of a new terrestrial purpose for mankind defined in the final day of the storytelling (...), love" (Mark Musa and Peter Bondanella, "The Meaning of *The Decameron,*" in *The Decameron: A New Translation* [New York: W. W. Norton & Company, 1977] 330).

[134] M. Pastore Stocchi, "Un antecedente latino-medievale di Pietro di Vinciolo," *Studi sul Boccaccio* I, (1963) 349-362.

[135] A. C. Lee, *The* Decameron, *its Sources and Analogues* (New York: Haskell House, 1909) 173.

> Realize her wishes, and so she made the acquaintance of an old woman who in appearance seemed as pure as Saint Verdiana who feeds the serpents, since she attended all religious ceremonies with her rosary in her hand, and would not talk about anything but the lives of the Church Fathers and the wounds of Saint Francis, and almost everyone thought of her as a saint.[136]

Unlike the case with the novel by Apuleius, this community does not know the old woman as a bawd. But the imagery is suggestive, and the reader is drawn instantly into a complicitous and easy knowledge with the narrator: the key for recognizing the old woman as a bawd lies in the not-so-latent kinship between visits to the church and amorous hunting. Ovid had long ago advised that temples and public gardens be toured in search of prey, and Jean de Meun followed up on this advice in great detail.[137]

The church represents a fertile ground for the wife, who maintains her control over the situation by communicating her exact requirements of a lover to the old woman. The latter agrees to help, justifying herself by voicing a lament reminiscent of the Vieille of *Le Roman de la Rose.* She wishes to help because in her old age she realizes that women must take every advantage of their youth while they can. Boccaccio endows the old woman with a livelier tone than the Vieille to communicate this; her portrayal of a disgraced old age has an embittered and yet spirited quality to it, connecting in a substantial manner to the realities of her own everyday life. Realistic descriptions, integral elements in Boccaccio's writing, make a significant contribution to the bawd's discourse. The detail used in her language provides legitimacy for her lament; whereas the Vieille of Jean de Meun utilizes an overwhelmingly vengeful language as both her lament and her technique of coercion, the realistic discourse of the "vecchia" now opens sufficient room for a serious consideration of

---

[136] "Per dare segretamente a ciò effetto si domesticò con una vecchia che pareva pur santa Verdiana che dà beccare alle serpi, la quale sempre co' paternostri in mano andava a ogni perdonanza, né mai d'altro che della vita de' Santi Padri ragionava e delle piaghe di San Francesco e quasi da tutti era tenuta una santa" (Giovanni Boccaccio, *Decameron*, edited by Vittore Branca [Torino: Guilio Einaudi, 1980] 696) (henceforth *Decameron*).

[137] In the *Roman de la Rose*, the Vieille suggests that women frequent the Church for the very simple reason that it promotes visibility: "For in those places the God and Goddess of Love hold their classes, and sing Mass to their disciples" ("Car en teus leus tient ses escoles/E chante a ses deciples messe/Li deus d'Amours e la deesse") (*Le Roman de la Rose* IV, 13517-13528).

her complaint. The theme of *contemptus mundi* becomes in her speech a palpable issue, posing legitimate material questions which matter to the old woman in urgent ways. The "vecchia" offers an image of bourgeois womanhood and its setbacks in old age, using scenes of domestic life to substantiate her claim: "when we are old, neither our husbands nor other men want to look at us, and they send us off to the kitchen to chit-chat with the cats, and to count the pots and pans."[138]

This legitimacy, even if proposed by a hypocritical old woman, receives further strength from one of the major specifications laid out by the literary project embraced in the *Decameron:* the author has made it clear from the outset that he has a female readership in mind for whom he wishes the tales to fulfill an entertaining and edifying function.[139] From the very beginning the book shows affinity with the frustrations of everyday life for this female readership. Women suffer from idleness, as opposed to men who have many opportunities for dispelling boredom.[140] The old woman's complaint represents the logical end of a life of idleness and frustration.

As a go-between, the "vecchia" finds herself in an unequivocally limited position due to a factor we have seen in other European and Classical texts. The disposition of her "client" dictates the bawd's every move. The old woman defines her function with confidence but shows awareness of the degree of control possessed by the young wife:

> (...) I tell you that you could not have spoken to anyone in the world who could have been more useful to you than me, for there is no man too refined for me to tell him what he should do, nor is there any man so crude and uncouth to stop me from softening him and bending him in the way that I want. I ask you to do one thing, show me which one you like, and let me take care of it.[141]

---

[138] "Quando c'invecchiamo, né marito né altri ci vuol vedere anzi ci cacciano in cucina a dir delle favole con la gatta e a annoverare le pentole e le scodelle" (*Decameron*, 697).

[139] This is initially made clear in the prologue, where the author indicates that he would like ladies to enjoy the tales, but also learn from them, and follow any advice which they consider useful in them (*Decameron*, 9).

[140] *Decameron*, 9.

[141] "Ti dico infino a ora che tu non potevi a persona del mondo scoprire l'animo tuo che piú utile ti fosse di me, per ciò che egli non è alcun sí forbito, al quale io non ardisca di dire ciò che besogna, né sí duro o zotico, che io non ammorbidisca bene e rechilo a ciò che io vorrò. Fa pure che tu mi mostri qual ti piace, e lascia poscia fare a me" (*Decameron*, 698).

The young wife enjoys considerable authority in this pact, since she chooses the man who interests her. The old woman's initial boasts of her own abilities turn out to represent a case of rhetorical posturing so as to promote herself better for the young wife. Effectively, the old woman goes after one chosen by the wife and delivers that which she is asked to bring. The rapidity of her subsequent actions (bringing in a number of young men to the wife described in one sentence) stands in contrast with the vivid picture she had offered of her talents in manipulating men.

Boccaccio here repeats a familiar pattern, adding a significant element in the poetics of mediation such as it is expressed by bawds: the old woman has promised much in speech and has carried out only a few simple actions. In this respect, no modification upon Apuleius' model can be discerned. Similarly, echoes of *Le Roman de la Rose* find their way into this text as the possible motivations of the old woman are explored in her own words, this time from an almost humble stance, allowing for some sympathy for her. Of greater importance is the old woman's awareness of her subordination to the will of the young wife; she articulates the boundaries set on the art of mediation and verbalizes the master-servant dynamic which commands the conception of this task. Her consciousness of this dynamic, although not heightened, draws attention to the go-between's image of the self as an entity tied down by material and class anxieties. The convincing, realistic insertion of material concerns into her task unravels, to some extent, the mechanism which connects mediation to a position of servitude. Countless bawds have declared their poverty and asked for financial help prior to this old woman: in that respect, her lament of old age and poverty is nothing new. Yet she advances the complaint from literary *topos* to a convincing material concern by linking it to a specific space and time, drawing attention to the dire circumstances which cause the mediator to undertake her task.

Moving away from the professional intermediary, Boccaccio also focuses his attention on the maidservant, recalling Ovid's mention of that possibility. The ninth story of the seventh day involves the "camariera" (maid) of a young lady in love. Lidia, wife of the older and sexually indifferent Nicostrato, confides in her maidservant regarding her intention to compensate for her husband's negligence. She knows the identity of her potential lover (the handsome Pirro, retainer to her husband) and conceives of the affair as a private and single-handed project.[142] She then proceeds to ask her maid to procure the lover.

The private realm of the household brings loyalty into play in the maid-mistress interaction and echoes the preoccupation with allegiance encountered in the courtly spirit. Yet Boccaccio modifies this feudal sentiment in terms of the new concerns of the middle-class housewife when the latter reminds the maid that obedience and loyalty are required in exchange for a roof over the maid's head. The relationship between fealty and material debt casts a shadow over the feudal and courtly model.

In this tale, Boccaccio takes a detailed look at the intermediary's discourse during the coercive process. The conversations between Pirro and Lusca reveal above all Lusca's bitter concern with questions of class and status. Pirro's main reason for refusal has to do with the fact that an affair with Lidia would mean the betrayal of his master Nicostrato. Against this, Lusca presents a critical perspective:

> Another thing is, servants should treat their masters as the masters treat them, if they have it in their power. You, if you had a beautiful wife or mother or daughter or sister whom Nicostrato fancied, do you really believe that he would be concerned with loyalty the way you are now with his wife? You would be a fool to believe that, because if his pleas and flattery did not suffice to seduce her, you would have no power, and he would take her by force. Let us treat them and that which is theirs as they treat us and that which is ours.[143]

She establishes a "they" versus "us" opposition: on this basis, Pirro's venture into the affair would mean revenge as well the more obvious material and physical gains. Vengeance motivated the Vieille of *Le Roman de la Rose* and, to a certain degree, the "vecchia" also. Here a shift has occurred in accordance with the vital context of Lusca: vengeance continues to provide the fuel for the go-between's discourse, but the argument now contains a blatantly subversive streak

---

[142] *Decameron*, 863.

[143] "E oltre a questo non si vuol quella lealtà tra servidori trattare, in quel che possono, come essi da loro trattati sono. Speri tu, se tu avessi o bella moglie o madre o figliuola o sorella che a Nicostrato piacesse, che eglessi la lealtà ritrovando che tu servar vuoi a lui della sua donna? Sciocco se' se tu 'l credi: abbi di certo, se le lusinghe e' prieghi non bastassono, che che ne dovesse a te parere, e' vi si adoperrebbe la forza. Trattiamo aduque loro e le lor cose come essi noi e le nostre trattano" (*Decameron*, 866).

against a particular ruling class.[144] Her point of view reflects her sensitivity to her own subject position, a feature encountered in Antiquity only when the *lenae* complained briefly of the cruelty of old age. Starting with the comedies and followed up in detail by *Le Roman de la Rose*, the medieval bawd focuses further on self-pity as an integral aspect of her coercive methodology. In a fashion similar to the *Roman de la Rose*, the bitterness of Lusca's complaint originally aims to manipulate; in the *Roman* it ends up showing the extent to which the Old Woman deserves pity and contempt. For Boccaccio, it offers a glimpse into the go-between's self-perception as a woman who knows full well her vulnerability to old age and unfair treatment. The actual impact of her mediation turns out to be questionable. Once Lusca has finished, the tale makes it clear that Pirro had already taken his decision prior to his meeting with her.

When taken into account together, both intermediaries considered above provide a commentary on their place within the community. Jean de Meun initiates this trait in his detailed look into the Vieille's contempt but discourages any further investigation by parodying her and setting up a series of commonplace motifs around her. As mentioned, these serve above all to stifle her popular philosophies on life and love. In Boccaccio's tales, the intermediary points at a concrete social situation and vitalizes the usual complaints of poverty in urgent persuasive ways by relating them to her inferior class position. All the well-known traits, courtly and non-courtly – loyalty, old age, encouragement for the pursuit of physical love – now engage an awareness of hierarchical powers at work in the city. The oft-signaled talent of Boccaccio for portraying the city and the concerns of its inhabitants comes across adequately in his portrayal of the female go-between.

Several other tales in the *Decameron* also discuss recourse to a maid for help with illicit affairs. Invariably, these recapitulate the essential factors that go back to Ovid. The wife determines a course of action, and the third party, who is always a maid, carries out specific orders.[145] In these tales no significant departure from Ovid occurs.

---

[144] It is also interesting to note that in her hypothetical case – based on her perception of reality – the master does not seek the assistance of go-betweens in his quest for the women, but rather resorts to force if all else fails.

[145] For instance, in the sixth and tenth stories of the fourth day. In the latter, it is made amply clear that every stage of the affair is in the wife's hands, with the maid carrying out what amounts to mere errands in the process; the wife searches, decides, and chooses for herself.

The question of mediation and love occupies an important place for Boccaccio, but not in the concrete shape of a go-between. In a fashion similar to the *Ars amatoria* and the *De Amore*, Boccaccio's text itself assumes the role of the real intermediary itself to impart relevant information to its supposed readership. The author of the *Decameron* reveals a sharp awareness of his status as intermediary in the preface to the hundred tales as well as in the alternative title of his work. The collection starts with the statement: "Here begins the book called Decameron, known also as Prince Galahalt[.]"[146] One of the traits associated with Galahalt (Galahad) concerns his function as go-between in the love affair of Lancelot and Queen Guinevere.[147] The *Decameron* thus announces itself as a guide in amorous affairs, especially for ladies in love, and, as mentioned, encourages them to follow or avoid those models which they deem (in)appropriate in the tales.[148]

Like Ovid and Andreas, Boccaccio differentiates between two activities undertaken by a third party: one involves assistance in logistical matters, while the other calls for the offer of guidance. The former contributes to the narrative at the level of the plot and allows for relevant transitions to come about. The latter emerges for the most part through the authorial voice in the shape of advice; for Boccaccio, it determines the direction taken by each anecdote and shapes the art of storytelling. The reader must seek the possible useful advice inherent in the fabric of the tale, and the *magister*'s role falls unequivocally on the author. Nonetheless Boccaccio dwells long enough on the actual go-between to illustrate some of the tensions and anxieties which inform her approach to the task of mediation.

(ii) *Geoffrey Chaucer*

(a) *The Transformation of the Go-Between in* Troilus and Criseyde

We have seen that, starting with the *Roman de la Rose*, the bawd of medieval literature begins to include some degree of reflection on

146 *Decameron*, 1.

147 The reference is specifically to Canto V, l. 137 of the *Inferno,* where a book is viewed as that which caused the love affair between Francesca and Paolo, setting up a comparison with Galeotto (Galahad). Both the book and Galeotto are perceived in the *Inferno* as wrongdoing go-betweens.

148 *Decameron*, 9.

the self such as it occupies the community. In Jean de Meun's allegorical romance and more so in Boccaccio's *Decameron,* the intermediary situates herself within a broader social scheme than that of texts from Antiquity by offering reasons for her type of behavior, even if she initially launches her laments as part of her scheme. The essence of the activity does not change in relation to basic Ovidian precepts; we have seen that in each case the disposition of her interlocutor determines the path and that the reflective nature of the intermediary's discourse produces each time a more complete portrait of herself.

In all the cases viewed above, the go-between remains an essentially secondary character. Pandarus, uncle to Criseyde in Geoffrey Chaucer's *Troilus and Criseyde*, brings about a veritable transformation in this pattern by reaching the level of principal character and occupying an unusually large space in the tale. Evidently, the character replicates Pandaro in Giovanni Boccaccio's *Il Filostrato.* The English writer adds a number of significant attributes to the intermediary.[149] The critic John V. Fleming maintains that Boccaccio's principal and original modification of the character has to do with the change of gender for the go-between.[150] Otherwise, the critic observes correctly that certain scenes with Pandaro – his first meeting with Troiolo, for instance – are handled in "a slightly brusque way (...) characterized by much of the shallow and maladroit ellipticism of the Italian verse romance, and there is little serious attempt to create a convincing psychological flavor for the scene."[151]

The change of gender does not constitute an original idea. Andreas Capellanus in the *De Amore* specifies the need for a same-sex confidant; Andreas recommends a helping friend, and Arthurian literature also emphasizes the completely non-mercenary aspect of

[149] Giovanni Boccaccio, *Il Filostrato*, and Geoffrey Chaucer, *Troilus and Criseyde*, parallel Italian and English texts, edited by B. A. Windeatt (New York: Longman, 1984) (henceforth *Il Filostrato* and *Troilus and Criseyde;* references will be to line numbers from these editions). For another variation on the character of Pandarus, see Aeneas Silvius Piccolomini (Pius II), *The Goodli History of the Ladye Lucres*, edited by E. J. Morrall (Oxford: Oxford University Press, 1996). This is a sixteenth-century translation of the *Historia de duobus amantibus.* Written in 1444 and influenced by Boccaccio's *Filostrato*, it makes some references to Pandalus, a figure who facilitates secret meetings between the lovers, but only after he is bribed.

[150] John V. Fleming, *Classical Imitation and Interpretation in Chaucer's* Troilus (Lincoln: University of Nebraska Press, 1990) 158 (henceforth Fleming).

[151] Fleming, 94.

assistance by setting up a clear contrast with the *lena*. In fact, Pandaro represents very much a dramatization of precepts laid out by Andreas: he shows care in justifying his actions on the condition of secrecy and does his best to avoid the negative associations of his task by repeating this condition throughout.[152] Additionally, he clarifies that his contribution to the liaison stems directly from his loyal love for his friend Troiolo. In this respect he situates himself within a safe distance from any connotation of mercenary procuring. He identifies himself primarily in terms of secrecy and allegiance, and, as Thomas A. Kirby has noted, coerces Criseida in an almost aggressive manner.[153] This proves his steadfast desire to please Troiolo and to disassociate himself from the identity of a professional go-between, quickly and at whatever the price, to substantiate his sentiment of loyalty.

The use of a male go-between relates to the courtly erotic spirit in another manner also. Georges Duby highlights this in a study entitled "L'amour qu'on dit courtois" ("The Love Called Courtly").[154] Duby considers courtly love an essentially masculine game in which men prove their worth to one another by performing well in the jousts of love, using the woman as one element in the game. The young man who fights for the attention of his *seigneur*'s lady has, in the long run, another goal in mind: "I am convinced that by serving the wife, young men sought to win the love of the prince (...) the laws of courtly love reinforced, in fact, the laws of vassalage."[155] Here

[152] "I can give each of you the same amount of comfort, but it must be kept a secret (...) Be wise about not revealing this to anyone else" ("E a ciascuno donar pari conforto,/Poscia che occulto il dovete tenere,(...) e tu sii saggio poi,/ Nel tener chiuso tal'opera altroi") (*Il Filostrato,* Canto II, 28). Stanzas 8 and 26 also show the same concern for secrecy and the preservation of honor. This necessity is voiced repeatedly across Canto II by Pandaro, Troiolo and Criseida.

[153] Thomas A. Kirby, *Chaucer's* Troilus*: A Study in Courtly Love* (Massachusetts: Peter Smith, 1958). The scholar provides a detailed, stanza-by-stanza comparison of the two poems in order to show the differences and similarities, at the plot level, between Pandaro and Pandarus. He concludes that the Italian version gives the reader a more abrupt and much less detailed picture; for example, Criseida's persuasion happens with remarkable speed in the Italian version, leaving little room for the development of Pandaro's eloquence; in fact, Pandaro succeeds in finally grasping her attention by cursing her. This process is shown to be a veritable challenge, and much more detailed, for the go-between in Chaucer's rendition.

[154] Georges Duby, *Le mâle moyen âge.*

[155] "servant son épouse, c'était, j'en suis persuadé, l'amour du prince que les jeunes voulaient gagner (...) les règles de la fine amour venaient renforcer les règles de la morale vassalique" (Duby, *Le mâle moyen âge*, 82).

Duby speaks of the triangle made up of husband, wife, young lover; his scheme applies just as well to the dynamics of the male go-between and his male friend, for, above all else, Pandaro seeks to prove his vassalage and friendship to Troiolo. Boccaccio's text does not offer visible reasons for this obsession with *amistat*, though the end sought by Pandaro may have to do with some type of political favor sought with his friend.[156]

As a third party privy to the love affair, Pandaro serves to highlight certain aspects of lovesickness as elaborated by Ovid and the *De Amore*. Troiolo's feelings render him so disoriented that he needs a helping hand to guide him through the path of love. Similar to Lunete in Chrétien's *Yvain*, Pandaro takes charge out of loyalty and acts as a foil to the lover's initial feebleness in the face of an all-consuming love. The ennobling power of love mentioned frequently by Capellanus surfaces in Troiolo only when Pandaro suggests that the lover divert his attention to other beautiful women.[157] This causes Troiolo to reiterate the depth of his feeling for Criseida, voicing his staunch fidelity to her and the benefits that he has gained from her love. In his role as interlocutor, Pandaro allows for the full articulation of such feelings. The overlap of mediation with listener to confidences is made clear in the person of Pandaro.

Both versions of the tale show a special concern with the idea of a doctrine of love: using dialogue, the works explore the rules, taboos, and limitations of such a doctrine. Boccaccio uses the character of the go-between to dramatize a role encountered in Andreas and Arthurian material as well as to underscore some of the effects of love on the male character as the latter expresses his feelings to this third party. Critics have noted Chaucer's considerable expansion of the character of the go-between. Some of the earlier scholarship on the figure suffers from the usage of vague and ultimately irrelevant psychological judgments upon Pandarus; critics have labeled him "a lively rascal," "an elderly gentleman with great experience of life,"

[156] Duby asks: "Disciplined by courtly love, was the desire of the male not used toward a political end?" ("Discipliné par l'amour courtois, le désir masculin ne fut-il pas alors utilisé à des fins politiques?") (82). As for Pandaro's allegiance, the extent of his loyalty is demonstrated on various occasions, but with the greatest intensity in Canto IV, where he weeps alongside Troiolo upon Criseida's disappearance.

[157] Kirby, *Chaucer's* Troilus, 105. The conversation in question takes place in Canto IV, 48.

"devoid of scruples," and "repulsive."[158] Moving away from such value judgments and focusing his attention on the world of the texts themselves, C. S. Lewis suggests that Chaucer's rendition of the tale represents a correction of the errors made by Boccaccio in the latter's treatment of courtly love.[159] Donald Howard sees the tale as "Chaucer's interpretation of the philosophy, or at least the morality, of paganism."[160] Recently, John V. Fleming has chosen to disagree with both views on the grounds that what Chaucer really does is to impose a strongly Christian viewpoint on Boccaccio's ancient pagan story of eroticism.[161] A homage to *Le Roman de la Rose* informs this tendency, and in Fleming's view, Pandarus represents one of the principal intertextual links between Jean de Meun's work and Chaucer's tale: "Pandarus' doctrines echo at different times nearly all of Love's preceptors from the *Roman de la Rose*, including Cupid, Lady Reason, Friend, La Vieille, Nature, and Genius."[162] Indeed, much of the advice given by Pandarus to the two lovers recalls the counsel found in Jean de Meun's work.

Fleming also sees in Pandarus an extension, although physically transformed, of the Ovidian bawd.[163] The darker connotations of Pandarus' activities cannot escape notice and repeat the insults aimed at the *lena;* Troilus even addresses the older man as a devil at one point.[164] In this respect Chaucer stands for "the literary conformist as well as the literary transformer."[165] The portrayal of Pandarus reminds the reader of several threads in the history of the go-between, brought together by Chaucer in a dialogue that engages Ovid, the courtly eroticism of *Le Roman de la Rose*, and the comic sexual *interpres* as exemplified by the (seemingly) diabolical but ultimately funny old bawd. The actual procedure used by Pandarus does not

---

[158] H. A. Taine, *History of English Literature* (London: Chatto and Windus, 1876) I, 34 and II, 93; J. J. Jusserand, *A Literary History of the English People* (London: G. P. Putnam's Sons, 1895) I, 302; Émile Legouis, *Geoffrey Chaucer* (London: J. M. Dent and Sons, 1928) 127.

[159] C. S. Lewis, "What Chaucer Really Did to *Il Filostrato*," *Essays and Studies by Members of the English Association*, edited by Sir Herbert John Clifford Grierson (Oxford: Clarendon Press, 1931).

[160] Donald Howard, *The Three Temptations* (Princeton: Princeton University Press: 1966) 135.

[161] Fleming, 91ff.

[162] Fleming, 98.

[163] Fleming, 162.

[164] *Troilus and Criseyde*, I, 623.

[165] Fleming, 161.

stand in great contrast to that of the go-betweens of elegiac comedy. He bases his coercion of Criseyde on an obvious lie, basing his approach to her on the device used in medieval Latin comedy, that is, a deceitful ploy. Before he meets with Criseyde he reflects deeply on the exact nature of his plan, as any trickster might.[166] In his conversation with her, he fabricates every detail of his meeting with Troilus as he tells her of the young man's love. Fleming has noted that in the entire poem "untruth in all its forms, from the verbal quibble to the bald-faced lie, commands the discourse."[167] In the case of the go-between, this indicates the continuation of the elegiac tradition in which lies are used to arouse interest.

The effectiveness of the go-between depends on the disposition of his prey, as we have seen time and again. In Boccaccio's version, Criseida falls in love with Troiolo very quickly. Chaucer offers a more complex perspective on Criseyde; the young woman decides to hesitate in the game before making any wholehearted commitment in an effort to buy time. Two elements finally bring about her genuine conversion: the first has to do with her sensitivity in the face of the power of fiction, a weakness manipulated by Pandarus as he makes up a story about Troilus.[168] The second concerns her friend Antigone's tempting song which describes love; hearing it produces a strong effect on Criseyde and changes her heart. The poem refers to this change as a conversion: "That she was quite able to convert" ("That she wex somwhat able to conuert").[169]

A combination of several elements brings about the surrender of Criseyde to the idea of love. Furthermore, Criseyde, a widow, possesses a strong awareness of the topic of love and is by no means inexperienced in its matters. Regarding Troilus she asks: "Can he wel speke of love?"[170] Chaucer offers us a variation on the disposition we have seen in the female characters of elegy and comedy; he presents the young widow's curiosity in terms of literary interest and

---

[166] *Troilus and Criseyde*, I, 1062-1071.

[167] Fleming, 94. As he states later, "Pandarus proves himself a cheerfully gratuitous liar time and again" (96).

[168] When her uncle first sees her on the day of the love declaration, she is reading a copy of *Le Roman de Thèbes* and shows herself to be sensitive to literary material. "She is, after all, just a bit like Emma Bovary; and the story he tells her is, after all, just as true as is the book of Lancelot de Lake" (Fleming, 97).

[169] *Troilus and Criseyde*, II, 903.

[170] *Troilus and Criseyde*, II, 503.

respect for her uncle's words.[171] But even if the text does indicate that her final surrender to love has to do with the result of cumulative elements at work around her, Pandarus still receives the bulk of attention in the narrative. The fact remains that Pandarus is a successful go-between. He extracts Troilus' secret and plays an important part in Criseyde's coercion. His success places him in a dubious light, blurring the line between courtly confidant and mercenary bawd. This diffusion of boundaries, itself a direct result of success, preoccupies Pandarus to some extent.

We have seen from the socio-religious background of the European Middle Ages as well as the perspectives offered by literature, that pandering is inextricably linked with prostitution. The non-courtly spirit manipulates this negative presupposition and takes it to the extreme: the bawds and go-betweens make no secret of the completely mercenary nature of their motivation, creating an atmosphere of sexual intrigue and comedy. The spirit of courtly love attempts to undo the negative associations by attributing mediation to loyalty and granting it a strictly limited, controlled space so as to avoid all unnecessary risks. The discourse of Pandarus frequently reveals an uncomfortable knowledge of these two modes of third-party operation: "And know well that this is a trick, for I would prefer that you and I and he were hanged, than to be his bawd[.]"[172] Elsewhere he complains to Troilus that he has become a procurer for the former's sake, even if he does not name the activity as such. The passage in which he confronts Troilus with the discomfort associated with intermediary activity expresses the anguish in remarkably clear terms:

> For you I have begun to play a game
> Which I shall never do for another,
> Even if he were my dear brother.
> That is to say, I have become, for you,
> Half-playfully, half-earnestly, the kind of man
> Who brings women to men,
> I will say no more, you know well what I mean.[173]

---

[171] It must be remembered that when at first she agrees to listen to her uncle's pleas, she does so as a result of careful planning and playing along in his game so as to calm him down; she shows considerable control over the situation, undermining to some degree the authority of Pandarus (*Troilus and Criseyde*, II, 449-462).

[172] "And also think wel that this is no gaude;/ffor me were leuere thow and I and he/Were hanged, than I sholde be his baude" (*Troilus and Criseyde*, II, 351-353).

[173] "ffor the haue I bigonne a gamen pleye/Which that I neuere do shal eft for

The concept of mediation between men and women carries such a shameful resonance that Pandarus will not even name it for fear of breach of decorum. In *Il Filostrato*, Pandaro conveys the anxiety more brusquely: "I have for your sake become a go-between, for your sake I have thrown my honor to the ground." ("Io son per te divenuto mezzano,/per te gittato ho'n terra il mio onore[.]")[174] In both cases, the go-betweens seek to frighten the lover so that he will guarantee his discretion when faced with this emotional blackmail. For Pandaro, the remark contains no self-judgment, for it is neither preceded nor followed by other instances of such anxiety. With Pandarus, the situation is different, since he reflects on the nature of his task;[175] the words "baude," "bauderye," "couetise," and "wikked dede" haunt his discourse and reveal the desire to keep a moral check on himself. Prior to the completion of his task, Pandarus resists the appellation of "baude," but once he has done his part to establish contact with Criseyde he lashes out at Troilus for making him "swich a meene as maken wommen vn-to men to comen" ("The kind of man that brings a woman to a man"). This constitutes a plea for Troilus' discretion in return for Pandarus' favors, yet it also implies that Pandarus cannot help but think of himself as a pimp, now that success has occurred. Having made the affair possible, Pandarus now finds himself closer to that perturbing designation. A paradox becomes visible in his mode of operation: as much as he stresses the importance of secrecy and Christian morality,[176] the mere fact that he has facilitated an erotic encounter banishes him on some level to the realm of bawds.

This momentary lapse impinges strongly on the courtly ethic, but Pandarus sees no way out of it. Chaucer's go-between articulates for the first time the paradox that one mode of third-party assistance (courtly) depends on the other (non-courtly). Chaucer reveals that

---

other,/Al-though he were a thousand fold my brother./That is to seye, for the am I becomen,/Bitwixen game and ernest, swich a meene/As maken wommen vn-to men to comen/Al sey I nought, thow wost wel what I meene" (*Troilus and Criseyde*, III, 250-256).

[174] *Il Filostrato*, Canto III, 6.

[175] Part of the difference is explained thus by Fleming; it is "clear evidence of Chaucer's *careful* adjustment from old to new in his normal fashion of softening and ambiguating Boccaccio's moral bluntness" (Fleming, 169).

[176] Pandarus makes frequent references to God and acceptable Christian behavior in his conversations with Troilus; see, for example, *Troilus and Criseyde* I, 939-945, and 1002-1008.

success requires the fusion of the two modes, and so Pandarus fits both in the tradition of the courtly go-between and the bawd, without the ability to solve the tension brought about by this convergence. The amount of space occupied by Criseyde's uncle allows for a clearer elaboration of this paradox to which previous writers had hinted: for example, Myrrha's nurse and Chrétien's Thessala both use mercenary-identified methods for a non-mercenary purpose. The *De Amore* determines the limits of third-party activity and shows a marked awareness of the slippery ground trod by the intermediary. Pandarus brings this uncomfortable fusion into full light by voicing his concerns about it.

As for the transformation in gender, Pandarus continues the same idea encountered in the character of his Italian predecessor. The principal relationship with the third party consists of the interaction between two men who grow to call each other "brother" and "friend," and who share the joys and sadnesses experienced by the male lover. In this system the woman becomes the addressee of prevarication, while the man benefits from an empathetic relationship with his mediator.[177] Duby's idea of courtly love as a "game for men" becomes quite apparent throughout this interaction and reaches its climax towards the end when the desperate Troilus loses his grasp over Criseyde. At this point, Pandarus suggests that they consider her abduction and rape, for even if this does cause some grief on her part, it will bring about the greater good of Troilus.[178] The task of the courtly male go-between, therefore, is to align himself all the more with the male lover and frame his activities in terms of brotherhood and allegiance. This constitutes an attempt to distance himself from the space occupied by the bawd.

In *Il Filostrato* and *Troilus and Criseyde* the medieval go-between undergoes two transformations. The first has to do with the change in gender, causing the effects we have discussed; the second, a logical continuation of the first, concerns the metamorphosis from go-between to friend. This progression does not apply to other intermediaries, largely due to the fact that no other third party studied so far occupies the text in the same way as Pandaro and his English descendant. Moreover, the female go-between appears too firmly rooted in

[177] For instance, among many other pieces of advice, Pandarus teaches Troilus to compose a decorous letter.

[178] *Troilus and Criseyde* IV, 533-539.

associations with either servitude or prostitution to aspire to the status of friend. Pandarus illustrates the nature and function of mediation (including all the tensions associated with it) when removed from the sphere of female and aged activity. It is once again Chaucer who calls for a closer look at the dilemma of the female bawd/amorous instructor in *The Canterbury Tales*.

(b) *The Transformation of the Bawd: Dame Alisoun in the* Canterbury Tales

In the course of his introduction of the story-telling pilgrims, the author of the *Canterbury Tales* presents the Wife of Bath as a woman who boasts five marriages and a life of great mobility: "She had crossed many a foreign river. She had been at Rome and Bologne, in Galicia at St. James', and at Cologne."[179] Her mobility places her in the realm of bawd-like activity, for it shows her freedom of movement alongside her love of intrigue and seductive scenarios. The poet rounds off the presentation with an acknowledgment of her familiarity with matters of carnal love, remedies for lovesickness and the art (skill) associated with these.[180] Later, in the preamble to her tale, she offers a lengthy description of her own life and many marriages in terms of the tricks played on each one of her husbands, always reiterating her voracious erotic appetite. These features identify Dame Alisoun as a bawd among other things, for each trait recalls an attribute seen in a *lena* and the old go-between of the *fabliaux* or elegiac comedy, with clear echoes of the Vieille. Chaucer does not limit the character to this identification, however.

Critics have interpreted the presence of Dame Alisoun in the tales in markedly diverse ways. To D. W. Robertson she illustrates "rampant femininity and carnality."[181] William Matthews regards the character as heir to two literary patterns: the comic old *lena* and the embittered old woman remembering a bygone life of luxury. He concludes that she continues in the spirit of the comedies of Plautus, Ovid, the *fabliaux*, and the Vieille of Jean de Meun, and that

[179] "She hadde passed many a straunge streem:/At Rome she hadde been, and at Boloigne,/in Galice at Seint Jame, and at Coloigne" (Geoffrey Chaucer, *The Canterbury Tales* [New York: Modern Library, 1994] 19, 465-466). Henceforth references will be first to page and then to line numbers of this edition.

[180] *Canterbury Tales*, 19, 475-476.

[181] D. W. Robertson, Jr., *A Preface to Geoffrey Chaucer* (Princeton University Press: 1962) 321.

Chaucer develops his version so that she becomes "the most individual, the most amusing of them all."[182] Richard Hoffman perceives the character as one who repeats the lessons taught by Ovid in the *Ars* as well as the ideas articulated by Jean de Meun's Vieille, noting little departure from these two sources in the portrayal of the lustful and experienced older woman.[183] More recently, several critics have chosen to debate the Wife of Bath's characterization in terms of its feminist or anti-feminist resonances.[184]

In these varied ways scholars have thrown light on the character from multiple perspectives, yet the assessment for the details of her characterization must also take into account a more panoramic understanding of the nature and function of intertextuality in the formation of her character. Matthews, for instance, offers a lengthy list of possible sources and inspirations, but his conclusion on the amusing nature of her character does not convince from an interpretive standpoint; such an evaluation relies only on individual aesthetic response. Similarly, Hoffman merely reiterates what he considers to be the sources by offering parallel passages from Ovid and Jean de Meun without searching for any possible changes brought about by Chaucer. Finally, the scholars who very correctly emphasize the need for a feminist perspective indeed raise many pertinent and important issues regarding the role of women in the texts, but might stress, in the case of the Wife of Bath, the role of a character within a literary tradition. The Wife's energetic and garrulous features may seem at first sight to derive from her refusal to remain silent and to articulate her erotic desire, perceivable (especially out of context) as gestures of independence. In fact, these are commonplace motifs that run through the portrayal of many a wife and

[182] Matthews, "The Wife of Bath," 443.

[183] Richard L. Hoffman, *Ovid and the Canterbury Tales* (Philadelphia: University of Pennsylvania, 1966) 129-144.

[184] Many scholars see the Wife of Bath and her tale as a reappropriation of a feminine space within a fundamentally patriarchal order. Such is the view of Carolyn Dinshaw, *Chaucer's Sexual Politics* (Madison: The University of Wisconsin Press, 1989) chapter four; a similar attitude guides the following studies: Priscilla Martin, *Chaucer's Women: Nuns, Wives, and Amazons* (Iowa City: University of Iowa Press, 1990); Mary Carruthers, "The Wife of Bath and the Painting of Lions," *PMLA* 94 (1979) 209-222. Among those who have disputed this view and argued that, in fact, Dame Alisoun represents the subordination of female discourse to a patriarchal authority are Elaine Tuttle Hansen, *Chaucer and the Fictions of Gender* (Berkeley: University of California Press, 1992); Ellen Schauber and Ellen Spolsky, "The Consolation of Alison: The Speech Acts of the Wife of Bath," *Centrum* 5 (1977) 20-34.

bawd in medieval literature, and not always with a feminist implication.

The Wife of Bath telescopes a number of different literary creations into one. She continues her role as wife, yet her entire discourse reveals a distinct affiliation with the medieval go-between: her bawd-like traits include her constant movement from place to place and her claim that she can fulfill the task of a first-rate teacher. Simultaneously, her focus falls on her own relationships with each husband, and she speaks only of her skills to gain their attention or their financial help with varying degrees of success. In this respect, she also fits into the category of "wykked wives," relating the dynamics of a strictly two-way interaction in her stories. Appropriately, then, her tricks and methods echo those sections of the *Ars amatoria* directed at the female lover more than Dipsas or any other *lena*.[185]

The Wife of Bath fits both categories (wicked wife and bawd) mainly because her audience chooses to perceive her as such. As her listeners, the other pilgrims expect a life story which will demonstrate much experience, and the Pardoner invites her to "teach us young men of your practice."[186] In this light the retelling of her feats becomes an act of mediation for a general public who temporarily bestows on her the role of erotic teacher, not without some ironic distance. With Dame Alisoun, Chaucer describes a trajectory in much the same way as *Le Roman de la Rose* has done for the Vieille and provides a background to the experience so often boasted by the go-between. In spite of his debt to Jean de Meun, Chaucer brings about a considerable shift in his unraveling of this trajectory.[187] Unlike the Vieille, Dame Alisoun is shown at a point in time in which she does not exclude the possibility of more sexual encounters, and announces her availability: "And blessed God, that I have wedded five! I welcome the sixth one, whenever he might come."[188] She

---

[185] Hoffman finds a number of evident parallels. For instance, the idea that a woman can meet a new husband at the ex-husband's funeral, or the use of fake tears for manipulating the lover's will (138).

[186] "teche us yonge men of youre praktike" (*Canterbury Tales*, 312, 187).

[187] Chaucer's close dialogue with *Le Roman de la Rose* has been investigated in several studies; particularly close analyses are Steven Allen Wright, "Literary Influence in Medieval Literature: Chaucer and the *Roman de la Rose*," (Ph.D. diss., 1986); Pierre-Yves Badel, Le Roman de la Rose *au XIVe siècle: Étude de la réception de l'oeuvre* (Geneva: Librarie Droz, 1980).

[188] "Y-blessed God that I have wedded fyve!/Welcome the sixte, whan that ever he shal" (*The Canterbury Tales*, 308, 44-45).

therefore perceives herself as an active sexual being, contrary to other bawds who convey their experiences only when they consider that their own sexual activity has become an impossibility. Chaucer's depiction of a figure hovering between the two boundaries allows for a sharper focus on the slippage which exists between the designations "wicked wife" and "bawd."

In the discourse of Dame Alisoun, experience constitutes the driving force behind telling her life story. She opens her tale with this word, and establishes a clear feedback with the Prologue which had identified her in that term also. In a mode reminiscent of the ancient and medieval bawd, the facts of Dame Alisoun's tale undermine her experience and authority. As she describes her husbands she indicates that none of her marriages have proven successful or gratifying, to the point that she needs to redefine the meaning of a "goode" husband in an unequivocally ironic manner: "goode" husbands mean old and almost impotent ones, for they inflict no harm and provide financial security. [189] Dame Alisoun clarifies that these men offered no sexual pleasure.[190] The subsequent utterance, that they "loved me so wel" emerges as doubly ironic when she specifies that her only motivation for intimacy was financial gain.[191] Given the erotically-charged prelude to this life story, during which Dame Alisoun sings the praise of sensual love, her revelation that her tricks brought her absolutely no carnal pleasure results in comic disappointment. The "badde" husbands, however, provided carnal pleasure yet demeaned and humiliated Dame Alisoun in other ways and failed to provide the type of security she sought.[192]

The Wife of Bath mentions several methods of combatting the difficulty of life with each husband, many of which recall techniques named in Ovid's *Ars amatoria* or La Vieille of *Le Roman de la Rose*, involving dissimulation towards financial gain. Dame Alisoun repeats the comic failure of such techniques: she has an unfulfilled relationship with one husband, yet chooses to repeat the experience with the next. Her "experience" and "auctoritee" thus prove tenuous. This particular twist recalls the Vieille of the *Roman de la Rose;* in addition, by documenting the misery of her youthful days, she subjects the

[189] *Canterbury Tales*, 311, 195-199.
[190] *Canterbury Tales*, 312, 202.
[191] *Canterbury Tales*, 312, 207.
[192] *Canterbury Tales*, 319, 504-525.

very notion of bygone beauty to an ironic inversion and implicitly questions the validity of such nostalgia.

The bawds of Antiquity, of Jean de Meun, and of Boccaccio voiced their lament as an integral part of their manipulative process to coerce a younger party into taking full advantage of youth and beauty. By minimizing the plot and discarding any idea of a specific task, Chaucer focuses all attention on discourse. In so doing, he intensifies the pattern of comic self-reflection seen in other bawds. Dame Alisoun projects an impression of erotic experience, which is quickly problematized by the chronicle of her failures. In other words, juxtaposition with other characters as well as her own retracing of her trajectory disclose a much more precarious subject position than suspected at first sight. Chaucer provides a premise for the understanding of this frailty insofar as he conveys the frustrations of the woman's life in her own words, albeit veiled by a semblance of optimism and authority. As Ruth Mazo Karras explains, the Wife of Bath makes a strong connection between sexual desire and "covetousness, greed, or avarice," and for her, "sex and money intersect in marriage, not in prostitution, but she still uses a vocabulary of sale and purchase[.]"[193] The critic continues: "Not all women may be commercial prostitutes, but any woman, whether a lady or a wench, who is 'dishonest of her body' is a whore; thus all may be assimilated to the image of the commercial prostitute."[194] This contributes to the strong impression of that which Karras labels the medieval impression of venality of feminine sexuality.[195] It imposes an infallible moral imperative, however latent, on the Wife of Bath as a fallen woman and throws light on the mechanisms which limit her existence to the sphere of women's deceits: once a wicked wife, she is now on her way, naturally, to becoming a bawd whose amorous instruction will involve only lessons in financial greed and the deception of the male. Inherently limited in scope because of the obsession with money, the lessons will undermine themselves in light of the Wife's failure to attain happiness for herself. This essentially circular and predeter-

---

[193] Ruth Mazo Karras, "Sex, Money, and Prostitution in Medieval English Culture," in *Desire and Discipline: Sex and Sexuality in the Premodern West*, edited by Jacqueline Murray and Konrad Eisenbichler (Toronto: University of Toronto Press, 1996) 201-216.

[194] Karras, "Sex, Money, and Prostitution," 203.

[195] Karras, "Sex, Money, and Prostitution," 204.

mined path is mapped by Chaucer in a vivid manner by drawing on numerous sources before him and expands the premise for her paradoxical characterization as weak yet wrongdoing.

VI. Conclusions

The medieval European go-between continues to share key conceptual elements with the models set up by Antiquity. One of the most important of these shared elements concerns the crucial role of the disposition of those with whom the figure interacts. Most medieval texts do not replicate the cast of courtesans seen in the elegies or the *Ars amatoria*, but rather, expand the range of characters who deal with third parties. Thus a few require visibly forceful coercion whereas others display latent or clear willingness to embark on a sexual relationship; in all cases the intermediary's impact relies on the volition of a more powerful agent.

On occasion, the bawd of Antiquity sets herself up as a cautionary example to inspire cooperation in the younger woman. Numerous medieval texts return to this gesture: from Lavine's mother to the Wife of Bath, discourse derives its force from the reconstruction of a personal trajectory. In the Middle Ages this autobiographical portrait takes up more space than in Antiquity: the go-between markets her autobiography as experience and attempts to use it as a manipulative technique. Yet the direction and ethical stance of the narrative point more strongly elsewhere: her autobiographical portrait sets her present behavior in the context of personal history and shows the how and why of her current status. The portrait, as we have seen, is painted using the same morally condemning perspective which applies to her in old age.

The medieval texts we have studied also use the figure of the go-between as an element within the debate on the nature of love and its consequences. Intermediaries offer the characters brief glimpses into possible scenarios for the evolution of love and enhance the impression of a debate regarding love: thus characters such as Lavine or Bel Accueil who listen to autobiographical teachings choose to pursue a direction contrary to the one prescribed by the third party. The young wife of Boccaccio's tale discards experienced maxims in favor of the practical help of the old woman and proceeds to fulfill her desire as planned on her own. At the utmost extreme,

Dame Alisoun ignores the moral of her own experiences and declares her willingness to take on a sixth husband. Mediation thus merges with pedagogy, only to be regularly undermined by textual strategies which seek to underscore the mediator's weakness as an agent.

The determination of courtly or non-courtly decides the tone with which the character enters the text and reaffirms some of the basic prerogatives of each genre. Yet the blurred fusion of types of intermediary activity from both spheres underscores the problematic nature of the very designation "courtly" as well as the act of mediation. Against the imperative of a morally driven reading, the noblest of third-party intentions becomes vulnerable to condemnation, thereby calling into question the nobility that was professed in the first place. With Pandarus, Chaucer points to the wrinkle in the idea of acceptable mediation (such as Chrétien and Andreas had proposed) showing that from a Christian point of view the task will inevitably raise criticism. For this reason Pandarus, the only go-between among the ones studied so far ever to occupy a central role, soon disassociates himself from his identity as such and integrates into the text as a friend of Troilus.

Jean Baudrillard observes that seduction has nothing to do with nature and energy and everything to do with sign and ritual.[196] Indeed, all the above texts link the poetics of love with ritual and game-playing and prove time and again that seduction equals the correct exploitation of signs which, themselves, possess a heightened consciousness of their artificiality. A gaping absence of spontaneity haunts the game of love in the texts studied above, maintaining the illusion of order and reason for a sentiment which, by the authors' own admission, does not allow itself to be grasped by human reason. The remarkable originality and artistic beauty of many of the texts discussed above do not preclude their tight links with past models and contemporary motifs played out in those areas where thematic concern is greatest. Seduction is one such area, and its players confirm the superficial suspicions of the reader, going on to redefine these suspicions in each text and only upon close reading. So, the priest in the *fabliaux* is expected to behave lasciviously, while the Arthurian knight, by definition, preserves his chastity until chivalric laws allow

[196] Baudrillard, *De la séduction*, 11.

him to discard it. This stands in great contrast with post-medieval notions of independence for the fictional character but explains quite well the impression of a lack of spontaneity. Whereas early modern and modern fiction accept the contradictions and ambiguities of falling in love or succumbing to seduction and attempts to do away with judgments on right and wrong in a character's decision-making, the medieval genres discussed here pay very close attention to the principal characters' correct or incorrect response to the signs around them. The textual scrutiny of this response generates the subtleties and variations which make the characters open to interpretation even today. By the same token, the secondary characters perform functions which seem increasingly predictable, for the lovers and the author possess the privilege of exploring the subtleties in the game of love.

From the *Romans d'antiquité* through to Chaucer, the lovers take it upon themselves to tackle the semiotics of seduction and, in the process, assign specific tasks to third parties. The third party turns into a sign that the lovers must interpret as they play out the game of seduction, and she must relinquish any powers of sign interpretation in her own right. Thus, while she performs an act of mediation, the definition of her task falls to the lovers who occupy the privileged space that affords them the interpretation of third-party activity. By involving the go-between in their interaction, the lovers complicate the language of seduction since they incorporate yet another mediating agent to the process of communication and challenge the self as well as the object of desire to the interpretation of this additional sign. We have seen that it is not so much what the go-between says or does, but the younger party's reactions to it, that defines the definition of seduction in the art of love. Despite the texts' efforts to endow the old woman in particular with an impression of power and skill, her words and actions never gain the status of a paradigm to follow in love: rather, they serve to reveal aspects of the lovers' capacity to handle mediation as a concrete act.

The treatment of the procuress in the literature of the European Middle Ages (excluding that of Spain, to which we will turn later) enhances our critical awareness of the historical context which produced the works studied above. The portrayal of the bawd in literature crystallizes into a series of static assumptions which, in fact, punish her for her old age, infertility, and lack of sexual impact. The classification of women in genres which favor sexual desirability causes the absence of the useful qualities of womanhood in the old woman. Every genre studied here points out the extent to which she exists only as a surrogate figure, be it as a mother or a sexual being. In sexual matters, she claims expertise, yet her own body has long since had to accept the absence of erotic fulfillment. She appears to have access to verbal skill, a tool necessary for seduction, though her words soon prove futile in light of the more dynamic eloquence of the lovers around her. Still, the character of the bawd persistently and relentlessly conjures up associations of evil, wrongdoing, and misdemeanor.

Why are the activities of a go-between so threatening? Legal and religious authority address the problem of proxenetism in brief terms, condemning it unanimously and moving on to the next topic. Whereas they show a willingness to debate the topic of prostitution, they adhere rigidly to the overwhelmingly negative view of the panderer and procuress and do not even encourage debate on the topic. Literature presupposes the essential evil inherent in the old woman and proceeds to paint her according to a set of supposedly universal attitudes. Contrary to the texts' willing problematization of principal characters such as young lovers or figures of authority, few of the works studied above show any consciousness of the contradictions created by their portrayal of the go-between.

The main contradiction, as we have seen time and again in our analysis, has to do with the bawd's essential weakness and lack of impact, which stand in such strong contrast to the image of power and evil projected when she enters the scene. This fact *per se* need not preoccupy us so much as its blatant denial. In other words, the works studied so far appear adamant in not acknowledging this contradiction: they allow little room for the construction of interpretive areas where this paradox might be addressed, and yet they insist on repeating her portrayal in these contradictory terms.

The indifference of the works to the go-between's problematic representation has to do with preconceived notions about the status of old women in all the literary genres discussed above. As texts concerned with love, sexuality, and erotic interaction, these works of literature define womanhood in terms of its relationship to masculinity and sex. Whether they like it or not, the old women in these works exist independently of men as far as those terms are concerned. Ruth Mazo Karras observes that prostitutes in the Middle Ages sexualized financial gain and therefore doubly threatened male control by giving an impression of independence (which may not even be necessarily true).[197] For their part, old women lack sexual appeal, do not promise fertility, and therefore cannot fit into an acceptable and unthreatening definition of womanhood. Ironically, this exclusion endows them with a curiously liberating independence because it severs their connections to the dynamics of love and places them in a realm where the poetics of seduction have no applicability, since men no longer identify them as potential erotic partners. Old women have no choice but to accept this paradoxical independence from men, since the central discourse of each text lacks the interest and the tools to find a place for them within the language of sexuality and seduction.

Independence, though, always carries a connotation of danger, for it indicates the ability to operate outside the control of a presumed authority. In the works we have studied, a male aesthetic defines womanhood according to her erotic potential: male poets, dramatists, and prose-writers set the boundaries of seductive appeal. If the objects of desire show initiative and independence, they do so to fuel the sexual imagination of the male poet/protagonist and to create an erotic game which engages the man as the central player. The often-mentioned independence of the courtesan or the courtly mistress, be it destructive or productive, exists within the boundaries of man's erotic wishes. The independence of the old woman, though, could potentially exist outside his boundaries.

For the male poet or writer, therefore, this independence connotes a threat. He faces a woman whom he cannot include in the realm of erotic interplay, and he is aware of her potential ability to draw attention to the territory uncharted by his sexual interests. As a result, he inscribes her within the poetics of love in the safest possible way so that she, too, can receive his magisterial gaze. Reduced to a series of landmarks raised by the poet or author, an area as potentially threatening and uncharted as that of mediation becomes a seemingly safe location well under the jurisdiction of the lover.

Be that as it may, a third party complicates and enriches the world of two lovers in diverse ways. The texts studied in this chapter display a subtle awareness of this potential, and each demonstrates to some extent the directions toward which intermediary activity might

[197] Karras, "Sex, Money, and Prostitution," 211.

pull the lovers' trajectory. The literature of the Islamic Empire offers an entirely different interpretation of the procuress, the go-between, and intermediary activity in general. The wealth of material available in two of the classical languages of Islam, Arabic and Persian, on the topic of carnal love allows for a needed and extended analysis of the phenomenon.[198]

[198] For the definition of the term "medieval" as used in conjunction with the history of Near-Eastern cultures, see David Morgan, *Medieval Persia: 1040-1797* (London: Longman, 1988)1.

CHAPTER THREE

THE MEDIEVAL NEAR-EASTERN GO-BETWEEN

I. Intermediary Activity and Society

We have seen in the previous chapter that medieval European society viewed the procuress as a figure beyond forgiveness because of the conviction that she associates with prostitution and illicit sexual behavior. The literary manifestations of the character took this particular connotation as the underlying idea upon which they constructed images of intermediaries and third-party activity. In contrast, the imaginative literature of medieval Islam depicts go-betweens based on an essentially distinct interpretation of the ethical implications of intermediary activity. These differences are by no means immediately apparent and require close study before they appear in the full view of the reader: similar to their counterparts from Romance texts (and Chaucer), Near-Eastern literary texts infuse their depictions of the go-between with strong doses of disapproval and, at best, amused reproach, in light of the character's dangerous affinity with unethical and adulterous activity.[1] Yet underneath the reproachful tone and the condemning epithets, Near-Eastern imaginative literature opens certain interpretative paths for the analysis of third-party activity for which Romance and Classical texts seem more reluctant to make room.

The first point a study of go-betweens must take into account is that for medieval Islamic society, intermediary activity enjoys a privileged position in political usage, reflected in thought-provoking ways in literary representation. The historian Bernard Lewis notes that the integration of a third party into the basic structures of political interaction constitutes a standard feature of medieval Islamic society. Islamic usage describes power relationships in terms of "near," "far," "center," and "periphery," the concept of "center" denoting a privi-

[1] Most of the literary texts considered here date from what is referred to as the Middle Period of Islam, from the tenth to the fifteenth centuries. For the socio-religious context, however, the periods preceding that era – that is, the Islamic conquest and the Umayyad and ʿAbbasid dynasties – have also been taken into account.

leged position with respect to God or a representative political power on earth. Lewis explains:

> Between the near and the far, there is the middle. And the Arabic term *wasat*, "middle," has given rise to a wide range of terms connoting mediation, intermediaries, intercessors, and interventions of various kinds. At the court of the Fatimid caliphs of Egypt, the *Wasit*, or "middleman," was a high court official, corresponding more or less to the wazir of the ʿAbbasid caliphate in Baghdad. Supreme sovereign power is at the center. The nearer to the center, the greater the power; the further from the center, the less the power. In the Ottoman Imperial Palace, the entire complex of buildings was divided into three zones known as the Inside, the Inbetween, and the Outside. The officers of the Inbetween, in Turkish *mabeynci*, in large measure controlled access to the seats of power and thereby themselves wielded great power and influence.[2]

Such a configuration allocates a privileged seat to the intermediary who, rather than represent a simple bearer of the terms of others, becomes a figure of authority in his own right. The power and influence exerted by those positioned in the "Inbetween" need not take on the guise of subservience: instead, they translate into the intermediary's full knowledge of legitimate and peculiar benefits inherent to the space of "Inbetween."

The act of mediation thus serves a powerful political purpose. Its potency becomes all the more apparent when it is shown, time and again in Islamic law and literature, to be a metaphor for the ideal type of communication between man and woman. The Prophet, whose declarations are collected in the vast and diverse body of *hadīth* – written reports of deeds and words which perform the function of legal codes – himself specifies this.[3] The scholar Fatima Mernissi quotes the *hadīth* reproted by the *Imam* Ghazzālī (1050-1111 A.D.), a significant authority on Islam in the Middle Ages, which stresses the importance of mediation between man and woman in carnal rela-

---

[2] Bernard Lewis, *The Political Language of Islam* (Chicago: University of Chicago Press, 1988) 13.

[3] For the full meaning of *hadīth*, see the entry in *E. J. Brill's First Encyclopedia of Islam* (New York, Leiden: E. J. Brill, 1987); also, Marshall G. S. Hodgson, *The Venture of Islam, Volume II: The Expansion of Islam in the Middle Periods* (Chicago: The University of Chicago Press, 1974) 63-66. Briefly, a *hadīth* is a relation of deeds and sayings of the Prophet as told by his companions. Collections of *hadīth* abound, and examples are often used by authorities to settle legal opinion on specific matters.

tions; here Ghazzālī reports that the Prophet advocated the following procedure prior to sexual contact between man and wife:

> "No-one among you should throw himself on his wife like beasts do. There should be, prior to coitus, a messenger between you and her." People asked him, "What sort of messenger?" The Prophet answered, "Kisses and words."[4]

Mediated intimacy, then, transforms the barbaric into the refined. This *hadīth* has not prescribed a human go-between, yet the personification of messengership has metaphorically placed a third person between the two, assigning the tasks of refinement and facilitation to this third element.

The metaphor serves to remind the reader of the segregation of man and woman that naturally calls for a mediator in order for any communication to occur. Both the political order and the metaphor employed in the *hadīth* must take into account the strength with which segregation commands the space between different spheres such as male and female, subject and ruler, in Islamic society. For the purposes of the study of the go-between, it is imperative that the notion of segregation be incorporated fully into the frame of reference, for it is primarily due to this phenomenon that intermediary activity assumes its particular energy. Segregation between males and females, in urban areas especially, is a visible and strong feature of life from the beginning of the Islamic conquest through to the end of the ʿAbbasid era, deriving much strength from the solid foundation it had enjoyed from pre-Islamic times. In fact, Islam inherited certain preexisting social structures in which "the mechanisms of control, seclusion, and exclusion of women from community affairs [were] already elaborately developed."[5] These mechanisms applied not only to community affairs, but also to married and sexual life.

The layout of the harem best exemplifies the hierarchization of women in terms of their sexual function and the segregation which determines the nature of their contact with the same and the oppo-

---

[2] Bernard Lewis, *The Political Language of Islam* (Chicago: University of Chicago Press, 1988) 13.

[4] Cited in Fatima Mernissi, *Beyond the Veil: Male-Female Dynamics in Modern Muslim Society* (Indiana: Indiana University Press, 1987) 40. This utterance of the Prophet can be found in many sources, especially didactic treatises of the medieval period.

[5] Leila Ahmed, *Women and Gender in Islam* (New Haven: Yale University Press, 1992) 45.

site sexes. The harem, an institution with clear roots in pre-Islamic civilization,[6] houses the female members of the wealthy ruling classes, and in its very layout points to the importance attached to mediation. It advances the pattern of sexual segregation to its fullest form and demonstrates the dynamics which result from the separation of the sexes.[7]

For the ruling classes of the Islamic empire, the indomitable boundary between inside and outside governed all interaction in the harem. As a result of this type of segregation the dependent females of a wealthy man

> had a world of their own in which women ruled over women, with the lone adult male as an often rather remote arbiter; or, often enough, willing tool of that woman who most charmed him at the moment. (...) Though visiting males could not be admitted, visiting females could be admitted all the more freely, whatever their social station; so each man's harem-home was linked closely to a wide network of feminine life from most of which he was rigidly excluded and even his own portion of which he was necessarily aloof from.
>
> The women's apartments, in these circumstances, tended to be the center of intrigues: intrigues for the master's love – which often went to young slave concubines by preference – or for his respect (and monetary favors).[8]

It was not always the desire for an illicit affair that moved women to find means of communication with the outside world; contact with a more powerful woman or with an offspring of the husband required access to a third party able to surmount the obstacles faced by those on the inside. The very architectural organization of the place

---

[6] "During the first Christian centuries the notion of women's seclusion – architecturally realized as a building or area for women in the residence, guarded by eunuchs – together with veiling and attitudes about the proper conduct of women, became features of upper-class life in the Mediterranean Middle East, Iraq, and Persia" (Ahmed, *Women and Gender*, 18). Many such practices were adopted by Islam due to the cultural exchanges which occurred between the Arab conquerors and their new subjects. The harem was therefore by no means an Islamic invention, for its existence is clearly documented as of the Achaemenid period (starting 550 B.C.). See Ilse Seibert, *Woman in Ancient Near East*, translated by Marianne Herzfeld (London: George Prior Publishers, 1975) 51-52; see also J. M. Cook, "The Rise of the Achaemenids and Establishment of their Empire," in *Cambridge History of Iran*, vol. 2 (Cambridge: Cambridge University Press, 1985) 226-227.

[7] Marshall G. S. Hodgson, "Sex, slavery and the harem system: the cult of masculine honor" in *The Venture of Islam*, 141 (henceforth "Hodgson").

[8] Hodgson, 142.

responded to the dynamics of a multi-leveled separation. A study of the architecture of the Topkapi Palace in Istanbul provides ample proof of this. As the layout of this structure shows, proximity to the center of power (that is, the Sultan) was coveted by all, with multiple intermediaries in between to represent special interests:

> Although the eunuchs oversaw the general administration, promotions and punishments in the Harem and the Sultan held the ultimate power of life and death over the inmates, it was the hierarchy of women that regulated the daily life, influenced the Sultan and the affairs of the palace and sometimes governed the rest of the Empire. Consequently, the hierarchy of women influenced and determined the spatial order and architecture of the Harem.[9]

This hierarchy of women shows the enormous significance attached to the position of intermediary, either between the Sultan and the numerous inmates of the Harem, or within the community of women. The Sultan's mother occupied the most powerful position and even entered the realm of politics by giving counsel on affairs of State. At lower levels where political decisions remained out of reach, women acting in the capacity of inbetween officials played an essential role in the Sultan's private life.[10] Even the protocol required for sexual intimacy was engineered by those acting between the husband and his wife or concubine, creating a hierarchy which stressed the crucial nature of any figure positioned between the spheres separating man and woman: "[for] the highest ranked woman [the Sultan's mother], her authority and power was justified by the central location of her apartments with the quarters of the women on one side and the Sultan on the other side."[11]

The importance of intermediary activity extended beyond the

---

[9] Cigdem T. Akkurt, "Social and Spatial Hierarchy of Women in the Architecture of the Topkapi Harem," *Traditional Dwellings and Settlements: Working Paper Series*, vol. XLV (Berkeley: Center for Environmental Design Research, 1992) 33-67 (34).

[10] As Akkurt explains, any particularly attractive young girl in the harem was brought to the attention of the Sultan's mother whereupon she and a number of harem inmates examined the potential concubine in the imperial *hammam* (bath). Consequently, after the Sultan's decision to summon the new young girl to his bed for the first time, she would undergo an elaborate ritual of socio-sexual instruction, bathing, and shaving carried out by women in the key position of liaison between her, the Sultan's mother, and ultimately the Sultan himself (Akkurt, "Social and Spatial Hierarchy," 50-52).

[11] Akkurt, "Social and Spatial Hierarchy," 50.

harem. Urban society depended on the figure for many types of interaction between the sexes, ranging from gaining information on a potential bride to matchmaking to facilitating an illicit relationship. With the passage of time, after the first centuries of the advent of Islam, the restrictions governing contact between the sexes became more firmly established in Islamic society, and the intermediary engaged in a variety of activities, some of which consisted of nothing other than simply exposing the house-bound urban women to the outside world. Sociological studies attest that the phenomenon occurred even in the modern period, showing the extent to which a go-between, called the *dallāleh* (literally, middle-woman) in Persian, helped maintain contact with people and events outside the home, as seen for example in this recollection from the turn of the century:

> Women, who lived in a state of semi-captivity indoors from morning to night, stepped out very rarely from the house. Inevitably they had needs which were partially fulfilled by *dallālehs* who moved from house to house every day. These *dallālehs* were often Jewish since even though they wore the *chador* (overall body cover) they were not veiled and could walk into homes and speak freely to the men in the family. They brought in accessories, toiletries, material, sewing equipment, jewelry and gold and silver to the women. They found husbands for the daughters, and sons sought their advice to ask for the hand of someone's daughter. Naturally the *dallālehs* received money from both sides for these transactions. Some of them set up secret love affairs between men and women and made very good money through this. (...) Women in harems and inside houses welcomed them with open arms. In these women's dull and monotonous lives, hearing about the outside world from the go-between was a pleasure. Sometimes these *dallālehs* became listeners to the problems and private sufferings of the women. They made up spells and prescribed potions to eliminate the women's difficulties, and in this way consoled the wretched ones. Finally, it was through the *dallālehs* that women found what was going on in town and among other families.
>
> These talking newspapers were a source of happiness for the prisoners of the house.[12]

[12] Badrolmuluk Bāmdād, *Zān-e Irānī* (*The Iranian Woman,*) (Teheran: Amīr Kabīr, 1966) 58-59. Also Jafar Shahrī, *Tārikh-e Ejtemā'iye Teherān-e Qadīm* (*the Social History of Old Teheran*), vol. I (Teheran: Ismailian Publishers, 1990) mentions old women indulging in both licit and illicit matchmaking.

Any woman engaged in a profession that allowed mobility was naturally welcome as a contact with the outside world. These women, though, also inspired the type of mistrust and disdain encountered in medieval European society. They inspired suspicion of corrupting elements in light of the ever-present conviction that they used their profession of seamstress, saleswoman, or beautician as a facade for the promotion of sexual intrigue. The Egyptian feminist Huda Shaarawi recalls female peddlers who visited upper-class Egyptian households:

> These women, Coptic, Jewish and Armenian, were assisted by young girls carrying wares (...) Displaying their goods to the members of the household, they urged them to buy various items, claiming that the wife of a certain *pasha* or *bey* had purchased a particular article. (...) the peddlers disclosed bits of gossip and were quick to elaborate if their listener appeared eager for more. I didn't like most of these peddlers – although some were quite witty – because they often damaged prominent families through their indiscretions and lies. They also charged exorbitant prices. As a young girl I was cautioned about the peddlers and told of the trouble they could cause. With the unfolding of the years I saw this borne out.[13]

Shaarawi does not specify the kind of "trouble" yet indicates that the peddlers exposed women to the danger of dishonor. A further strain of suspicion is evident in both memoirs as they identify the go-betweens in terms of their religious or racial difference, placing them implicitly on the margins of a supposedly unified and mainstream society. At the same time, one detects easily an acknowledgment of useful elements in both accounts: Shaarawi concedes that these women possessed wit and therefore entertained the household, and Bāmdād regards them as a consolation for women trapped night and day in the home. The sense of condemnation does not emerge in the overwhelming ways seen in European accounts of procuresses, nor is there an awareness or indication of any legal reproach applicable to these women. Rather, the memoirs chose to observe the go-betweens from a more ambiguous standpoint, one which at once sees the benefits but worries about honor. The liberating quality of encounters with go-betweens is articulated fully, revealing the powerful ambiva-

[13] Huda Shaarawi, *Harem Years: Memoirs of an Egyptian Feminist (1879-1924)* translated by Margot Badran (New York: The Feminist Press at the City University of New York, 1986) 48.

lence that guides her perception on the part of feminist sociologists in particular. Literature maintains this ambivalent attitude, thematizing it to a considerable degree with fictional texts that often assume a seemingly reproachful posture as the most visible point of departure for the intermediary's portrayal. The character is frequently represented as an old woman.

It is fitting here to return to a point brought up earlier in this study regarding the selection of texts. As has been mentioned, the purpose of this study is not to offer a comprehensive catalogue of go-betweens in the Classical languages of Islam. Rather, with the full acknowledgment that no text selection is ever complete, nor can one pretend in literary studies to master a full set of data, the aim here has been to pick out those literary manifestations of intemediary activity that allow for a particularly fruitful analysis of the figure. The choices have been made based upon the extent to which third-party involvement appears to guide the text's conception of seduction and insofar as it engages the questions of genre and tradition sufficiently enough to show the workings of intertextual development. The texts studied below are in Arabic and Persian only and by no means claim a quantitatively exhaustive tackling of the subject. The literature of medieval Islam is unusually rich in genres and texts which take carnal love as their subject-matter, and an attempt at exhaustive study would, undoubtedly, confront the scholar with the problem of diminishing returns at some point, not to mention the overwhelming task of categorizing the vast number of fictional and non-fictional texts that deal with sexual and amorous relationships. In this study the texts chosen represent significant and thought-provoking contributions to the topic of mediation, and its agents, in the Near-Eastern literature of the medieval period, with enough of a meaningful connection to literary tradition and the collective idea of a *topos* to allow for the creation of a rigorous frame of reference for study.[14]

On the most visible level, it was said, the portrayal of the old woman underscores her marginal position in society as well as the common attitudes towards old women seen in folkloric and learned sources. The ambiguities articulated by the two feminists cited above

[14] For the question of research methods in medieval Islamic history and law in particular, and for the problems presented by the vast scope of materials and methods available in these areas, see R. Stephen Humphreys, *Islamic History: A Framework for Inquiry* (London: I. B. Taurus, 1991).

emerge in literary texts in a multitude of uncertain though significant ways, almost always launched from the platform of amused mistrust or even contempt. The presuppositions attached to the figure of the old woman abound in popular wisdom, and their comprehension facilitates our understanding of one of the basic tenets in the conception of the *ʿajūz*, that is, the old woman acting as intermediary.

II. The Perception of the Old Woman in Popular Literature and Society

Both pre-Islamic Mesopotamia as well as early and medieval Islamic society viewed women primarily in terms of their relationship to sexual activity and fertility.[15] Old women, no longer able to fulfill requirements in either category, found themselves in an altogether undesirable position. Within clear limits, they undertook employment such as midwifery, home medicine, peddling, or informal teaching; they helped out in general within the walls of the harem, always carrying a connotation of intrigue: "[the Caliph] Al-Ma'mūn (813-833) reportedly employed several hundred old women to infiltrate and report on his harem."[16]

An old woman could, therefore, partially overcome her lack of productivity by somehow making herself useful in the harem or the household. Her often crafty skill with manipulative speech comes in medieval literature and other sources to replace every other facet known as feminine and occupies an ambivalent space, depending on the agenda of the author who presents her. The medical literature of the Islamic Middle Ages, for example, assigns a productive task to her, based on a conviction that she can perform many tasks using speech and on her general knowledge of the community in which she lives. The tenth- and eleventh-century physician Avicenna, in his influential compendium *Canon on Medicine* – which contains an exten-

[15] Ahmed, *Women and Gender*, 15-16; the Mesopotamian laws that confirm the view are found in "The Code of Hammurabi" and "The Middle Assyrian Laws," translated by Theophile J. Meek, *Ancient Near-Eastern Texts Relating to the Old Testament*, edited by James B. Pritchard (Princeton: Princeton University Press, 1955). Many laws concern the restrictions placed upon women in matters of marriage and involvement in the community. See also S. N. Kramer, *The Sumerians: Their History, Culture and Character* (Chicago: The University of Chicago Press, 1963).

[16] Ahmed, *Women and Gender*, 84.

sive section on lovesickness as a mental disorder – acknowledges the therapeutic influence of the *ʿajūz* (the old woman) in cases where the malady calls for the patient to "fall out of love." In the chapter entitled "Illnesses of the Mind and their Harmful Effect Upon the Senses," Avicenna describes the symptoms of love in the patient and first lists the cures that directly affect physical well-being: the patient must eat well, avoid irritating situations, and sleep. If possible, he must fall in love with another, obtain her consent in a licit fashion, and forget the first love. Among the many solutions offered, Avicenna suggests a certain type of therapeutic dialogue which will bring about a change of heart in the patient:

> If the one in love is a wise human being, the following might be useful: he should be exposed to advice on the one hand, mockery and reproach on the other, and be told that his object of desire is only temptation and a cause of insanity. Dialogue can be effective in this case.[17]

Avicenna next selects the figure who would best engage the patient in dialogue:

> Bring old women to surround the patient. They will talk behind the beloved's back, and attribute things to the beloved so as to inspire the disgust of the patient, with mentions of the cruelty and the tyranny of the beloved. They will soothe the fever of love with these words. But, some lovers fall even more in love upon hearing such descriptions.
>
> The old women could impersonate the beloved and show things which would diminish the beloved's beauty in the eyes of the lover. They could continually repeat that the object of desire is ugly. Old women are more adept than men at such tasks. Also, there are people who are neither man nor woman and they are referred to as neuters, who are not unskilled at such false propaganda either.[18]

His choice reveals an intrinsic belief in the old woman as the perfect manipulator;[19] in this case, he prescribes an activity contrary to that of the go-between, yet the techniques that he singles out call for the type of skill useful in mediation. In fact, he acknowledges that verbal manipulation can have the reverse effect and cause the intensifica-

---

[17] Abū-Alī Sīnā, *Qānūn dar Tibb*, Book III, part 1 (Teheran: Soroush Editions, 1987) 136 (henceforth *Qānūn*).

[18] *Qānūn*, 137.

[19] Note that he even acknowledges the danger that the patient may fall deeper in love upon hearing her words.

tion of passion: the old woman's capacity to divert the purpose does not escape unnoticed. Impersonation, insistence, and continuous talking indicate a talent with words which Avicenna attributes naturally to the old woman, and for this reason he chooses her above everyone else, knowing full well that risks do exist in such a choice. The old woman's marginal status is emphasized in the parallel drawn between her and the "neuters," serving as a reminder that she and her counterparts occupy essentially sexless worlds in which any form of amorous or carnal power can occur only through speech. This power does not lead to consummation and immediate physical gratification for those sexless beings; nonetheless, Avicenna appears to be aware of its potential breadth of reach in the area of mediation.

Whereas Avicenna invests in the old woman's skill and supposedly nonexistent sexuality toward the progress of a medical cure, common folkloric attitudes often mingle her lack of visible sexuality and her manipulation of words with the penchant for intrigue. This produces an altogether negative image of the old woman, even in cases where the portrayal seeks to amuse the reader. In her study of folkloric ideas about the place of women in North Africa, Fatima Mernissi notes that for folk wisdom, age has "entirely opposite effects on men and women."[20] She quotes from Medjoub, the sixteenth-century Maghrebine poet whose words have entered the body of popular wisdom: "A man who reaches eighty becomes a saint/A woman who reaches sixty is on the threshold of hell."[21] Elsewhere the poet states: "What takes Satan a year to do/ Is done by the old hag within the hour."[22] The other view of advanced age in women takes into account the predilection for scandal and intrigue: "When the woman grows old/ She becomes obsessed with intrigues;/ Whatever she sees, she wants to get involved in./ May God curse her, alive or dead." [23]

In such written and oral sources the inclination for intrigue suggests a strong sense of frustrated sexual desire. This trait renders the old woman all the more vulnerable to the mockery of the text. For exam-

[20] Mernissi, *Beyond the Veil*, 124.

[21] Cited in Mernissi, *Beyond the Veil*, 124.

[22] Mernissi, *Beyond the Veil*, 124.

[23] Mernissi, *beyond the Veil*, 124. Note, though, that a mocking attitude towards old age in men also emerges at times in Arabic literature. In the treatise-writer al-Wassa's work, there are several disparaging remarks about old men, for example. See Al-Wassa', *El libro del brocado*, traducción, estudio e índices de Teresa Garulo (Clásicos Alfaguara, Madrid: 1990) 162.

ple, in his collection of moral tales in verse, the thirteenth-century poet Jalāl al-Dīn Rūmī paints a grotesque portrait of the old woman consumed by carnal desire, "her face full of trembling wrinkles, her color the same as saffron."[24] The poet describes her absurd predicament as that of "an empty cauldron with a full fire beneath."[25] In vain, the crone makes every effort to change her appearance with makeup so that the male sex will notice her. Deeply frustrated with her failure, she curses the Devil, who immediately appears unto her and advises her to abandon her efforts and to stop blaming him for her ugliness. The very denomination of *ʿajūz*, used often to designate the old woman, carries connotations of wrongdoing and misguided desire. In one of the notes to his translation of the *Thousand and One Nights* Sir Richard Burton writes: "Ya 'l-ʿAjūz: (...) the address is now insulting and would elicit 'the old woman in thine eye' (with fingers extended). In Egypt the polite address is 'O lady (Sitt), O pilgrimess, O bride, and O daughter' (although she be the wrong side of fifty)."[26]

In their treatment of the topic of carnal love, a variety of genres in Near-Eastern literature showcase the old woman's interest in erotic love and intrigue, drawing on the traits reflected in medical and anthropological sources; at the same time they problematize the portrayal of the old woman due to the special place devoted to third-party activity in the poetics of love and seduction. The broad context for the elaboration of this poetics is the Islamic conception of seduction, sexuality, and carnal love, which, while obviously impossible to reduce to a single ideological framework, presents many important distinctions from the medieval European perspective.

III. (i) *The Topic of Earthly Love in Medieval Islamic Texts*

Physical love and sensuality have received considerable treatment in Persian and Arabic literature from standpoints that would strike the

[24] Jalāl al-Dīn Rūmī, *Masnavī-ye Ma'navī*, edited by R. A. Nicholson (Teheran: Amīr Kabīr, 1984) vol. III, 344.

[25] Rūmī, *Masnavī*, 344.

[26] Sir Richard Burton, *A Plain and Literal Translation of the Arabian Nights' Entertainments, now Entitled the Book of the Thousand Nights and a Night*, (Printed by the Burton Club for Private Subscribers: 1885) vol. V, 163. In volume VIII of the collection, Burton writes a footnote to the description of an old woman: "among Eastern women age and ugliness are synonymous. It is only in the highest civilisation that we find the handsome old woman" (Burton, volume VIII, 86).

Western-centered reader as altogether more permissive, especially as regards detailed discussion of the topic, than medieval Christian standpoints on the issue. Franz Rosenthal articulates this difference succinctly in the following terms:

> Islam always took care to admit that sexuality existed as a problematic element in the relationship of individuals and society and never hesitated to leave room for the discussion of approval or disapproval. Traditional Christianity was inclined to pretend that sexuality's legitimate right of existence was limited, and further discussion was to be avoided as much as possible. [27]

Throughout the history of medieval Islam, the discussion of physical intimacy takes place time and again in religious, scientific, and literary sources. Authoritative, prescriptive, polemic, scientific, humorous, and literary treatments of seduction and sexuality abound in the body of the *hadīth* as well as in other religious writing, in addition to medical, legal, and imaginative literature. A wealth of information on prevalent themes and attitudes comes to us, for example, in erotological treatises dating from the eleventh century onwards. These collections anthologize a large body of anecdotes and observations on the topic of sexual (mis)behavior. The treatises consist of compilations of stories, reflections, and ideas brought together in one place:

> It is well known that this branch of literature is hard to define. It consists of topically arranged accumulations of aphorisms, prose mini-essays, and snatches of verse. It deals with a large variety of problems of language and literature (...). A distinguished scientist and physician of the twelfth century indicates the purpose of his erotic work in these words: "I have decided to write a book serious as well as humorous, literary and entertaining as well as practical, conversational as well as philosophical."[28]

The anecdotes encountered in erotological treatises range in inspiration from popular to courtly material and sometimes date back to tales or motifs from the pre-Islamic period. Such treatises on love

---

[27] Franz Rosenthal, "Sources for the Role of Sex in Medieval Muslim Society," in *Society and the Sexes in Medieval Islam*, edited by Afaf Lutfi al-Sayyid-Marsot (Los Angeles: Gustave E. von Grunebaum Center for Near Eastern Studies, UCLA, 1977) 3-22 (4).

[28] Franz Rosenthal, "Sources for the Role of Sex," 16. The author quotes from an unpublished manuscript of the work of Yahyā al-Maghrībī.

constitute an established literary genre which draws on a variety of frameworks; their range includes "theological works, belle-lettristic compositions with an ethical and sociological bent (...); early ascetic and mystical texts (...); and an assortment of literary anthologies."[29] Specifically erotological treatises form part of the literature of *adab*[30] which in the case of amorous topics assumes a refined posture for the expression of ideas on love and harks back to the Indian erotological traditions such as the *Kāma Sūtra* of Vatsyayana.[31]

The Sanskrit manual pays close attention to many aspects of sexual interaction stressing that the go-between plays a significant role in the careful approach to relations with the opposite sex. Persian and Arab writers also worked to elaborate a framework for the discussion of carnal love, using graphic detail, much linguistic wit, and the technique of cataloguing in an organized fashion to discuss various aspects of physical intimacy: positions, methods, tricks, choice of partners, and third parties. Among the architects of this amorous system are Ibn Hazm of Córdoba, Sheikh Nafzāwī, Alī al-Baghdādi, and Ahmad al-Tifāchī, each of whom contributed to the genre of the erotic treatise by providing selections of anecdotes and reflections on the matter of sexual relations.[32] In this detailed treatment of carnal love, the treatises reveal that which Luce López-Baralt refers to as a hybrid quality, mingling a scientific stance with a literary one or bringing a religious perspective into the scientific treatment of

---

[29] Joseph Norment Bell, *Love Theory in Later Hanbalite Islam* (Albany: State University of New York Press, 1979) 8.

[30] Definitions of *adab* are found in several works, among the more important of which are Gustave E. von Grunebaum's *Medieval Islam: A Study in Cultural Orientation* (Chicago: the University of Chicago Press, 1953) and Jean-Claude Vadet's *L'esprit courtois en Orient: les cinq premiers siècles de l'Hégire* (Paris: Maisonneuve et Larousse, 1968). A concise and useful definition in Spanish appears in Al-Wassa', *El libro del brocado*, xxxi-xxxii, cited earlier. As the editor explains, *adab* comprises the refined attitude and etiquette as well as the use of eloquent language in a topic of interest such as love, clothes, food, hunting, to name a few.

[31] Luce López-Baralt, *Un Kāma Sūtra español* (Madrid: Ediciones Siruela, 1992) 235.

[32] Because well-translated and annotated versions of some of these treatises are now available in French and Spanish, I have drawn on those versions for this study. Alī Ibn Ahmad Ibn Hazm, *El collar de la paloma: tratado sobre el amor y los amantes*, translated by Emilio García Gómez (Madrid: Alianza, 1985); Ahmad al-Tifāchī, *Les Délices des coeurs*, translated by René R. Khawam (Paris: Phébus, 1981); Umar ibn Muhammad al-Nafzāwī, *The Glory of the Perfumed Garden: The Missing Flowers* (London: Neville Spearman, 1986); Alī al-Baghdādi, *Les fleurs éclatantes dans les baisers d'accolement*, translated by René R. Khawam (Paris: Éditions Phébus, 1989). Henceforth, the texts will be referred to using the last name of the author.

[33] López-Baralt, 230.

sexuality.[33] Stylistically, they are marked by a predilection for wit and a willingness to infuse the anecdotes with humor where appropriate.

Islamic literature thus covers a vast territory in dealing with sexuality with many texts as yet unexhausted by modern criticism. These texts confirm that medieval Islamic culture does not share Christianity's preoccupation with abstinence and chastity. As López-Baralt and other scholars have observed, medieval Islam's notion of sexuality differs greatly from Patristic teaching which proposes resistance to pleasure for the sake of pleasure.[34] For the scientific and religious authorities of the early and middle periods of Islam, sexual relations meant a natural and necessary aspect of life, within certain limits which shifted continually according to the perspective of the writer.[35] Several *hadīth* and examples confirm this view, and construct a fundamental frame of reference for a more open discussion of sexuality.[36]

In some examples and *hadīth*, it is shown that the spirit need not be overwhelmed by preoccupation with chastity. The evil inherent in desire is acknowledged, but satisfactory compromises for the believer are offered at many junctures, providing a marked contrast with the restrictions imposed upon carnality in Christian writings. A fundamental frame of reference is constructed in which the use of legitimate authorities, known examples of sensual but acceptable behavior, and the legitimate place of sexuality in life are foregrounded as significant tenets. In many *hadīth* and writings, it is amply clear that the spirit need not be overwhelmed with the preoccupation for chastity, and that while evil can be present in desire, there are satisfactory compromises available that do not involve abstinence. As Fatima Mernissi notes, Muslim religious authorities of the Middle Ages expressed no hesitation in recognizing the pleasure brought by sexual contact.[37]

The most open and frank discussion of sexuality in Islam occurs in medical literature, which enjoys even more freedom from ethical

---

[34] López-Baralt, 214.

[35] See for instance the declaration in Ibn ʿArabī's *Fusūs al-hikām* (Cairo: Isa al-Bābī, 1946) 214.

[36] See, for example, the *hadīth* cited by James A. Bellamy, "Sex and Society in Islamic Popular Literature," in *Society and the Sexes*, 30.

[37] Fatima Mernissi, *Sexe-Idéologie-Islam* (Rabat: Les Éditions maghrebines, 1985); this matter is discussed in the first two chapters of volume 1.

constraints. Physicians such as al-Jazzārī, al-Rhāzī (Rhazes), and Avicenna – all of whom wrote between the ninth and the eleventh centuries – develop this scientific perspective and provide detailed insight into views on sexual activity from a non-religious standpoint. Significantly, in the *Canon on Medicine* where love comes under the heading of an illness, Avicenna recommends consummation as the best possible cure for the malady before the resort to old women as detractors.[38] Scholars have observed that as an heir to Aristotle, Galen, and Hippocrates, Avicenna stands firmly within the tradition of physicians who lent attention not only to the physiological but also the emotional components of sexual activity.[39] Again, this indicates a probing vision of sex in comparison to mainstream Christian attitudes.

In the chapter of the *Canon on Medicine* entitled "Reproductive Organs and the Sexual Instinct in Men," Avicenna lists the advantages of sexual activity without even considering the question of love. Here, under the subheading "The Benefits of Intercourse," he regards physical intimacy as a preventive measure against poor physical and mental health.[40] He follows this with a section entitled "Damages caused by Intercourse" that, far from condemning physical intimacy, concerns excess in such matters, stressing that men ought to refrain from immoderate indulgence. Avicenna gives no

[38] "Once you have found out the identity of the beloved, help the patient and the beloved to be reunited in licit, religiously acceptable ways. I have seen men in love who have lost weight, suffered prolonged fever, and been ill, and this is all the result of weakness from love. But I have visited them soon after they have attained the beloved, and I have seen wonders: the man has gained weight, recuperated his strength, and I have understood once again that our physical well-being depends on our emotional state" (*Qānūn*, Book III, 136).

[39] For an overview of the Eastern tradition and its reception by the West, see Mary Frances Wack, *Lovesickness in the Middle Ages: the Viaticum and its commentaries* (Philadelphia: University of Pennsylvania Press, 1990); see also López-Baralt, the chapter entitled "La erotología como una rama de la medicina," *Un Kāma-Sūtra español*, 250-253. In this tradition we find Maimonedes, the twelfth-century Ibn Yahyā, and the fourteenth-century Andalucian Ibn al-Khātib. Avicenna's influence on Western medicine is chronicled in Danielle Jacquart and Claude Thomasset's *Sexuality and Medicine in the Middle Ages*, translated by Matthew Adamson (Princeton: Princeton University Press, 1988).

[40] *Qānūn*, Book III, 223-224. Having stated that intercourse purifies the body and ensures well-being and strength, Avicenna concentrates on useful psychological effects: "Intercourse rids the man of his dark thoughts, makes him courageous, dispels useless anger, and improves composure. It rids the brain of harmful vapors, and is therefore most useful for melancholic and depressive people." After this he goes on to list further benefits for the body.

ethical or religious reason for this, expanding his argument purely in terms of a medical rationale.[41]

He expresses these views in the chapter on male sexual behavior and bases them upon his study of male anatomy. In his treatment of gynecology and obstetrics, he does not emphasize the benefits of intercourse with the same vigor. On one occasion he even blends his medical arguments with a recognition of the ethical aspect involved in the discussion of female sexuality.[42] Yet he confirms the benefits of sexual activity, albeit in less direct terms. He attributes a number of physical disorders to the married woman's deprivation of intercourse and recommends lovemaking as one possible remedy against maladies of the uterus.[43] He quotes a "learned physician" on the unexplained nature of some illnesses of the uterus with the observation that such ills occur in "women who are greatly desirous of intercourse, and deprived of it; girls who have reached puberty but have not had their maidenhood taken; or, have been married but have not yet consummated the marriage."[44] Evidently, like his predecessors, he considers sexual activity a valid cure for certain female ailments. Avicenna also acknowledges the therapeutic impact of simply inspiring sexual pleasure in women without always prescribing actual intercourse.[45]

---

[41] "Those who have intercourse in excess and far more frequently than is usual, will become cold and dry in the body, experience fatigue and weakness (...) due to excess they are more vulnerable to pain, might suffer stomach aches, and have bad breathe(...)" (*Qānūn*, Book III, 324-325).

[42] For instance, Avicenna considers that menstruation has at least one good effect on female sexual desire: "When the woman menstruates on time, she is less inclined to desire intercourse and in this way preserves better her honor and sense of shame" (*Qānūn*, Book III, 351).

[43] The eleventh chapter of the section on the female reproductive system is entitled "The Interruption or Disappearance of the Monthly Cycle," an affliction for which Avicenna counts sixteen reasons. The last reason for this condition is that "the woman has been deprived of intercourse, because her husband might have gone away." *Qānūn*, Book III, 371. With regards to the uterus, Avicenna suggests that surgery followed by "ample lovemaking" will resolve any problems therein (*Qānūn*, Book III, 376).

[44] *Qānūn*, Book III, 386.

[45] His definition of pleasure is not related to intercourse only and encompasses a broader range in the case of the woman. He suggests alternate ways which do not involve a spouse by assigning a surrogate when necessary, in the shape of a midwife or a female nurse (*Qānūn*, Book III, 391). In the section on gynecology, Avicenna either specifies that a midwife or nurse apply the medicine, or uses the general second-person form ("You must do such a thing") when discussing procedure. But by no means does he recommend consistently that another woman conduct detailed examinations or administer the treatment.

In the chapter on gynecology, the comments on the utility of sexual activity and pleasure appear in less systematic fashion than the clear-cut section on the "Benefits of Intercourse." He couches them in purely medical terms and stays well away from psychological observation. But a thorough reading of both chapters shows that Avicenna regards sexuality as a basic curative element in both male and female physiology. In addition he points to the importance of accurate knowledge and its direct impact on marital happiness; one of his comments reveals his sense of social responsibility when dealing with sexual matters:

> Doctors are often ashamed to discuss [intimate details] or women's pleasure in intercourse and such matters, and they avoid explaining such things. They do not understand that this kind of withholding can only harm the people. They do not know that this is all directly related to procreation. Or maybe they know, but are ashamed; but these are important issues, and it is ridiculous to feel ashamed about them.[46]

Thus, while the bulk of Avicenna's discussion has to do with medical issues, he also pays attention to the social and emotional aspects of marital sexuality. He maintains an authoritative but concerned tone as a physician who wishes to offer an important community service as well as an open discussion of sexuality within a legalized framework. With the *Canon on Medicine* Avicenna confirms and perpetuates the visible status of sexuality as a subject of discourse and investigation, and his multifaceted approach to the subject-matter reveals the existence of elaborate structures for the sociological, scientific, and even partially anecdotal discussion of the topic.

Religious sources also express the theme of sexuality as an acceptable part of life. One of the most influential expositions of this view appears in Ghazzālī's influential treatise, *Revival of the Religious Sciences*. Here, he discusses questions of ethically acceptable behavior in relation to the issue of religious responsibility, yet continues to acknowledge the importance of sexuality. As J. C. Brügel has observed: "Ghazzālī clearly states that coition, though its primary sense is progeniture, has a value of its own, its unrivaled but always all too brief delight arousing man's longing for the lasting one in the world to

[46] *Qānūn*, Book III, 260.

come."[47] As a religious authority, he warns against the temptation towards adultery.[48] Only in this respect does al-Ghazzālī interpret desire as an evil sensation, emphasizing the importance of marriage. His view confirms the prescription by Avicenna that, only if the loved one cannot come to the lovesick patient in a "licit and religiously acceptable" fashion, must one do everything to dispel the feelings of love in the patient right away.[49]

Medical and religious literature do not fully develop any ideas on the role of a third party in sexual matters, for they deal for the most part with licit situations in which access to a sexual partner does not constitute a problem nor does it require the help of a third party. As we saw earlier, Avicenna engages the third party as an anti-intermediary, and his view indicates that social and scientific authority need to emphasize the importance of sexuality within a licit or marital framework, directing readers to slave girls and wives. The go-between cannot come to life in such a context, for legal and religious arrangements will obviously have preempted her input. Not all sources discussing carnal love reveal the same sense of ethical responsibility, however, for they do not share the prescriptive concerns of science and religion. Furthermore, the relatively open discussions of sexuality punctuated by brief moral caveats in medical and legal sources shape, by way of intertextual influence, the conception of the go-between in other genres.

(ii) *The Further Exploration of Carnal Love and the Go-Between: Treatises on Erotology*

Erotological treatises whose anecdotal accounts often reflect popular inspiration enjoy the advantage of a narrative stance that permits

[47] J. C. Brügel, "Love, Lust and Longing: Eroticism in Early Islam," in *Society and the Sexes in Medieval Islam*, 81-117 (87).

[48] "(...) sex, though being useful as an incentive for the two lives as was said before, is nevertheless the strongest instrument of the Devil against the sons of Adam" cited by Brügel, "Love, Lust and Longing," 87. See also López-Baralt, 211, where the similarities between al-Ghazzālī's views on abstinence and some currents of modern psychoanalytic thought are emphasized.

[49] It must be recalled that one of Avicenna's recommendations for dispelling the feeling is that the patient engage in lovemaking with several other girls; this proves once again that the physician does not have qualms about the positive effects of erotic activity.

some character development, and can therefore delve more deeply into the social and interpersonal dynamics of sexual activity. In terms of plotline, these collections of tales and observations on erotic love often revolve around the clever ruses employed by men and women who wish to engage in nonmarital affairs. Here the treatises lend attention to the social components that aid or impede the quest for intimacy and demonstrate that a third party helps lessen the burden of shame and honor for those who hesitate in embarking on the path of seduction by encouraging them in several ways to do so. The third party is an integral element of the amorous system constructed in the treatises, even if her assistance often facilitates an illicit encounter. The old women who assume the role of intermediary project several of the qualities assumed in social and anthropological documentation: a love of intrigue, great skill with words, and close familiarity with sexual matters. The go-between of the treatises uses these qualities to dispel suspicion on the part of adversaries – often the overprotective husbands – to an illicit situation, namely, adultery.

For topics related to intermediary activity, several significant treatises on erotological topics such as Ibn Hazm's *Tawq-al hamāma* (*The Dove's Neckring*) and Sheikh Nafzāwī's *Rawd-alʿatīr* (*The Perfumed Garden*) offer a systematic categorization of the figure's scope., Other writers assimilate the figure into their anecdotes in ways that also denote an intrinsic belief that illicit quests invariably require the help of a third party. The treatises do not wholeheartedly condone the acts of procuring and pandering, yet they recognize the need for it and acknowledge that a subtle and entertaining type of intelligence is required for mediation between lovers.[50] Such treatises therefore reveal a marked ambivalence with regards to their treatment of the go-between. The fourteenth-century al-Baghdādī, for example, reports the ruses and activities of an old hag with relish, only to round off the descriptions with curses and diatribes against her.[51] Indeed, the moral ambivalence of narrators commands the description of every *ʿajūz*.

The *ʿajūz* of the treatises rarely advertises herself as a go-between,

[50] *Orígenes y sociología*, 42.

[51] Al-Baghdādī, 92. This text of popular inspiration draws on city life and everyday activities for its subject matter. The book comprises twenty-five adventures, erotic in nature, recounted by various male narrators who pass time by telling stories involving amorous encounters and the insincerity, deception and cunning of women.

counting on the implicit knowledge of the initiated members of the community regarding her potential services. The thirteenth-century North-African Ahmad al-Tifāchī, who offers a glimpse into the scope of social identity covered by her, makes this clear by enumerating the many guises assumed by the go-between: she can pose as a religious old woman, an ascetic, a hairdresser, a musician, a seamstress.[52] Nafzāwī also lists the disguises taken on by the *'ajūz* in her effort to divert suspicion.[53] In the anecdotes from these and other treatises, her basic methodology consists of projecting a professional identity which masks her true objectives. At the same time, the guise is rendered entirely invalid by the text's (and the community's) full awareness of the falsity of such postures, thereby equating all types of professional activity with pandering. That is to say, a survey of erotological treatises soon trains the reader to read "procuress" for any profession announced by the old woman. This blatantly transparent codification suggests that the old woman's disguise represents a mere element in the lengthy ritual of seduction, all of which consists of the correct interpretation of codes and signs by those who wish to embark on an illicit affair.

The one person who remains a stranger to this otherwise accessible codification is the husband who is duped by the illicit affair. This peripheral status undermines the husband considerably, even if he is morally in the right. For example, in the sixteenth tale of al-Baghdādī's compilation, a wife is challenged by her lover to have sexual relations in the presence of her husband. To help satisfy this whim, she solicits the help of an *'ajūz,* who immediately comprehends the best way to go about fulfilling the seemingly impossible task of including the unsuspecting husband in the scheme. She generates enough panic in him so as to lead him to agree that his wife, who feigns an illness, sleep with the lover to obtain the cure supposedly possessed by the latter. The old woman's repeated threats regarding the gravity of the wife's illness[54] and her confident posture as home doctor ensure the success of the trick. The power of her pseudo-scientific discourse leads the husband away from suspicion by luring him into the very fabric of her trick. He ends up granting willingly that which would

---

[52] Al-Tifāchī, 43.

[53] *The Glory of the Perfumed Garden: The Missing Flowers,* translated by "H. E. J" (London: Neville Spearman, 1975) 75.

[54] Al-Baghdādī, 147-148.

otherwise be impossible for the wife to attain. His fear and ignorance, exploited to the full by the well-timed words of the old woman, prompt this concession. Her dramatic discourse mingles scientific authority with maternal compassion and thereby secures the husband's cooperation. A similar situation occurs in the eleventh tale, in which the *ʿajūz* bases her entire scheme on the anxiety and ignorance of a husband regarding medical matters and thus can carry the wife from the closely guarded house with the spouse's unsuspecting consent.

In such anecdotes the old woman's deceit involves a central ruse that achieves the desired objective. Blatant lies such as a feigned illness, an artificial threat, or a false message help to construct the decoy. To a certain degree, the employment of artifice recalls the old woman's counterparts in medieval Latin comedy and the *fabliaux*. Another similarity with the Western go-between has to do with the *ʿajūz*'s clear requirement for financial recompense. But the Near-Eastern *ʿajūz* possesses considerably more eloquence in speech and holds together the integrity of the ruse without simple repetitive or formulaic constructs. Her discourse follows a well-delineated narratological path with specific effects at appropriate moments: in the sixteenth tale of al-Baghdādī, for example, she begins by offering comforting words to an adulterous wife in distress before venturing into action. Her next step involves manipulating the husband into believing a false premise that will lead the lover into the house. Her words ensure her continuous presence before and during the implementation of the scheme, and she monitors the accountability of the situation by never ceasing to ensure that her lie adapts to transitions.

Another special feature brought out in full in the Near-Eastern go-between has to do with the magnitude of her complicity with the younger woman. Her portrayal in the treatises is based on the conviction that the go-between has a legitimate place in the broad tradition of women's deceits. Much of the narrative momentum in the anecdotes derives from vivid descriptions of the traps and decoys set up by the partnership of women, and young wives often devise ingenious plans for ventures into adultery. For example, the fourteenth-century Syrian ʿAbd al-Rahīm al-Hawrānī, in his *Kashf asrār al-mouhtalīne wa nawāmis al-khayyālīne* (*The Unveiling of Deceits Engineered by Women who Set Traps Using their Imagination*), dedicates a collection of twenty-one tales to depictions of carnal love, giving much attention to the stratagems of the wives and daughters.[55] Complicity between young and old women is a key element in the go-between's conception, where the talent of the latter for manipulative speech serves to set up the principal trap, always counting on the alertness of the young wife.

This complicity stems from the conviction, apparent in the texts, that both women inhabit the same segregated space and share a special knowledge of its environment, faced with spouses and lovers who are portrayed as having little or no information on the goings on within that space. As we have seen, the old woman takes advantage of this ignorance to advance her plans; significantly, in her interaction with the young wife, she attempts to teach and learn all the more on the art of duplicity. In al-Baghdādī's sixteenth tale, the adulterous young wife learns the details of a plan from the *ʿajūz* as a student would from an expert teacher; she is said to appreciate the prose and verse by which the old woman's ruse is constructed.[56] The appreciation of the young woman goes beyond her relief at the resolution of this particular predicament. It derives also from the fact that she has just learned a useful lesson, which will prove of value to her in her evolution as a "wicked" wife.

The relationship works in reverse also, although by no means as often: in al-Baghdādī's eleventh adventure, an adulterous wife is introduced to the reader as intelligent, sensible, clever, competent in poetry, able to recite many poems as well as historical anecdotes from memory.[57] When faced with a challenging circumstance, the wife calls on an old hag, a well-known intermediary amongst women. The two operate through an equal partnership, since the young woman elaborates the scheme and the *ʿajūz* follows through conscientiously by reading all the signs correctly. As the young woman feigns an urgent need to leave the house, the old woman confronts the husband and summons all the necessary anxiety and compassion to expedite the departure. The tale ends with a reflection by the old woman on the lesson she has drawn from the episode; she declares that she did not know what ruse to employ when first called upon by the wife, but that the latter showed her exactly what to do.[58] Recip-

---

[55] ʿAbd al-Rahīm al-Hawrānī, *Les ruses des femmes*, translated by René Khawam (Paris: Phébus, 1993).

[56] Al-Baghdādī, 145.

[57] Al-Baghdādī, 93.

[58] Al-Baghdādī, 116.

rocal lessons in deceit help both parties to improve their techniques. The lively and playful dynamics of complicity receive substantial attention in these accounts, establishing a thematically strong link between third party and wife.

Old age also plays an important part in determining the nature and function of the Near-Eastern go-between. More than in financial recompense, the old go-between experiences joy in the very act of bringing two parties together.[59] The pleasure taken in arranging clandestine meetings constitutes a basic sentiment for the *ʿajūz* on par with her need for financial reward. The two types of desire may seem distinct at first sight, yet they point to a similar motivation. The texts' insistence on showing the old woman's pleasure in both areas indicates some sensitivity regarding her fulfillment: her trade allows her to make a living and hence to remain productive, while her mediation between lovers compensates in part for her own lack of sexual productivity. It allows her to live sexual adventures vicariously, and no profession will bring her closer to an impression of sexual activity than that of go-between. Her financial achievement and her desire to facilitate sexual contact increase the sense of social and personal fulfillment that her age otherwise prohibits. The transgressions committed by the *ʿajūz* in facilitating illicit love reveal a more threatening shade when her productivity and enjoyment are taken into account, these two elements being precisely those to which she is not entitled. No treatise on erotology announces this threat as such, but includes the old woman's productivity as an integral part of her identity as go-between. This fact produces two puzzling results: one, it sets up a contrast with the idea of the old woman as unproductive, and, two, relates productivity to threat. It is quite possible within the framework of these tales to discern the rebellious agenda of the go-between whose tactics solidify her sense of self and whose disintegration into an empty *topos* is challenged by her tremendous productivity.

To further complicate the old woman's representation, none of the erotological treatises establishes a consistent ethical posture in her portrayal, for they oscillate between marvel and amusement at her

[59] This fact is observed in *Orígenes y sociología del tema celestinesco,* 42, with examples from the works of both Ibn Hazm and Nafzāwī, who acknowledge the old woman's pleasure at bringing lovers together. Also in al-Baghdādī's eleventh adventure, the go-between is described as one who loved nothing better than to bring two people together under illicit circumstances (87-88).

skills, and mistrust and disapproval as regards the topic of adultery. It will be recalled that while Islam maintains a relatively open attitude towards sensuality and sexuality, adultery receives the condemnation of authorities. Given that the old woman simultaneously facilitates the celebration of sensuality and promotes illicit encounters, it comes as no surprise that medieval erotologists are unable to resolve or even consolidate their ethical stance towards her.

In the context of narratological processes, the old woman of the treatises serves to underscore a major thematic and stylistic concern of the genre: her fast-paced thinking, immediate access to ruses, and way with words reflect the genre's interest in fast and witty scenes that give the anecdotes their appeal. The short narratives maintain an altogether amused and lively attitude toward the exploits they describe, and the *ʿajūz* contributes significantly to this tone. As such, the artistic potential of her character subordinates the morally dubious quality of her endeavors and begins to elevate her to the status of a literary character whose ethical implications are overshadowed by artistic concerns. The process is by no means smooth or clear, and the contradictions between moral and artistic projection remain; nonetheless, her capacity to satisfy the contours of a literary figure is a major component of her makeup for the treatises.

As Joseph Bell observes, the greatest treatment of love is found in the imaginative literature of Islam in anecdotes, romances, and verse.[60] This corpus constitutes a fertile terrain for the go-between; love tales and narrative poems draw on her for a wide range of purposes and engage her as a literary character within the amorous system constructed by the text.

IV. The Literary Representation of the Go-Between

(i) *Tales in the Popular Spirit*

(a) The Forty Parrots

Similar to medieval European letters, the literature of the medieval Islamic period was rich in intertextual contact ranging from obvious borrowing to ironic transformations of a recurrent theme. From the

---

[60] Bell, 6.

eighth through fifteenth centuries, artists produced a court culture, a learned culture, and a popular culture, all of which interacted with and informed one another in significant ways. The first dealt above all with protocol and courtly etiquette for princes and rulers, and the second comprised "the culture of religious scholars (*'ulamā*), belletrists (*udabā'*) and other 'men of the pen.'"[61] As is to be expected, it was not uncommon to see one genre find inspiration in a "lower" or "higher" cultural source. Collections of tales, for example, display the intermingling of popular and learned in their subject matter, and variations on the same basic story can be found both in folkloric and learned sources. By extension, the literary manifestation of the Near-Eastern go-between occurs in both popular and learned literature. Two widely circulated collections of popular tales in which the go-between appears prominently are the Arabic collection *Alf Laylā wa Laylā* (*The Thousand and One Nights*) and the Persian *Chehel Touti* (*The Forty Parrots*), some of whose tales date from pre-Islamic times.[62]

The collection of tales entitled *The Forty Parrots* goes back to the *Sūkasaptatī*, a Sanskrit book of tales on the ruses and deceits of women. The most complete version from the medieval period is the fourteenth-century translation into Persian.[63] It follows the Sanskrit format of independent stories told daily by a parrot so as to stop its young married mistress from going out to meet her lover.[64] All stories contain narrations of deceitful behavior by women as cautionary examples for the wife. These are told against a backdrop of three players who interact with the parrot: the young wife, her often absent

---

[61] For this basic division into three groups and for some examples of the ways in which they influenced one another, see Boaz Shoshan, "High Culture and Popular Culture in Medieval Islam," *Studia Islamica* LXXIII (Paris: Maisonneuve-Larose, 1991) 67-109.

[62] On the sources and evolution of the *Thousand and One Nights*, see Nabia Abbott, "A Ninth-Century Fragment of the 'Thousand Nights': New Light of the Early History of the *Arabian Nights*," *Journal of Near Eastern Studies* (1949) 129-164; Muhsin Mahdi, ed., *The Thousand and One Nights (Alf Laylā wa-Laylā) from the Earliest Known Sources*, 2 volumes, (Leiden: E. J. Brill, 1984).

[63] The collection is edited, with an introduction to the history of the tales, by Shams Āl-Ahmad, *Jawāhar al-Asmār* (Teheran: Asadi, 1973). The tales enjoyed great popularity before and during the Islamic period in the Near East and were translated into a number of languages in variant forms.

[64] As Rameline E. Marsan states in *Itinéraire espagnole du conte médiéval* (Paris: Librairie Klincksieck, 1974), these tales often go back, in terms of content, to Indian texts such as the *Panchantantra*, *Hitopadesa*, *Sūkasaptatī*, and continued to be in vogue in Persia until well into the 17th century (136). The writer does not refer specifically to the *Forty Parrots*, yet her statement holds true for that collection also.

merchant husband (who offered her the parrot as a gift), and an old woman who fulfills the function of go-between in a number of seemingly contradictory ways.

The old go-between assumes a central role as she generates the momentum in the frame story: she first encourages the reluctant merchant to take a wife, finding for him the exact spouse whom he has in mind. Initially, then, she plays the role of a legitimate matchmaker with great mobility in the community around her, a fact reconfirmed by her free access to the merchant and her instant ability to seek out the kind of girl that he is willing to marry. After the wedding, this role is transformed immediately when the merchant sets off on a trip. The old woman continues to visit the young bride with news of a young man, ill with love, who is most enthusiastic to be her lover. The legitimate matchmaker has now become a go-between for illicit situations, with no explanation in the text for this change in priorities. The same adamant insistence used in coercing the merchant to take a wife appears in her demand that the bride now take a lover. On both occasions she requires payment for services rendered.

The shift in her identity from matchmaker to procuress is explicable to a certain degree. The Near-Eastern go-between operates in an urban environment where segregation requires her presence for a wide range of services: almost every type of male-female relationship will at some point call for assistance, and the promise of financial reward compels her to change the nature of her activities according to where the next source of income may be found. The society around her remains well aware of her familiarity with sexual matters from both male and female perspectives and of her talent for both licit and illicit arrangements. The young man who falls ill with the love of the newlywed woman declares that only a crafty old woman can cure him of the illness: his recognition of the fact reveals the extent to which the cure for love is associated with an old female intermediary.[65] In this respect the old woman provides a community service even when the task in question involves treading on unethical ground. Also, in the same way that the *ʿajūz* presents herself in terms of another profession such as saleswoman, midwife or home-doctor

---

[65] The young man's request recalls Avicenna, with the variation that he wishes the *ʿajūz* to bring about a reunion.

as a pretext for other activities, it can be considered that legitimate matchmaking constitutes one of her disguises to help her integrate herself further into the private lives of others. The illicit interests of the old go-between leave a stronger mark on every narrative than her help with more regular arrangements, showing her special emphasis on illicit love in spite of the shifts in her posture.

In *The Forty Parrots*, the bird is identified with the interests of the husband and portrayed in a favorable light, which enhances all the more the impression of vice in the old woman who ends up killing the parrot's mate.[66] The strong identification of the parrot with the husband's standpoint overshadows the memory of the go-between's legitimate matchmaking for the same man. By the end of the frame story, no doubt remains as to the reproachful tone of the omnipresent narrator with regards to the go-between. The tales in this collection are significant for the literary history and typology of the go-between insofar as they establish the range of her activities, her shifts in posture, and her full integration into the community portrayed in the stories. They generate an altogether condemning tone in her portrayal but offer no resolution for the contradictions inherent in the portrayed society's tolerance, and even need, of her. The collection of tales in *The Thousand and One Nights* presents similar ambivalent attitudes and confirms the notion that a silent ambivalence governs the portrayal of the old go-between.

(b) *The* Thousand and One Nights

The thematic range of these tales is much broader than that of *The Forty Parrots*, and their subject matter is quite varied, including tales from diverse origins such as Indian, Persian, and Arabic. Husain Haddawy explains that in spite of the diversity of origins, the tales reveal "a basic homogeneity resulting from the process of dissemination and assimilation under Islamic hegemony, a homogeneity or distinctive synthesis that marks the cultural and artistic history of

---

[66] The negative image of the go-between is further reinforced in the sixth tale told by the parrot, about an old go-between who brings misfortune to an entire household by encouraging the wife to commit adultery.

[67] *The Arabian Nights*, translated by Husain Haddawy based on the text edited by Muhsin Mahdi (New York: W. W. Norton and Company, 1990), xi. An observation on editions and variants used in this study is needed at this point. As Ferial J. Ghazoul explains in *Nocturnal Poetics: The Arabian Nights in Comparative Context* (Cairo: The

Islam."[67] Another unifying factor concerns one of the thematic features of the work: the theme of women's deceits occupies a prominent place in the tales, again with emphasis on the ruses employed to deceive a figure of authority such as a husband or father.

Old women who act as go-betweens or assistants to tricks can be found in several tales.[68] Often disguised as a pious old woman, the character takes on a variety of illicit tasks in favor of a wide range of clients. Similar to the *ʿajūz* of the treatises, a strong sense of ready confidence and an admirable ability with speech constitute the basic traits of the old woman. A feature more prominently present in the *Thousand and One Nights* is the old woman's continuous reference to God as a reminder of her piety: this becomes a basic aspect of her discourse, and guarantees her access into homes in addition to securing the confidence of suspicious parties.

The ability to impose her will on others, either by way of verbal insistence or through a well-planned trick, is identified throughout with the figure of the old woman, so much so that it becomes the

---

American University in Cairo Press, 1996), the textual history of these tales is intricate and "the major problems of origin and genesis remain unresolved" (1). Many manuscripts of the tales exist, yet no complete edition of any has been made: "*The Arabian Nights* is an artistic production of the collective mind (...) [T]he variation in texts is not an accident due to inadequate transmission, but is rather a fundamental aspect of the narrative performance of *The Arabian Nights* and an intimate characteristic of the received texts" (Ghazoul, *Nocturnal Poetics*, 2, 4). Similarly, as Aboubakr Chraibi, *Contes nouveaux des* 1001 Nuits: *étude du manuscrit Reinhardt* (Paris: Librairie d'Amérique et D'Orient, 1996), succinctly explains, the *1001 Nights* is not one author's text; it is an open corpus, which expands or changes like a "geometrical progression," always offering new variants. Depending on one's area of inquiry, one would have to decide whether to study only one version/manuscript, or several. Thus, Chraibi continues, one scholar (Muhsin Mahdi) is justified in basing his edition on the oldest manuscript available, while another, David Pinault, in *Story-telling Techniques in the* Arabian Nights (Leiden: E. J. Brill, 1992), is equally justified in drawing on several editions and manuscripts as well as tales in the spirit of the *1001 Nights* (Chraibi, *Contes nouveaux*, 12). For our purposes, we have opted for a strategy similar to the latter, that is consideration of a variety of editions, since the object here is to analyze cases where mediation occurs. Editions consulted are: *Kitab Alf Laylā wa-Laylā*, edited by Muhsin Mahdi (Leiden: E. J. Brill, 1984); *Los más bellos cuentos de las mil y una noches*, traducción directa del árabe del Dr. Juan Vernet (Barcelona: Editorial Labor, 1965); Sir Richard Burton, *A Plain and Literal Translation of the Arabian Nights' Entertainments, now Entitled the Book of the Thousand Nights and a Night*, volume V (Printed by the Burton Club for Private Subscribers, 1885). Henceforth, references to each text will be to the title or part thereof, followed by page number.

[68] See Samuel G. Armistead and James T. Monroe, "Celestina's Muslim Sisters," *Celestinesca* 13, 2 (1989) 3-27. See also Fernando de Toro Garland, "*La Celestina* y *Las mil y una noches*," *Revista de Literatura* 29 (1966) 5-33.

salient expected trait. In the tale of the "Crafty Dalila," an old woman invents a seemingly unending sequence of tricks, lies and artificial promises for various members of the community. Her very *raison d'être* appears to be the necessity to indulge in deception using piety as a disguise: "Her tongue praised the Lord while her heart galloped in fields of wrongdoing, and, meanwhile, she kept looking for ways to bring about intrigue in the city."[69] Later, having conned four different people out of their possessions, Dalila says to her daughter: "Zaynab, my daughter, I'd like to get up to more tricks."[70] Her daughter sees no need for unnecessary risk, yet the old woman declares her immunity to all danger and goes off searching for more victims ("intending to cause trouble").[71] The clear impression created by the tale points to Dalila's search for intrigue, showing no signs of motivation by a crisis or a problem. This absence of a causal link further hones the image of the old woman as naturally drawn towards intrigue and dismisses, albeit implicitly, the need for any logical explanations of her behavior other than the simple fact that she is an old woman. That is, her image allows definition only in the strictest of auto-referential terms, discouraging the search for motive or causality in her case. This inhibition of inquiry represents an attempt to negate the contradictions apparent in her portrayal, or, at the very least, to draw attention away from these as much as possible.

The portrayal of Dalila the Crafty centers upon the emphasis on particular skills: she roams the city, displays familiarity with people, and strips each new victim of his or her possessions using the previous victim as bait. Motive is entirely subordinated to plot, and her construction of stories-within-stories (to lure unsuspecting parties each time) also serves to distract the reader from questioning the composition of her character. Her rich imagination produces a tale on the spot every time trouble is near, to the point that she even escapes execution by producing a story on the spot. As a weaver of seemingly infinite, fabricated tales, Dalila distances herself from any coherent and complete notions of her own self, becoming in a vehicle for the transmission of stories that aim to mislead not just the characters, but also the reader. Her tales indicate her remarkable skill with invention yet conceal those areas that would afford the reader some

[69] *Los más bellos cuentos*, 420.
[70] *Los más bellos cuentos*, 429.
[71] *Los más bellos cuentos*, 429.

clues regarding her motivations. Dalila is a figure so intensely mediated by her own tales that the reader's grasp of her sense of self is negligible.

As far as her inscription within the plot is concerned, this go-between offers a wealth of material for study. Her smooth mobility within the city parallels the itinerary of stories in her mind, showing that rapid movement from one abode to another makes up the foundation for her methodology. The lack of stability provides a marked contrast with the stationary and housebound women of the city, enhancing the sense of marginality that accompanies the *ʿajūz*. More importantly, though, it increases the potential for entertainment and subordinates the wrongdoing to a more visible comical character of her tricks: again, this denotes a latent push by the narrative structure to divert attention from the question of motive. Ultimately, Dalila turns the tale into an amusing one by leading other characters into predicaments of a slapstick nature: as she tricks one character after another, she creates a trail of angry victims who chase her across town, reclaiming their property as she further confuses the situation by continuing to prevaricate to the authorities who fail at every turn to bring her to punishment. She also directs her own discourse along comic lines. Blatant exaggeration constitutes a basic part of this discourse; assuming the identity of a pious old woman dedicated to a life of poverty, she tells one victim who has offered her food: "My child, I only take the food of Heaven. I am continually fasting, and break it only five days a year."[72]

Dalila is not just a go-between, for she assumes this disguise as one among many to facilitate her ultimate financial goal.[73] Yet the elements of her discourse, such as on-the-spot prevarication and comic exaggeration, as well as her consistent search for movement and further intrigue, facilitate this very disguise. Similar to the case of *The Forty Parrots*, the mediating *ʿajūz* of *The Thousand and One Nights* talks her way across a remarkably wide scope, generating at times an illicit situation, and on occasion a conventionally happy ending. No explanation is given for the changes in her focus, implying that the shifts in type of activity are simply an integral part of her identity. Another sequence of tales repeats this puzzling absence of causality

[72] *Los más bellos cuentos*, 422.

[73] For instance, she begins the deception of one victim by claiming to have found a desirable wife for him.

with some variation, warranting an inquiry into the implications of this absence.

The sequence, titled "The Porter and the Ladies," contains the story recounted by "The Second Lady, the Flogged One."[74] The tale reveals some of the reasons for the indeterminate moral nature of the decisions made by the *ʿajūz*. The narrator, a lady from Baghdad, recalls that an *ʿajūz* came to her insisting that they go to a wedding party where, as it happens, the lady met her future husband. Nothing of an illicit nature has therefore occurred, yet the initial description of the old woman belies a suspicious tone in the narrative: " 'One day, as I was sitting at home, an old woman came to me, and what an old woman she was, with a pallid, scabby skin; a bent body; matted gray hair; a gray, freckled face; broken teeth; plucked out eyebrows; hollow, bleary eyes; and a runny nose.' "[75] In addition to an impression of evil, this portrait emphasizes the great distance between the old woman and any indications of feminine youth and beauty, directing her all the more towards an act that would only vicariously bring her into contact with the world of youth and love. The ravages of old age are marked to the point of becoming parodic, reinforcing the notion that the *ʿajūz* lends herself amply to poetic objectification.

The old woman's first words stress one particular talent: a remarkable skill for insistence. Her plea that the lady attend the wedding party is calculated to inspire sufficient pity and a well-timed dose of self-importance, both useful techniques in manipulation.[76] Even though the first appearance and words of the *ʿajūz* do not in themselves lead to an illicit arrangement, the scene is implicitly set for a further exploitation of her talents in that direction. A short while after the lady has married the son of the *ʿajūz*, whom she had met at the wedding party, the old woman accompanies her to the market and leads the young wife to the stall of a handsome fabric merchant. The interaction between the three characters deserves full citation in order to convey the dynamic created by the *ʿajūz:*

> I said to the old lady, "Let him show us some nice fabric." She replied, "Ask him yourself." I said, "Don't you know that I have sworn

[74] *Arabian Nights*, 142.
[75] *Arabian Nights*, 142.
[76] She begs the lady to attend her daughter's wedding on the grounds that she (the old woman) and her daughter know no-one, and that all the other ladies in town will come if this lady attends (*Arabian Nights*, 142).

> not to speak to any man other than my husband?"[77] So she said, "Show us some fabric," and he showed us several pieces, some of which I liked. I said to the old woman, "Ask him for the price." When she asked him, he replied, "I will sell them for neither silver nor gold but for a kiss on her cheek." I said, "God save me from such a thing." But the old woman said, "O my lady, you needn't talk to him or he to you; just turn your face to him and let him kiss it; that is all there is to it." Tempted by her, I turned my face to him. [78]

Aware of her daughter-in-law's promise that she must never allow another man near her, the *ʿajūz* makes an attempt against the promise with the laconic but suggestive "Ask him yourself." Even though the plea is not realized, it appears to have paved the way for a positive response to the old woman's next suggestion. Effectively, the *ʿajūz* has gained the trust of her daughter-in-law in abiding by her rule and agreeing to speak with the merchant. She also manipulates the young bride's words on the subject of not speaking to other men by presenting the logical yet manipulative argument that a kiss does not equal speaking. The old woman's discourse focuses on techniques for coercion and successfully changes the will of the young woman.

Her motivation for so doing remains unclear, particularly in light of the fact that her act militates against her own son's honor. It does, however, correspond to one of the main presuppositions attached to the figure of the *ʿajūz*, namely the love of intrigue and the pleasure taken in witnessing flirtation between young people. That her act has to do with a seemingly natural, involuntary penchant for intrigue is confirmed by her next move. The fabric merchant surprises both women by taking a bite out of the young wife's cheek, causing a serious wound. The horrified old woman is quick to propose a solution so as to avoid the wrath of the husband.[79] Her regret appears genuine, especially after her son inflicts a violent punishment on his wife, subsequently calling for her death. Here the *ʿajūz* steps in and begs for her daughter-in-law's forgiveness. Her plea with her son, witnessed by the battered daughter-in-law, targets his conceptions of honor and duty:

---

[77] Her husband asks her for this pledge on their wedding day, strictly forbidding her from any contact with other men.

[78] *Arabian Nights*, 145.

[79] The old woman instructs the wife to pretend to be sick and to cover herself and promises to bring powders which will heal her cheek (*Arabian Nights*, 145).

> I grew certain of death and gave up myself for lost, but suddenly the old woman rushed in and, throwing herself at my husband's feet, said tearfully, "O son, by the rights of rearing you up, by the breasts that nursed you, and by my service to you, pardon her for my sake. You are still young, and you should not bear the guilt of her death, for as it is said, 'Whoever slays shall be slain.' Why bother with such a worthless woman? Drive her out of your hearth and heart." She kept weeping and imploring until he relented (...)[80]

This marks the third occasion upon which we encounter the old woman in a position of adamant insistence. Like her other efforts at changing minds, this entreaty touches on sentiments that cannot be disregarded: the *ʿajūz* singles out duty to the mother and the sense of self-preservation from guilt, achieving success in changing her son's will without once departing from her assumed posture as a weak, inferior being. In spite of her varying interests, the *ʿajūz* demonstrates at every turn a remarkable talent for persuasion blended with a desire to affect the interactions between people. Her multifunctionality showcases both the talent and the desire, with the strong implication that her very subsistence relies on this type of interference. At the same time, the lack of any moral consistency shows her to be in possession of talents which she cannot put to a straightforwardly productive use. The poetics employed for the construction of the old woman's image create a severe imbalance by endowing her discourse with great power and momentum while stripping her conception of any curiosity on the part of the text. Beyond the suggestion that she is purely motivated by a love of intrigue, the character puts up resistance against the search for any other causes for her behavior. As a result, she serves as a convenient mechanism for the introduction of major transitional points in the tale, allowing for the subsequent dramatizations of various sentiments such as passion, jealousy, and fear.

The tale of "Niʿamah bin al Rabiʿa and Naomi his Slave-Girl" emphasizes the community's perception of the old woman's indiscriminate posture: here, she confronts characters who differ in motivation yet converge in their need for the persuasive skills of an *ʿajūz*. Initially she is portrayed in a morally reprehensible capacity as one who makes a living by procuring girls for clients. An inhabitant of the same city as the beautiful Naomi, a slave girl married to Niʿamah, the

---

[80] *Arabian Nights*, 147.

old woman receives the order to "foregather with the girl Naomi and combine means to carry her off" by the Viceroy of Cufa, who would like to send the girl to his ruler as a gift.[81] The *ʿajūz* is simply presented as "an old woman of the duennas of his [the Viceroy's] wives," and his casual recourse to her indicates the degree to which she is identified with the "carrying off" of young girls. To this end she disguises herself as a pious old woman and enters the girl's house, gradually inspiring much affection by feigning piety and wisdom until she secures the right to daily visits to the house. Having obtained the girl's trust after a month of regular visits, she fools Naomi into following her outside the house and hands her over to the Viceroy. Sir Richard Burton footnotes this description of the *ʿajūz* in a manner that reveals his presuppositions from a textual and social point of view:

> The old bawd's portrait is admirably drawn: all we dwellers in the East have known her well: she is so and so. Her dress and manners are the same amongst the Hindus (...) as amongst the Moslems; men of the world at once recognize her and the prudent keep out of her way. She is found in the cities of Southern Europe, ever pious, ever prayerful; and she seems to do her work not so much for profit as for pure or impure enjoyment. [82]

For Burton, the figure clearly represents wrongdoing and appears so familiar to her audience that a general mention of her work suffices to indicate the act of procuring. Yet the portrait offered in popular literature does not always connote an overwhelmingly negative tone, even if such an association remains the strongest.[83] Shortly afterwards, Naomi's predicament is resolved by another old woman who resides in the slavegirl's new and involuntary home. The recourse to this *ʿajūz* by both Naomi and her distressed husband Niʿamah indicates an intrinsic trust in the *ʿajūz*'s capacity to bring two parties together in much the same way that the Viceroy had entrusted his old woman with a similar task. As Niʿamah says to the *ʿajūz*: "we know not how to bring this affair to a happy end save through thee."[84]

---

[81] Burton, *Alf Laylah wa Laylah*, iv, 3.

[82] Burton, *Alf Laylah wa Laylah*, iv, 4, n. 1.

[83] When the city's Chief of Police launches a search for Naomi, he also looks for the old woman "whom he knew for al-Hajjaj's procuress" (Burton, *Alf Laylah wa Laylah*, iv, 9).

[84] Burton, *Alf Laylah wa Laylah*, iv, 13.

This old woman, referred to as an old nurse, displays the confidence also encountered in the previous *ʿajūz*: "O youth," she says to Niʿamah, "thou shalt owe thy reunion with her to none but myself."[85] Indeed the procuress from the Viceroy's household, when initially refused entry to Naomi's house, had lashed out with a similar confidence to the doorman: "Shall the like of me be denied admission to the house of Niʿamah bin al-Rabiʿa, I who have free access to the houses of Emirs and Grandees?"[86] The tone recalls Dalila the crafty, in the following conversation with her worried daughter: " 'Mother, I am worried for you.' – 'I am – insisted the mother – like the strings in beans, which resist fire and water.' "[87]

The firm authority and confidence projected by the *ʿajūz* always stand on tenuous ground. The angry words to the doorman follow her declaration that she is a chamberwoman of the palace, a fact that diminishes the glamor of her free entry into the houses of "Princes and Grandees." She is later admitted into the house because Niʿamah hears the loud argument at the door, laughs and orders that she come in.[88] The old woman is a source of amusement for others, and her aura of authority is subject to a comical twist. Similarly, the nurse to whom the couple turns after the abduction offers her reassuring words only after she has received a thousand dinars for her services. The fluctuating levels of her authority indicate the tenuous nature of her position as a marginal member of the community: the degree of her control over a situation has much to do with the tolerance of the community.

In the tale under discussion, the old nurse brings about the union of the lovers by cleverly disguising Niʿamah as a handmaiden and talking her way past various levels of palace security. Essentially, she has performed a task that requires lying and deception, only this time for a morally acceptable cause. The narrative treats her favorably, staying away from any pejorative indications, in light of her contribution to the happy ending. In this respect her portrayal counterbalances the general assertion made by Burton as well as the impressions of the *ʿajūz* that occur throughout the erotological manuals or the popular tales of *The Forty Parrots*. In full possession

85 Burton, *Alf Laylah wa Laylah*, iv, 15.
86 Burton, *Alf Laylah wa Laylah*, iv, 4.
87 *Los más bellos cuentos*, 429.
88 Burton, *Alf Laylah wa Laylah*, iv, 4.

of the ingredients for successful go-between activity – confidence, financial recompense, rapid arrival at a solution and use of deceit, all of which can raise moral indignation – she emerges in a different light at the end. The tale therefore stresses the utility of the character for any type of reunion, be it against or in favor of the lovers' will.

It was seen above that the tales also derive some comic force from her depiction. This note enhances the sense of ambiguity in her portrayal and intensifies the impression that the entertaining aspect of her character at times overcomes the ethical concern associated with her acts. In addition, the absence of a causal nexus that would explain her contradictory behavior plays a significant role for the lack of resolution in her image; the *ʿajūz* enters every tale in terms of the narrative's emphasis on her wrongdoing and evil, a concern countered by two types of acknowledgment: her presence is needed if the love-affairs and reunions are to take place, and she can advance morally acceptable tasks just as much as unethical ones. Consequently, the ultimate impression left by the old woman of these popular tales is one of ethical indecision on the part of the text, the tension of which emerges increasingly as more genres incorporate her into their thematic scheme. It is important to note that in the genres considered so far, the continual shifts of focus and behavior on the part of the old woman are aligned with the intricate and ever-changing direction of the tales, whose endings and beginnings are often obscured in their Chinese-box framework. In other words, in addition to a colorful character in the stories, the *ʿajūz* represents an aspect of the poetics of the treatises and *Thousand and One Nights:* she parallels the sense of fluidity and improvisation which governs the language and plot of the tales.

(c) *The "Sindbād" Cycle*

Another thought-provoking example of the go-between's shifting types of influence occurs in one of the collections stemming from the Sindbād cycle of tales. This cycle, of Sanskrit origin, designates those collections which revolve around the principal frame story of a Prince accused of violation or trespass by a high-ranked woman in the court and subsequent tales on the deceits of women used in the Prince's defense against the accusation. As is well known, the Sanskrit *Book of Sindbād* gave rise to numerous variations and translations of these tales across the East and Europe.[89] One such variation, entitled the *Bakhtiār Nāma*, entered Islamic letters via Persian translation and was later rendered into Arabic and Turkish.[90] Existing manuscripts of the work date from 600 A.D. to 1296 A.D., indicating the wide time-span covered by the stories and the popularity which they enjoyed.[91] The version of the *Bakhtiār Nāma* considered here consists of nine stories told by the Prince in his own defense against evil viziers who wish him dead – in the *Book of Sindbād* the stories are told by the ministers who defend the prince.[92]

The seventh tale told by Prince Bakhtiar in his own defense portrays an old woman in an unexpected context. Here, she witnesses the grief of a king whose wife has come under serious suspicion of betrayal. For her part, the queen feels alienated and frightened by the accusation, which in fact stems from an innocent secret from her past.[93] As a result of this misunderstanding the king and his wife maintain a strict and unhappy code of silence with one another. The one person privy to the grief of both is the old woman, who has the ability and initiative to meet with them separately, of her own choice, and promise both that the conflict will reach a resolution through her magical powers. The king receives a talisman from her which she assures him will make the queen speak the truth in her sleep. The queen on the other hand is instructed to feign sleep, and disclose the truth under the supposed effect of the charm. Following these

[89] The evolution of tales that made their way from Sanskrit into Persian, then Arabic and subsequently the European languages has been traced both in the East and the West. See María Jesús Lacarra, *Cuentística medieval en España: los orígenes* (Zaragoza: Universidad de Zaragoza, 1979); see also Marsan, the chapter entitled "Auteurs et oeuvres d'origine musulmane," 120136. In the next chapter we will look more closely at the Western reception of the tales.

[90] *Bakhtiār Nāma*, anonymous, edited by Mohammad Roshan (Teheran: 1969). Two English versions are available: *The Bakhtyar Nama, a Persian Romance*, translated by Sir William Ouseley (Privately printed: 1883); *Bakhtiar nameh, or, The Royal Foundling* (Philadelphia: Edward Parker, 1813).

[91] Some, but not all, editions of the *Thousand and One Nights* provide a variant of the tale under the heading of "The Story of the Ten Viziers."

[92] Quite possibly, the *Bakhtiār Nāma* harks back to a different collection of tales in Tamil entitled *Alakeswara Katha* in which four ministers are falsely accused of violation and go on to tell stories in their own defense. This is explained by W. A. Clouston in the introduction to the 1883 English translation of the *Bakhtiār Nāma* cited above.

[93] The details are complex and not entirely relevant to our purpose here; briefly, the queen, who has been wedded to the king by force, has an adolescent son from a previous marriage and causes much suspicion by having him brought to her new home and treating him with great affection without explaining the kinship.

instructions, the misunderstanding is resolved that same night, and the couple resume a happy relationship.

This tale shows the use of intermediary activity in the context of a married couple's problems and indicates that strict notions of honor, shame and secrecy have the same degree of hold over the intimate realm of husband and wife's life as they would in an illicit situation. The transposition of the ordinarily illicit-minded old woman to this licit setting yields positive results and shows the extent to which third-party activity can bring about the resolution of a difficult problem. The old woman's gentle persuasive power over both parties comes across in her clear speeches to both, and to gain further trust she adds the safety net of the illusion of magic (which, as the reader knows, has no true effect in the tale). The influence exerted by her in the private world of husband and wife, revealed by her very presence at the king's court and by the two spouses' natural willingness to follow her instructions, distances her considerably from any immoral connotation even if the appearance of deceit remains in the shape of the talisman and the old woman's confident promises. Here she momentarily fuses the sphere of women's deceits with that of utility within a realm completely separated from illicit concerns. Her role as such reflects the significance attached to mediation in the political language of Islam, where proximity to the source of power ensures a privileged position thanks to which truthful dialogue occurs between two estranged or distant parties.

The favorable notion of mediation converges, in the figure of the old woman, with her affinity with the world of women's deceits. These two informing currents stand at polar opposites of one another, since one suggests artful political power while the other has to do with the realm of comical and clear-cut negative meanings. The apparent irrelevance of motivation and ethical sensitivity in the old woman seems, then, to be the result of a fundamental disparity between the elements which create her composite image. Her role requires access to a strategy associated with ingenious expertise and power (that is, mediation), while her actual tasks occur within the limits of a predictable, exhausted topic (that is, women's deceits). The incongruous coming together of the two transforms the designation of "old woman" into a problematic signifier associated with entertaining verbal skills and clever scheming, yet unlinked to a context that would explain the uncertainties of the texts in her regard.

This lack of resolution is addressed to a certain degree in works of fiction in the learned spirit, in which plot, engaging as it may be, takes second place to theme and poetic invention. The narrative love romances of the medieval period involve the go-between in their schemes against the backdrop of courts and inner sanctums of monarchs. In the upper-class households portrayed by these texts, her special place as a political and amorous advisor comes under deeper scrutiny. In these tales, mediation is of a custom-made nature and suits the needs of only the two main characters, departing from the world of entire communities who draw collectively on the pre-exisiting structures of third-party activity. The go-between therefore adapts her discourse to the special needs of few people and in so doing creates new definitions for her own identity.

(ii) *The Learned Spirit*

Between the eleventh and fifteenth centuries the cultural world of Islam was witness to the creation and re-elaboration, in the form of narrative poetry, of several love stories with roots in the pre-Islamic period. Those responsible for these creations pertained to the class of belletrists (*udabā'*) for whom the topic of love was a continuous source of artistic and philosophical inspiration. In the re-elaborations, these men addressed philosophical or theological points in addition to the intricate discussions of love within the narrative. With the fragmentation of Islamic culture around various clusters, the stories told by the *udabā* were cultivated in more than one language, resulting in a wealth of literary production in another classical language of Islam, that is, Persian, which provided some of the best-known love tales of the Near East.[94] In addition, it constituted the natural link between

[94] This role is explained by Hodgson in "The Bloom of Persian Literary Culture and Its Times," 293-328. Hodgson points out that as of the eleventh and twelfth centuries Persian became the language of polite culture in a great part of the Islamic empire, serving in many ways as a model for much literary activity. This "new Muslim Persian" naturally was "very much under the influence of the Arabic of the High Caliphate (itself, of course, partly of Pahlavi inspiration)" thereby revealing the closeness with which languages interacted with one another as of the Middle Period (12th-15th centuries) of Islam. Also Jean-Claude Vadet, in *L'esprit courtois en Orient dans les cinq premiers siècle de l'Hegire* notes that at least one aspect of *'isq* – earthly love – derives from a Persian influence, given that for centuries Persia had known a tradition of love stories involving particularly individualist perspective on the fate and behavior of lovers (48). Similarly in R. Grousset, L. Massignon, and H. Massé's

pre-Islamic material from Sanskrit and other languages and Islamic letters, and played a significant role in the growth of the concept of *adab*, the intricate protocol and codified pattern of representation.

By and large, the topic of love plays a prominent role in long narrative poems (romances) in Persian. These devote much space to dialogue as well as monologue and depict the principal characters with remarkable complexity and detail by focusing on inner sentiments as much as external experiences. In addition they lend close attention to the qualities of language and imagery in the poems. Colorful plotlines allow for diverse interpretations, and the evolution of the characters is traced using great detail and shifting standpoints. It would not be far-fetched to say that most of the lovers celebrated by the romances of the period ranging from the tenth to the sixteenth centuries are, and have been, household names, thanks to the wealth of interdisciplinary and intertextual re-elaborations by way of music, poetry, drama, and other forms of retelling.

(a) *Typology by Default: The Case of* Laylā and Majnūn

The intermediary is conspicuously absent from one of the most famous love stories of the Islamic world. The tale of the doomed lovers *Laylā and Majnūn* goes back to the seventh century and is retold in numerous versions by biographers, historians, and poets familiar with the Arab and Persian traditions.[95] The absence of the intermediary, however, is significant for our study.

Briefly, the story concerns two Bedouin cousins in love with one another but not permitted to marry each other; upon the young girl's betrothal to another, the young man, whose nickname Majnūn denotes his insanity, drives himself to madness and death. In every version of the tale, and throughout the tribulations of their love, the two cousins communicate face to face and through letters. In some

---

L'âme de l'Iran (Paris: Albin Michel, 1951) the essays headed "Les penseurs iraniens et l'essor de la civilisation arabe," by Massignon (69-89) and "Les sept princesses de Nizāmī," by Jan Rypka, illustrate the Persian impact on Islamic letters.

[95] The unhappy love story is recorded in the tenth-century compilation of texts and memoirs of the tenth-century Abu l-Faraj al-Isfahānī entitled *Kitāb al-Aghānī* (*The Book of Songs*), and recounted by numerous writers in Arabic and Persian throughout the centuries, as recently as the Egyptian playwright Ahmad Chawqi's version entitled *Majnūn Laylā* (Cairo: s.n. 1916). The detailed chronology of this famous tale is given in André Miquel and Percy Kemp's *Majnūn et Laylā: l'amour fou* (Paris: La Bibliothèque arabe Sinbad, 1984).

renditions a third party by the name of Nowfal appears as a close friend of Majnūn, offering his assistance in resolving the latter's dilemma. However, his interference bears no similarity to that of a go-between, for his solution concerns the invasion of Laylā's tribe with an army and the abduction of the girl for his friend. He aborts the plan at Majnūn's plea.

The absence of a go-between serves to remind the reader of the character's dependence on an urban culture in which segregation constitutes the accepted norm, whereas the two cousins inhabit the realm of desert Bedouins untouched by the restrictions of hierarchized urban systems, be they pre- or post-Islamic. The *Kitāb al-Aghānī*, by the tenth-century compiler and biographer al-Isfahānī, states that the two cousins interacted freely and in mixed groups of young people.[96] Even the subsequent versions produced by high-culture urban poets respect the standard set by the Bedouin context of the tale and omit the go-between. Such, for instance, is the case with the twelfth-century poet Nizāmī, all of whose love tales include a significant intermediary, with the exception of his version of *Laylā va Majnūn*.[97] This famous love tale, then, confirms the unfaltering attachment of third-party activity to segregated and artificially conceived spaces in which distance is created by authorities so as to render direct communication difficult.

(b) *The Private and Public Go-Between:* Vīs and Rāmīn

The go-between's scope and the qualities of her discourse receive the fullest treatment in love romances that take place in the ritualized, codified and closed setting of the court, where mediated communication governs the direction of political and amorous encounters. In such a context, the discourse of the third party not only brings about the union of the lovers, but also marks an important stage in the education of the young ones. The eleventh-century romance of *Vīs and Rāmīn* by Fakhr al-Dīn Gorgānī offers one of the most detailed and complex representations of this role.[98]

---

[96] Abu-al Faraj al-Isfahānī, *Kitāb al-Aghānī*, (Teheran: Scientific and Cultural Publications, 1989) vol. I, 144. Miquel and Kemp also take note of this fact.

[97] Nizāmī Ganjavī, *Kulīyyāt-e Khamsa-ye Hakīm Nizāmī Ganjavī* (Teheran: Amīr Kabīr, 1962).

[98] Fakhr al-Dīn Gorgānī, *Vīs o Rāmīn*, edited by Mohammad Jaffar Mahdjoub (Teheran: The Ibn Sina Library, 1959).

Completed in 1055 A.D., this lengthy narrative derived its basic plotline from pre-Islamic Parthian sources yet continued to meet with great popularity throughout the Islamic world and became sufficiently well known to allow speculation on its possible links with the European romance of *Tristan*.[99] The tale is excessively complicated to be summarized here in detail; briefly, it concerns Vīs, a young girl already betrothed to her brother, nonetheless taken away and wedded against her will to a king named Mobed upon his victory in a battle.[100] While Vīs is on her way to her new husband, Mobed's younger brother Rāmīn catches a glimpse of her and falls madly in love. As it happens, both Vīs and Rāmīn were brought up by the same nurse who now continues to accompany Vīs. At an opportune moment, Rāmīn confides his love to the nurse who, after much effort, arouses the young girl's interest in pursuing an affair with her brother-in-law. In their attempts to hide the affair, Vīs, Rāmīn, and the nurse devise many stratagems throughout the tale. They undergo numerous tribulations until, at the suggestion of the nurse, Rāmīn invades his brother's army and takes his place on the throne, after which he lives happily with Vīs.

The major conflicts in the tale result directly from the barriers imposed by strong notions of honor and shame on the principal characters. In other words, every clash with the central antagonist Mobed derives from a transgression against him as brother, husband or political ruler. To help overcome any sense of regret or guilt in the young and often confused lovers, the nurse applies her powerful discourse to the redefinition of some of these notions in favor of the lovers, and there lies her greatest skill. Thus when Rāmīn asks her to speak to Vīs on his behalf, she begins indirectly to do so, having found herself alone with the girl: slowly but consistently she instructs Vīs on the idea of womanhood, undaunted by the young bride's violent rejections at the first mentions of Rāmīn. Her seduction involves

---

[99] The pre-Islamic sources of the tale are discussed both in the introduction by the editor and in *History of Persian Literature*, edited by Yunus Jaffery (Delhi: Triveni Publishers, 1981) 129-152; the possible *Tristan* link is discussed in Pierre Gallais' *Genèse du roman occidental: essais sur* Tristan et Iseut *et son modèle persan*, (Paris: Éditions Tête de Feuilles et Éditions du Sirac, 1974) as well as in Lucie Polak, "*Tristan* and *Vīs and Ramin*," cited above.

[100] The custom of marriage between siblings dates back to the Zoroastrian period.

[101] It must be noted here that Vīs's marriages to her brother and Mobed are unconsummated.

no use of magic or sorcery whatsoever, even if some of the adjectives used in her description define her as a witch. Rather, the nurse patiently couches her advice for taking a lover in terms of Vīs's duty as woman and queen, thereby redefining exactly those concepts that inhibit the young woman's venture into adultery:

"You were born human,
Not demon, not fairy, not angel,
(...) No man has sought pleasure with you as yet,
For until today you have given your body to no-one. [101]
(...) You have not known this pleasure, you are not aware,
Without it life is not enjoyable.
God has created female for male,
And you are a female,
Wives of great men and leaders,
Wives of the illustrious and the noteworthy
Are all happily married (...)
And although they have husbands of great fame,
They all have lovers in secret."[102]

The go-between's words to the young girl represent an important step in the latter's sexual and social education. At first sight and for Vīs, the nurse seems to recommend a transgression, but in fact, the nurse claims, she pleads for the adoption of a pattern dictated by society and human nature. In this way, the undertaking of an affair will, paradoxically, represent the fulfillment of an expected duty, since every wife has a lover, particularly if married to a powerful man. In the three lengthy visits to the young girl, the nurse continues to reason in terms of examples from nature to further clarify this paradox and makes ample use of social models and the requirements made by nature and society of the young woman.[103] Her task consists of deciphering certain codes for the young girl, who hitherto has chosen to read the signs of honor and shame in more literal ways. It is thus no longer a question of employing ruses to facilitate a clandestine sexual encounter, but of a young woman's education within a system whose elaborate codes of conduct are prone to entirely con-

[102] *Vīs o Rāmīn*, 106, vv. 125-142.

[103] Carefully monitoring the young girl's every reaction, the nurse becomes increasingly explicit as time passes: "You have not had a man, you are not aware./ If you have intercourse with a man once,/ I swear to you that you will no longer avoid it" (*Vīs o Rāmīn* 116, vv. 13-16).

tradictory interpretations. An eloquent and powerful discourse guarantees the success of this education and, for the reader, throws light on the complexity of the poetics of love which the text seeks to construct: love in *Vīs and Rāmīn*, as in subsequent learned genres, is a field of study which calls for the careful education of the novice lover.

To gain power and credibility within the pedagogical poetics of love, the third party draws on a variety of factors. These include a projected sense of experience and authority in sexual matters as well as the respect generated by her older age. One other factor, hinted at in Ovid's work, receives ample treatment in *Vīs and Rāmīn* and forms a significant aspect of the go-between's identity. It concerns the erotic persona of the third party herself.

In his ardent entreaties that the nurse help him, Rāmīn makes a decidedly charged plea to the go-between, filled with erotic drive; the text leaves little room for doubt as to the nature of the initial relationship between the adult Rāmīn and the nurse. Once he has fallen in love, he arranges to meet the nurse and receives her in the garden, a traditional *locus amoenus* for lovers. He states his case, asks for her help, and

> He said this and held her tight
> Kissed her a few times on the head,
> Then kissed her on the mouth and face,
> The demon came and went inside her body,
> Rāmīn showed his desire to the nurse,
> As though he had planted the seed of love in her heart.
> When he had shown desire to the woman once,
> The nurse was moved to helping him.
> It was then that the veil of shame was torn,
> Her cold speech became warm.[104]

The poem offers no additional explanations for this encounter. Out of context, it would appear as if the young man were scheming to obtain the go-between's consent, yet the rest of the narrative shows him to be ingenuous, inexperienced, completely ill with love and at a loss for a solution. His appeal to the go-between's erotic capacity therefore has to do with his sentimental education, just as Vīs's encounters with the nurse constitute lessons in love. As he pours out his anguished heart to the nurse, Rāmīn accompanies this secret feel-

---

[104] *Vīs o Rāmīn*, 91-92, vv. 251-255.

ing with an explicit show of physicality which, in a certain manner, turns the go-between into a surrogate lover for that brief period. That is to say, not only does Rāmīn reveal his first words of love to the intermediary (long before he even speaks to Vīs), but he also experiences an instance of intimacy with the one person who has access to the sealed-off world of his beloved. The go-between inspires the construction of amorous discourse and behavior in the young man. The encounter between Rāmīn and the nurse marks a process of initiation for the young man, not without its own delight for the third party:

> She said "(...) You were my friend, O light of the heart,
> But today I have become more of a friend to you.
> Excuses have now disappeared between us (...)
> Henceforth, command all that you wish,
> For I will not disobey any orders.
> I shall make your will overcome Vīs,
> I shall make that beautiful one accept your love."[105]

In spite of her obvious enjoyment, the go-between comprehends fully her role in the affair and proceeds to exert her influence on Vīs. The meeting with Rāmīn does not confuse the issue but rather reinforces the central role of the third party as a necessary guiding and educating force. From this point onwards, Rāmīn concentrates all his amorous attention on Vīs. The complete lack of any subsequent mention of the erotic aspect of their encounter indicates the extent to which it forms a part of the construction of amorous discourse for the young man, without any emotional or ethical side-effects.

The poem continues to showcase the intermediary's flexibility and her talent to adapt her discourse to every situation. The nurse seduces Vīs with words while she establishes, at least initially, a more physical relationship with Rāmīn: in this way she provides both parties with the appropriate outlet for their sentiments. An earlier example of the older woman's skill for adapting to the circumstances occurs when the nurse, as yet unaware of Rāmīn's feelings, advises Vīs on her marital duties. The young wife, wedded by force, is reluctant to consummate the marriage, whereupon the nurse, ever the educator, declares:

---

105 *Vīs o Rāmīn*, 92, vv. 256-259.

Oh light of my eyes, my daughter,
It is right that you should weep for your brother.
For he was both your brother and your lover,
And you two never had the opportunity to be intimate.
What can be worse than two faithful lovers
Who spend months and years together,
Stay happily together night and day,
And yet do not join? [106]

This comment serves as a preamble to the suggestion that Vīs should now experience intimacy with her husband, Mobed. The nurse continues to speak gently about the recognition of grief and then calls for the joy of living for a new future. Her logical tone blends a pragmatic and emotional attitude as she tells Vīs about responsibility and public image. Gradually, she injects force and assertiveness in her speech; she alerts Vīs to people and how they will talk if a young queen does not comply with her husband's needs, ending her argument on a kindhearted note that expresses the possibility of happiness: " 'In the eyes of Mobed, what is ugly in you is beautiful/ For he loves you with all his life and heart.' "[107] This illustrates the intermediary's ability to serve as a third party between man and wife and to adapt her discourse to the needs of that particular estrangement. More importantly it reveals the degree to which the older woman is identified with the explication and unraveling of codes of sexual conduct for other characters. The privileged space of third-party activity finds itself repeatedly confirmed in these examples.

The romance by Gorgānī also offers one of the rare occasions in which the third party extends her abilities beyond the realm of love and into the world of politics without changing the basic tenets of her discourse. Towards the end of the tale, when all three, exhausted from the continuous dissimulation and movement, look for further solutions to the obstacles raised by Mobed, she advises Vīs to remove Mobed altogether and to make Rāmīn the king of the land. Characteristically, she presents her argument with examples, logic, and clear options. Vīs conveys the decision to Rāmīn, and the tale reaches a happy ending for the lovers. Evidently, the nurse's interference in political affairs pales in comparison with her other activities in the

106 *Vīs o Rāmīn*, 72, vv. 1-5.
107 *Vīs o Rāmīn*, 74, v. 30.

amorous terrain, yet it underscores the extent of her control over the lovers. The last turn of the plot demonstrates that her type of persuasive language has an applicability beyond sentimental concerns. Her proximity to various sources of power facilitates communication between those sources for amorous or political reasons. One notion confirmed time and again by the narrative is that at certain times, communication is close to impossible without her: the actual sources of power are curiously bound by their rigid locations, while she, as a mediator, enjoys great facility for movement and for the transmission of ideas from one party to another. It comes as no surprise that the poetics of seduction is synonymous with the poetics of power: *Vīs and Rāmīn* demonstrates the workings of this equation fully.

As a literary character, the go-between in *Vīs and Rāmīn* attains a certain level of complexity which eludes clear identification with any specific ethical standpoint. Never motivated by material greed, she approaches the young lovers with a visible sense of compassion. Her words to Vīs in particular are maternal and full of concern.[108] The tensions in representation result from the fact that the text always follows her with admonishing moral words uttered by the omniscient narrator. When she finally succeeds in making a case for Rāmīn, for example, and alerts Vīs to the possibility of love with him, the narrator labels her a "sorceress" and a member of "the army of the devil." Whereas she makes use of absolutely no magic in arousing the interest of Vīs for the young man, once the girl does agree to a meeting, the narrator declares: "Now the old witch of a wetnurse knew/ That from her bow she had struck on target/ By magic that fair one had been tamed/ The prey had finally fallen into her trap."[109] The poem equates the power of her language with magic and adds a decidedly threatening aspect to her activity with the references to hunting and witchcraft. This judgment recalls the crafty *ʿajūz* of popular tales with the negative connotations of deceit.

---

[108] For instance, after Vīs is married off by force to Mobed, the nurse addresses her thus:

"Your mouth still smells of milk,
Yet your story is in every mouth.
Your two breasts have not yet fully grown
Yet seven countries are filled with your presence.
You are so small, why is your name so great?
You are a gazelle, why does your spouse have to be a wolf?" (*Vīs o Rāmīn*, 69-70, vv. 7-12).

[109] *Vīs o Rāmīn*, 110, vv. 23-24.

Further in the poem, King Mobed makes the most puzzling gesture toward the nurse; in one of his many efforts to keep Vīs away from Rāmīn, he imprisons his wife in a fortress and goes on to hand the keys to the nurse: an odd choice, given how well he knows the nurse's loyalties. He then says:

> O sorceress, mistress of demons,
> I have seen much betrayal from you.
> For once, try to show loyalty.
> I am going away for a few months,
> Keep this building closed for me,
> For I who closed it should be the one to open it.
> I am giving you the keys under your oath,
> For once, respect your oath.
> You know yourself that breaking an oath
> Is not a commendable act.
> I wish to test you this time,
> And be as good to you as you might be to me. (...)
> But I have chosen you because
> I have heard it said that if you give your possessions
> To the burglars to keep,
> You will find them to be very efficient guards.[110]

The passage offers an instance of interaction with the go-between from the point of view of an adversary and permits a new reference point for the evaluation of the character. The adversary believes that the go-between alone has the power to exert genuine influence on the young lovers. He therefore adapts his tactics to recruit her for his struggle, as he has come to understand that without her support he cannot establish any contact with his own wife. He operates on the basis of the belief that the intermediary does not adhere to a single frame of mind and that she can modify her position in accordance with each situation. As a result, his trust for the go-between is fraught with wariness and reluctance, further enhancing the intermediary's complexity as a character in the drama. Mobed's attitude reveals the privileged place of mediation as a vehicle of communication and draws attention to the perception of the go-between as a powerful advocate through whose language otherwise indecipherable codes between two people are translated.

---

[110] *Vīs o Rāmīn*, 205-206, vv. 7-17.

We have devoted special attention to the romance of *Vīs and Rāmīn* since it offers a remarkably detailed and complex depiction of the go-between. The nurse provides continuous education for the two lovers and fully develops many features repeated in subsequent depictions of the go-between. When grouped together and expressed in dialogue form, the wide range of attributes such as compassion, erotic energy, hints of sorcery, and older age create a full-fledged literary character. In Gorgānī's romance, each of these is explored in its own right to create a particular impact: the go-between emerges as a lover, a mother, a close advisor, and even a sorceress, while the sum total creates a vehicle of communication without whom dialogue between others is, at times, impossible.

As mentioned, the poem counter-balances the significance of the nurse with pejorative and disapproving references which, although not overwhelmingly abundant, appear with some frequency throughout. The intrinsic belief that her skill with words connotes sorcery and evil has to do with her status as an older woman, infertile and potentially dangerous due to her primary preoccupation with the language of love at the expense of ethical concerns. These elements inform her characterization in implicit ways, present in the epithets used in her description ("sorceress," "charmer," "manipulator") while her actions promote the well-being of the lovers. This constitutes a sophisticated manifestation of the problem posed earlier, that of a respected art, that is mediation, emerging in an undesirable vehicle, that is, an infertile, unattached woman. *Vīs and Rāmīn* pushes the discomfort and irresolution associated with these contradictions to the forefront. In this romance, in spite of the gaping absence of any background information on the nurse, and in spite of the simple fact that she remains unnamed throughout the poem, the moral contradictions of her functions are afforded some room for interpretative reflection. The nurse's presence underscores the impossibility of unmediated communication to an extraordinary extent; if the transmission of words between two parties can occur almost exclusively through a third party, then it must not come as a surprise that this mediation will take on contradictory connotations depending on the nature of the ideas which are being conveyed. By showing the nurse in an impressively wide range of positions in which she fulfills the role of third party, the text draws attention to the fact that mediation is such a basic staple of dialogue that it assumes the ideological nature of each individual interaction. Thus, when used for adultery, it connotes immorality, but when used for the happiness of lovers, it exudes productivity and fulfillment. Mediation in this romance is an amorphous body that must take on the contours of the task to which it is responding: it is a tool used by everyone and shaped by their needs to fit their ethical postures.

Such flexibility is at once restraining and liberating for the mediator. Within textual poetics, the older woman fufills an actantial role categorized by her ability to mediate, and should as such be immune to moral considerations. But the text's continual references to her in moral terms do not allow this and restrain her by hinting that the art of mediation appears to excel only against the resistance of an ethical stance which observes or reports it. The more complex or difficult the moral issues (in this case, the happiness of lovers who are in fact committing adultery), the more multilayered the art of triangulation: for this reason the nurse of *Vīs and Rāmīn*, inhabiting a world of complicated loyalties and paradoxical moral decisions, is entirely devoid of comic potential, unlike her counterpart, the *ʿajūz* of popular tales. The absence of humor marks the text's shifting and even fragile ethical stances, for the type of humor projected on a female go-between would indicate a degree of confidence in the work vis-à-vis right and wrong, comedy deriving in part from the text's nonchalant recognition of light immorality.

Courtly and learned literature grapples with this connection in subsequent love tales also to a greater degree than in erotological treatises or popular literature; it is fitting to study the mechanisms of this problematic representation in two other prominent cases.

(c) *Matrimony and the Go-Between: The* Seven Princesses

The harem is a promising location for inquiry into ambivalent attitudes toward the go-between. The twelfth-century Persian romance of the *Seven Princesses* by Nizāmī Ganjavī showcases this attitude in a typical story-within-story where the *ʿajūz* acts as an agent between husband and wife.[111] An old woman in the harem has the habit of turning the king's concubines against him; shortly after they arrive,

[111] The narrative poem uses the typical structure of tale-within-a-tale, the frame story being a king's demand that each of his seven wives tell him a tale every night of the week. This particular narrative is presented on the second night by the Greek wife.

she gains their confidence and inspires such indifference and arrogance in them that the king, unaware of her machinations, experiences deep disappointment and frustration with all women.[112] The old woman's scheme is discovered by his most recently acquired concubine whereupon the king throws the crone out of the harem. As it happens, the same concubine has an intense aversion to physical intimacy, while in every other respect she remains an ideal companion to the king. The old woman hears about this aversion and seeks revenge by finding a means to confront the young girl with consummation. She makes her way back to the court with advice for the king on how to secure the girl's consent. The advice (that he should inspire jealousy in the concubine by sleeping with his other wives and thereby arouse her interest in him) leads to successful results for the king and secures the concubine's sexual favors for him.

The initial presentation of the old woman situates her firmly in the realm of women's deceits, given her predilection for trouble and vengeance. Yet the king's reaction to her after she has been expelled invites more speculation on her exact role in his marital life and raises questions on his perception of her. Even after the trouble she has caused, she walks back into the court and gives him advice on a highly intimate matter, one that is closely tied with his masculine identity and his control over the object of desire; still, the king listens to her. The old woman's interaction with the king becomes, simultaneously, a display of her skill with words. When she addresses him, she shapes her discourse in such a way that it promotes his understanding; to teach him how to inspire jealousy, she uses an extended metaphor with a specially familiar resonance for him: "If you wish to tame a wild foal, bring a tame foal to the wild one's presence, place a saddle on its back and ride and caress it in front of the wild foal. This is how the experts tame the unbroken young horses with success."[113]

The power of her words derives from the authority and experience she projects in matters related to sexuality, in addition to the intrinsic belief that, just as much as she has a talent for causing trouble, she possesses a talent for bringing about a successful carnal relationship

---

[112] "There was in that house a hunchbacked old hag/A stupid woman, looking for more stupid victims/ Whenever the king purchased a new slavegirl/ The old woman found profit in flattering her/ She showered the new bride with compliments/And told her she was better than any queen or sweetheart/Once the slavegirl had heard those words/She forgot all notion of duty and obedience" (Nizāmī, 716-717).

[113] Nizāmī, 723.

by making the necessary mediatory arrangements. In a gesture similar to Mobed's bitter acceptance of that authority, the king displays the inherent conviction that the key to communication with young women rests in the hands of the older, experienced intermediary. On the level of praxis, the go-between is ultimately too essential an element in the foundation of his household to be discarded permanently, even if her reputation as troublesome precedes her. On the level of textual poetics, the old woman represents the language of seduction: in the highly elaborate code of love and intimacy, she occupies the space to which one or both lovers must come, from different directions, to face the phenomenon of seduction. Clearly, her suggested method is open to any number of moral objections, especially from the modern reader's point of view. It does not take the concubine's desires into account, nor does it represent a comprehensive or complex view of female sexuality. Be that as it may, she constructs a space in which, according to the text, the king finds himself comfortable and able to communicate with his beloved.

One wrinkle remains. The narrative poem does not clarify the exact way in which the outcome of events gratifies the old woman's desire for revenge, since the consummation is not described as a particularly traumatic event for the concubine. The tale does not pursue the benefits of the ending for the old woman and chooses instead to concentrate on the couple. This recalls a characteristic shift of focus seen in popular and learned sources: once the go-between has completed her task, even if it started due to her personal motivation, attention turns to the resulting situation of the lovers. It must be assumed that an underlying structure in the narrative accounts for the old woman's satisfaction in vengeance: the very fact that her plan has led to success ought to imply that she has attained her goal and that further delving into the ambiguities of this success are not deemed necessary for the focus of narration.

(d) *Feminine Sexuality and the Go-Between:* Yūsuf and Zuleikhā

In the love literature of the medieval period, with the passage of time it appears that the higher the social rank of the characters, the more rigorous the isolation of the female protagonists who occupy luxurious but lonely spaces, where inner struggles and anxieties constitute the principal drive for the character's self-expression. In this context the go-between might fulfill a maternal role, for her relationship with the younger woman often involves nursing during childhood and a lifelong accompaniment that elicits confidences and the revelation of secrets in moments of distress. From this emerges a sense of compassion not encountered in the *ʿajūz* of popular tales whose intentions are often purely mercenary in nature. At the same time, in moments of action, even the court or harem go-between displays the type of knowledge which carries a strong hint of past (and dubious) sexual experience. The social context of narrative romances does not offer clues on the background of the old woman; her presence in the house is either taken for granted, as is the case with *The Seven Princesses*, or explained by way of her capacity as former wet nurse. Either way, the character projects enough sexual know-how and energy of her own to mix her maternal nature with that of an erotic teacher. And, as we have seen, her identity contains an aspect which continues to push her in the tradition of women's deceits, visible in her ready capacity for devising crafty stratagems in cases of distress. This act often inspires the designation of "sorceress" even if the ruse itself reveals no otherworldly traits. Negative presuppositions are discerned at this point in the focalizing voice of the tale that does not seem able to refrain from a disapproving ethical judgment against the nurse, even if her schemes work in aid of the lovers.

In addition to that, the focus on one of the go-between's associations (maternal compassion, clever planning, or sexual know-how) draws attention to a particular thematic aspect of the romance itself. For example, popular tales tend to stress the entertaining ruses of women as a major thematic concern, enhanced by the clever plans of the *ʿajūz*. Or, the more theoretical, decorous approach to politics and love occurs in the careful discourse of the nurse in the ambitious *Vīs and Rāmīn*.

The reflection of broader thematic concerns through the go-between's role is seen amply in a late variation on the tale of Joseph and Potiphar's wife, a story recounted by numerous writers throughout the early and medieval periods of Islam, Judaism, and Christianity.[114] The master-narrative has served many purposes for inter-

[114] As is well known, the tale appears in the Talmud, the Bible, and the Koran. Outside religious sources, the Orientalist Auguste Bricteux counts seventeen Persian variants as well as a dozen Turkish ones, in addition to the Spanish versions, and even a Judeo-Persian text in the Hebrew alphabet. Auguste Bricteux, *Jāmī: Youssouf et Zouleikha*, Les Joyeux de l'Orient, tome V (Paris: Librairie Orientaliste Paul Geuth-

preters, ranging from moralization to the exposition of a particular religious philosophy, yet as the critic James Kugel notes: "for ancient readers of the Joseph story, the adulterous proposal of Potiphar's wife, and Joseph's virtuous refusal to cooperate, came to loom larger and larger in the imagination."[115] Completed in 1509 A.D., the version of *Yūsuf and Zuleikhā* of Abdul-Rahmān Jāmī expands the details of the well-known tale considerably and pays close attention to the central amorous intrigue.[116] In so doing, he adds the character of wet nurse (to Zuleikhā) and dwells at length on the symptoms and effects of unrequited love on the young woman.[117]

In Jāmī's version, prior to her arranged marriage to Potiphar the young woman falls in love with a vision of Yūsuf in her dreams, becoming ill with the intensity of the emotion. The wet nurse enters the scene at this point; she notices Zuleikhā's grief and begs for the revelation of her secret. The presentation of the nurse merges two contrasting attitudes; initially, she is introduced in terms of magical powers:

> Now Zuleikhā had a wetnurse well-versed in magic,
> the long practice of which had given her much experience
> in matters of love,
> and made her skillful as a go-between for lover and beloved,
> and a tamer of the most reluctant objects of desire. [118]

Immediately following this presentation comes a lengthy description of the nurse's feelings for her "daughter," softening the effect of the somewhat pejorative connotation of sorcery. She expresses her feelings skillfully and combines maternal instinct with devoted servitude:

> I am that brook coming from the sea of loyalty which raised you
> I was the first to see your face, I cut your umbilical cord with the knife of love

---

ner, 1927) i-xvii. See also the introductions to Ottokar de Schlechta-Wesseherd's *Jussuf und Suleicha* (Vienna: Druck und verlag von C. Gerold's sohn, 1889) and H. Bacher, *Zwei Jüdisch-Persische Dichter* (Strasbourg: K. J. Trubner, 1907). More recently, James L. Kugel in *In Potiphar's House: The Interpretive Life of Biblical Texts* (Cambridge: Harvard University Press, 1990) provides a detailed analytical look into the many early accounts of the story.

[115] Kugel, *In Potiphar's House*, 22.

[116] Abdul-Rahmān Jāmī, *Yūsuf va Zuleikhā* (Teheran: Amīr Kabīr, 1961).

[117] Kugel notes that the name Zuleikhā is not from early Jewish sources nor does it appear in the Koran: "It is apparently of Persian origin and was popularized by post-Qur'anic Muslim writers" (*In Potiphar's House*, 61, n. 7).

[118] Jāmī, *Yūsuf*, 43.

> (...) I offered my milk to your sweet lips and nourished your body with vitality
> (...) Later, where you went, I followed you like a shadow
> (...) and now too I am your servant, as devoted as ever. [119]

Throughout the romance the poem stresses her role as mother in the words of the younger and the older women, given that with the exception of actual birth the nurse has fulfilled every duty of a mother for Zuleikhā. On the one hand this reveals trust and compassion on both sides, yet on the other it connotes a negative undercurrent for two reasons: the mother is also traditionally identified with ruses and clandestine amorous advice, and the very identity of a nurse points to infertility. The convergence of these implications keeps the nurse confined in a space vulnerable to moral reproach on the part of the text.

Jāmī renders this traditional stance more complex by endowing his go-between with a markedly acute sensitivity to erotic appeal: the old woman's discourse abounds in lavish praise of Zuleikhā's feminine perfection, and once she discovers the young woman's love for Yūsuf, she produces rapid suggestions for luring him through overt physical messages:

> Attract him by showing your heavenly face
> Then sit with him alone such that your knee touches his
> (...) let out the laughter from your honeyed lips, so that he will approach you
> Enhance the whiteness of your skin with black silk, which will burn him with desire.[120]

She places Zuleikhā's sexual potential at the core of her argument, and her final extravagant method reveals her deep trust in the power of sensuality.[121] This attitude reveals a maternal pride in Zuleikhā's beauty: her allegiance to the young woman is expressed in terms of the appreciation of physical perfection, and her methods for seduction revolve solely around her conviction that feminine beauty will

[119] Jāmī, *Yūsuf*, 43.

[120] Jāmī, *Yūsuf*, 125. Much of the dialogue between Zuleikhā and the nurse revolves around the latter's detailed portrayal of the young woman's physical sensuality, in the shape of advice on how she should employ each part of her body towards the seduction of Yūsuf.

[121] Causing much work and expense, she has Zuleikhā build a palace decorated with images of her and Yūsuf in intimate embrace, confident that the contemplation of these drawings will weaken the young man's will.

overcome any type of resistance. In light of her utter trust in Zuleikhā's physical perfection, it is no surprise that the nurse refers continually to the body and the power of sexuality. Similar to Zuleikhā herself, the nurse nurtures an obsession with carnal love which conceives of the ideal male-female dynamic as a physical relationship. Mediation, for her, takes inevitable success as its point of departure, determined by absolute faith in the imperative of sexuality. The text accounts for this faith in several ways, the most important of which is the fact that Zuleikhā loses her heart to the young man purely as a result of the latter's remarkable beauty, and in defiance of verbal interactions with him which leave her no hope for the fulfillment of desire.

The overwhelming carnality thus celebrated by the text, and visible in the acts and discourse of the two women, sets up a strong contrast with Yūsuf's deferential restraint, even though his beauty plays a crucial role in determining the direction of his fate. The intermediary identifies strictly with a posited feminine point of view, intensifying the perception of his beauty by underscoring his virtue (she fails to connect with him as an interlocutor, reconfirming his reluctance to be integrated into the carnal universe of the women). The failure to engage Yūsuf in dialogue, it must be noted, does not highlight her weakness but rather Yūsuf's extraordinary control which surpasses the human norm, as the poem makes clear. Yūsuf's exceptional control recurs in every rendition of the tale, and has become "the one particular virtue that [he] came frequently to be connected with."[122] The failure never diminishes the impression given to the reader of Zuleikhā's beauty or the nurse's skills in seduction; on the contrary, both attributes are viewed as compellingly powerful, thereby provoking even more admiration for Yūsuf, who faces them as a difficult trial.

The go-between in this tale shows a concern for physicality which surpasses that of counterparts studied so far: she is perfectly integrated into a conceptual system in which the body governs motive and poetics; in this respect, she represents an ally of the text, which also celebrates virtue, love, and desire in terms of physical beauty. She also

---

[122] Kugel, *In Potiphar's House*, 21. As the author also mentions, this is noted by L. Ginzberg in *Legends of the Jews*, volume 5 (Philadelphia: Jewish Publication Society, 1925): "There can be no doubt that this title ["Yūsuf ha-Saddiq:" Joseph the Righteous"] was conferred on Joseph on account of his virtuous victory over the wiles of his master's wife" (325).

advances the dynamic feminine trait which the tale has chosen to elaborate and set up against the fortitude of Yūsuf. The poem, much like a trainer aware of the opponent's dazzling strength, propels the nurse and Zuleikhā into battle with Yūsuf, all too aware that the battle is already lost. The narrative, then, betrays the decided mark of an unhappy love story, not one of moralism or religious ideology. Every detail and plot twist serves to push the tale further in the direction of an amorous adventure, sustaining the faith in beauty and desire. Significantly, for example, a vivid portrait of an ever passionate Zuleikhā shows her to differ greatly from the traditional wanton wife:

> Such was Zuleikhā, who dedicated her whole life to love,
> As a young child, she played with her dolls and was filled with love for them,
> She was not interested in any game that did not embrace love.
> If she sat face to face with her dolls
> She named one "lover" and the other "beloved." [123]

In spite of the evidently physical nature of her passion, the narrative adds enough detail to her portrayal to depict her as a woman genuinely smitten with Yūsuf, with an otherwise innocent track record. Furthermore, her desire almost justifies itself in light of the unusual beauty of Yūsuf; Kugel notes that many early rabbinical sources even go as far as to hint that Joseph was quite aware of the power of his own beauty, indulging at times in "dandy-like" behavior at Potiphar's house.[124] Added to the fact that Zuleikhā's relations with her own husband never betray an impression of tenderness or understanding, the question of guilt regarding Potiphar's wife becomes ever more slippery. Her moral guilt is of course emphasized in their first encounters, but diminished in light of these attenuating circumstances. Yūsuf turns out, paradoxically, to portray the antagonist as well as the hero, for he refuses to yield to the laws of the text's amorous poetics. This is resolved when after many years Yūsuf and Zuleikhā finally marry and live to have a family together. As James Kugel observes, the relationship between Joseph and Potiphar's wife is the element most repeated in all versions of the tale.

---

[123] Jāmī, *Yūsuf,* 198.

[124] Kugel, 96. The chapter of his study entitled "Joseph's Beauty" demonstrates how some rabbinical versions portray Joseph as a young man whose innocent purity is open to question.

How do these elements affect the conception of the go-between? If anything, Jāmī's *Yūsuf and Zuleikhā* hails the nurse as a character who tries, genuinely and earnestly, to perform a necessary task and to facilitate the celebration of love and beauty as best she can. The questions of wrongdoing, moral flaw, and even the initial hints at sorcery lose all momentum when it is understood that the poem itself is, implicitly, on the side of the nurse, and in awe of Yūsuf's resistance. With Jāmī's poem, the power of desire is finally articulated with such strength that the previous paradoxes between morality and sensuality come close to a resolution. In his poem, he places the utmost representation of virtue in battle against the natural force of desire, subtly showing that the questions of fault and guilt cannot apply in a universe governed by the human being's desire to be close to beauty. In this context he unravels mediation as a necessary and lively force that assists the expression of desire and undoes as much as he can the negative associations of the task. He posits that in the battle between desire and morality, even if the former is vanquished, it has had every right to carry itself as it chose to, for it is a natural and uncontrollable force. The great stress placed by the nurse and Zuleikhā on physical matters comes to represent the feminine (and natural) point of view in the tale, and the intermediary's advice conforms to a legitimized preoccupation with the fulfillment of desire. This represents an innovation in the conception of the go-between, for it takes into account the fact that within the poetics of desire, the third party must shed moral weights and proceed in the natural direction of fulfillment.

Additionally, the poem belongs to the genre of romantic narratives in which an older companion to the young heroine always takes on the task of giving advice or surmounting the obstacles of segregation. In fact, hardly any love tale of the medieval Islamic period develops the plot without mention of a nurse, an old woman or a mother who gives help at some point in the love affair. These older women might offer graphic advice on sexual matters or, on some level, facilitate planning for a particularly difficult encounter.[125] The important con-

---

[125] Examples of this are simply too numerous to mention; it suffices to name a few sources where the figure appears extensively although by no means as a principal character: the fifteenth-century *Abu-Muslim Nama*, by Abu-Tālib 'ibn 'Alī 'ibn Hossein Tartūssī, an episodic tale of adventures in which an old aunt arranges for the reunion of a young man and his beloved; the ancient Sanskrit tale of "Padmavat"

tribution of Zuleikhā's nurse to this common paradigm consists of Jāmī's sensitivity to the fact that where desire governs a text's poetic makeup, morality becomes at best a peripheral issue in the perception of the third party's role.

But the text also assumes, *ab ovo*, that Yūsuf will not relent to sensual charms except on his own terms and much later in life. This assumption heralds the failure of the go-between's task from the outset: she thus inhabits the poem not as a facilitator, but rather as a cataloguer of methods of seduction. The predestined failure of her methods diverts attention away from the outcome of her plans, and encourages focus on the nature of her role in the obviously flawed seductive project. Yūsuf's superhuman power of resistance confirms the intricate bond which ties the go-between's strategies to the disposition of the interlocutor, underscoring the fundamentally dialogic nature of her interaction with others. The artifice of seduction has no meaning – indeed, cannot exist – when set up before an adversary untouched by desire. To lay any moral blame on the intermediary, then, is to ignore the extent to which mediation derives its strength from the consent (or, at least, the friction) afforded by the so-called "victim" of seduction. Jāmī's *Yūsuf and Zuleikhā* brings about a reconfiguration of the triangle pursuer/pursued/go-between by separating the pursued from the realm of profane love altogether, thereby depriving the mediator of the most basic premise on which she might operate. Her failure is the obvious result of the damaged structure of the triangular setup in which she finds herself from the start, in light of Yūsuf's remarkable alienation from the province of seductive discourse. Jāmī's contribution to the topic of mediation consists of his sensitivity to the irresolvable clash brought about by the encounter of a moral (here, religious) stance and one rooted in the world of desire and profane love. In the poetic register, the go-between enjoys every asset available to mediation, from a dazzlingly beautiful pursuer to a rich background of loyalty, concern, and compassion for the pursuer's objective. Technically, this arrangement must not lead to failure, for that would defy the intrinsic logic which dictates that armed

put into poetic form by Malik Mohammad Jaessi in 1540, where an escaped parrot describes the beauty of its former mistress to the new owner, causing the latter to fall in love, and then goes on to act as intermediary for the two; similarly in the eleventh-century epic of Firdawsī, entitled the *Book of Kings*, several of the love stories make use of the older female intermediary.

with such advantages, seduction will occur. By revealing the mechanisms of this seduction and then chronicling its failure brought about by superhuman factors, Jāmī highlights the fundamentally unsatisfactory results of the blend of two registers hailing from the moral and the poetic universe. Yūsuf's wedding to Zuleikhā at the end of the tale serves as a rather explicit compensation for the earlier failure of poetics: the defeat of the seductive scheme makes little sense from a poetic point of view and is justified only by the divine intervention that renders Yūsuf so resistant to desire.

Mediation's moral failure, so often emphasized by writers especially in the "women's deceits" tradition, is presented by Jāmī as a flawed concept. *Yūsuf and Zuleikhā* might be read as the deliberate exaggeration of a scenario in which the extra-poetic factor – that is, the moral imperative (chastity, resistance to women) – overrides the otherwise well-designed and logical poetic structure, thereby uncovering the incongruity of imposing ethical parameters on a poetic structure. A credible, narratological armature that would explain the nurse's failure is blatantly missing from *Yūsuf and Zuleikhā:* Yūsuf's holiness (unaccounted-for in poetic terms) has the power to annul the well-invested energy of mediation, leaving an unsatisfactory and unexplained textual gap in the tale. In this regard, Jāmī's poem serves as a compelling articulation of the misguided application of ethical concerns to mediation: by detailing the plans for a successful mediation and then allowing them to fail, Jāmī's poem enacts the persistent blindness which commands the construction of mediation in literature, as though encouraging the reader not to pose excessive questions about its outcome, for it is immoral and therefore must fail. In this enaction however, the poem affords the reader enough clues to its own inconsistencies, thereby calling attention to the fact that the literary representation of mediation is unduly stifled by extra-literary moral concerns. The poem thus indicates the existence of a fundamental problem: that of resistance to the expression of the go-between's multi-layered presence in the text and the recourse to moral judgment as an inadequate explanatory framework for her failures.

V. A Necessary Counterpoint for Literature: The *Bahr al-Favā'id* and the Question of Right and Wrong

The simultaneous acknowledgment of the go-between's entertaining, skillful, and morally reprehensible presence is a part and parcel of the Persian and Arabic love tales and treatises studied here. To a certain degree the moral suppositions found in literary texts hail from attitudes found in other genres, to which it is fitting to turn our attention for a broader appreciation of the question of the go-between's identity. One of the most fruitful areas for the broadening of the scope is homiletic material of an explicitly Islamic nature, a valuable example of which is the anonymous twelfth-century Persian compilation known as the *Bahr al-Favā'id*. The text's editor and translator, Julie Meisami, explains that this compendium of didactic instruction and inspirational anecdotes represents the views of

> the pious, orthodox class, possessing a religious rather than a secular education, and putting the values enjoined by the Sharī'ah and its sources above humanistic or philosophical considerations. It is thus of interest not only for what it conveys of medieval ethical and political thought, popular religious lore and folk wisdom, but also (...) for the insights it provides into attitudes that have changed little in the centuries since it was written[.][126]

Some of the sources for this collection may be identified, as Meisami specifies in her introduction to the text. The work is unequivocally Islamic in tone and content, and in addition to its known sources (mainly other didactic compendia) it derives material from

> innumerable collections of Hadīth, *fiqh*, manuals dealing with rituals such as prayer, fasting, and pilgrimage, and many other works of this sort that, since the material they treat is so general and their manner of treatment so standardized, would be difficult if not impossible to identify.[127]

Not only does this fact attest to the work's general agreement with a broad religious, orthodox current of thought and therefore justify its

---

[126] *The Sea of Precious Virtues: Bahr al-Favā'id, a Medieval Islamic Mirror for Princes*, translated by Julie Scott Meisami (Salt Lake City: The University of Utah Press, 1991) xiv (henceforth "Meisami").

[127] Meisami, xvi.

selection as a counterpoint to literature, but also – and rather incidentally – it confirms once again the wealth of Islamic anthologized materials which are a genre in and of themselves and have no genuine counterpart in the medieval European tradition.

As with so many Islamic treatises, the *Bahr al-Favā'id* mingles anecdotes and examples with discursive passages in which various right and wrong life choices are discussed. The text addresses, among many other topics, the issue of family life, the upbringing of children, the correct behavior of kings, etiquette, pilgrimage, the law and piety, to name but a few topics. With a confident tone regarding right and wrong, the text places people and phenomena inside structures which evaluate these as desirable or undesirable.

The *Bahr al-Favā'id* presents a series of judgments on certain attributes, people, and activities which, while they do not touch directly on the go-between, are reminiscent of her characteristics in markedly obvious ways. In other words, in certain sections, the compendium brings up issues for which anxiety, disapproval, and repression are deemed necessary as responses; interestingly enough, these issues impinge considerably on mediation and third-party activity as well.

The *Bahr al-Favā'id* dismisses medicine as a viable manner of tackling one's problems. In the section devoted to the "Conduct of Kings," the compilation lists seven evils from which a father must protect his son, the first of which concerns frequenting "astrologers, poets, and physicians."[128] Physicians, according to the text, do not take the Law (Sharī'ah) into account and allow doubt to enter the heart. Consequently, in a section dedicated to the "Lawful and the Unlawful," the text forbids the reading of medical texts by Avicenna and Rāzī, referring to the physicians as an infidel and a heretic, respectively. The dismissal of the physicians clearly implies a lack of interest in their therapeutic methods, including that of lovesickness, in which for Avicenna, the old woman played a significant role.

The compendium mentions wet nurses and nurses on several occasions, setting up an ideal image of the figure and emphasizing the extent to which nurses determine the fate of the children whose care they undertake. The text's construction of an ideal nurse acts upon the image of the nurse in literature, for it takes into account the influence exerted by her as well as the privileged space of contact

---

[128] Meisami, 80.

which she enjoys with the child (and later, adult) in her care. In the section on the conduct of kings, the proper education of children is addressed, the first condition of which consists of the child's suckling by a pious woman (not a Christian or a loose woman), for the child's nature will be determined by the way of his nourishment. The Prophet is quoted here as saying that "wet-nursing alters natures,"[129] and these assertions throw new light on the image of the wet nurse in *Yūsuf and Zuleikhā* as well as in *Vīs and Rāmīn*, for they show that within this orthodox and religious way of thinking, the nurse is responsible for the most basic inclinations of those in her care. She is, therefore, a powerful agent whose influence must not be underestimated.

The *Bahr al-Favā'id* makes a number of decisions on the question of literature and poetry, all of which throw light on the clash of moral and poetic registers in the literary texts studied above. In a section devoted to the etiquette of Islam, it is declared that children must not read poetry and any verses that speak of love or describe women. The point that young people attain refinement through the study of such poetry is discarded as incorrect.[130] In the chapter on the conduct of kings, the fifth evil from which children must be protected concerns reading Persian books which have no relation to the Law: the author names *Vīs and Rāmīn* and several other epics and love tales as undesirable books, for they present indecency and unbelief.[131] The anxiety towards love tales gains further meaning in light of the many other concepts which adorn the text's moral armor: not only does the question of wetnursing impinge upon the preoccupation with love tales (in which wet nurses play important roles) but also, imaginative literature's conviction of love as an illness worthy of discussion supports the theoretical works of physicians deemed dangerous by the compendium.

A web of dread and disapproval thus envelopes readings of medicine, love literature, and on the practical side, suckling by unpious women. These three concerns touch directly on the topic of mediation which engages them at some point; the *Bahr al-Favā'id* makes references to a series of other factors which further target intermediary activity as dangerous: the first of these factors, predictably, is women.

---

[129] Meisami, 81. The importance of suckling by pious women reappears in the section on the "Etiquette of Islam," 154.

[130] Meisami, 154-155.

[131] Meisami, 80.

The text touches many times on the issue of women's fickle nature, their vulnerability to Satan, the dangers associated with leaving children in their exclusive care, and questions of the sort seen in any body of work which deals with women's deceit. Of specific importance is the compendium's concern with power and language, two phenomena which, when in the possession of women, lead to disastrous results. Thus the section on the "Conduct of Kings" concludes after an exemplary anecdote that "he who gives women power and command must pay dearly for it, and does a great wrong."[132] This assertion ties in with the many references to the potentially destructive effect of language: the section on the "Character of the Pious" specifies that hypocrites are best recognized through their manipulative use of language – for example, their false oaths (it will be recalled that this constitutes one of the basic traits of the *ʿajūz* of popular Arab tales).[133] That women are specially predisposed to wrongful exploitation of language is underscored in a section entitled "Stories of Pious Men," in which a pious woman who has to her own knowledge never sinned, is reminded in a violent and aggressive manner that she has indeed sinned, for "'you are ungrateful; you speak rudely to your husband; you disturb your neighbor, and gossip about people.'"[134] Language, then, is a dangerous tool which in the mouths of women in particular leads to corruption: so far, we have seen how many provinces of mediation, such as the literature in which it portrayed, medicine, language, nursing, and womanhood are held up by the didactic work as corrupt.

As regards old women, the work does not address their evil potential. In a chapter on "Exchanging Greetings," the author says that while one must take every care to greet one's fellow Muslims as politely and sincerely as possible, one must not greet women. The implication here is twofold: women are not worthy of greeting, but more importantly, greeting women may lead to immoral complications. The text then specifies, very briefly and parenthetically, that one can greet a woman if she is old; no reasons are given.[135] The subtext to this exception is of great importance for our study of the *ʿajūz:* by sanctioning this type of brief communication with an old woman, the author exiles her from the realm of femininity and sexuality, for she

---

[132] Meisami, 78.
[133] Meisami, 59.
[134] Meisami, 73.
[135] Meisami, 90.

presents no possibility of temptation. Set against the abundance of crafty and sly old women in literature, this implicit assertion by the text fulfills the function of a cursory denial of the old woman's powers: it establishes, in one short sentence, its firm reluctance to acknowledge the old woman as a source of power or temptation. This denial mirrors the literary representation of the *ʿajūz* insofar as it posits the refusal to elaborate on the reasons for treating the old woman in this particular way, suggesting that the reasons are clear enough for every reader to see in an existing body of presuppositions.

The territories occupied by the mediator are thus marked as dangerous and unlawful. Such a stance is complicated by the work's explicit recognition of lust and desire as forces which exist in man, and which cannot be eliminated. That is to say, the *Bahr al-Favā'id* consents to the reality of physical desire with which every man lives, and offers certain strategies to divert this force from that which it considers the wrong direction. Contradictions arise immediately, when the text makes assertions such as "[it is] lawful for women [to] increase their beauty, for women are objects of adornment and beauty," (when discussing the issue of physical ornamentation) or the specification that one of the attributes of the ideal wife is her physical beauty, so that she may inspire love and affection.[136] One short chapter discusses the "Etiquette of Intercourse with Women," stating the importance of mutual pleasure.[137] A section on singing and music approves of singing as long as (among other restrictions) it is not carried out by women, for they are objects of lust.[138] Even in the section on "The Cure for Carnal Desire," while the author suggests remedies for eliminating lust, his language remains quite clear on the existence of the phenomenon and the many areas in which it arises in man.[139] The text's denunciation of specific topics such as medicine, love literature, bad wetnursing, women, goes hand-in-hand with its characteristically Islamic recognition of sexual desire as a fact of life which must be addressed in one way or another. Its oscillation between offering advice on how best to enjoy sexual intercourse within a lawful (religious frame) and how to avoid carnal desire altogether throws light, to some extent, on the literary representation of

[136] Meisami, 144, 162.
[137] Meisami, 164.
[138] Meisami, 171.
[139] Meisami, 188.

mediation which is an activity intensely centered upon carnal union. In both genres, explicit areas such as women's deceits, medicine, social roles, are represented to expand the discursive field: in literature, these help the plot and the themes to move forward and take shape; in the didactic work, they act as zones of danger to be avoided or reprehended. Underlying both genres is an obvious perception of carnal desire as a basic fact of life: while literature uses explicit figures such as medicine, lovesickness, and women's deceits to create an ever-shifting and complex space for mediation, thereby attempting to negotiate the questions of seduction, poetics, and dialogue, the didactic text attempts to empty the space of mediation (by condemning women, language, nursing, medicine) of every possible element, in order to put an end to the possibility of encounters between the sexes. Both genres come to this in-between space of mediation where the encounter between man and woman is made possible with the intention to explore the power of a series of specific tropes, which they do to greatly varying degrees; neither is able to walk away from it having resolved the struggle between morality and poetic creativity, though. At least the *Bahr al-Favā'id* shows us the areas in which anxiety is created for a didactic genre, vis-à-vis the facilitation of carnal dialogue.

VI. Conclusion

We have seen that Near-Eastern medieval genres dealing with profane love designate a space for mediation that covers a wide range of functions and figures. The works studied above have been selected for the special attention they lend to some or all of these elements and for the detail with which they have portrayed the figure. As our analysis shows, the literary writings on carnal love often stress one of the many traits of the old woman in order to emphasize a certain thematic aspect such as women's deceits or the feminine preoccupation with sensuality. At the same time, any mention of the go-between's own motivations indicates a desire to compensate for old age and lack of sexual productivity by encouraging sexual contact between others, always suggesting a deep love of intrigue. However, rarely do the works offer a glimpse of the old woman's interior world except in the context of her function within the community. The reader comes to know of this function in terms of the perceptions of the narrator or the surrounding characters: words such as "sly," "crafty," and "sorceress," frequently inserted by the narrators, recall the weight of the extra-textual presuppositions, hailing from the didactic world, attached to the old woman's identity, even if at odds with her actual impact on the tale. Furthermore, the old woman is seldom named, and across the texts the terms *ʿajūz* or "nurse" and their synonyms conjure up a set of expected characteristics.

The predictable elements associated with her cohabit somewhat uncomfortably with her role in the construction of a poetics of love and seduction. Translated into words or ruses (or both), this role reflects the privileged space given in politics to the "Officer of the Inbetween," yet finds itself undermined in light of the senses of suspicion, mistrust, or at best comic amusement, which permeate the texts in which she appears. The unrelenting nature of these presuppositions, even as features in the background, endows the figure at times with the static qualities of a stock character. This association impedes the full evolution of the go-between into a central literary character.

Once the reader becomes familiar with the configurations of the court, the marketplace, or the harem, he or she comes to expect the insertion – at some point – of a crafty old woman whose advice or ruses will cause a major transition to occur in the love affair. In this regard, the texts present her as a motif rather than a dynamic character. The aim in the study of the texts above has consisted of showing the hidden layers underneath this seemingly predictable motif. Our study of courtly literature in particular has shown how the go-between reflects and highlights, in each tale, a particular thematic concern of that story by conceiving of the discourse of seduction and desire in terms of the text's own thematic direction. For example, a deep concern with feminine sensuality in *Yūsuf and Zuleikhā*, a close involvement with the role of king as spouse and sexual being in *The Seven Princesses*, and a strong inclination for amusement and wit in the erotological treatises. In each one of these genres and texts, the old(er) woman is meticulously attuned to the work's thematic concerns, yet will only allow a close observation of this fact once the veil of her stock features and predictable traits has been cast aside. The go-between's contribution to the discourse and poetics of love of each text is, ultimately, her most significant trait in the Near-Eastern tradition.

A final point that warrants attention has to do with the special place of the nurse in *Vīs and Rāmīn* for the typology and literary history of the figure. All the works considered above have been chosen due to significant references made to the figure of the third party: it is clear that the romance by Gorgānī designates the most comprehensive and multi-layered space to the character. In light of its relatively early date of composition, its influential status as a literary work, and its clear intertextual links with pre-Islamic sources, the romance inspires the question of why subsequent portrayals of the go-between do not occupy a similar scope in love tales. The answer to this question is of great relevance for the critical evaluation of the go-between.

The nurse of *Vīs and Rāmīn* touches not just the world of love but also that of politics. She infiltrates those spheres that, for a person of her rank, would instantly suggest dangerous ambition and a desire for power well beyond any acceptable range for a woman of lower rank. While the nurse never exploits any gains in her own personal favor, the potential threat of her access to the highest level of sovereignty lurks in the background at all times. Her characterization reveals the ease with which her talent for the construction of a poetics of love is equally applicable to the domain of politics, at least insofar as literary representation is concerned. That subsequent texts do not pick up fully on this multiple applicability is indicative of the inherently disturbing implications of such a talent and of an implicit reluctance to experiment with the go-between's influence on the several registers of the text. The literary traditions of medieval Spain provide a useful frame of reference for the study of the go-between's impact on the text, and to these we turn our attention in the next chapter.

CHAPTER FOUR

THE MEDIEVAL SPANISH *ALCAHUETA*

I. Preliminary Observations: A Reassessment of Near-Eastern and European Go-Betweens

The study of medieval European and Near-Eastern intermediaries reveals a basic polarity in the conceptions of the character in each tradition. This contrast becomes visible above all in the type of discourse used for the purpose of mediation. In the Western tradition, the go-between's discourse is subordinated to her input in matters of a logistical nature. When developed, as with the Vieille of *Le Roman de la Rose* for instance, discourse deals with matters peripheral to the seductive component of mediation, such as financial motivation or a cynical attitude to old age. Mediation *per se* therefore does not guide the direction of the discourse; rather the third party's utterances offer a glimpse of a different, more weary perspective on carnal love and find themselves ultimately overshadowed by the attitudes of the main characters. To a certain degree, this indicates a continuation of the models proposed by Antiquity. In cases where old age and money do not form the basis of the intermediary's discourse (Pandarus in *Troilus and Crisseyde* for example), the character focuses attention on the sentiment of allegiance to one of the parties involved in the affair to divert emphasis from the mercenary connotations of mediation. In this manner, the dissimulation of true purposes becomes a crucial task of the intermediary in dealings with the other parties.

A similar pattern emerges in the approach of the talkative go-betweens of Latin comedy or the *fabliaux* who operate only along the lines of a central lie to one party. They mediate via misleading, ignoring the challenges of seductive mediation in favor of the faster and more profitable strategy of lying. Moreover, the task is almost invariably facilitated by an intrinsic favorable disposition in the female or duped party. The figure of the go-between in Antiquity and medieval European letters thus stands on the periphery of seduction in the "art of love," and provides instead a secondary task often determined by one of the principal characters or required at a specific instance for practical purposes.

The go-between as portrayed in medieval Islamic literature emerges as a figure completely integrated within the amorous system constructed by the lovers. The nature of her interaction with the principal characters reveals the extent to which third-party assistance accompanies amorous involvement as an indispensable factor. The intermediary possesses a discourse of mediation guided by different types of impulse: the need to preserve a central ruse or to contribute to the art of seduction by way of dialogue and argument. Curiously, all the texts we have studied show some resistance to the development of the *ʿajūz* into a full-fledged literary character. In the overwhelming majority of texts she remains unnamed, referred to as nurse, *ʿajūz*, or any term synonymous with "old woman," indicating the stress, albeit misplaced, on the essential predictability of her role, and the texts' compulsion to project a predetermined meaning for whichever signifier is used to denote her. The ambivalence which runs through her representation renders her more complex and vivid than her European counterparts. The ambiguities, especially regarding her oscillation between good and evil activities, receive some attention at times, remaining out of focus at others, as though the text wished to discourage their subjection to a depth of scrutiny. Both the veiling and the unveiling of the ambiguities constitutes Islamic literature's sensitivity to the shifting ground on which the figure stands, indicating the focalization which begins to thematize the ambivalences in each case. The Persian and Arabic works studied throw some light on the conflicting dynamics at work in her portrayal. Medieval Spanish literature articulates the ambiguity inherent in the go-between as a topic in and of itself and provides a critical framework for the evaluation and understanding of the figure as a full-fledged literary character.

II. The Special Case of the Medieval Spanish Go-Between

In the works of Juan Ruiz and Fernando de Rojas, the *alcahueta* emerges as a principal player with substantial influence on the thematic and structural configurations of the text. Trotaconventos and Celestina, the two bawds portrayed so vividly by the fourteenth-century Ruiz and the late fifteenth-century Rojas, respectively, expand the limits of significance for the *alcahueta* in literature partly because they derive inspiration from a remarkable range of literary and extra-literary traditions.

The characters of Trotaconventos and Celestina forge the image of the bawd. But the wealth of examples of *alcahuetería* available in legal, didactic, and literary works prior to the fourteenth-century *Libro de buen amor* reveals the awareness of Eastern as well as Western parameters for the characterization of the figure, given not only the sensitivity to scholastic and Christian frameworks, but also the widely circulating sources from the East such as the *Disciplina clericalis*, *Calila y Digna*, and the *Libro de los engannos y assayamientos de las mujeres* as well as the condemnations of the figure in Alfonso X's *Cantigas* or Pedro Pascual's didactic writings.[1]

Documents available from the time of Alfonso X through to the fifteenth century help us trace the evolution of prostitution and therefore *alcahuetería* in Spain.[2] In such documents, revelations of the bawd's strategies go hand in hand with an unequivocal moral lament. Of particular importance for the conveyance of attitudes and anxieties is the role of legislation that made every effort to restrict or punish mercenary sexual activity, as observed for example in the *Fuero Juzgo*. Alfonsine laws categorized the *alcahueta*'s types of activity in detail, warning of her presence in every walk of life and giving concrete examples of how she might go about her business; subsequently the annals of the Inquisition offered the names and specific deeds of accused go-betweens, chronicling such women's methodology within the framework of legal punishment.[3]

---

[1] *Orígenes y sociología*, 76-87. See also Francisco Sánchez Castañer, "Antecedentes celestinescos en las Cantigas de Santa María," *Mediterráneo, Guión de literatura* 1, 4 (1943) 33-90; Jules Piccus, "Consejos y consejeros en el *Libro del cauallero Zifar*," *Nueva Revista de Filología Hispánica* 16 (1962) 16-30. For the background to Eastern tales in Spain, see Marsan's *Itinéraire espagnol du conte médiéval*. Marsan lists the tales which deal with the topic of old women in the body of the prose narrative, including examples from *El conde Lucanor* and *El libro de los exenplos* (527-540).

[2] María Eugenia Lacarra, "La evolución de la prostitución en la Castilla del siglo XV y la mancebía de Salamanca en tiempos de Fernando de Rojas," in *Fernando de Rojas and* Celestina: *Approaching the Fifth Centenary*, edited by Ivy A. Corfis and Joseph T. Snow (Madison: Hispanic Seminary of Medieval Studies, 1993) 33-78. For a comprehensive bibliography on *La Celestina* see Joseph T. Snow, La Celestina *by Fernando de Rojas: an Annotated Bibliography of World Interest 1930-1985* (Madison: Hispanic Seminary of Medieval Studies, 1985). See also, by Joseph T. Snow, La Celestina *by Fernando de Rojas: an Annotated Bibliography of World Interest 1899-1999* (forthcoming).

[3] *Orígenes y sociología*, 115-137. Lacarra also cites a number of passages from the *Partidas* confirming the prevalence of proxenetism and mercenary sexual activity, lamented by Alfonso X as a grave sin and a serious crime (34 and further). The annals of the Inquisition provide a detailed look at the type of procuring carried out by women accused of sorcery, as shown by Julio Caro Baroja, *Vidas mágicas e Inquisi-*

Legal texts also illustrated the difficulty in eradicating the problems of prostitution and *alcahuetería*, showing their preoccupation with the many benefits delivered to various parties, namely relatives of prostituted women or corrupted officials. The *Fuero Juzgo* highlighted the corrupting power of those who acted as agents in mercenary situations and emphasized the temptation which they provided for law enforcers or judges to reap some benefit from prostitution.[4] The law made use of considerable detail in depicting the go-between to bring home a series of dangers and negative connotations.

In Spain, like other European countries, the prevalent view of the go-between branded her a criminal. Invariably, she conjured up the world of prostitution and sorcery. The latter implied interference in amorous affairs as well as other problems, and sorcerers found themselves accused of "doing or undoing things, making people fall in love, curing or killing people, attracting men for erotic purposes, summoning wolves to devour children, and other bizarre things."[5] With the advent and evolution of the Inquisition, the links between sorcery and love magic became solidified in the minds of legal and religious authorities, such that "[i]nquisitorial proceedings clearly distinguished [a] group of women as involved in magical practices, with the primary goal being seduction and conquest of a suitor."[6] Julio Caro Baroja's important study of the Inquisition highlights trial records in which a third party's interference in erotic matters always appeared to include some degree of witchcraft. The scholar Sánchez Ortega has brought together numerous examples of the practices

---

ción (Madrid: Taurus, 1967). Baroja chronicles the evidence available on the trials of "hechiceras" (sorceresses) to establish a typology (volume II, 11). This evidence, which is drawn from the meticulous records of the Inquisition, offers considerable detail regarding the sociological context, the immediate circumstances, and the everyday interactions of Toledan and Manchegan women with so-called witches. Caro Baroja notes that in the urban milieu *alcahuetería* became a prevalent phenomenon and was identified with witchcraft in general. Toledo offered a fertile ground for this kind of activity, according to the number of accusations brought against "hechiceras" from that city. The exact categorization of the *alcahueta*'s types of activity is also mentioned by Lacarra (34-36).

[4] Lacarra notes that the corruption of officials and judges, who drew an income from prostibulary activity imposed on women, was a serious problem (34).

[5] Anwar Chejne, *Islam and the West: the Moriscos, a cultural and social history* (Albany: State University of New York Press, 1983) 131.

[6] María Helena Sánchez Ortega, "Sorcery and Eroticism in Love Magic," in *Cultural Encounters: The Impact of the Inquisition in Spain and the New World*, ed. Anne J. Cruz and Mary Elizabeth Perry (Los Angeles: University of California Press, 1991) 58-93 (58-59).

and incantations used for the purposes of seduction, stressing that from the law's standpoint "love magic meant also extramarital magic, one in which erotic relations always carried a sinful, condemnable connotation[.]"[7] The immoral associations were aggravated by the non-Christian aura of some of the incantations used in love magic, so that the practice became increasingly identified with non-Christian, heterodox, and Satanic rituals.[8]

Non-literary sources indicate that the medieval Spanish go-between constituted a high profile presence in society, her connections taking her from the clergy through to students' rooms at the universities as well as the into households of urban married women.[9] The law emphasized the criminal slant to her character while society added the strong presupposition of sorcery; these perceptions, as always, came into conflict with what legal authorities saw as the reality of everyday recourse to her on so many levels of everyday life.

Literature broadens the premise of mediation by resisting the unanimous perception of intermediary activity as necessarily connected with sin and sorcery. While these connotations appear in many important instances of the go-between's portrayal, not all literary go-betweens appear in the professional and business-like guise feared by non-literary texts. In the case of the early Spanish lyric, the third party, often referred to as "madre," assumes a wide range of positions in relation to the love-stricken young woman.[10] The mother as a corrupting agent surfaces in the Spanish *cuentística* (short prose narratives) also, but the lyric explores the motif of the mother as confidante in a nonmarital situation, with little or no attention paid to the older woman's potential as a crafty character and with a marked irrelevance to the taxonomy of women's deceits. The poetic voice

---

[7] Sánchez Ortega, 83.

[8] One Juana Dientes from Castile, brought to trial in Toledo, was known to have recited a conjuration which made clear references to Satan and Beelzebub, in the form of pleas for success in love (cited in Sánchez Ortega, 75). What the critic refers to as the "basic recipe book" of these "sorceresses" has also been compiled, as she notes, by Sebastián Cirac Estopañán, *Los procesos de hechicerías en la Inquisición de Castilla la Nueva (tribunales de Toledo y Cuenca)* (Madrid: Diana, 1942).

[9] The links between the clergy, students, and prostitution are documented elsewhere in Europe also, as mentioned by Roussiaud in *La prostitution médiévale* and by Leah Lydia Otis, *Prostitution in Medieval Society: The History of an Urban Institution in Languedoc* (Chicago: University of Chicago Press, 1985).

[10] See Aurora Juárez Blanquer, "Madre y cantiga de amigo," *Estudios románicos* 1 (1978) 295-311 (henceforth "Juárez Blanquer").

evokes her with sentiments ranging from intimate trust to firm defiance, exploring the affective aspect of a feminine relationship with the third party. This aspect goes on to make its mark on the more famous Peninsular bawds who, as stated earlier, engage a wide range of literary traditions.

III. The Mother as Third Party in the Early Lyric of Spain

Across the principal types of the early Spanish lyric – the Mozarabic *jarchas*, the Gallego-Portuguese *cantigas d'amigo* and the Castilian lyric – the reader encounters numerous instances of appeal by the principal poetic voice to the mother in an amorous situation.[11] In many of the lyrics, the mother provides the impression of a guide, confidante, or simple listener for the first person who speaks. Examples abound, from the desperate question of the *jarcha* on what to do in the absence of the lover, to resistance to a mother's will,[12] to the dialogue of the *cantiga d'amigo* in which the mother listens and then offers advice. The mother is used as a trope for silent listening or active participation in dialogue, in either helpful or hostile capacity.[13]

It is important at this point to mention the risk of counter-produc-

---

[11] For the background to the early lyric, see Ramón Menéndez Pidal, "La primitiva poesía lírica española," *Estudios literarios* (Madrid: Espasa Calpe, 1957); *Poesía árabe y poesía europea* (Buenos Aires: Espasa Calpe argentina, 1941); see also the following five titles by Margit Frenk: *Lírica hispánica de tipo popular* (México: Universidad Nacional Autonoma de México, 1966) (henceforth *LH*), *Las jarchas mozárabes y los comienzos de la lírica románica* (México: El Colegio de México, 1985), *Estudios sobre lírica antigua* (Madrid: Editorial Castalia, 1978), *Corpus de la antigua lírica popular hispánica (siglos XV a XVII)* (Madrid: Castalia, 1987), *Corpus de la antigua lírica popular hispánica, suplemento* (Madrid: Castalia, 1992); Lucy A. Sponsler, *Women in Medieval Spanish Epic & Lyric Traditions* (Lexington: The University Press of Kentucky, 1975); Pilar Lorenzo Gradín, *La canción de mujer en la lírica medieval* (Santiago de Compostela: Universidad de Santiago, 1990). For observations on sexual initiation and the court lyric, see Alan Deyermond, "Sexual Initiation in the Woman's-Voice Court Lyric," in *Courtly Literature: Culture and Context*, edited by Keith Busby and Erik Kooper (Amsterdam and Philadelphia: J. Benjamins Publishing Company, 1990) 125-158.

[12] *LH*, 4, #4, and LH, 71, #122. In the second example, the daughter refuses to become a nun in defiance of the mother.

[13] Sponsler, 61. The critic divides briefly the roles of the mother as follows: "(...) never was the mother pictured as objecting to her daughter's wishes in the *kharchas*, though this was always the case in Castilian lyric. In the Gallego-portugués lyric the mother appears in both roles." See also J. G. Cummins, in *The Spanish Traditional Lyric* (Oxford: Pergamon Press, 1977) 54, in which the author makes a very brief reference to the mother/daughter relationship.

tive generalizations when considering the lyric from a point of view in which characters play important narratological roles; this imposes a "reading for plot" on the lyric, which may well produce misguided results. It is thus necessary to clarify that even in the context of narrative structure, the central element in the young daughter's sentimental and erotic development has to do with a personal and poetic articulation of an amorous situation, which the poetic voice on occasion expresses by the apostrophization of a figure referred to as "mother." A reading of the lyric in light of the positions of different lyric voices vis-à-vis one another does not suggest that the lyric contains a deep narrative structure. Lyric poetry, after all, operates under rules which often have little to do with characterization and plot in the narrative sense. However, as far as mediation in love is concerned, the early Spanish lyric is significant, for it reveals the processes involved in the act of sharing intimate information with an older female interlocutor and as such inscribes itself in the tradition of portrayals of mediation.

By addressing a figure other than the lover the voice of the young woman seeks on the literal level to share an experience and perhaps ask for guidance from the older woman. In cases where the young woman faces reprimand, she puts up a strong verbal resistance against the mother. More importantly the voice strives to create a poetics of amorous expression, elaborated principally in the addresses to the lover but incomplete without the apostrophes to and conversations with the mother figure. By addressing the mother, the girl's voice fulfills a basic requirement in the poetics of love, described thus by Roland Barthes:

> Love's atopia, the characteristic which causes it to escape all dissertations, would be that *ultimately* it is possible to talk about love only *according to a strict allocutive determination*; whether philosophical, gnomic, lyric, or novelistic, there is always, in the discourse upon love, a person whom one addresses, though this person may have shifted to the condition of a phantom or a creature still to come. No one wants to speak of love unless it is *for* someone.[14]

The early lyric does not tell a story with beginning, middle, and end, nor does it paint characters in such a way as to justify investigations

---

[14] Roland Barthes, *A Lover's Discourse: Fragments*, translated by Richard Howard (New York: Hill and Wang, 1978) 74.

into psychological motive. The figure of the mother, in its compliant or defiant manifestation, constitutes a trope for the exploration of the poetics of love as articulated by a young female voice: in this poetic process, to talk of love is at least as important as the expression of the sentiment itself because it enables the principal poetic voice to experiment with concepts of rebellion, complicity, and despair at a safe distance from the beloved and addressed to a less implicated focalizer. The literal role of the mother within a presumed storyline, while a useful point of departure for analysis, is not her most significant feature. The brevity of the lyrics and their emphasis on symbolism, repetition, and rhythm, indicate that language is utilized in the songs not so much to tell a story or to unravel motive, but to explore the qualities of amorous discourse and expression.

In those cases where the mother is portrayed as a silent listener, the poetic voice strives to create a trusting relationship between the main character and the semblance of an older female interlocutor. The *jarchas* formulate problems in the shape of brief questions, revealing the poet's trust on both a pragmatic and emotional level and the youthful need to explore tropes which allow for the exposition of palpitating questions and concerns. The mother, for example, is construed as a third party able to comprehend her daughter's concern for physical appearances, as the daughter explains her preferences in jewelry and colors to the older woman. [15]

The trust also extends to an appreciation of the lover's mien, shared with the mother as intimate friend, as one who understands the basic sensitivities to a lover's beauty.[16] Confidence in the interlocutor's authority also appears in these lyrics, such as the lament of sleeplessness or the question "¿Qué faréi?" ("What will I do?") These laments and questions constitute the foundations of lyric expression for the daughter: more than quests for an actual reply, they represent the daughter's struggle to create a poetics of love, an integral part of which is the expression of laments, questions, and anxieties, directed at a third party.

With the *cantigas d'amigo*, the dynamic between mother and daughter expands at times into dialogue and casts the mother in the role of an experienced party who can give advice on amorous matters. The critic

---

[15] *LH*, 4, #5. Here the daughter expresses her concern with the effect of jewelry on the color of her skin.

[16] *LH*, 4, #6.

Aurora Juárez Blanquer points out that the interference of the mother can assume two basic paths: she either helps (as a kind listener and confidante) or hinders the loves of her daughter. For both categories, the information on the mother's stance comes to us by way of monologues on the part of the daughter, who either confides in or stands in defiance of the older woman, declaring for example that she resents being confined to the house.[17] Some declarations appear almost as willful confessions, as in the poem "Madre, passou per aqui un cavaleiro" ("Mother, a young man [knight] passed by here"),[18] which defy the mother's supposed reproach by boasting the illicit nature of their love.[19] In fact, the mother's status as addressee promotes the articulation of desire in the girl in ways which the lover would inhibit. The above examples from the *jarchas* and the *cantigas* have to do with the young woman's esthetic choices, her indecision as to how to behave with the lover, her hot-headed debates on absence and separations. These are areas which she chooses to explore with the mother as addressee, turning the latter into a foil for the lover and highlighting those figures and tropes of love which are better received by a third party than by the lover. This is seen for example in the proud boast that she has initiated the love affair herself,[20] or in the stubborn insistence in a *jarcha* to decorate herself as she pleases for the lover.

In those lyrics where the older woman does speak, the implications of her past experience provide a sense of continuity in the lyric, showing that the authority in the third party's voice is inextricably linked with the impression of personal experience in similar matters. "Tal vai o meu amigo" illustrates the mechanisms of this type of dialogue.[21] The daughter relates her impressions of her beloved to the mother; the latter offers cautionary advice, based on a similar experience. This does not amount to reprobation, but rather appears to solidify a bond between the two generations because the dialogue serves to bring to light a shared experience.[22] The mother's warning

[17] *LPH*, 22, #38. Juárez Blanquer provides other examples of both types: 133, 134, 142, 143.

[18] *LH*, 22, #39.

[19] *LH*, 23, #39; the poetic voice indicates her desire to be even more "love-struck" than now.

[20] *LH*, 23, #39. The young woman states that she sought out his love herself.

[21] *LH*, 20, #36.

[22] *LH*, 20, #36; she reminds the daughter of a similar experience she (the mother) has had and warns her of a possible deception.

involves a confession of her own amorous history and subjects her authority to a gentle ironic twist. The result, again, has little to do with actual advice and emphasizes instead the different spaces in which the young voice may explore figures for the expression of love.

Juárez Blanquer opens a third category for those *cantigas* in which the mother steps beyond her capacities as a sympathetic listener to offer advice on how to sustain the amorous interest of the male lover: "the mother [is] the center and the motor of the action. Her advice has an aim: to secure love for her daughter."[23] The more active mother engages in a dialogue process which creates the semblance of narrative form and places the sentiment of love within a context, albeit a highly schematic one.[24] Juárez Blanquer concludes that the mother in this last group – comprising relatively few *cantigas* – is not, in fact, conceived as a biological mother but rather as none other than a go-between for lovers in nonmarital situations.[25]

Also, both Juárez Blanquer and Margit Frenk warn against the temptation to discern a mother's presence in every single composition which includes the word *madre*. Juárez Blanquer points out that the word contains phonetic qualities which enhance the rhythmic flow of the lyric, and Frenk advises that this utterance may well represent a simple cliché, placed within the poem in a purely rhetorical capacity.[26] The warning made by these critics must be taken further: it does not really matter what the exact nature of the relationship with the mother might entail. The lyrics do not pursue a narrative line for which such clarifications would be important. What the conversations with and addresses to the mother emphasize is the crucial place of a third party, that is, a character other than the lover who can assume the role of interlocutor. The triangular configuration created in this way promotes lyric expression, setting up one interlocutor as the foil for another and inspiring the young woman to test her sentiments against a listener whose implied interference or judgments are entirely separate from the lover. This third party elicits the type of discourse from the young woman which helps touch on issues such as rebellion, anger, complicity with a female interlocutor, esthetic

---

[23] "la madre [es] centro y motor de la acción. Sus consejos tienen una intencionalidad; conseguir el amor para su hija" (Juárez Blanquer, 150).

[24] Examples of this, in which the mother tells the girl what she must do (albeit very briefly) are cited by Juárez Blanquer (150).

[25] Juárez Blanquer, 151-152.

[26] Juárez Blanquer, 142, and Frenk, *Estudios sobre lírica antigua*, 300.

choices, and anxious indecisions, all of which form fundamental tenets of a discourse on love, but are inhibited in the presence of the lover.

The prose narrative of the thirteenth century converges with the lyric only insofar as it focuses on the mother's interest in illicit desire and the daughter's understanding of the potential for complicity with the older woman. In the *cuentística* – the body of prose narrative with tales from diverse origins – the mother's role in the love life of the daughter links up with the broader theme of women's deceits; professional *alcahuetería* also surfaces in the prose narratives and places the focus on the third party's penchant for intrigue to which the lyric pays no substantial attention.

IV. The Go-Between in the *Disciplina clericalis* of Pedro Alfonso, *Calila y Digna*, and the *Libro de los engannos*

The evolution of these prose tales from their Indian origins to their reception in medieval Spain has been traced in detail.[27] These prose narratives touch on a variety of topics including women's deceits with occasional references to a cunning female third party. The tales do not delve into the go-between's motives; rather, they integrate her into the plot based on the assumption that lack of moral scruples constitutes a known component of her character aggravated by greed and old age.

The clearest illustration of the link between old age and wrongdoing appears in the variants of the tale "la vieja e la perrilla" ("the old woman and the small dog") or "de canicula lacrimante" ("the weeping puppy") in the *Libro de los engannos* and the *Disciplina clericalis* respectively.[28] The "vieja" of the *Libro de los engannos* represents a natural recourse for the man who wishes to pursue a married woman,

[27] See María Jesús Lacarra, *Cuentística medieval en España: los orígenes* (Zaragoza: Universidad de Zaragoza, 1979); see also the introduction to *Calila e Dimna*, edited by J. M. Cacho Blecua y M. J. Lacarra (Madrid: Castalia, 1987).

[28] *Libro de los engannos y asayamientos de las mugeres*, a cura di Emilio Vuolo, I (Messina: Peloritans, 1971) (henceforth *Libro de los engannos*); Pedro Alfonso, *Disciplina clericalis*, edición y traducción del texto latino por Ángel González Palencia (Madrid: Consejo Superior de Investigaciones Científicas, 1948). The theme of a woman's transformation into an animal is encountered in the *Thousand and One Nights* as noted by Marsan, 543, n. 55.

since his plea for her help comes as a natural gesture: "He asked for her love; and the wife said that in no way would she give it to him. So he went to an old woman who lived close to the wife and told her everything as it had happened (...) and asked that she make the woman his, saying that he would give her as much as she would like." [29] The ruse employed by the old woman fits into the narrative in the same manner as the tricks encountered in popular Islamic literature, conveying at once her immorality, skill, and ability to prevaricate on the spot. However, the trick does not occupy the only central position in the tale, for the wife also displays remarkable resourcefulness once her husband enters the scheme by accident. The wife's instant deflection of the situation to her favor parallels the spontaneous method of the "vieja" and confirms the message in the title of the collection: women in general are deceitful.

In the *Disciplina clericalis* of Pedro Alfonso the same tale undergoes a significant variation. The virtuous wife stands in exact opposition to the "vieja," and the latter's wholehearted dedication to wrongdoing stands out more visibly. To begin with, contrary to the version discussed previously, here the old woman forces herself into the situation upon witnessing the young man's distress and reveals her attraction to any possibility of intrigue.[30] The opposition between innocence and corruption is intensified when the young man confides in the old woman "thinking that she was a knowledgeable person"[31] since she has set herself up as an authority: "she tells him: ' – The patient who does not wish to show his illness to the doctor, will suffer all the more.'"[32] The analogy with a physician increases the aura of her authority and science in matters of love. In light of contemporary laments by university-certified physicians that too many unqualified people engage in healing, the old woman's allusion to her healing abilities would have attracted more reproach from the educated male physician or anyone sympathetic to mainstream and

[29] "demandole su amor; y ella [the wife] dixo que en ninguna manera lo harya. Entonces fue a una vieja que moraua çerca della, y contogelo todo como le conteçiera (...) y rrogole que ge la fisiese aver y que le daria quanto quisiese" (*Libro de los engannos*, 22).

[30] "(...) lloraua de sus ojos, al qual andando assí encontró una vieja, honesta de cara, con hábito de religiosa, de la qual fué preguntado de la causa de su tristeza, e lloró él non queriendo descubrir el secreto a la vieja" (*Disciplina clericalis*, 127).

[31] "considerando que era persona graue," (*Disciplina clericalis*, 127).

[32] "ella le dize: ' – El enfermo que no quiere mostrar su enfermedad al fisico, más adolescerá'" (*Disciplina Clericalis*, 127).

certified approaches to medicine.[33] Throughout the narrative, the old woman operates on the basis of concealing true intentions, aided by the fact that the characters surrounding her remain genuinely unaware of her purpose. Thus when she visits the young wife, the latter receives her with an innocent joy, thinking of her as a pious old woman: "she received the religious woman happily and honored, feeling very joyful about the visit for [the old woman] had a reputation as a person leading a good and pious life."[34]

The "vieja" here falls within a category encountered in Arabic erotological writing as well as in the *Thousand and One Nights*, that of the go-between whose true function hides behind religious disguise.[35] The nature of the disguise emphasizes the conflict of immorality with the purity of heart: from this perspective, the old woman's marginal position is stressed, for she stands alone in knowledge of the lie and imposes her presence on people based on a misleading disguise. (The semblance of piety, incidentally, will play an important part in the representation of Celestina, showing her debt to her thirteenth-century forerunners). The two variants of the tale show different attitudes in their vision of the *alcahueta*'s dishonesty, representing two types met in Near-Eastern sources: one sought out by the community, the other, more evil, interrupting a situation in order to exert her own pressure using a disguise. The versions contribute to Spanish literature's familiarization with the simultaneous recognition of utility and the sense of disdain which permeate the conception of the figure.

The tale "Example of the woman and the go-between, the man, and the merchant,"[36] also portrays the go-between as an expert in disguises and ruses, aided all the more by the innocence of the young wife. Here the old woman provides a service fully acknowledged by one party, since the man in love seeks her out by going to her and

---

[33] For contemporary views held by physicians on the interference of "undesirable" parties in the healing sciences, see the last part of the section on *Le Roman de la Rose* in chapter 2 of this study.

[34] "rescibió a esta religiosa con cara alegre e honrradamente, teniéndose por muy contenta en ser visitada della porque era reputada e avida por persona de buena e religiosa vida" (*Disciplina clericalis*, 127).

[35] Marsan makes a note of this fact in *Itinéraire espagnol.*, 528. She also observes that old age is associated in the tale with evil, since the chastity and beauty of the young wife are at all times stressed in the narrative (532).

[36] "Enxenplo de la muger y del alcaueta, del ome, y del mercador" (*Libro de los engannos*, 26).

asking for help in conquering his object of desire.[37] A variation on the figure has to do with the initial reluctance of the "vieja" to help, a resistance that is overcome with the promise of financial reward. In all likelihood, the unwillingness to assist signifies an indirect plea for compensation when faced with a man who reads the sign with no difficulty: "I will give you as much as you like."[38] The financial transaction confirms the integration of the *alcahueta* into the community and shows the exchange of her favors for money as an established routine; the deep structure of the narrative implicates the client in the scheme as much as the old woman.

In addition to the professional *alcahueta*, in the collections of prose narratives the old mother fulfills the task of a third party. The sense of intrinsic moral corruption emerges strongly, since no professional motive stands behind the woman's behavior. Her acts betray basic aspects of her character, mentioned briefly and left largely unexplained, as in the title: "Of a very deceiving old woman who did not wish her daughter to be chaste."[39] The depth of the transgression committed by the mother is accentuated in a manner unseen in the *alcahueta*'s case: once she has arranged for her married daughter's encounter with the lover, she stays with them to enjoy some of the pleasures of this reunion by eating and drinking copiously with her daughter and the latter's lover at their "posada" ("home"). The vicarious compensation she receives relates directly to sensual, as opposed to material, pleasure and contains no trace of a financial advantage which might ultimately help justify her actions in the way Celestina does two centuries later.[40] The tale points to the defective nature of her sexuality by revealing the thrill she experiences indirectly. At the same time, the old woman's visible pleasure in the company of the illicit lovers confirms the go-between's multi-layered implication in the love affair; it points, though crudely and schematically, to one of the fundamental elements of mediation in illicit love: the integration of the third party in the physical sentiment of desire

[37] *Libro de los engannos*, 26.

[38] "yo te dare quanto tu quisieres" (*Libro de los engannos*, 26).

[39] "De una vieja muy engañosa que non quería que su fija guardasse castidad" (*Disciplina clericalis*, 202).

[40] Celestina, whom we will study further, at one point defends her position by stating that her career is the key to her livelihood. Fernando de Rojas, *La Celestina, tragicomedia de Calisto y Melibea*, Edición de Dorothy S. Severin (Madrid: Alianza Editorial, 1990) 81 (henceforth "*Celestina*").

and her reliance on this force as both motivation and reward. Mediation therefore depends upon the promise of an emotional sensation for the third party in order to function successfully. This fact points in turn to the implication that there is a continuity in feminine amorous experience: old age and inactivity do not annul the craving of sexual contact, a desire which appears blatantly comical or immoral in schematic portrayals. So far, we have seen that medieval Spanish literature has laid the foundation for the problematization of this absurdity in prose narrative and the early lyric.

The idea of continuity in female experience also fuels the plot in "Of the young woman and her husband and the mother-in-law and the adulterer," in which the old mother's support allows for the survival of the adulterous love affair.[41] The complicity of the older and younger women, an element found in abundance in popular tales of the Near East, sways the theme in the direction of women's deceits in general, but the idea of a naturally corrupt instinct in the older woman stands out prominently. Here, too, she shares the meal which is the prelude to consummation with her daughter and the latter's lover.[42] The displaced enjoyment of the love affair, a recurrent trait of the old female third party, assumes with the mother a more sinful connotation, for it involves trespass in the home (the use of the "posada" as a setting is repeated several times) and therefore a more visible violation of morals.

The overall tone established in the *Libro de los engannos* and the *Disciplina clericalis* betrays a basic assumption that the old woman, regardless of the nature of her affinity with the lovers, is deceitful enough to produce a ruse at every turn and employ it to their advantage. The tales aim to heighten the reader's consciousness of the need on the part of the "vieja" for this type of behavior, as it obviously provides her with great pleasure. As to methodology, she attends first to the pacification of the husband (calling him "my beloved son," "Honorable son") and then a seemingly ingenuous, linear narrative which aims to rule out all possibility of suspicion ("it's like this: three men came here, and..."), as the daughter and the lover stand aside, watching. The implication is that the silent

[41] "De la muger moça e su marido e de la suegra e del adúltero" (*Disciplina clericalis*, 122).

[42] "(...) estando este jouen e la madre e fija comiendo con grand plazer(...)" (*Disciplina clericalis*, 122).

daughter's observation of her mother's tactics initiates the former in the tradition of deceit.

In *Calila e Digna* the word *alcahueta* covers a wide range of unethical behavior, not excluding an entirely negative view which associates the profession with a clear lack of moral scruples. In one tale a traveling religious man witnesses the murder of a young woman in the hands of her *alcahueta* in reaction to the young prostitute's refusal to charge a client with whom she has fallen in love.[43] The old woman can only tolerate a mercenary type of relationship in her house and destroys every sign of real love. Her visible lack of guilt or shame in planning and executing the murder before the very eyes of the religious man enhances the brutality of her crime. The narrative matches the old bawd's hostility with an unequivocally reproachful stance, allowing for no redemption in her case. The act of murder takes the bawd's capacities for wrongdoing to their utmost extreme and generates a mistrustful and condemning reaction from the text, without the grain of admiration seen on occasion in the accounts of misbehavior.

Immediately following this portrait of evil, *Calila e Digna* moves on to a tale in which go-between and wicked wife tread on very similar ground; the religious man who witnessed the murder now lodges with "a good carpenter and his wife," finding out immediately that "this woman had a lover, and a neighbor's wife was their go-between."[44] The simple fact that the wife is a go-between denigrates both figures in one sweep, in particular due to the clearly negative connotation of the word *alcahueta* carried across from the preceding tale. Yet the equation "wife equals go-between" also indicates the interchangeability of the two functions among women: should one wife require the help of another in the game of deception, the latter may easily don the identity of third party. The task therefore encourages the participation of a wide range of candidates. The first implication is that all women are capable of performing evil deeds; the second, and more significant, indicates that illicit love needs a go-between and cannot exist without one.

The third party in this tale exhibits a makeshift quality, since once her function as such has been completed, she changes her role yet

---

[43] *Calila e Digna*, 62.

[44] "esta muger avia un amigo, e era alcahueta entre ellos una muger de un su vezino" (*Calila e Digna*, 62).

again and trades places with the adulterous wife to protect her all the more.[45] The move leads to her accidental bodily mutilation, intended for the adulterous wife, which she now has to explain ingeniously to her own husband. Introduced into the tale as wife and go-between, this character occupies the story in terms of her shifting identities. The unifying thread consists of the inclination for rapid problem-solving in each case. But her skill is flawed since she suffers great bodily harm in the process. A darkly humorous, almost slapstick tone governs the scenes of mistaken identity and the cutting off of her nose, suggesting that the ersatz go-between has fallen victim to her own thoughtless miscalculation and that her mediation has failed. Even if she succeeds in explaining the mutilation to her own husband, the damage has been done, betraying a partial failure on her part. Her struggle to fit every new situation thus results in some degree of comic defeat.

This vision complements the entirely evil portrait of the *alcahueta* witnessed by the religious man the previous day. Seen together, the two narratives offer a cumulative perception of the figure of the *alcahueta.* The implication that third-party activity is necessary does exist, as does the inevitability of this task for the perpetuation of illicit love. But the end result indicates a definitive immoral tendency with little room left for the type of narrative ambivalence and admiration encountered in popular material from the Near East. The lack of a latently admiring point of view on the part of the narrator has to do with the absence of ingenious discourse and ruses; both *alcahuetas* have very basic approaches to illicit love, one leading to murder and the other to irreparable self-damage. The standpoint of the *Calila e Digna* regarding the go-between involves an evident moral condemnation mingled with slapstick humor at the expense of the figure. The dynamic component of the portrayal resides in the shifting identities of the second go-between: her position shows that the function of the third party may be assumed by anyone with a logistical advantage.

Our study of the above examples from the popular lyric and the *cuentística* reveals that the lyric touches on the affective possibilities of the relationship with the mediator. It explores briefly the mutual build-up of a shared discourse between younger and older women

---

[45] *Calila e Digna*, 63.

with little room left for ethical judgments. The genre focuses on the fertile ground available for the development of language and poetics when a third party enters the picture in an erotic journey. Conversely, prose narrative relates actions rather than feelings in its depiction of the go-between, recording the effects of mediation on specific members of the community. The judgmental posture of the frame-stories guides the direction of the tales and focuses on the disruptive impact of mediation on morality. Yet mediation as one of the keys for the survival of illicit love does enter the picture and adds important momentum to the portrayal of love. Ethically, little room is left for speculation: there are few connotations of affection or sympathetic understanding in the mother-daughter relationship. They display instead a business-like approach to adultery with emphasis on the logistical problems it might entail. The third parties here deal with money, food, objects, and other everyday realities as opposed to the evocative or intangible qualities of language. The tales thus trace both the disorder and the energy generated by the interferences of a third party.

Nevertheless the contributions of the early lyric and the *cuentística* to the literary history of the go-between go beyond a mere reiteration of familiar motifs. The prose narratives draw attention to the old woman's visible presence inside and outside the *posada* ("home") and display the community's natural recourse to her as a mediator, thereby forging her image as a regular source of help whose immorality is a given character trait. The popular lyric accentuates the significance of a third-party addressee for the expression of amorous sentiment. Both genres also demonstrate the adaptability of the character to generic contours and her contribution to the realization of a genre's favorite themes such as women's deceits or the poetics of love. This type of flexibility, which will make its way into the works of Juan Ruiz and Fernando de Rojas, can also be seen in the *Cantigas de Santa María*.

V. An Uncharacteristic Case from the *Cantigas de Santa María*

The financial greed and immoral tendencies of the go-between in the *Cantigas de Santa María* of King Alfonso X provide the literary substantiation of the figure delineated in his legal writings. Alfonso X's lyrics paint the portraits of greedy and crafty go-betweens whose roots are clearly in the world of prostitution.[46] The lyrics complement the cautionary and descriptive passages from legislation with a brief but firm mention of a number of basic corrupt elements in the go-between's makeup: her affinity with unmarried love, her willingness to procure, and her demand for financial reward.

But one *Cantiga* provides a foil to the image of the professional, greedy third party by describing an altogether different type of intervention in earthly love. The title of the poem refers to how Santa María delivers from dishonor two young people promised to one another.[47] Here a young girl who has promised marriage to a childhood sweetheart is married off by her parents to a rich man, who understands her grief and decides to reunite her with her beloved. On their way they are kidnapped by another rich man who, upon imprisoning the husband, attempts to spend the night with the young wife; at this point the Holy Virgin interferes and causes the kidnapper to fall asleep, and he wakes up completely reformed the next day. Both now accompany the young virgin wife to her original beloved, whereupon a wedding takes place and the new couple consummate the marriage happily.[48] As Keller remarks, in this poem the reader finds the Virgin "actively abetting lovers and bringing them together in a romantic marital passion in defiance of the wishes of their parents." The scholar notes the rarity of such a theme, since, by and large, the Virgin of the *Cantigas* attempts to "lead people away from carnal desire and into the paths of chastity and devotion to her[.]"[49]

Keller's simultaneous study of the two pages of illuminations which accompany this poem leads the scholar to yet another surprising find. The panel corresponding to the consummation of the final wedding has all the markings of a "traditional representation of carnal love" which describes the groom and bride's action with "sim-

---

[46] See Francisco Sánchez Castañer. See also *Orígenes y sociología*, 75-77, where Alfonso el Sabio's portrayal of the type is discussed alongside the presence of the go-between in the *cantiga d'escarnho e de maldezir* in the context of the thirteenth century.

[47] "[C]omo Santa Maria livrou de desonra dous que sse avian jurados por ela quando eran *men~yos* que casassen ambos en uno, e fez-lo ela conprir"(J. E. Keller, "*Cantiga 135:* The Blessed Virgin as a Matchmaker," in *Florilegium Hispanicum: Medieval and Golden Age Studies Presented to Dorothy Clotelle Clarke*, ed. John S. Geary [Madison: Hispanic Seminary of Medieval Studies, 1983] 103-117). The citations from the *Cantiga* are taken from *Cantigas de Santa María* (3 vols.), edited by Walter Mettman (Madrid: Editorial Castalia, 1986-1989) (Henceforth "Mettman"), #135.

[48] Mettman, #135, v. 155.

[49] Keller, 103. (Both citations).

plicity, naiveté, and explicit frankness."[50] The critic points out the startling quality of placing such a scene in a "work in which the Virgin repeatedly prevents such love[.]"[51] But as Keller himself speculates, this *cantiga* "may derive from one of those romances in written form in French and Spanish prose which seem to have been modeled upon the Byzantine romance."[52] The type of third-party assistance offered here corresponds to the model encountered in French romance, where financial gain does not enter the picture and an inherent sense of justice and loyalty motivates the intermediary. The carnal aspect of the relationship thereby gains perfect legitimacy and is happily recounted in some detail as attested also by the romances of Chrétien de Troyes, for example.

Against the landscape of wrongdoing go-betweens in the *Cantigas*, then, the Virgin Mary as matchmaker recalls the traditions in which assistance to lovers does not imply an inherently evil disposition. What Keller refers to as the "unusual (...) romantic regard for the young couple under her protection"[53] might indeed appear unique as an aspect of Holy Mary's character; yet in the context of the *Cantiga* as a love tale, the Virgin fits the model of the experienced and helping confidante able to produce miracles (such as the impotence of an evil spouse) to save the lovers. The depiction provides a foil for the established notion of the wrongdoing third party insofar as it justifies the aid given to the lovers, setting up a contrast to the more prevalent image of the go-between. Additionally, the husband who feels pity for his young wife and decides to help her find her original sweetheart represents yet another manifestation of third-party assistance not guided by material gain. As a man his role is facilitated by his control and power over the young wife, and so it is not loyalty or indebtedness which motivate him but rather compassion and pity. Material gain is replaced in the *Cantiga* by the Virgin's blessing for all those who have helped facilitate the rightful marriage.

This particular vision of matchmaking, which ends in marriage and therefore is not ultimately immoral, alerts the reader to the exis-

---

[50] Keller, 113.

[51] Keller, 113. As the critic observes, the context of marriage may not in and of itself provide a strong reason for such a depiction since in other cases, even if legally married, lovers have not benefitted from the Virgin's aid. (See also Keller, 115, n. 2)

[52] Keller, 103.

[53] Keller, 114.

tence of a space in which go-between activity leads to the joyful resolution of conflict. A far cry from the sly old *alcahueta*, the Virgin nonetheless fulfills a task that overlaps with the go-between in terms of the perpetuation of carnal desire, not to mention the annulment of the first marriage through the use of a miracle, which treads on ground surprisingly close to sorcery when observed from a strictly textual angle. This glimpse of the beneficial results of mediation proves the possibility of a positive ethical response to the activity and discreetly inscribes such a response in the tradition of *alcahuetería*.

In the *Cantigas*, the boundary which separates the two types of response maintains a clear definition, all the more emphasized here due to the interference of none other than the Virgin who represents the exact opposite of the *alcahueta* in terms of intention and image. In the *Cantigas* and elsewhere, slippage between the two ethical reactions occurs only when the reader asks a series of specific questions about the contradictions inherent in the act of mediation, especially when portrayed positively against an overwhelming context of negative representations. By and large, literary texts dated before *El libro de buen amor* opt for the exposition of the morally condemnable traits of the go-between and appear to deny the existence of that slippage; a case in point is the Arthurian and Eastern-inspired *El caballero Zifar*, which maintains an unequivocally reproachful stance in regard to the *cobigera* ("go-between"). A close reading of the passage in which the wicked woman appears allows for the perception of the text's own conflicts in her portrayal.

VI. A Question of Discourse: The Case of *El caballero Zifar*

The author of *El caballero Zifar* draws on a religious perspective to conceive of go-betweens as moral dangers to society, yet for the sake of propriety chooses not to delve too deeply into a description of the figure. Rather, the author provides an obvious moral gloss to the brief passage where *cobigeras* appear to make his own stand on the issue quite clear.[54] The bawd serves as a figure for the voicing of extra-textual concerns made up of moral observations and complaints.

The *cobigeras* of *El caballero Zifar* take up limited space and go about

[54] See *Orígenes y sociología*, 83-88.

their task in a seemingly straightforward manner. Yet a glance at their speech suffices to establish one type of rhetorical device which indicates the alertness of the women to the effectiveness of language as opposed to sorcery or resort to a decoy. In their attempt to entice their reluctant mistress, "a very beautiful lady (...) loved by many,"[55] into an affair with a married knight, the female attendants referred to as *cobigeras* counterattack the lady's resistance to the affair with aggressive questions and arguments, contending that the refusal to indulge in the affair would denote a violation of protocol and natural human response.

The *cobigeras* provide a very basic and minimal, though logical, structure for the support of this argument, protesting that first, resistance to amorous advances would betray her impoliteness and second, the knight's handsome mien and great love must provoke a positive reaction in her. The women evoke God and religious duty a number of times to lend credence to the argument, stating that it is a sin to turn him down and that God has given her gifts which she must put to good use.[56] In other words, they appeal to her on the basis of logic and reason, inserting God and religion into the scheme and turning their objective into a question of duty and necessity. The author's commentary follows the women's speech and attempts to invalidate the content of their words: he laments the existence and activities of such females. *El caballero Zifar* therefore contributes to the identification of the go-between with evil and turpitude. But it offers a sampling of a rhetorical skill which both Trotaconventos and Celestina will develop to the full: that of logically identifying what is right (because God has decreed it) with that which is more than often considered wrong (nonmarital intimacy).

By the time Juan Ruiz, the Archpriest of Hita, composes his *Libro de buen amor* the go-between constitutes a familiar presence associated with women's deceits, legal misbehavior, affective confidence, and a mutual bond with the community around her. This last feature seems especially unacknowledged in all texts. The monumental contribution of the Archpriest of Hita to the history and typology of the go-between derives from the fact that his poem begins an intricate

---

[55] "una dueña muy fermosa (...) amada de muchos" (*Libro del caballero Zifar*, edición, introducción y notas de Joaquín González Muela [Madrid: Castalia, 1982] 218).

[56] *Libro del caballero Zifar*, 219.

process of problematization for the very meaning of mediation and she who carries it out. In *El libro de buen amor* various elements from different traditions come together to affect the nature of the *alcahueta*'s presence in the work, so that the figure emerges as more than a simple sum of her parts.

VII. The Emergence of Go-between as a Literary Character: Trotaconventos in *El libro de buen amor*

(i) *The Meeting of Traditions: Genre and Meaning*

The ever-growing scholarship on Juan Ruiz's *Libro de buen amor* covers a vast range of topics, not the least important of which has to do with the place of the Archpriest's work within a literary tradition. As a text which simultaneously celebrates carnal love, offers instruction in that area, and yet maintains a heightened religious consciousness (that according to Christianity would condemn the lessons of the book), the work has given rise to much speculation on the reasons behind this apparent ambivalence. The recurrence of terms such as "ambiguities, inconsistencies, and dualities" characterizes a great portion of the studies on this work, with many an effort to discover a "missing link," an "elusive prize" that may clarify the work's purpose and genre.[57] Eduardo Urbina points out correctly that a survey of the bibliography on the *Libro* will demonstrate the impressive number of occasions on which scholars have questioned the inconsistencies of the text in an attempt to find a message which would resolve the ambiguities.[58]

---

[57] Eduardo Urbina, "Now you see it, now you don't: The Antithesis *corteza/meollo* in the *Libro de buen amor*," in *Florilegium Hispanicum: Medieval and Golden Age Studies Presented to Dorothy Clotelle Clarke*, 139-150 (139).

[58] Roger M. Walker, "'Con miedo de la muerte la miel non es sabrosa': Love, Sin and Death in the *Libro de buen amor*," in *Libro de buen amor Studies*, ed. G. B. Gybbon-Moneypenny (London: Tamesis, 1970) 231-252, attributes the duality in the Archpriest's Book to a superficial recommendation of worldly love subordinated to a serious and ultimately stronger orthodoxy which condemns that kind of love wholeheartedly. Some other scholars follow a similar line of thought and suggest that there is a general movement in the Book "from love to death, from sin to salvation," and in it there can be seen "the duality of human nature and the cyclical patterns it presents, the journey and struggle common to all men" (Urbina, 140). One other study which confirms this standpoint is G. B. Gybbon-Monypenny's "The Two Versions

On one level, it is rather puzzling that the ambiguities of *El libro de buen amor* continue to generate so much debate: the Archpriest's poem is a full-fledged literary work, the mark of which is none other than its open quality. *El libro de buen amor* is a writerly text, a *texte scriptible*, open to a multitude of definitions and interpretations. Much of the work's lively multi-layeredness must be attributed to its ability to represent ambiguity as a theme in and of itself with great flair.

But on the level of intertextual and contextual connections there are ambiguities which can indeed be resolved. The question of the work's intertextual derivations is now an established part of bibliography on the *Libro de buen amor.* Those scholars who have chosen to focus on the purely Christian, scholastic roots of the work have offered enlightening remarks on some of the reasons behind the *Libros de buen amor*'s apparent contradictions: Richard P. Kinkade, for example, perceives the work as inscribed in the Christian tradition of didactic eroticism in which profane and earthly images are used to illuminate aspects of divine love.[59] This assertion is premised on the idea that the *Libro de buen amor* contains an "eros-agape dichotomy" that follows the two apparently contradictory currents of "the religious and the ribald."[60] To a certain degree, the scholastic background of the Archpriest's book explains the use of *exempla* and the sources for some of the materials used to convey a moral question. But the entirety of the book's scheme and its themes cannot be explained only by its Christian and scholastic background. The dichotomy perceived by Kinkade and others exists on one level, that of the textual game of offering the reader thoughts on "good" and "bad" love without apparently siding with one or the other from a moral point of view. This dichotomy, however, is not all-encompass-

of the *Libro de buen amor*: The Extent and Nature of the Author's Revisions," *Bulletin of Hispanic Studies* 38 (1962) 205-221; Gybbon-Moneypenny perceives a strongly didactic element in the Doña Endrina episode in another study, "Dixe la por te dar ensienpro': Juan Ruiz's Adaptation of the 'Pamphilus'," in *Libro de buen amor Studies* 123-147. Eduardo Urbina regards the *Libro* as a performance-text, suggesting the following resolution to the ambiguities in the text: "The book transforms itself and serves as a creative object and instrument of redemption while remaining all along a string of humorous parodies and satires; it is itself an artistic object of deception and vehicle through which the author allegorically exemplifies the reversal of the fall, the original deception" (Urbina, 141). See also Oliver T. Myers, "Symmetry of Form in the *Libro de buen amor*," *Philological Quarterly* 51 (1972) 74-84.

[59] Richard P. Kinkade, "A Thirteenth-Century Precursor of the *Libro de Buen Amor:* the *Art d'Amors*," *La Corónica* 24: 2 (1996) 123-139.

[60] Kinkade, "A Thirteenth-Century Precursor," 124, 123.

ing: the book does not posit the conflict of good and bad love as the central enigma to which the reader must find an answer. Rather, the poem weaves the two tendencies, love of God and love of women, into a flowing narrative which embraces both tendencies without generating an ongoing, essential conflict between the two and presents these as equal though different ingredients in the composition of the work's poetics. That is to say, while the two distinct currents of religiosity and carnality are discernible in the poem, they do not exist solely to create a sense of conflict.

That the conflict between carnality and religion is in fact a false one is borne out when one considers the multicultural heritage of Juan Ruiz's poem. A clearer sense of the coexistence of both topics may be found using Américo Castro's suggestion that from a Muslim perspective the "continuous transition from one plane to another" is quite natural.[61] A comparative approach to medieval Spanish literature soon faces the reader with the fact that the Archpriest's Book contains many Hispano-Arabic traits and derives many themes from Arabic writings known in Spain in his period.[62] The simultaneous existence of sexual love and religion in a medieval text is not a problem if one considers that there is a non-Christian tradition which for the most part has posited the coexistence of the two without much discomfort at all.

The very fact of being a Peninsular clergyman in the fourteenth century implied some familiarity with Eastern elements in both lifestyle and intellectual activity.[63] The abundance of political, architectural, philosophical, scientific, interpersonal, economic, and artistic interaction between the Archpriest's Christian world and the very close territories in which Islamic life flourished is by now an indisputable fact, as studies in various disciplines have shown and continue to show.[64]

---

[61] Américo Castro, *Realidad histórica de España* (México: Porrúa, 1954), 387. On this point, see also López-Baralt, 158

[62] López-Baralt's own work, her edition of the *Kāma-Sūtra española* in particular, delves into the issue of Spanish contact with Arabic material in the realm of erotology.

[63] *Orígenes y sociología*, 88-98.

[64] See in particular *Primeras jornadas: estudios de Frontera Alcalá la Real y el Arcipreste de Hita*, coordinadores: Francisco Toro Caballos y José Rodríguez Molina (Jaén, 1996); *The Legacy of Muslim Spain*, edited by Salma Khadra Jayyusi (Leiden: E. J. Brill, 1992); *VI Simposio Internacional de mudejarismo: Actas* (Teruel: Centro de Estudios Mudéjares,1995); Mercedes García-Arenal and Béatrice Leroy, *Moros y judíos en Navarra en la Baja Edad Media* (Madrid: Libros Hiperión, 1984).

The scholar Roger Boase expresses succinctly that some medievalists are still reluctant to acknowledge that "Arab culture had an impact on medieval Europe which went far beyond the acquisition of certain luxury goods."[65] Fortunately, the bibliography on the vast and multi-leveled contact between Christians and Muslims in medieval Spain is impressive and on the rise, showing that the coexistence of Christians with Muslims in medieval Spain was by no means limited to the areas which have been traditionally acknowledged. That is to say, in addition to philosophy, natural sciences, and medicine, interchange and communication occurred between Muslims and Christians in many areas with relentless consistency ranging from mundane daily activities to considerable intellectual exchange. Today the most useful studies for the appreciation of the extent of contact between Islam and Christianity are works on various disciplines such as architecture, literature, philosophy, medicine, town-planning, the arts, legal issues, intermarriage, conditions during war and peace, and border-life in regions which knew both Christian and Muslim rule. Such works help construct a comprehensive picture of all the areas in which Muslims and Christians had dealings with one another and show time and again that there was hardly a site in which the two religions did not meet. The work of the scholar Mercedes García-Arenal, for example, draws on archival material to bring to light numerous instances of this interaction, one interesting example of which (among many) is Christian royalty's implicit trust in Muslim and Jewish medicine and midwifery.[66]

In the fifteenth-century compilation of legal problems and advice, the *Kitāb al-Mi'yār* by the jurist al-Wansarīsī, the focus falls on North-African and Andalusian communities with numerous examples of legal issues and how these have been commented on or resolved by jurisconsultants in positions of authority. Some of the examples recorded by al-Wansarisi deal with ordinary people's questions on interaction with Christians and Jews and reveal the widespread, inti-

---

[65] Roger Boase, "Arab Influences on European Love-Poetry," in *The Legacy of Muslim Spain*, 458-482.

[66] García-Arenal points out that in the Trastámara dynasty for example, Queen Leonor's children were all delivered by Moorish midwives. As mentioned, this is one example only: using primary sources and archival material, García-Arenal is one of the many scholars to show that Christians in medieval Spain turned to Muslims for recourse for numerous reasons and that contact between the two groups was widespread.

mate, daily nature of coexistence in Andalusia in particular but also other "fronterizo" ("border") communities. For example, in one section of the text, the author refers to the ninth-century Cordoban jurisconsultant Yahyā ibn Yayha is quoted as speaking of the "night of the first of January which people call the nativity of Jesus" and expressing his intense disappointment with the fact that Muslims have taken to celebrating the date, accepting gifts from Christians and taking the day off from work. Yahyā goes on to enumerate a series of other practices which in his opinion ought to cease immediately: these include the tendency of Muslim women to bathe on Saturdays and Sundays and to take a rest from housework on such days, the participation of Muslims in Solstice celebrations (the feasts of St. Julian and St. John), and their acceptance of invitations from Christians on New Year's Eve.[67] In spite of itself, this example and numerous others in the compilation point out that on the level of religious and legal authority, Christians and Muslim authorities felt anxiety at the widespread nature of interaction between religions but that on many other levels, all kinds of people went about their daily lives communicating, conducting business, even marrying members of the "other" religious group. The very political geography of medieval Spanish communities, especially in the central and southern regions which so often changed hands from Christian to Muslim and back, required that people adapt themselves to border life. This does not imply that all religious groups lived in an exquisite harmony together: naturally, conflicts, anxieties, hate and violence permeated everyday life as much as they do in any area where ethnic diversity is intense and politically thematized by authorities. Yet it is indispensable that the other side of coexistence, that is, the fact of a rich and complex exchange of ideas to and fro, also be acknowledged, for conflict and anxiety vis-à-vis a different group do not signify a full-proof resistance to the osmosis of ideas with that group.

Studies on medieval Spanish agriculture, urban development, culinary arts, ceramics, irrigation, linguistics, and other disciplines, when taken together point in the same direction: they prove beyond any doubt that the mutual influence of religions on one another exerted itself at times quite smoothly and sometimes even unnoticeably, on

---

[67] Vincent Lagardère, *Histoire et société en Occident musulman au Moyen Âge: analyse du* Mi'yar *d'Al-Wansarisi* (Madrid: Casa de Velazquez, 1995) 476.

intellectual and mundane areas and was by no means restricted to the well-known domains of medicine and philosophy.[68] Yom Tov Assin reminds us that long after the 1085 conquest of Toledo, for example, Arabic remained the language of the ordinances of Toledo and that even in the fourteenth century it was a commonly known language among the élite of that city.[69]

As mentioned earlier coexistence also implies tension, conflict, and mistrust, all of which can be distilled from primary and secondary sources when studying the literature and history of medieval Spain. David Nirenberg's study of medieval minorities in the Crown of Aragón (and France) provides an articulate and compelling expression of the tensions and conflicts resulting from coexistence and draws attention to the dangers perceived by one community when faced with interaction with the other.[70] For the representation of the *alcahueta*, Juan Ruiz shows considerable sensitivity to the curiously contradictory nature of the blend of *mudéjar* currents with Christian ones and thematizes the simultaneous existence of interaction and conflict in the shape of the old go-between.

To return to the *mudéjar* framework, it is important to bear in mind that Arabic erotological writings were not unknown to Peninsular clergymen, nor were the latter excluded from intimate contact with Islamic lifestyles.[71] Regarding the seemingly insoluble conflict between

[68] For a series of valuable essays in the disciplines mentioned, see *V semana de estudios medievales, Nájera 1994* (Logroño: Instituto de estudios riojanos, 1995). In this collection, attention is given to technical aspects of medieval irrigation, urban development, ceramic art, among other areas, always revealing the intricate links which bound Muslim and Christian communities to one another. Also in *VI simposio internacional de mudejarismo* (Teruel: Centro de estudios mudéjares, 1995), by analyzing technical aspects of town-planning and architecture, the essays show the integration of Muslims and Christians in medieval Spain. One study points out, for example, that many thirteenth- and fourteenth-century convents in Castilla and León made use of Muslim artists and masons in their design and construction, mingling *mudéjar* craftsmanship with Christian planning. Pedro J. Lavado Paradinas, "Mudéjares y moriscos en los conventos de clarisas de Castilla y León," 391-419.

[69] Yom Tov Assis, "The Judeo-Arabic Tradition in Christian Spain," in *The Jews of Medieval Islam: Community, Society, and Identity*, edited by Daniel Frank (Leiden: E. J. Brill, 1995) 112-124.

[70] David Nirenberg, *Communities of Violence: Persecution of Minorities in the Middle Ages* (Princeton: Princeton University Press, 1996).

[71] For the kinds of Eastern readings which were readily available to the Peninsular clergy see Francisco Márquez Villanueva, "Las lecturas del deán de Cádiz en una 'cantiga de mal dizer'," *Studies on the "Cantigas de Santa María," Art, Music and Poetry, Actas del Seminario Internacional sobre las Cantigas de Santa María*, edited by I. J. Kotz and J. E. Keller (Madison: Hispanic Seminar on Medieval Studies, 1987) 329-354.

sexuality and religion in its content, Juan Ruiz's Book will puzzle the reader much less if he or she takes into account the body of *adab* literature which constituted a substantial part of the Archpriest's literary and intellectual environment: texts such as the one labeled today as the *Kāma-Sūtra español*, the *Speculum al foderi*, the *Historia de la doncella Teodor* or the *Libro conplido en los juizios de las estrellas*, Ibn Hazm's *Tawq al-Hammama* (*The Dove's Neck-Ring*) address human sexuality and its accepted place within the Divine scheme. The subject matter of these links up invariably with the medical and erotological traditions found in medieval Islam which, while not subject to a homogeneous assessment of attitudes to sexuality, has maintained a more open and all-encompassing view than Christianity of the place of carnal love in man's life.[72] Inscribed in the outlook which has few problems reconciling erotic energy with religious concern, the Archpriest's book takes the view that sexuality has a place within the scheme devised by God and that its discussion and enjoyment need not conflict with religious belief.

In light of these findings, it would be difficult to challenge the notion that the *Libro de buen amor* belongs to a *mudéjar* framework that is simultaneously Christian and Muslim and that assimilates numerous Eastern attributes alongside a "clear clerical consciousness and sincere Christianity." [73] Such a reality defines much of the *Libro de buen amor*, indicating that the work stands at the crossroads of several different traditions. That is to say, the reader must not lose sight of the unique Spanish framework of the text created by the Archpriest's vital style and by the cultural diversity on which he drew during his creative process. As Julio Rodríguez Puértolas has said, the *Libro de buen amor* integrates elements from various contexts, Christian, Moslem, and Jewish.[74] López-Baralt also specifies:

> It is important to clarify that those of us who perceive Islamic traces in the work of Juan Ruiz do just this, and no other thing; I do not think that anyone would think of inscribing Juan Ruiz within Arabic literature (...) Of course not, and naturally the Archpriest is more Western

---

[72] In addition to Luce López-Baralt's study, see Michael Salomon, *The Mirror of Coitus: A Translation and Edition of the Fifteenth-Century "Speculum al foderi"* (Madison: Hispanic Seminar on Medieval Studies, 1990); Walter Mettmann, *La historia de la donzella Teodor* (Mainz: Akademie der Wissenchaften und der Literatur, 1962).

[73] "conciencia de clérigo [y] de sincero cristiano" (*Orígenes y sociología*, 88, 100-101).

[74] Julio Rodríguez Puértolas, *Juan Ruiz, Arcipreste de Hita* (Madrid: EDAF, 1978).

than Eastern. But his Arabic cast is crucial for understanding his work[.][75]

The presence of Islam in medieval Spanish literature is a fact, yet one must not assume that thematic ambiguities are instantly solved when Islamic influences are taken into account. The acknowledgment of Islamic presence in key medieval Spanish works helps formulate more productive and pertinent questions, and to understand the nature and function of puzzling representations or nagging ambiguities.

To understand the place of the bawd Trotaconventos in the typology of the *alcahueta,* one must therefore take into account two factors: the multiple intertextual elements which inform her portrayal and the nature of her association with the characters and themes around her. Her very first appearance warrants the study of these two elements, as it establishes a link between the *Libro de buen amor* and the medieval Latin comedy *Pamphilus de amore;* yet the intertextual relationship soon displays clear and deliberate divergences from the so-called original source and raises questions as to the Archpriest's motives for turning away from the source in several ways. Concomitantly, the divergences impinge directly on style and the qualities of discourse endowed upon the characters, the analysis of which throws light on the Archpriest's motives for the changes he chooses to make.

(ii) *Trotaconventos and the Bawd of the* Pamphilus

It cannot be denied that the general plot of the *Pamphilus* repeats itself in the Archpriest's poem: even a quick glance at the medieval Latin comedy will show that the Spanish poet follows it quite closely in terms of plot progression, distribution, and design. Juan Ruiz's departures from the source however emerge in obvious ways, many of which relate directly to the portrayal of the old bawd. Earlier this century, both Marcelino Menéndez y Pelayo and Félix Lecoy noted

[75] "Conviene aclarar que los estudiosos que proponemos huellas islámicas en la obra de Juan Ruiz hacemos justamente eso y no otra cosa; creo que a nadie se le ocurriría inscribir a Juan Ruiz dentro de la literatura árabe (...) Claro que no y claro que el Arcipreste es mucho más occidental que oriental. Pero su impronta árabe es determinante para entender la obra" (López-Baralt, 434, n. 219).

that Trotaconventos bore little resemblance to the old bawd of the *Pamphilus*.[76] Anthony M. Zahareas also perceives the substantial differences between the players in the Latin comedy and the Spanish poem.[77] More recently, in a verse-by-verse comparison of the two texts, Gail Phillips confirms that Juan Ruiz departs from the Latin comedy in the overall tone and linguistic register which he creates for the imagery used in the episode.[78] In an excellent study on the implications of widowhood in the episode (given that in the *Pamphilus* Galatea is a virgin whereas in Juan Ruiz's version Endrina is a widow), Louise O. Vasvari draws attention to the wealth of poetic tradition which informs Juan Ruiz's treatment of his subject matter and points out the meaningful transformations brought about by Endrina's widowhood in the tale.[79]

These changes in portrayal have provoked various interpretations. Some critics have viewed them as efforts towards achieving a livelier tone in line with the general atmosphere created by Juan Ruiz in the doña Endrina (that is, the *Pamphilus*) episode.[80] Others have perceived a didactic motivation behind the changes, asserting that the posture of the narrator creates a fundamentally moralizing stance which warns against carnality. Thus Jorge Guzmán discerns a didactic tone in Juan Ruiz's work and concludes that the depiction of Trotaconventos serves to enhance the warning against carnal love and those who lure people into it.[81] Lázaro Carreter and Gybbon-Monypenny also view the episode as a confirmation of Juan Ruiz's moralizing agenda against carnal love and in favor of religious devo-

---

[76] Marcelino Menéndez y Pelayo, *Orígenes de la novela* III, 310-311; Félix Lecoy, *Recherches sur le* Libro de buen amor (Paris: Librairie Droz, 1938) 318-322. (Henceforth *Recherches*).

[77] Anthony N. Zahareas, *The Art of Juan Ruiz, Archpriest of Hita* (Madrid: Estudios de Literatura Española, 1965) 159ff.

[78] Gail Phillips, *The Imagery of the 'Libro de buen amor'* (Madison: Hispanic Seminary of Medieval Studies, 1983) 11-94 (henceforth "Phillips").

[79] Louise O. Vasvari, "Why is Doña Endrina a Widow? Traditional Culture and Textuality in the *Libro de buen amor*," in *Upon my Husband's Death: Widows in the Literature and Histories of Medieval Europe*, edited by Louise Mirrer (Ann Arbor: University of Michigan, 1992) 259-287.

[80] Such is the view of Georges Cirot, "L'épisode de Doña Endrina dans le *Libro de buen amor*," *Bulletin Hispanique* XLV (1943) 139-156; see also Joseph de Morawski, *Pamphile et Galatée par Jehan Brasdefer* (Paris: Champion, 1917) 54; Félix Lecoy also perceives Juan Ruiz's adaptation as a more successful stylistic endeavor (*Recherches*, 309-317).

[81] Jorge Guzmán, *Una constante didáctico-moral del* Libro de buen amor (Iowa: State University of Iowa Studies in Language and Literature XIV, 1963), chapter 2.

tion.[82] Zahareas sees in Trotaconventos the signs of great artistic achievement, calling her "the paradox of the bawd," since the range of attitudes governing her description leads to a mingling of "cynicism and sentimentality."[83] For Zahareas this mixture of contradictory postures "allows for a pervasive suggestiveness (...) to which the reader is then free to assign any number of meanings." Conclusive remarks on the moral posture governing her description, according to this scholar, are made close to impossible since she is "criticized and praised, rejected and accepted at the same time."[84]

Gail Phillips concludes that the Spanish poet's handling of imagery reveals a deep concern for characterization whereas the *Pamphilus* provides its three characters with a comparatively cursory treatment.[85] The conclusion reached by Phillips is an elaboration of the observations of Gybbon-Monypenny; she perceives an unmistakably didactic purpose behind the changes from the *Pamphilus* that lead the reader to "appreciate the evil of lust, which negates all that is good and which reduces men to the level of beasts."[86] Later, under the heading "The Negative Portraits," the critic classifies Trotaconventos as an "enemy of womankind[.]"[87] This classification enables her to stress further the didactic purposes of the *Libro de buen amor* since "the poet not only utters explicit warnings against this archtemptress of the flesh, but also uses imagery to reinforce the identification of the bawd with the forces of evil and treachery."[88]

Phillips, who produces by far the most detailed comparison of Trotaconventos with the bawd of *Pamphilus*, understands the differences in terms of a much clearer association with evil in Juan Ruiz's portrayal of the old woman than in the original.[89] That the Archpriest's creation bears little substantial similarity to the medieval Latin bawd cannot be disputed; however, the differences do imply more than a visible didactic purpose. As Phillips herself observes, Juan Ruiz matches imagery to character in a careful and disciplined manner.[90]

---

[82] Fernando Lázaro Carreter, "Los amores de don Melón y doña Endrina," *Arbor* 62 (1951) 210-236.
[83] Zahareas, *The Art of Juan Ruiz*, 171, 172.
[84] Zahareas, *The Art of Juan Ruiz*, 171.
[85] Phillips, 94.
[86] Phillips, 94.
[87] Phillips, 135.
[88] Phillips, 142.
[89] Phillips, 135-142.
[90] Phillips, 94.

This leads to a complex characterization of the bawd which charges the latter with a significance that extends beyond any didactic purpose within the work.

Prior to the entrance of the old bawd, the *Libro de buen amor* establishes a premise for the third party's crucial role in every love affair.[91] In a previous episode a messenger is sent to another one of the narrator's objects of desire. The young woman's answer to the messenger indicates her clear understanding of the functions of a go-between. Her brief conversation with the latter initiates the dynamic which goes on to become an integral part of the text: that of the pursued female and the third party, an interaction so indispensable to the *Libro de buen amor* that it overshadows the communication between the lovers.[92] The next messenger, Ferrán García, deceives the narrator by conquering the pursued lady for himself; it therefore becomes clear to the narrator that only a female third party must enter into one's amorous plans, a fact confirmed by the encounter with don Amor and his advice on sexual conquest. Part of this advice has to do with the importance of acquiring an efficient go-between. (Don Amor even credits himself with providing the principal guidelines for Ovid for his art of seduction).

In the *Pamphilus,* recourse to the third party appears as one of the last pieces of advice given by the Goddess of love to Pamphilus as he prepares himself for seduction and conquest. In the *Libro de buen amor*, immediately after describing the ideal woman, don Amor specifies that success in love requires a special type of go-between; it will be recalled that for Ovid this factor existed on the margins of his advice, with a composite third party made up of doormen and maids inserted into the *Ars amatoria* as a helpful detail along the lines of wine or seductive poetry. Don Amor, however, attends to the matter of the go-between at the very outset, lending it primary importance. He makes it clear that the task belongs to a particular kind of old woman: the description occupies strophes 436 to 449, enlightening the narrator with many a detail on the old woman's duties. One radical departure from Ovid consists of the explicit instruction that the

---

[91] Juan Ruiz, *Libro de buen amor* (henceforth *LBA*) edición crítica de A. Blecua (Barcelona: Planeta, 1983). References are to the line numbers from this edition.

[92] "dixo la duenna cuerda /a la mi mensajera:/' yo veyo muchas otras/ creer a ti, parlera, /e fállense mal ende; /castigo en su manera/bien como la comadre/en ajena mollera" (*LBA*, 81).

third party not fulfill the position of servant or confidante to the pursued woman, but rather remain completely identified with the narrator's interests.[93] Furthermore, don Amor delegates considerable authority to the go-between by filtering the beloved's beauty entirely through her judgment: the lover must listen to the third party's reports on the young woman's physique and pursue her only if the old woman reports no defects. The principal interaction at these initial stages of the love affair involves only the two women, with the lover standing by and observing the evolution of the circumstances.

Don Amor enumerates a series of qualities for the go-between which clearly indicate her upper hand in the initiation of the love affair, a factor which, as we have seen, does not concern Ovid in his approach to seduction. The God of Love stresses the moral irresponsibility of such go-betweens, yet by no means does he diminish their power for that reason. Next, when the narrator seeks the help of doña Venus, the latter also reiterates the importance of go-betweens.[94] Once the narrator has found Trotaconventos, he makes a most revealing statement on the type of relationship he maintains with this bawd as opposed to the situation found in the *Pamphilus:* "doña Venus did not do more for Pamphilus."[95] This significant remark hints at Juan Ruiz's awareness of his own carefully-designed departures from the original and complements the build-up to the entrance of the go-between, who by now, even before she has done anything, has come to represent substantial differences with the bawd of the *Pamphilus*. Phillips' findings highlight differences in the following elements: Trotaconventos' use of language, her passionate – one might say love/hate – relationship with the narrator and with Endrina, her vivid storytelling, her continual references to erotic and popular imagery, and her deeper integration into the fabric of the love affair.

As mentioned earlier, on the basis of the go-between's portrayal in the doña Endrina episode, Phillips, drawing principally on previous observations by Gybbon-Monnypenny, reaches the conclusion that the character emphasizes "loco amor" ("bad/carnal love") and therefore reconfirms the work's warning against physical love. Yet the

[93] "La mujer que embïares/ de ti sea parienta/ que bien leal te sea;/ non sea su sirvienta/ non lo sepa la dueña/ porque la otra non mienta" (*LBA*, 436).

[94] *LBA*, 645.

[95] "doña Venus por Pánfilo non pudo más fazer" (*LBA*, 698c).

bawd's presence does not limit itself to the doña Endrina episode: Trotaconventos goes on to become a companion of the narrator in several other adventures. The critique of her impact on the *Libro de buen amor* must therefore take into account her presence throughout the text, and this comprehensive assessment will reveal that the tale does not maintain a consistently reproachful attitude towards her. Rather the relationship she maintains with the narrator and the women he pursues evokes a much wider range of attitudes in the text.

The significance of these different attitudes depends upon a detailed characterization of the bawd in narrative structure and discourse. The process of characterization for the bawd simply begins in the Endrina episode, with the *Pamphilus* acting as a useful reference point which would indicate the areas where Juan Ruiz has chosen to elaborate on his go-between. The characterization then continues as the poem leaves the *Pamphilus* episode behind: subsequent interactions with the bawd occur in several situations, each of which engages a different aspect of her presence within the narrative.

In the *Pamphilus*/doña Endrina episode, Juan Ruiz expands the old woman's speeches, frequently inserting passages that have no equivalent in the Latin comedy;[96] he also makes room for the development of the third party's associations – such as witchcraft or pseudo-religiosity – as perceived by the narrator and Endrina.[97] Another element elaborated in the doña Endrina episode has to do with the bawd's relationship with both parties and the special place she occupies within the configuration of the proposed affair.[98] It must also be borne in mind that Trotaconventos offers glimpses into the perception of her own sexuality, diverting attention to her own identity as a

---

[96] For example, stanzas 740-765 where the bawd exchanges tales with Endrina, or the opening speech of the go-between, 704-705. Phillips points these out (50 and 56).

[97] Phillips, 58, 62.

[98] In Juan Ruiz's version, there are more dialogues between the old woman and both characters. Phillips points out that don Melón has a less restrained relationship with the bawd (e.g., stanzas 783-784, where he lashes out at her angrily), and Endrina, of course, has many an exchange with her in the form of exemplary fables. Elsewhere don Melón sees her as his mother-figure, or an esteemed, wise woman, thereby adding to the layers of perception which she is able to evoke in him (*LBA*, 799-800; 886). Phillips points these out but comments only very briefly on them: the designation of "mother" reduces the lover to a child figure and touches on the popular form of respectful address, and the reference to the old woman as "wise" is seen by her as a flippant gesture, as it underplays the plight of the fallen woman (Phillips, 85 and 62).

sexual being. This produces a comic effect, as Phillips proposes, but the implication extends further because the thread continues through the rest of the poem with wider meaning.[99] Another difference is that she does not reproduce the "deferential and meek" [100] attitudes of the old woman of the *Pamphilus*, making clear the availability of her services in exchange only for money. Phillips does not comment on the religious elements in the bawd's discourse.[101]

In Juan Ruiz's version the overall interaction among the three characters conjures up a strong sense of interdependence. Trotaconventos elaborates considerably on her relationship with both don Melón and doña Endrina: her initial storytelling with the latter allows for a slower, more careful introduction into the young woman's world. Similarly, the narrator, in spite of his angry outbursts, continues to demonstrate his basic dependence upon her and to refer to her as his "good old woman" and "Lady and old mother."[102] In Juan Ruiz's version, this mutual dependence is stressed alongside the emphasis on the bawd's skill with language.

(iii) *Trotaconventos and the* Mudéjar *Tradition*

The very inclusion of the *alcahueta* as a significant player in the game of love throughout the book must be considered one of the footprints of *adab* literature in *El libro de buen amor*, this being a "canonical requirement" of the genre.[103] The privileged position given to the go-between by don Amor and the subsequent full integration of the old woman in the narrator's affairs clearly indicate the work's conception of a triangular setup in amorous pursuit that includes a go-between for the purposes of seduction. Similarly, the use of religious overtones in her speech corresponds to the identical feature encountered in so many Eastern tales involving the *ʿajūz*.

Regarding the issue of self-perception, when Trotaconventos refers to herself as a pursued maiden ("çierva corriendo")[104] she does indeed strike a comic note. But as mentioned, the comic note does

---

[99] Phillips, 68.
[100] Phillips, 66.
[101] Phillips, 62.
[102] "buena vieja" and "Señora madre vieja" (*LBA*, 806a).
[103] *Orígenes y sociología*, 92.
[104] *LBA*, 826a.

not exclude a glimpse into the bawd's self-image as a sexual being: the go-between's own erotic potential comes to light in Eastern texts in a variety of contexts. Evidently, the humorous aspect serves an important purpose here, yet there is more to the erotic projection of the Spanish and Near-Eastern bawd. An inherent assumption runs through every Islamic text where the old bawd appears: to carry out her task, she must have firsthand knowledge of sexuality. Trotaconventos translates this into her methodology in addition to using it as a form of auto-reference. Later in the work when she attempts to seduce the nun doña Garoça on behalf of the narrator, she marks her discourse with blatant physical passion, enhancing the suggestive overtones by interjecting it with exclamations and a sense of frenzy experienced by herself at the very thought of sexual thrill.[105] She thereby attempts to evoke a certain complicity from her female interlocutor on the basis of a shared physical reaction.

The *Libro de buen amor* problematizes the idea of the go-between's unquestionably evil disposition to the full. The transformations undergone by the bawd in Juan Ruiz's text in this regard feature amongst the most significant contributions of medieval Spanish literature to the representation of mediation in non-marital love. As the poem moves through the narrator's subsequent love affairs, Trotaconventos creates a deep bond with the characters around her due to the interdependence which guides her dialogues with others; this close, often affectionate, yet still dubiously inspired bond invalidates the idea of her as a figure working in isolation and therefore subject to relentless criticism. She expands the limits on the identity of the *alcahueta;* this development in turn brings about a change in the predetermined nature of her qualities, mostly thanks to the complexity bestowed upon her by the narrative structure of the poem.

(iv) *Narrative Structure and the Go-Between*

After Trotaconventos makes her initial appearance, the poem settles into a pattern marked by the narrator/lover's ever-growing dependence on the bawd, displaying each new pursuit in terms of the increasingly close contact between the two. Seduction falls under the

---

[105] *LBA*, 1492.

old woman's jurisdiction while the lover, like the reader, stands aside to await the results. In the process, the lover and his go-between develop an ongoing dialogue on matters related to his situation. In such instances the poem offers a glimpse into the affective bond she has created with the narrator. Starting with references to her as "madre," the lover later specifies that "That messenger was a faithful old woman,"[106] and, prior to one of his later adventures, he reveals the degree of complicity and comfort in the following words: "I called Trotaconventos, my wise old woman;/ ready and willing, she came gladly."[107] The appellation "madre" recalls the daughter's quest for a language of love in the early lyric, as well as the unscrupulous "madre" of prose narrative. The composite and conflicting nature of these currents indicates the extent to which the signifier "madre" is open to contrasting interpretations if taken from a strictly ethical standpoint. Juan Ruiz begins the process of transcending purely ethical interpretations of such recurrent signifiers, as is the case with the adjective "plazentera" ("willing") also.

It must be noted that the word "plazentera" appears at the very beginning of the *Libro de buen amor* to describe the ideal female sexual partner.[108] The next use, for Trotaconventos, does not imply an identical meaning, but it problematizes the gesture of repetition, endowing the designation "vieja" with an unexpected but logical meaning among the many which she will receive throughout the poem. Characterized at this specific moment from the standpoint of the lover/narrator, the go-between emerges as an object of affection and, more importantly, as a woman whose long history with the lover validates the prominence of her presence all the more. The relentless moralist objectification of the *alcahueta* as sly, crafty, and corrupt thus yields to the expression of a bond which has formed between her and the narrator without which the articulation of *eros* would be impossible. The old woman too is desirable and willing, in the taxonomy of the narrator: mediation is itself a desirable act.

Juan Ruiz never ceases to problematize this affectionate picture

---

[106] "Aquesta mensajera fue vieja bien leal" (*LBA*, 914a).

[107] "Fiz llamar Trotaconventos, la mi vieja sabida;/ presta e plazentera, de grado fue venida" (*LBA*, 1317ab).

[108] "As Aristotle says, it is true/ the world moves for two reasons: the first/ to have food, and the other to couple with a willing female" ("Como dize Aristótiles, cosa es verdadera,/ el mundo por dos cosas trabaja: la primera,/ por aver mantenencia, la otra cosa era juntamiento con fembra plazentera") (*LBA*, 71).

and assumes a playful moralist posture every now and then, showing his full awareness of the presuppositions which accompany his bawd. Flanking the notion of his bond with Trotaconventos with detailed examples of the old woman in action and interrupting the more intimate, approving views of her with cautionary asides such as "beware of the false old woman,"[109] he creates a wider perspective for the appreciation of her role and does not destroy her place within the well-known tradition of *alcahuetería.* In so doing he allows for the bawd's perception from a number of different standpoints so that her distinct effects on each character may be discerned accordingly. The narrator's own accounts of the shifting nature of their relationship reveal the necessity for the existence of many perspectives for gauging the bawd's impact. The narrator and the procuress construct a passionate relationship of their own marked by angry outbursts and affectionate dialogue, as seen in their exchanges in which he calls her anything from "killer" to "dear old mother." This attests to the multifaceted nature of their relationship, pointing out the complexities in a bond constructed upon financial and emotional investment. To some degree, the fluctuating nature of their relationship mirrors the coexistence of Muslims and Christians. The shifting attitudes of the narrator indicate the difficulties of filtering the bawd through a consistently reproachful or deferential attitude and open the path for the critique of any uniformity of interpretation. The wide range of appellations also points to the challenges set up poetically in involving a third party in the discourse on erotic love. As listener, helper, confidante, with everything except an erotic attachment to the lover, the third party is apostrophized by the lover in ways which enable the exploration of frustration and hope in the absence of the true object of desire. Mediation equals the crucial dialogue about love, reflecting in each instance the vicissitudes lived by the lover.

To widen the critical scope further, the text also offers ample opportunity to observe the third party from the perspective of the pursued women, adding yet another layer to the composite picture of the bawd. The traditional modes of address to the bawd found abundantly in Eastern and Western literature include insults and accusations directed at the go-between and the younger woman's declarations that she remains perfectly aware of the crone's ulterior motives.

---

[109] "guárdate de falsa vieja" (*LBA*, 909c).

Juan Ruiz's poem subjects this antagonistic dynamic to careful observation. The work continually points to the degree of the old woman's inclusion into the fabric of everyday life and to the interdependence, with women just as much as men, upon which the bawd builds her career. This interdependence blurs the usual opposition of bawd/victim, although not in the parodic fashion of elegy or the *fabliaux* where the go-between's final impact had little to do with the art of seduction. Rather, the interwoven dynamics of reliance which link the *alcahueta* to those who surround her subject the very idea of the old woman's inherent evil, as well as the pursued woman's victim-status, to critique. The encounter with Garoça illustrates that for the solicited woman, the bawd represents more than just an evil element from the outside world; Garoça first addresses the go-between thus: "How are you, my old woman? How is life?" The bawd starts the reply with the phrase: "Since I left you (...)"[110] Subsequently, when Garoça refuses to acknowledge the seductive message in the first exemplary fable told by the old woman, the latter exclaims: "Why am I so badly treated? When I bring gifts, then I am treated so well;/ today I come empty-handed, and I am bad-mouthed."[111] The aura of familiarity between the two women transforms the bawd's public image into a more integrated and less evil one, since the customary reaction of anger soon develops into a relatively peaceful dialogue.

Moreover, doña Garoça introduces an element of respect in her dealings with the "vieja":

> "Old woman," said the lady, "I did not lie:
> You hurt me with the words you said;
> What I told you, I regretted later,
> Because I can see that you are a very worthwhile person,
> But, I am very fearful of being duped."[112]

Even though Garoça at this points resists the advances made by Trotaconventos, she indicates her desire to avoid fighting with the old

---

[110] "¿Cómo te va, mi vieja,/ cómo passas la vida?" "Desque me partí de vós" (*LBA*, 1345a).

[111] "¿Por qué só baldonada? Quando trayo presente, só mucho falagada;/ oy vin manos vazías, finco malestultada" (*LBA*, 1356).

[112] Vieja, dixo la dueña, cierto yo non mentí:
por lo que me dixiste yo mucho me sentí;
de lo que yo te dixe luego me arrepentí,
porque talento bueno entiendo yo en ti;
Mas témome e recelo que mal engañada sea (*LBA*, 1368-9a).

woman: "may the fight end."[113] These gestures on Garoça's part contribute to the elaboration of the perspective crafted by Juan Ruiz for the critical appreciation of his bawd: the narrative of her biography, coming to us in lively dialogues and occasional flashbacks as opposed to the linear and embittered paths we have seen in *Le Roman de la Rose* or Chaucer's Tale, now includes an amiable past history as well as a present interaction with others that allows playfulness and familiarity. These, in addition to Garoça's subtle respect, make for the creation of a new and complex premise for the depiction of the bawd.

In his lively portrayal of the go-between, Juan Ruiz also shows how the bawd's familiarity with the woman can lead to mockery and failure. The procuress's excessive faith in this acquaintance ends with comical results when the *alcahueta* greets a Moorish girl whom the narrator would like to seduce with exaggerated enthusiasm, mentioning the last time they saw one another.[114] The approach fails right away, creating a momentarily pathetic image of the bawd, reminding the reader that a past history does not necessarily imply sincerity on the old woman's part. She concentrates first and foremost on the professional advantage of this familiarity and in this case faces the immediate dismissal of this move by the Moorish girl.

El libro de buen amor contains several depictions of the bawd from other characters' perspectives in dialogue with or without her. These multiple focalizations enrich the character of the *alcahueta* yet do not create a paradoxical image.[115] They exist for different reasons, corresponding to the hidden agendas of characters who operate at odds with one another's interests, each of whose discourse on carnal love differs from the next one. As a result, the go-between encounters both praise and reproach for her work and is characterized as anything from a kind mother to a ruthless old devil. Rather than create a puzzling or inconsistent image of her, these conflicting qualifications bring to light the differences in attitude when dealing with a third party implicated in one's private life: financial commitments or past history further complicate this relationship, and by reporting the various attitudes towards the bawd, Juan Ruiz thematizes this complication as a basic factor in the triangulation of desire.

---

[113] "e finque la pelea" (*LBA*, 1369d).

[114] *LBA*, 1509b.

[115] See Zahareas, *The Art of Juan Ruiz*, 171, who concludes that Trotaconventos remains at all times a puzzling presence in the work.

In stanzas 924-927, the Archpriest brilliantly displays a condensed and highly charged parade of all the different stances available to himself and the reader regarding the procuress.[116] Evidently, the list serves a fundamental comic purpose, drawing on contemporary legal and sociological references.[117] Whatever the "now-lost" context of the nicknames, their humorous qualities maintain considerable effectiveness, and Juan Ruiz recalls the bawd's continuous links with laughter.

At the same time, along the margins of the passage looms the narrator's own acknowledgment of his utter dependence on the old woman, coming to the reader in the stanzas immediately preceding and following the list of nicknames. In these, the narrator makes no secret of the influence exerted upon his own language by the bawd: after all, one gesture by her (in line 919) triggers off the poet's listing of her potential nicknames in the spirit of fun, "as though in a game."[118] Her anger upon hearing the words uttered in jest reverses the narrator's tone of playful insult and modifies it to the point of arriving at the designation of the crone as "Good Love" ("Buen Amor") itself.[119]

In the space of a few verses, then, Juan Ruiz has spanned the vast range covered by the signifier "vieja" from such notions as dishonorable and malevolent to the affectionate "my old woman" and the charged epithet "Buen Amor." The barrage of adjectives and names in these lines recalls at once the perspective of those women with whom the bawd has dealt as well as the narrator's playful yet dependent attitude towards the go-between. The old woman's chief fea-

---

[116] Lists figure often in the *Libro de buen amor*, as María Rosa Lida de Malkiel had observed in "Nuevas notas para la interpretación del *Libro de buen amor*," *Estudios de literatura española y comparada* (Buenos Aires: Editorial Universitaria de Buenos Aires, 1966) 32-33.

[117] John K. Walsh, "The names of the Bawd in the 'Libro de buen amor,'" in *Florilegium Hispanicum: Medieval and Golden Age Studies Presented to Dorothy Clotelle Clark*, 151-164. Walsh analyzes the parodic and comic elements at work in the list of nicknames, concluding that it is a continuation of the animal imagery associated with seduction throughout the work and hence quite comic, and that the modern reader cannot appreciate every nuance in the same way as "a now-distant original audience" (162). According to Walsh, one "possible frame for parody," for example, is "that of a specific legal formulation" as found in so many local *fueros* of the time, in which "there are sub-sections prohibiting insults and abusive names – especially, those with sexual connotations" (156).

[118] "como en juego" (*LBA*, 920a).

[119] *LBA*, 933b.

tures come together and remain ever open to various interpretations in a single sweep.

Juan Ruiz points out that her impact, therefore, must be gauged in terms of the complex relationships which she sets up with various parties, all of whom shape their discourse in relation to her. The poem contains several formulaic or expected reactions to the bawd, yet more importantly and consistently it establishes the idea of a shifting dynamic with each character. The complexity provided by narrative structure is complemented by the old woman's own discourse in situating herself within the history and typology of the medieval *alcahueta*.

(v) *Elements of Discourse*

Trotaconventos makes use of language with special vitality and focus, handling verbal manipulation with a vigor that no critic has failed to point out.[120] Taken not in isolation but as a milestone in the evolution of *alcahuetería* in literature, the bawd's discourse acquires special significance: Trotaconventos, an evolved heir to the "madres" of the lyric and the go-betweens of the *cuentística* among others, takes speech to a new level and makes it her most prized asset. Thus the ever fragile connotations of sorcery are cast aside more forcefully.

Initially, for the embittered narrator, this eloquence signifies nothing but evil, as made by clear by his reproach to don Amor when the poet imagines the type of procuress who works at the service of Love: "Your go-between will find a way [to seduce a girl for you]/ she will use 'mouth,' 'tongue,' 'mind' to attack her and corrupt her mind."[121] Once Trotaconventos appears and begins the actual process of seduction, the narrator expands this vision and takes note of the old woman's complexity. Significantly, the go-between's very first speech has no counterpart in the *Pamphilus*. The tone set by her at this point veers towards a popular and crude register, colorful in its recourse to

---

[120] The special vitality of Trotaconventos is mentioned by several critics, for instance Lecoy in *Recherches*, 317; Zahareas, *The Art of Juan Ruiz*, 158-172; María Rosa Lida, *Dos obras maestras españolas* (Buenos Aires: Editorial Universitaria de Buenos Aires, 1966) 37, 39. All are correct in pointing out that she possesses dynamic qualities; yet these critics do not delve deeply into the elements of her discourse.

[121] "tu católica allá cata manera que la trastorne;/*os, lingua, mens la envade,* seso con ardor pospone" (*LBA*, 379).

"raw imagery."[122] She conjures up experience and confidence, with little respect for the possible resistance of woman. She produces a lively and uninhibited language designed to express the basic fact that carnality takes precedence over all else. Phillips sees in her "use of crude euphemisms, double entendres, and well-known erotic symbols" the intention to "debase completely the traditional courtly picture of a cool, remote heroine."[123] Yet the text has hardly raised the reader's expectations to await a "courtly heroine," given the unmistakable images of sexual and distinctly non-courtly love established so far in the dialogues with don Amor and doña Venus.[124] These images are continued by Trotaconventos, who with her double entendres and playful symbols also provides relatively clear innuendoes.

For the seduction of doña Endrina, the go-between reveals the trademark of her strategy, which consists of approaching the young woman from a variety of directions, simultaneously creating several coexisting images that generate erotic, practical, and visceral responses. Trotaconventos does not limit herself to a particular type of discourse for each, but draws on both metaphorical and direct terms to drive her points home. Metaphors related to food or animals make for sensual titillation without posing any blatant, unethical threats. The bawd demonstrates that she derives great strength from an unfaltering belief in the premise of her own argument: that the physiological aspect of love takes precedence over all else, and physicality is a necessary, natural phenomenon.

In the passages where she explains the delights of love, Trotaconventos selects her images more carefully than her Latin counterpart; at one point, Juan Ruiz adds two stanzas (863-864) to develop the theme. Phillips remarks that these "provide further evidence of the go-between's almost hypnotic persuasiveness."[125] More importantly, they touch on a purely sexual matter, whetting Endrina's appetite for an encounter. Whereas the *lena* of the Latin play had tempted Galatea with fruit and nuts, in the Spanish bawd's case, "many of the foods she lists are traditionally associated with sexual love, and it is

[122] Phillips, 51.

[123] Phillips, 51.

[124] For the abundance of such imagery in the book, see Louise O. Vasvari, "Festive Phallic Discourse in the *Libro del Arcipreste*," *La Corónica* 22:2 (Spring 1994) 89-117.

[125] Phillips, 79.

significant that she makes these delicacies available specifically to 'las loçanas' [862a]."[126]

On the practical level, the bawd shows her skill for evoking cautionary realistic scenes and relating them to a general, infallible truth which would apply to doña Endrina's situation. In stanzas 754-758, the old woman enumerates the advantages of allowing a man into one's life by touching briefly on the many things that can go wrong in the absence of a man both practically and emotionally. Demonstrating a special aptitude for conjuring up particular scenes from daily life, she illustrates her point by using brief scenarios which show the woman suffering from solitude or legal helplessness at home. Subsequently she strengthens the image by linking it to a generalization, painting the dismal picture of a life lived without a man, alone and afraid.[127]

She mingles imagery with direct communication, adding constant references to both general and particular situations, and thus formulates a very competent strategy. Trotaconventos maintains a balance in all areas, ensuring that her utterances do not lose a visible pertinence to doña Endrina's personal resistance or vulnerabilities. Again, a comparison with the *Pamphilus* helps underscore the different nature of Trotaconventos' skills. For instance, stanza 837 of the *Libro de buen amor* (which corresponds to verses 568-570 of the *Pamphilus*) shows both bawds speaking on the effects of love to the younger woman, yet Trotaconventos is quick to connect the general idea to the specific case of doña Endrina.[128] In the last stage of her dialogue with Endrina prior to the meeting with don Melón, Trotaconventos renders her appeal to don Melón's love object all the more effective by siding with the younger woman, creating the illusion that she – the older woman – only wishes to be Endrina's sympathetic companion.

As early as the doña Endrina episode, Juan Ruiz demonstrates the essentially triangular shape of seductive discourse when he plays it off against the male protagonist. In other traditions, on the whole, the recurrent features of the dynamic between male lover and go-between have shown that the man monitors the progress of the third party, expressing sentiments ranging from anger to panic to hope. Accordingly, the professional bawd – in both Eastern and Western works – offers recognizably reassuring or despairing words to the man as a req-

[126] Phillips, 79.
[127] *LBA*, 757.
[128] Phillips, 71.

uisite of her job. It will be recalled that in the Near-Eastern tradition the erotic energy of the go-between at times emerges as one facet of her relationship with the man, leading to ridicule or a darker sexual tension according to the tone of the work. Juan Ruiz downplays this aspect but elaborates the verbal exchanges between the two to demonstrate the ways in which the old woman manipulates the man's supervision, advancing mediation to the forefront of the seductive process.

This expansion contributes significantly to the emergence of Trotaconventos as a literary character, especially in terms of the textual poetics of love and seduction. While certain aspects of her interaction with the narrator remain necessarily predictable, the old woman reveals her strategies in more detail through her dialogues with the lover. The most important strategy constitutes an ongoing exploitation of seductive discourse: in her second meeting with don Melón, which concerns an account she gives of doña Endrina's reactions to the advances so far, she provides "slyly titillating comment[s]"[129] and indications of how Endrina has been reacting. Gybbon-Monypenny and Phillips both note, for example, that the bawd "adds one or two extra touches" to the description of an impatient Endrina, that she emphasizes secrecy, and that "she stresses her power over the girl and her willingness to exercise it if properly paid."[130]

These factors and others related to departures from the *Pamphilus* warrant further interpretation. The Archpriest's bawd imposes an idea of herself on others as an absolute professional while conveying to the lover her instinctive understanding of the delightful temptations of beauty and physical love. Doña Endrina's position requires that the bawd shape her discourse according to notions of feminine complicity and gentle persuasion by means of metaphorical or anecdotal appeals. With don Melón, the flexibility of that discourse comes into full view when the go-between endows her utterances with features designed to suit a masculine frame of mind according to the poem: she describes physical beauty in titillating and direct terms, displays a business-like gravity by sharing aspects of her methodology (808c), and boasts of a predatory type of power over the girl.[131] She

[129] Gybbon-Monypenny, "'Dixe la por te dar ensienpro'," 140. She tells him: "Pareçe que con vusco non se estaría dormiendo" ("It looks like with you she will not catch much sleep") (*LBA*, 811d). No parallel to this exists in the *Pamphilus*.

[130] Gybbon-Monypenny, "'Dixe la por te dar ensienpro'," 140.

[131] *LBA*, 868d.

tells him to "act like a man" according to an idea supposedly understood by them both as reiterated in her firm command to him: "be a man tomorrow, so that you are not taken for a mere actor."[132] She aligns herself as accomplice to both the male and the female parties by lending the appropriate seductive slant to the components of her discourse in both cases.

Often in her conversations with both don Melón and doña Endrina, as well as in her later encounter with doña Garoça, which reveals the solid continuity with which the old woman is portrayed, the old woman resorts to popular and folkloric imagery in order to convey her ideas. The critic John Dagenais regards this device as one of the "*formes simples* of ethical reading in medieval scripta."[133] He observes that the chaining and amplification of proverbs becomes

> a characteristic "mode" of writing in Castilian in the Middle Ages and after. (...) the character of the go-between seems almost to have been chosen for the known penchant among such old crones for spouting proverbs(...). Trotaconventos' character allows the author to lard his text with a maximum number of proverbial expressions.[134]

This is a useful and astute observation, but must be complemented by the recognition that the language of Trotaconventos does not limit itself merely to an identification with simple forms, given that her tactics of seduction engage more than just one form of address. When she draws on proverbs and popularisms, the simple authority of such utterances functions well because she mingles these with direct, sexually charged appeals to project the validity of personal experience backed by general proof. Thus, when breaking the good news to don Melón that doña Endrina will see him, she says: "It is quite true, that which is said in the proverb/ that the pilgrim who persists will always attain his bread."[135] The proverb retrospectively justifies her sense of confidence in an implicit announcement to the lover that she has known all along that hard work will always pay off. The proverb and its concrete proof also serve as a lesson in persever-

---

[132] "sed cras omne en todo, non vos tengan por tenico" (*LBA*, 869c).

[133] John Dagenais, *The Ethics of Reading in Manuscript Culture: Glossing the* Libro de buen amor (Princeton: Princeton University Press, 1994) 65.

[134] Dagenais, 66.

[135] "Sé-que bien diz verdat vuestro proverbio chico/quë 'el romero hito/siempre saca çatico" (*LBA*, 869ab).

ance, in whose delivery she briefly assumes the role of his teacher by demonstrating the uses of steadfastness to him.

As the poem moves forward, the *alcahueta* continues her engagement of several traditional features of her literary antecedents from such sources as the lyric, short narrative, and Eastern material. In each case she brings about significant evolutions because of the multileveled connection she has established with other characters by means of language. She adapts her utterances to particular situations and explores the possibilities of seduction relentlessly. Juan Ruiz unfolds the many layers which inform the nature of the *alcahueta*'s interactions with others: the poet shows the relationship between the financial, pedagogical, and personal networks created in the triangular positioning of the players.

As a literary character, Trotaconventos develops in terms of the complexities which she adds to the language of mediation with each new task, aware that she must defend her methodology and her choice of words every time. So, after a string of failures shared by both lover and bawd, starting in stanza 1332, Trotaconventos suggests to the narrator that he contemplate the love of a nun. This is a familiar *topos* for medieval literature and, in this case, serves partly to recall the connection of the old go-between with the world of the convent.[136] Trotaconventos personalizes the theme by giving specific examples of the nuns' behavior and uses this professed insider knowledge to lend considerable authenticity to the content of her speech. She mentions recipes, herbs, spices and stimulants used by the religious women in their quest for physical fulfillment, equating her knowledge, not without a touch of humor and irony, with the mainstream and morally acceptable facts which circulate from known scientific centers such as Montpellier, Alexandria, and Valencia.[137]

The old woman translates her familiarity with the lifestyle of the nuns into an aura of feminine mystery for the male interlocutor, seducing him into desiring them by means of a tight focus on the nuns' interest in exotic medicine and their rampant sexual desire.[138] Cleverly, she reports on their know-how without once implicating herself as an agent in their conception of the art of love, thus enhancing the sense that she stands in some awe regarding their practices,

---

[136] For the *topos* of nuns and sexual love, see Graciela S. Daichman, *Wayward Nuns in Medieval Literature* (Syracuse: Syracuse University Press, 1986); also *Recherches*, 266-270.

[137] *LBA*, 1338d.

[138] For instance, *LBA*, 1341-1342.

speaking of the rich and strange foods which they eat.[139] She presents an exoticized truth, based on visible images of food and drink, separating herself from the facts by expressing naive enthusiasm, thereby lending much credibility to her assertions. By personalizing the situation, providing exact details yet stepping aside with wonder alongside the narrator, the old woman turns the literary *topos* of the sexually active nun into an immediate, dynamic fact, endowed with new life through her words. The lover stands tantalized and convinced, now only concerned with how he may penetrate this abode.[140]

Her subsequent encounter with the nun doña Garoça produces successful results because the same vitality and identification with the interlocutor run through the conversation with the nun.[141] Even if the sequence of exemplary stories provokes resistance on the part of Garoça, the latter also acknowledges the enticing quality of the bawd's storytelling, referring to her utterances as "these good words, these sweet charms[.]"[142] The go-between goes directly after the point which most perturbs the younger woman, causing her to put up resistance. So, once Garoça has recounted the fable of the fox and the crow and expressed her fear of becoming an unchaste nun, Trotaconventos replies that fear is a known characteristic of nuns and that she must not allow it to dissuade the suitor.[143] The assertion prefaces an anecdote that cleverly avoids any further elaboration of this particular fear, but the bawd has indeed managed to reduce the gravity of the nun's anxiety with a casual yet firm generalization which, in one sweeping gesture, acknowledges and dismisses the fear.

The old bawd chooses the correct path for the seduction of the younger woman by addressing the latter's main concern with her ethical obligations as a nun. Trotaconventos attacks these reservations from personal and general angles, again resorting to proverbs and tales, but always keeping alert to Garoça's own circumstances. For example, Trotaconventos provides an observation regarding the daily behavior of the young woman and other nuns, condemning Garoça's notion of propriety. She expresses disappointment with the

---

[139] *LBA*, 1333cd.

[140] *LBA*, 1343.

[141] This episode also reveals significant links with Islamic techniques of debate and reasoning; see my "Trotaconventos, Doña Garoça, and the Dynamics of Dialectical Reasoning," *Bulletin of Hispanic Studies*, LXXVI (1999), forthcoming.

[142] "estas buenas palabras,/estos dulces falagos" (*LBA*, 1436a).

[143] *LBA*, 1444.

nuns' habit of sitting sadly, singing or reading, fighting amongst each other, and never allowing themselves to have fun.[144]

This represents a far cry from the image she had evoked for the Archpriest when inciting him to consider a nun-mistress; gone are the references to wild and titillating behavior aimed at whetting the man's appetite. For the moment, gone also are proverbs and generalizations. Instead, here the *alcahueta* demonstrates another talent by creating a series of very simple, private images to communicate the sense of boredom and underachievement with the added pretense of a deep personal concern for the nun's dull lifestyle. Even her exclamation "¡Yuy, yuy!" as she describes nuns' lives conveys a simple yet urgent worry brought about by observing the dullness of a nun's existence. The young woman therefore hears an unfavorable report on her own image. Cleverly, Trotaconventos follows up the assessment with proof when she shows Garoça a sample of what really goes on in the rectory after mass, that is, nuns and priests indulging fully in hedonistic pleasures.[145] Faced with the old woman's concern, her wealth of substantiating proverbs and tales, and the proof of living examples around her, Garoça may well be questioning her own normalcy as a nun at this point, aware that she fails to correspond to the textual *topos* of her image. The old woman finally attains success, and, in a gesture of awe, the narrator declares his great debt to her utterances: "(...) from good words/came good results."[146] Concomitantly, she offers the narrator step-by-step advice on how to go about his treatment of the young woman.[147] The precise instructions provide a visible contrast with the vehement and excited tone of the previous lines to doña Garoça, demonstrating the bawd's talent for changing the tone and structure of her sentences to suit the particular interlocutor.

With Trotaconventos, the limits for the typology of the Spanish go-between expand to include language as the driving force behind an intricate strategy of seduction. Those components associated with the go-between – magic, past experience, and financial greed – act in Trotaconventos as elementary qualities which, when subordinated to a lively and powerful discourse, turn the bawd into more than the sum of her parts. A wide variety of signifiers turns the old woman into

---

[144] *LBA*, 1396cd-7abc.

[145] *LBA*, 1399.

[146] "de buena fabla/vino buena cima" (*LBA*, 1498d).

[147] *LBA*, 1495-1496.

a central figure in the poem, evoking different responses at different times. Rather than interpret these as either unresolvable ambivalence or didacticism, the conclusion must be reached that the *alcahueta* of Juan Ruiz raises questions on the legitimacy of strict, ethical judgment of a literary character and marks the poet's consciousness of the power of ambiguity in representation. In his use of dialogue in particular, the Archpriest draws attention to the poetics of seduction at work and underscores the validity of the go-between as a literary persona whose dialogic position with other characters engages the age-old preoccupation of moral wrongdoing from a vantage perspective.

The critic Michael S. Macovski refers to "the status of dialogue as an inquiry into otherness" in his study of Romantic literature and illustrates the ways in which a character's capacity to "investigate both themselves and some central, noumenal character" have to do with the externalized vantage of dialogue.[148] Macovski's readings of selected Romantic texts show that the very use of dialogue by characters turns this form of communication into an interpretive rhetoric since it causes "a rhetorical displacement that effectively enables characters to stand outside themselves, to see themselves from the 'third' perspective."[149] He adds:

> We are now in a position (...) to discuss this externalized vantage in terms of that investigative stance often sought by cultural anthropologists – an anthropological distance that strives for a kind of cultural otherness. By thus comparing both literary and cultural investigations, we will be able to reframe our (...) conclusions about interpretive dialogue within the larger context of literary hermeneutics and cultural studies.[150]

In spite of its special reference to Romantic literature, Macovski's critique of dialogue as a rhetorical device is applicable to the case of the Spanish *alcahueta,* for it signals the device's potential for tracing the development of new perspectives for auditor and speaker. We have seen that Trotaconventos's methodology derives its greatest strength from her capacity to "stand outside" herself and to respond to her interlocutors within frames of reference with which they are suppos-

[148] Michael S. Macovski, *Dialogue and Literature: Apostrophe, Auditors, & the Collapse of Romantic Discourse* (Oxford: Oxford University Press, 1994) 172. (Henceforth *Dialogue and Literature*).
[149] *Dialogue and Literature*, 172.
[150] *Dialogue and Literature*, 172.

edly more comfortable. Her use of dialogue is a genuine attempt at communication, refined and reworked each time to suit the moment. The process requires her appreciation of other perspectives and her willingness to assume the roles of speaker and auditor in dealings with others, which she accomplishes with ease.

Macovski observes that the dialogic position of the auditor in dialogue signifies his or her "outsideness," promoting the investigation of the central characters in light of the outsider's ability to confront the central issue or character from a different interpretive location.[151] Curiously enough, in spite of her love of chatter and her relentless identification with speech, Trotaconventos simultaneously occupies the position of an auditor in the poem, for she exists to listen to lovers' demands, to transmit them to the objects of desire, and in turn to absorb the latter's reactions and thereby gauge the chances for success or failure in the seductive process. The inextricable links which connect her task to the act of listening and noticing endow her with the qualities of an auditor who, according to Bakhtin, understands the situation better than anyone else:

> In order to understand, it is immensely important for the person who understands to be *located outside* the object of his or her creative understanding – in time, in space, in culture. For one cannot even really see one's own exterior and comprehend it as a whole, and no mirrors or photographs can help; our real exterior can be seen and understood only by other people, because they are located outside us in space and because they are *others*.[152]

Macovski sees this as a pertinent statement with regards to literature also, explaining that "the external interlocutor is able not only to stand outside a textual enigma but to launch an investigatory dialogue into it."[153] The critic points out correctly that this endeavor may or may not lead to actual understanding, but it does instantiate dialogue, "the rhetorical encounter that (...) can confront both textual and cultural meaning."[154]

As an old woman, a third party, and a figure charged with negative imagery, Trotaconventos stands outside the boundaries inhabited by young lovers in pursuit of carnal pleasure. But her integration

---

151 *Dialogue and Literature*, 173.
152 Mikhael Bakhtin, cited in *Dialogue and Literature*, 173.
153 *Dialogue and Literature*, 173.
154 *Dialogue and Literature*, 173.

into their world as the best architect of the artifice of seduction places her in a location which implies distance and intimacy at once: technically, the results of the seductive processes have nothing to do with her, yet their failure or success is accounted for by her. Likewise, the lovers ought to engage in dealings with one another, and yet for the most part the poem shows them in dialogue with the old woman. These seemingly paradoxical and shifting positions – all of which are translated into dialogue – show the poetics of love to be founded entirely on the interdependence of three and not two figures. This interdependence is no longer fueled by the overdetermined assumptions of Eastern texts to the effect that where there is illicit love there is an old woman. Rather, it takes that requirement as a point of departure and ventures into the space of poetic creation with it, showing that the communication of lovers comes to existence only when mediated by a third party rich in resonances from the lyric, legal writings, moralist narrative, and other genres. The character is simply too prevalent in medieval Spanish and Islamic literature to go unnoticed by an artist of Juan Ruiz's caliber, and with Trotaconventos he pursues the pathways which link her textually and culturally with her predecessors. The shape and nature of her organic links with others – left largely untouched by other Eastern and Western writers – are, indeed, explored fully by Juan Ruiz.

Textual and cultural paths of investigation intersect again, more than one century later, when Fernando de Rojas creates Celestina by making ample use of the wealth of literary traditions available to him. He pursues an altogether different direction than Juan Ruiz yet continues the Archpriest's work insofar as the elaboration of a main literary character is concerned. Rojas expands the range of referential meaning for Celestina to the point of transforming her into an indispensable reference for the typology of the medieval go-between.

VIII. The Go-between as Principal Literary Character: *La Celestina*

(i) *The Essential Frameworks of* alcahuetería *for* La Celestina *of Fernando de Rojas: Sources and Traditions*

The mindframe and time period of *La Celestina* stand at a considerable distance from the world of *El libro de buen amor*. However, the two literary creations form significant links to one another since Rojas, while positing a new series of problems in his work and also bringing in a humanist perspective, continues in the vein of a tradition known also to Juan Ruiz.[155] López-Baralt, having outlined the traces of Eastern presence in the *Kāma Sūtra español*, states that *La Celestina* appears to be the only Spanish and even European work (other than *El libro de buen amor*) inscribed in the erotico-spiritual universe of *mudéjar* concerns.[156]

Some transformations in the *mudéjar* character of erotology can be gauged in Celestina, most of which occur within the old woman's own realistic representation, a feature which many critics have noticed.[157] After all, the *alcahueta* existed as a familiar figure in urban and university life, and Rojas had many models on which to draw. The image of the procuress in society has always evoked mercenary sexual exchange, greed, and corruption. At the same time, her identity conjured up the idea of a certain type of knowledge, highly relevant to sexuality in general and the female body in particular, that treads a gray area between procuring and the science of gynecology. By the time of the publication of *La Celestina*, much medical information on human sexuality had circulated in Spain and the rest of Europe, utilized among others by midwives who exercised great influence in the field of women's health but whose control was consistently on the wane as of the fifteenth century.[158] This simultaneous access to and loss of control is dramatized by Celestina.

The circulation of sexual information of Arabic provenance had begun in the West in the eleventh century with the *De coitu* attributed

---

[155] *Orígenes y sociología*, 180.

[156] López-Baralt, 163.

[157] Several aspects of this "verisimilitude" are analyzed in María Rosa Lida's *La originalidad*; also, Stephen Gilman, in *The Art of* La Celestina (Madison: University of Wisconsin Press, 1956), discusses the realistic quality of the dialogue, which enhances the dramatic nature of the work. The insertion of many realistic details is also noted by M. Criado de Val, "Melibea y Celestina ante el juicio de Don Quijote," *Anales Cervantinos* IV (1954) 187-198.

[158] Daniel Jacquard and Claude Thomasset, *Sexuality and Medicine in the Middle Ages*, translated by Matthew Adamson (Princeton: Princeton University Press, 1988) point out that a woman doctor named Trotula practiced at Salerno in the twelfth century: she exemplifies the type of medical practice and expertise monopolized in the Middle Ages by women. Trotula was essentially a midwife, and three treatises on female anatomy are wrongly ascribed to her but have continued to be identified as her works (71). See J. F. Benton, "Trotula, Women's Problems, and Professionalization of Medicine in the Middle Ages," *Bulletin of the History of Medicine*, 59 (1985) 30-53.

to Constantine the African.[159] With the advent of this genre, that is, medical treatises which dealt in detail with the physiological and sometimes psychological aspects of sexuality, the discourse on sexuality developed its own special lexicon.[160] The links between Western sexual knowledge and the Arab contributions to the erotico-medical field strengthened continuously, since in the medieval West this material remained essentially in the province of translation. Based on the translations of writings by scientists such as Avicenna, a medical discourse on sexuality established itself as an instrument for the graphic yet serious discussion of female and male sexuality.[161]

Among the medical writings on sexuality which circulated in the Middle Ages existed three treatises, written probably in Salerno towards the end of the twelfth century, attributed to the famous midwife Trotula.[162] In these, the author discusses gynecological problems and solutions, many of which refer directly to issues related to intercourse in addition to problems regarding the menses, childbirth, and the like. Trotula mentions that several of her health and beauty tips come from witnessing the ways of Saracen women: for example, she draws on the latter for the cure for bad breath as well as advice on hairdressing. This type of non-medical advice constitutes the premise to pleasurable erotic activity (note Celestina's advice to Lucrecia in Act IV, in which she announces her knowledge of powders which eliminate bad breath).[163] The Saracen women from whom Trotula learns exemplify one of many currents of the influence in Europe of the Arab approach to sexuality, which connects physiological drives to a heightened consciousness of skills and talents destined to yield

---

[159] López-Baralt, 182. Jacquard and Thomasset consider the original to have been by Ibn al-Jazzar. The full text by Constantine appears in *Constantini Liber de coitu. El tratado de andrología de Constantino el Africano*, estudio y edición crítica de Enrique Montero Cartelle (Santiago de Compostela: Universidad de Santiago, 1983). Of special importance is the fact that in his *De coitu*, Constantine speaks of the pleasure of carnal love as sanctioned by God, a declaration which would ring unfamiliar to the Christian mentality of his time.

[160] Jacquard and Thomasset, 116.

[161] Jacquard and Thomasset offer a useful overview of this kind of textual production: for example, Gentile da Foligno's *Expositiones in Librum Tertium Canonis Avicenne*, Bernard de Gordon's *Lilium medicine* (14th century), and Jean de Gaddesden's *Rosa anglica* (14th century).

[162] Jacquard and Thomasset, 121. The authors point out that an examination of the manuscripts indicates a male author, yet the texts continue to be attributed to Trotula.

[163] *Celestina*, IV, 101. (Henceforth references will be to act and page number).

greater pleasure. This concept of pleasure includes both physical and aesthetic response; as Jacquard and Thomasset explain, few were the Arab doctors or scolars who did not explore the erotic and pleasurable aspect of sexuality in their writings.[164]

Concerning the anatomy and sexuality of women, Trotula assumes a presupposed honorable stance articulated when she links her remarks on restored virginity to a firm medical reason. The same would have to apply to the observations on the adverse effects of abstinence. However, this type of knowledge possesses every quality of a double-edged sword: it can easily fuel the discourse of those who, according to a mainstream ethical position, carry a more unethical agenda, for it brings with it an unequivocal aura of scientific authority and can impress the listener. It attracts the laywoman's diffidence for science, facing her with open yet titillating discussions of the mysteries of the body.

An essential framework for the identification of Celestina's audience (to a much greater extent than Trotaconventos) concerns her claims to a science of erotic love, based on the unfaltering conviction that love above all concerns the body and that none other than the old woman has enough experience to guide others through it. The ever-recurrent evil image of the old woman inevitably ties in with exploitations of such scientific know-how, subtly turning the science into a deceitful art of erotic love. Literature, if it transmits that knowledge, offers useful and detrimental information to readers.[165] *La Celestina* plays an important part in unveiling the workings of this dynamic to its readership.

Both in the context of medicine and that of prostitution, society assumes that an old woman who possesses knowledge stands witness to the sexual act and becomes an interested spectator to the procedure. On this premise, the writers of *Sexuality and Medicine in the Middle Ages* hint at the intricate bond between knowledge and old women:

> Outside the framework of prostitution, there was another character who witnessed the sexual act in the Middle Ages – the matron, the midwife who was required particularly in proceedings for the annulment of marriage. The surgeon Guy of Chauliac describes her as administering aphrodisiacs, making free with her advice and being

[164] Jacquard and Thomasset, 123.
[165] Jacquard and Thomasset, 112.

> present "for a few days" at relations between husband and wife, so as to be in a position to make a report to the doctor who in turn would be able to give his opinion to the judicial authorities (...).
>
> There were thus two types of women who had expertise in sexuality: the procuress and the midwife, whom literature often fused into a single figure.[166]

In the later Middle Ages, even the presuppositions attached to the very profession of midwifery began suffering unfavorable press.[167] Knowledge of folk medicine, which constituted an important aspect of the midwife's task, brought about accusations of witchcraft, as attested, for example, by treatises on demonology.[168] One of the recurrent anxieties about midwives derived from the suspicion that they were lax, indifferent, or hostile to the baptism of newborns. Their identity engaged the notions of religious unorthodoxy so that by the middle of the sixteenth century, an ordinance issued in Flanders by the Duke of Alba stated that no midwife would be admitted to the profession unless she showed herself to be "Catholic and of good name."[169]

As the Middle Ages reached their end, medical knowledge in women became synonymous with a series of visibly negative assumptions, always stressing the threat it posed for the orthodox Establishment. Celestina, of course, is highly identified with certain types of medical knowledge, as repeated by the reports of the characters

[166] Jacquard and Thomasset, 115.

[167] "Among the the cultural changes that mark the later Middle Ages was the beginning of a decline in the art of midwifery. Medieval midwives earned the reputation of being backward, superstitious and dangerous; their activities were increasingly restricted by the law" (Myriam Greilsammer, "The Midwife, the Priest, and the Physician: the Subjugation of Midwives in the Low Countries at the end of the Middle Ages," *Journal of Medieval and Renaissance Studies* 21 [1991] 285-324 [285]). Greilsammer points out that looking back at the Middle Ages, even some modern critics speak disapprovingly of midwives; she mentions Thomas Forbes, who, in *The Midwife and the Witch* (New Haven: Yale University Press, 1966), calls the medieval midwife "often ignorant and superstitious" (112), while Keith Thomas, in *Religion and the Decline of Magic* (New York: Scribner, 1971), also regards them as unqualified. Greilsammer argues that these women must be credited with a useful knowledge of female anatomy and childbirth, given the common recourse to them by many women.

[168] Greilsammer, 304.

[169] Greilsammer, 309. The critic adds that the Church's preoccupation with baptism eventually took precedence over all else, limiting the powers of midwives as time went on. In this way, not only did midwives slowly lose the privileges of their status but also were utilized "in the battle against the Reformation" (309).

around her and as attested by her own clinical approach to the topic of desire.[170] This fact constitutes one of the principal bases for the shape of her public image; her contact with medicine automatically places her in the realm of unorthodoxy and sorcery yet shows her to be in possession of desirable knowledge.[171] She thus articulates to the full the relationship between mediation and knowledge: just as mediation serves at once an unethical and a necessary purpose, the knowledge on which it draws occupies licit and illicit grounds.

Above and beyond the realm of her public image, Celestina engages a number of themes which relate to preoccupations of a philosophical nature, revealing issues pertinent to the mindframe of the *converso* writer Rojas. These relate partially to a state of mind and being which does not explain the particular characterization of Celestina to the full, yet constitutes a fundamental aspect for understanding her place in the author's work.

(ii) *Celestina: The Creation of a New Frame of Reference*

The clear presence of a *converso* tenor in the work of Fernando de Rojas stands confirmed today thanks to previous and ongoing research.[172] The writer's *converso* frame of mind infuses his work with a subversive tone, raising questions on issues which he perceives as problematic in his society, namely, mercenary sexuality, religious and class prejudice, and the philosophical preoccupation that there is no

---

[170] For example, Pármeno's description of the old woman in Act I stresses her knowledge of herbs, potions, and medicines; later, when Celestina explains Calisto's condition to Pármeno, she makes it clear that sexual desire is primarily a physiological, natural symptom inherent in all living beings.

[171] The question of Celestina's reliance on withcraft has been debated by numerous scholars, given in particular her monologue with the Devil prior to her seduction of Melibea. A number of scholars adhere to the belief that her pact with the Devil has much to do with her success with Melibea; see in particular Peter E. Russell, "La magia como tema integral de la *Tragicomedia de Calisto y Melibea*," *Studia philologica: Homenaje a Dámaso Alonso, III* (Madrid: Gredos, 1963) 337-354; Javier Herrero, "Celestina: The Aging Prostitute as Witch," in *Aging in Literature*, edited by Laurel Porter and Laurence M. Porter (Michigan: International Book Publishers, 1984) 31-47. The present study attaches meaning to Celestina's powers as a witch only insofar as it concerns the old woman's public image and the assumptions made by the community about her. It is our opinion that the text offers no viable evidence that Celestina's success with Melibea stems from the bawd's magical powers.

[172] See in particular Stephen Gilman, *The Spain of Fernando de Rojas: the Intellectual and Social Landscape of* La Celestina (Princeton: Princeton University Press, 1972) 495.

Higher Power which might offer protection to those who do not conform to the prerequisites of *limpieza de sangre* (purity of blood). The resultant effect on textual poetics is the creation of a profound sense of irony, as Gilman has noted, and the identification of violence as one of the fundamental themes of the work.

Irony, violence, and a concomitant fear of abandonment determine many of the directions taken by the old bawd Celestina in her interactions with others. Of equal significance for the representation of the bawd is the *converso* author's unhappy confrontation with patterns of sexual behavior in his urban setting. Márquez Villanueva points out the highly disturbing implications contained in matters related to sexuality for any erudite *converso* who saw Christian clergy making full use of the services of procuresses and prostitutes.[173] Even for less transgressive matters such as that of sexuality within marriage, a perspective colored by Judaism could but clash with the Christian viewpoint.[174]

Given this basic difference in outlook, almost any formalized aspect of the Old Christian's view of sexuality would have conflicted with that of the *converso*, let alone in matters regarding prostitution.[175]

---

[173] This comes to us in the testimony of literature: as observed in *Orígenes y sociología*, the strong note which prevails in Gil Vicente's work is one of sadness and clear sympathy for the *converso* who ends up facing gross misjustice in his conflict with a go-between, while in the *Laberinto de Fortuna* the licentious conduct of the clergy does not go unmentioned (143-146, 151).

[174] In a comprehensive overview of medieval marriage rituals in Judaism and Christianity, Esther Cohen and Elliot Horowitz write: "The radically opposed views of Judaism and Christianity concerning marital sexuality indicate the deep differences underlying the superficially similar processes (...). Judaism had always considered marriage a positive force. Therefore, the sacralization of of Jewish marriage was not an attempt to purify and distance it from mundane pressures. To the contrary, it meant the further imbuing of everyday life with the holy. Conversely, Christianity viewed marriage as essentially the poorer choice and therefore used symbolism to justify marriage (...). Insofar as all sexual relations were an enslavement of the human will, marital sex could not be completely exonerated (...). No such [idea] existed in Judaism, which neither elevated nor condemned marriage to any such extent" (Esther Cohen and Elliot Horowitz, "In Search of the Sacred: Jews, Christians, and Rituals of Marriage in the Later Middle Ages," *Journal of Medieval and Renaissance Studies* 20 [1990] 225-249 [237, 239]).

[175] María Eugenia Lacarra notes that rather than attempt to eradicate it totally, Christian authorities sought to supplement income with prostitution, by legal or illegal means, always concentrating on the financial benefits it might contain for people in various positions of authority. Lacarra documents this with evidence starting with Enrique III, whose imposition of a levy would have been a genuine attempt to control the problem in 1398. In the fifteenth century, this was known as the "derecho de perdices" and bore testimony to the fact that municipal Christian authorities

All the factors mentioned above – medical knowledge in women, prostitution, the reactions of the *converso* to an alienating attitude to sexuality in a hostile society – make up the contexts for the conception of Celestina as a literary character. Celestina weaves the many anxieties projected by these contexts into her discourse and her very identity: by her existence, and more importantly by the nature and function of her discourse, she articulates several levels of apprehension both within and without the text.

The critique of Celestina's function in light of Rojas' *converso* background requires the understanding that a balance must be maintained between contextual and textual research. Concentrating more specifically on the *converso* situation, Stephen Gilman has pointed out:

> no incidents or characters [in *La Celestina*] are going to be explained anecdotally. But, by considering Rojas in his family as a member of a caste, we may at least gain some comprehension of the larger relationship between the *converso* situation and the prehistory of fiction. (...) What [the *conversos*] contributed to the world was nothing less than the possibility of the major literary genre of modern times: the novel.[176]

Gilman's assertion has to do with the importance of considering the question of artistic imagination in the development of Celestina as a literary character. The particular vision of Juan Ruiz initiated the process of endowing the bawd with qualities which took her beyond the force of pre-established notions. With Rojas, this process of characterization continues, this time calling more urgently for a problematization of every principal trait associated with the figure of the

attempted to control the women via taxation in exchange for certain legal guarantees (Lacarra, 38-39). In 1476 the Catholic Monarchs established a fixed amount for this "derecho de perdices" (women known as "rameras" paid 24 maravedís per annum, while "public" prostitutes paid 12). The scholar explains that officials, according to archival sources, appear to have been quite corrupt, as were other executors of municipal legislation. In this way fines ended up being larger for prostitutes than stipulated by law (39). The interest in the financial benefits of the "mancebía" was shared by the authorities at even the highest levels, as illustrated by some of Lacarra's examples (40-41). The idea of the institutional centrality of *alcahuetería* is also reflected by George Shipley, who in "Authority and Experience in *La Celestina*," *Bulletin of Hispanic Studies* 62 (1985) 95-111, writes that in the community of people such as Calisto and Melibea, "Celestina is an institution more central and vital than the Church (...) more adored for her miracles and mediation than its saints, and more sought after, even in church and on holy occasions, than its clerics." (98).

[176] Gilman, *The Spain of Fernando de Rojas*, 154.

go-between and offering the most detailed look into her language and methodology.

With a discourse reminiscent at times of the Eastern *ʿajūz*,[177] both Trotaconventos and Celestina approach the question of sexuality in terms of an absolute necessity and go about the task of seduction on the basis of this conviction. In addition they convey the distinct sense that their presence is indispensable for the success of the amorous quest. Rather than simply reproduce the Near-Eastern model, however, these two Spanish *alcahuetas* surpass it by formulating their convictions in careful accordance with the discourse of others and with a marked awareness of mediation as a task which is grounded within a dialogic framework. This gives rise to the individualized portrait of the character, whose interactions with others form the basis, not the end result, of her utterances. In the case of Celestina, the process of individualization has also to do with the creation of substantial links and conflicts among the main thematic concerns of the work. Celestina inhabits an urban society where money, power, and class difference continuously impose their influence on everyday life and where the *alcahueta* can no longer limit herself to the resolution of amorous problems on their own terms. Rather, she must incorporate into mediation an awareness of urban realities and the contentions of characters other than the lovers. Her interlocutors have multiplied in number and in type, and her survival depends on more than just a knowledge of amorous matters.

(iii) *Elements of Discourse*

(a) *The Reappropriation of the Commonplace*

The old bawd of Rojas draws on proverbs, aphorisms, humor, science, and philosophy to influence those around her, providing in

[177] It is interesting to note that Celestina makes frequent references to God when she speaks; many of her remarks are prefaced or interspersed with phrases such as "la gracia de Dios sea contigo," "De Dios seas perdonada." ("May God's grace be with you," "May God forgive you"). Even when talking about Pármeno's mother, who was a witch, she automatically inserts a reference to God (*Celestina*, I, 67). María Rosa Lida, in *La originalidad*, regards Celestina's religious beliefs as basically popular in nature and quite empty, devoid of any effect on her moral behavior (310-313). It will, however, be recalled that the reference to God is a basic tenet of the speech of the Eastern *ʿajūz* who in similar fashion repeats the name of God on every possible occasion.

simultaneous fashion a running commentary on her own understanding of her place in the community.[178] The construction of this self-image through dialogues with others (and occasional monologues) represents one of Celestina's most significant contributions to the literary history of the medieval go-between; some of her highly complex and accomplished techniques come into play for the elaboration of her own image and subsequently link up with her more immediate task of seduction.

An intriguing method employed by Celestina in the expression of her identity consists of the usage of degrading terms to describe herself; when she recognizes Pármeno, for example, she exclaims in a seemingly jolly tone: "May the fire of Hell burn you, your mother was as much of an old whore as I!"[179] Elsewhere, the notion of her own sexual desire becomes subject to such treatment as well, revealing a complete awareness of the absurd effect created by an old woman's articulation of sexual desire. She shows no qualms in exploiting its comic potential; during a visit by Pármeno and Sempronio, she calls out to the women in her house: "Get yourselves down here, hurry, there are two men here who are trying to have their way with me!"[180] On one occasion, when Pármeno asks if she would like to be walked home, she sneers: "I am not afraid of being raped on the street."[181] Along similar lines, her descriptions of her trade make full use at times of blatantly negative connotations with no attempt at disguise or concealment. As she portrays Pármeno's dead mother to him in an outburst of loving and faithful sentiment,

---

[178] For specific rhetorical skills, see Malcolm Read, "The Rhetoric of Social Encounter: *La Celestina* and the Renaissance Philosophy of Language," in *The Birth and Death of Language: Spanish Literature and Linguistics (1300-1700)* (Madrid: Porrúa Turanzas, 1983) 70 and further; George Shipley, "El natural de la raposa: un proverbio estratégico de *La Celestina*," *Nueva Revista de Filología Hispánica* XXIII (1974) 35-64; Dorothy Sherman Severin, *Tragicomedy and Novelistic Discourse in* Celestina (Cambridge: Cambridge University Press, 1989) 63-89 in particular and "Celestina as a Comic Figure," in *Fernando de Rojas and* Celestina, *Approaching the Fifth Centenary*, 165-181; the use of a form of popular sorcery known as love magic in the bawd's speech is discussed by Olga Lucía Valbuena, "Sorceresses, Love Magic, and the Inquisition of Linguistic Sorcery in *Celestina*," *Publications of the Modern Language Association of America* 109, 2 (March 1994) 207-225.

[179] "Fuego malo te queme, que tan puta vieja era tu madre como yo!" (*Celestina*, I, 67).

[180] "Andad acá abajo, presto, que están aquí dos hombres, ¡que me quieren forzar!" (*Celestina*, IX, 143).

[181] "No he temor que me fuercen en la calle" (*Celestina*, VII, 132).

she mentions the cemeteries they raided together and the public humiliations they suffered.[182]

The immediate effect produced by these apparently ingenuous or self-deprecating references is of course humor. The reflections on Pármeno's mother in particular bring about a comical shock in that they associate feelings of admiration and nostalgia with activities such as pulling dead men's teeth out of their mouths in the middle of the night; the ethical standards of the old women appear as grotesquely reversed versions of supposedly correct ethical postures. But the comic effect does not reduce the strength of a strategy that in today's language is known as "empowering." By presenting herself in an epithet such as "puta vieja," ("old whore") or in terms of an incongruous sexual drive, Celestina shows full awareness of the discourse which has been used to denigrate her type. Her loud and clear use of these belittling terms to designate herself represents her invasion of a terrain hitherto reserved to non-*alcahuetas* who gave themselves the right to ridicule her. She thereby protects herself from the insulting power of those terms, having reappropriated them into her own discourse and replaced their judgmental or offensive force with humor.

Celestina's reappropriation of the negative commonplaces occurs in other ways also. These come to light when she discusses the details of her profession with others in terms which appear initially to deny the standard ethical implications of her trade. In Act IX, where Celestina reminisces at the dinner table about her bygone good fortune, she evokes the feelings of honor and nostalgia which reigned in her thriving brothel, complete with love and understanding, free of any hardship: "Hard work, my dear? Relaxation and relief, in fact. They all obeyed me, they all honored me, I was held in everyone's esteem, not one of them was unloved by me, what I said was right, and I gave each one her own dues."[183] There follows a detailed, yearning description of the respect she inspired in the distinguished men of the community, especially in the clergy. This reminiscence recalls her conversation with Pármeno on the subject of his mother and how the latter enjoyed fame and recognition for what she did without having to disguise it.[184]

---

[182] *Celestina*, VII, 122-125.

[183] "¿Trabajo, mi amor? Antes descanso y alivio. Todas me obedecían, todas me honraban, de todas era acertada, ninguna salía de mi querer, lo que yo decía era lo bueno, a cada cual daba su cobro" (*Celestina*, IX, 151).

[184] *Celestina*, VII, 123.

At first sight, the effect suggests irony and deprecation at the expense of the *alcahueta.* To link such activities as pimping and restoring virginity with nostalgia, honor, respect, and love creates a humorous effect at the expense of the one who establishes that link with no apparent awareness of its problematic nature. But the construction of self-image in such terms also delivers a serious jab at the community which so visibly makes use of the services provided. At Celestina's first mention in the text by Sempronio and Pármeno, the impression revolves distinctly around her dark, evil, and mysterious activities. She does not discard that image in her own words, yet in a calculated, innocent tone draws attention to the fact that those goings-on provided a service to the community. Society therefore needs her, and Celestina's aside to that effect makes for an implicit critique of her community.

Here, her contribution to the criticism of the community derives from the ingenuous tone she assumes in articulating the extent to which society has come to depend on her type. Rather than formulate it as a reproach, Celestina acknowledges the need for an *alcahueta* in nostalgic and loving terms and in fact succeeds in building a convincing image of the happiness and affluence of her bygone life, not to mention the security granted to her by men in high places. Her lengthy description at the dinner table evokes all those positive sentiments in adequate fashion and with a generous dose of irony for the reader who is aware of the increasingly staunch posturing of late medieval Spain vis-à-vis mercenary sexuality. Celestina's flattering redefinition of her own wrongdoing indicates the extent to which she feels comfortable perceiving herself as a legitimate member of a community which does not cease to lament her existence.

(b) *Persuasion and Violence*

Celestina's treatment of her own image constitutes a reappropriation of commonplace attitudes about her and also indicates her shrewd reflection on the community of which she considers herself a product. The bawd does not operate by reflection alone, however. Her observations in the scenes mentioned above disclose her ability to turn a situation in her favor by implicating others in her universe. She continues to enhance this ability by counterbalancing the joking references to her own sexuality with darker references that reveal the extent to which a preoccupation with physical love guides her world-vision. To Pármeno she says: "No chance of letting you near me, even though I am old! Your voice is getting deep, and your beard is growing!"[185] Her sexual gaze upon him, even if expressed half-jokingly, indicates full awareness of the body as the center of attention for amorous matters. It also helps inscribe her more firmly into the sexual universe of others as a valid but almost intrusive presence. This heightened sensitivity comes into full view in her encounter with Areúsa, with whom Celestina's sexual discourse takes free reign because of the hierarchical power she holds over the young woman.

As she prepares Areúsa for the meeting with Pármeno, Celestina unravels significant tenets of her dogma, the principal one of which is that the very language used by her contains an intensely sexual tenor, overwhelming the listener with its clearly suggestive words and tonalities. The authority lent to this voice derives from the old woman's posture as a medical expert familiar with female ailments; she creates a space of female complicity entirely rooted in sexual experience and reveals to Areúsa as well as to the reader the bare essence of her strategies, which revolve around the all-importance of sexual desire.

Celestina translates the power of sexuality and the boast of her own familiarity with it primarily into verbal expression but also makes use of the sense of touch. As she touches the young woman's body with the half-true pretext of finding her ailment, she accompanies the gesture with a mesmerizing tirade on pleasure and merges medical discourse with an intensely personal, erotic one, the intention of which becomes immediately apparent in one gesture not seen but perfectly understood by the reader. Searching for the reason for Areúsa's pain, Celestina continues to touch the young woman:

> Celestina – Give me some room, and I'll take a look. For I still know a thing or two about this ailment, since we have all have a womb and have suffered because of it.
>
> Areúsa – I feel it a little higher, over the stomach.[186]

The check-up continues but changes direction momentarily to draw attention to Aréusa's capacity for arousing desire: "How plump and

[185] "¡Mas rabia mala me mate, si te llego a mí, aunque vieja! Que la voz tienes ronca, las barbas te apuntan" (*Celestina*, I, 66).

[186] "Celestina: – Pues dame lugar, tentaré. Que aun algo sé yo de este mal, por mi pecado, que cada una se tiene (o ha tenido) su madre y (sus) zozobras de ella.
Areúsa: – Más arriba la siento, sobre el estómago" (*Celestina*, VII, 127).

fresh you are! What breasts and what softness! Oh to be a man and get to enjoy a good look at you!"[187] Areúsa continues to complain of her pain, whereupon Celestina reverts to a medical standpoint (the negative connotations of the woman's knowledge of medicine are engaged by the imagery of this scene), displaying great familiarity with the condition and suggesting a number of remedies ranging from powders to herbs and incense.[188] These, she says, will put the womb back in its place and stop the pain; Celestina treads on purely medical ground, showing incidentally that her identity comprises more than just go-between activity and that to be an efficient procuress one must have ample knowledge of medicine.[189]

She continues her suggestions for a remedy by stating that she considers another cure even more effective; at Areúsa's inquiry she snaps: "Come on, you know what I mean, don't act stupid with me!"[190] The medical solution – and it will be recalled that Avicenna recommended intercourse in such cases of uterine pain – now overlaps with the strategy of seduction; impatience stems from Celestina's familiarity with Areúsa and the young woman's relatively inferior status. To break her resistance, however, Celestina does not use force: having piled a series of sexual compliments mingled with medical reasoning on Areúsa, she now resorts to folk wisdom in order to overcome the final obstacle. A succession of proverbs on the misfortunes associated with loneliness now follows, whereupon Pármeno, pushed forward by the old woman, enters the room.

The manipulation of the other's will does not stop there. Aware of Pármeno's inexperience and Areúsa's partial reluctance, Celestina remains in the room. As she has no concerns for any objections they may have, her tactics take on a more aggressive form. Celestina shows her absolute control over the situation but also ties her arguments in with the inherent idea that sexuality and violence do go

---

[187] "[¡]qué gorda y fresca estás! ¡Qué pechos y qué gentileza! (...) ¡Oh, quién fuera hombre y tanta parte alcanzara de ti para gozar tal vista!" (*Celestina*, VII, 127).

[188] *Celestina*, VII, 128.

[189] The wandering womb as illness was a well-known diagnosis in medieval medical practice. See Laurinda S. Dixon, "The Curse of Chastity: The Marginalization of Women in Medieval Art and Medicine," in *Matrons and Marginal Women in Medieval Society*, ed. Robert R. Edwards and Vickie Ziegler (Rochester: Boydell Press, 1995) 49-74. For Celestina's identity as more than just a go-between, see my "'... y otros treynta officios:' The Definition of a Medieval Woman's Work in *La Celestina*," *Celestinesca*, 1998, forthcoming.

[190] "¡Anda, que bien me entiendes, no te hagas boba!" (*Celestina*, VII, 128).

hand in hand. To Pármeno she exclaims aggressively that he should get close and stop being so shy. She follows this with a direct, violent instruction, ordering him to take possession of the young woman on the bed.[191] The incompatibility of this type of sexual love with politeness or decorum emerges in the bawd's sarcastic remark to Areúsa's feeble objection: "So, now you're all caught up with politeness and permission, are you?"[192]

The animal imagery used by Celestina enhances the frenzy which guides her discourse in moments of seduction as well as the wealth of images on which she is able to draw for descriptions of physical intimacy; of Pármeno she says that he resembles a fighting cock who will not lower his crest even after three consecutive nights.[193] She elaborates the metaphor with food imagery, increasing all the more the sense of physicality by recalling how she too partook of this remedy at the suggestion of physicians when she had "better teeth."[194] She reiterates all her arguments in terms of her own sexual experience and indicates a very real desire on her own part, taking her leave of the young couple by mentioning the extent to which seeing them has excited her, for she still remembers quite well the taste of what they are about to do, even if she has lost her teeth.[195]

The scene confirms Celestina's self-perception as a sexual being whose task consists of reliving thrills through others and, more importantly, her understanding that a discourse composed of scientific authority, folk wisdom, and some measure of violence will guarantee the successful coercion of others. Celestina places her own experience at the center of mediation, thereby rendering it all the more effective by personalizing the general drives about which she speaks. This affords the reader a provocative glimpse into the mediator's sexual identity and the extent to which it is bound up with the activity she masters.

The violence inherent in her encounter with Areúsa and Pármeno also acts as a foil to the principal seduction which she carries out in the work, i.e., that of Melibea. With the latter, it becomes necessary to customize the elements of speech to a mentality unfamiliar with the par-

---

[191] *Celestina*, VII, 131.
[192] "¿En cortesías y licencias estás?" (*Celestina*, VII, 131).
[193] *Celestina*, VII, 131.
[194] *Celestina*, VII, 131.
[195] *Celestina*, VII, 132.

lance of the brothel and of servant life. Having exposed her guiding principles, not the least important of which is a financial purpose, in a more naked form to Pármeno and Areúsa, Celestina goes on to refine and focus the tactics to suit the case of Melibea. The key operative concept in Celestina's approach to the seduction of Melibea comes to light in cruder form in the scene with Areúsa and Pármeno. The concept has to do with the translation of violence into words, rendered easier in Areúsa's case because of the bawd's license to touch the young woman and exploit the sense of familiarity. The violent nature of carnal love and the implicit understanding of that fact appear to exist already in the minds of all characters. Mediation gives this violence a language: Celestina's role consists of bringing out the expression of such feelings in various people, educating them, filling gaps in those places where they struggle with uncertainty and unawareness. The question of the "victim's" disposition, seen across other genres previously, assumes a regenerated importance in this case with the added significant feature of the instructional value of the bawd.

The sense of violence does not limit itself to the seductive strategies of the old bawd: rather, she represents one in many reflections of a strong tone of fury which reigns over the play in general, starting in the very prologue and continuing throughout the work. Its inevitable presence occurs as a result of the fundamental hopelessness which pervades the play from the disturbing centrality of the *alcahueta* to the general lack of any viable alternative for a society filled with "internal contradictions and vices."[196] The absence of didactic intention in the work enhances the sense of violence all the more, for Rojas offers no solution to the moral problems which he posits.[197] Examples of fury abound in the work, denoting a dynamic conceived in anger and frustration between all the characters.[198] Within this atmosphere, love

[196] *Orígenes y sociología*, 158 and 164, respectively.

[197] On the lack of didactic spirit – which would constitute a refutation of Marcel Bataillon's thesis – see also Gilman, *The Spain of Fernando de Rojas*, 360-367; María Rosa Lida, *La originalidad*, 297. The final proof of the absence of any compensation for the absurdity of life is found in Pleberio's lament where he categorically denies the consolation provided in the after-life.

[198] The text of *La Celestina* makes no secret of a deep-rooted and consistent preoccupation with fury from every single character's point of view. The very first encounter in the work – that of Calisto and Melibea in the orchard – is marked with severe harshness on the part of Melibea, who lashes out at Calisto with abusive words (*Celestina*, I, 47). The air of fury maintains its intensity in the next scene where Calisto converses with Sempronio: the passage abounds in brusque imperatives and

also transforms into a brute force, a physical illness in need of remedies and capable of generating an income for those who facilitate access to the cure. Celestina never loses track of the latter capacity and betrays in her dialogues with others a deep-seated conviction that love, expressed verbally or physically, means a considerable degree of violence. Curiously, mediation is a form of keeping this violence in check and taming it so that it will fit within a manageable framework.

In the course of Melibea's principal meeting with Celestina, the young woman's secret desire for Calisto comes into full view guided by the old bawd's careful direction. Scholars have examined the encounter as a successful exercise in the manipulation of rhetoric; Erica Morgan observes that Rojas challenges Cato's definition of rhetoric, "vir bonus dicendi peritus," by extending it to characters who by no means speak with honorable intentions.[199] Otis Handy also views the passage in light of its rhetorical features, explaining Celestina's use of such figures as litotes, distribution, syllogisms, and enthymeme, which deflower Melibea prior to the young woman's actual intercourse with Calisto.[200] Malcolm Read points out the use of innuendo and the reliance on double-entendre, which allow for the communication of real meaning, observing that in *La Celestina* language transforms itself into a powerful, tangible object.[201]

In addition to the effective use of rhetorical devices, Celestina's

---

cruelly sarcastic asides. In Act II, Calisto's overwhelmingly aggressive address to Pármeno causes the latter to finally decide in favor of joining Celestina's group (*Celestina*, II, 77-78). The young servant, who until this moment voiced some degree of moral caution, now bursts out in a frenzy of anger, cursing those around him as he stands alone (*Celestina*, II, 79). Celestina herself has not a single kind word for members of Calisto's class, subjecting them to a resentful tone and recalling their cruelty towards others once they are out of earshot (*Celestina*, I, 69).

[199] Erica Morgan, "Rhetorical Technique in the Persuasion of Melibea," *Celestinesca* 3.2 (1979) 7-18.

[200] Otis Handy, "The Rhetorical and Psychological Defloration of Melibea," *Celestinesca* 7.1 (1983) 17-27.

[201] Malcolm K. Read, "Fernando de Rojas' Vision of the Birth and Death of Language," *Modern Language Notes* XCIII (1978) 163-175. See also D. J. Gifford, "The Place of Verbal Fascination in *La Celestina*," *Medieval and Renaissance Studies on Spain and Portugal in Honour of P. E. Russell*, edited by F. W. Hodcroft, D. G. Pattison, R. D. F. Pring-Mill, R. W. Truman (Oxford: The Society for the Study of Medieval Language and Literature, 1981) 30-37. Gifford observes that in her encounter with Melibea, Celestina makes use of the hypnotic techniques of incantation, "investing particular power in *names*," (32) specifically that of Calisto, which causes Melibea to faint. The art of persuasion is discussed also by Edward H. Friedman, "Rhetoric at Work: Celestina, Melibea, and the Persuasive Arts," in *Fernando de Rojas and* Celestina: *Approaching the Fifth Centenary*, 359-370.

persuasive technique draws once again on the authority of medicine, this time in a much more elaborate manner than with Areúsa. The latter suffered literally from a physical pain best cured in Celestina's opinion by intercourse. With Melibea, the basic idea remains, even if the details have changed; the bawd conveys the remedy in a manner which compensates for the lack of access to touch or familiarity available to her in the case of Areúsa.

The elaborate medical metaphor here evoked by the bawd leaves little room for doubt as to the nature of her suggestion.[202] As mentioned, scholars rightly note the rhetorical powers of Celestina here; yet it must be observed that the strength of the procuress lies in matching her rhetoric to the register set by the young woman. The go-between's skill consists not only of her ability to communicate her ideas but equally of the essential suitability of her words for an interlocutor such as Melibea.[203] Celestina waits cleverly for the young woman to set the tone of the exchange and, upon receiving Melibea's own frenzied and pained discourse, plunges into the type of verbal communication which would correspond suitably to the latter's state of mind. After all, Melibea herself clearly perceives her condition as a burning illness and introduces graphic imagery to describe it;[204] her references to wounds and pain, her plea for a doctor and the restoration of her health find a suitable outlet in Celestina, who follows the young woman's train of thought along those very lines. The *alcahueta* reveals a remarkable capacity for active response to the elements of dialogue, establishing a firm and organic link between the utterances of her interlocutor and her own. She thus distances herself from the realm of formulaic or predictable responses and gauges the exact requirements of dialogue as she goes along. Her debt to Trotaconventos cannot escape unnoticed in this regard.

This skill goes hand in hand with the elaboration of the kind of violence encountered in the Pármeno-Areúsa scene; the discussion with Melibea carries more power due to the mystery and trepidation

---

[202] Otis Handy offers the corresponding sexual meanings for the bawd's imagery in detail.

[203] For the "dialogic" genre of the work, see Severin, *Tragicomedy and Novelistic Discourse*, 2-3.

[204] In fact, Luce López-Baralt correctly regards Melibea's attitude as an indication that the young woman knows more than she claims (161). María Rosa Lida in *La originalidad* considers Melibea far from "chaste in soul" (419) and stresses the young woman's passion for love, even if it overlaps with a certain horror (406-470).

associated with medicine, a sense exploited to the full by Celestina. The bawd rapidly educates the young woman, her new patient and a virgin, into seeing that carnal love belongs to the domain of physical illness. Starting with the notion of a "llaga" ("wound") introduced by Melibea herself, the bawd moves on to the cure offered by a needle ("mi sotil aguja" meaning "my discreet needle") and effectively telescopes medical procedure and sexual intercourse into one and the same. Celestina surrounds the idea of the cure with the highly suggestive imagery of pain, the first wound, patience, and suffering. "[T]emer la melecina" ("fearing the medicine") comes to signify the fear of intercourse; yet Melibea, now at the end of her tether with anxiety and longing, refuses even to acknowledge a specific name for the cure: "Say what you like, do what you know."[205] Celestina has efficiently placed herself in the position of the seducer who paves the way for the physical act, maintaining at all times an underlying sense of violence by relating the experience to pain.

She matches this skill with a careful delivery which draws on various tones, ranging from that of the doctor scolding the uncooperative patient to the older woman versed in this female experience.[206] The result overwhelms Melibea, whose frenzied state meets with complicity and authority on the part of the bawd. With such an attitude, the go-between prompts and aggravates the young woman's state on its own pathological terms. Having understood the tenor of Melibea's language of violent desire, Celestina has responded accordingly and provided the young woman with more images which can now act as points of reference.

In a manner reminiscent of the prologue to the work, Celestina equates man and beast in terms of her imagery, justifying her firm belief that sexuality governs men and women just as much as it controls other animals. This conviction goes on to constitute the principal directive idea of the work, leading in turn to the creation of differences between the Spanish bawd and her Eastern counterparts. Before delving into the further significance of this idea for the representation of the bawd, it is important also to address the issue of Celestina's perception of herself, for it bears in a meaningful way on the overall characterization of the go-between.

---

[205] "Di (...) *lo que* quisieres, haz *lo que* supieres (...)" (*Celestina*, X, 157) (emphasis mine).

[206] *Celestina*, X, 158-159.

(c) *The Humanizing Aspect of Discourse*

One of the most important contributions of Celestina to the literary history of the medieval go-between concerns the focus on the image of the self. Around her, the unequivocal tone of those who describe her establishes an ostensibly clear and predictable image of the go-between: Sempronio, Pármeno, and Lucrecia each impart information on the bawd in terms of her physical activities followed by disapproving moral judgment. The construction of her identity in the words of others therefore centers upon the bawd's actions and the speaker's standard ethical posture that, even in moments of recourse (as is the case with Sempronio), not once loses track of her inherent evil associations.

Set against this unified public image with its stress on potions, magic, and misguided medical procedure, Celestina herself ponders the nature of her task in ways which challenge the unanimous voice of others. The traditional image of the go-between, regardless of origin or heritage, has always implied an unfaltering confidence on the part of the bawd, who guarantees success to her client. When confronted with others, Celestina does not once betray a sense of doubt since an integral aspect of her profession consists of a relentless show of confidence in the success of a familiar project.

But the bawd also inhabits a space dedicated to private reflection. Act IV opens with a monologue inspired by fear and doubt, demonstrating how the old woman's language tailors itself to the expression of such uncharacteristic sentiments. The passage engages many of the stylistic and discursive techniques associated with the language of the go-between: proverbs, exclamatory remarks, imagined scenarios, and highly rhythmic series of repetitive phrases with a cumulative effect.[207] The monologue successfully creates a sense of fear and doubt precisely due to its persuasive power seen elsewhere in the completely different context of seduction.

In this passage Celestina discloses a deep understanding of the dangerous implications of her public image of herself. Whereas others have portrayed her in terms of evil power, here she reminds the reader that the ultimate power rests with the person who pays for the operation, in this case, Calisto. Her fear of his reprimand indicates

[207] *Celestina*, IV, 86-87.

the subordination of her supposedly otherworldly skills to his financial power. The insulting forms of address which she imagines no longer represent amused reappropriations on her part; rather, they illustrate her complete grasp of the tenuous nature of her situation:

> He will say to me: "You, old whore, why did you increase my passion with your promises? False go-between, for everyone else you have feet, for me just a tongue; for others deeds, for me words; for others a cure, for me pain; for others you have energy, for me it failed you; for others light, for me darkness. So, you old betrayer, why did you offer your services to me?"[208]

In this imagined diatribe, Celestina defines "words" as useless features in the mind of a man who requires action. They fall within the same category as pain and darkness, thereby proving the bawd's own sense of their potentially feeble status and creating a marked contrast with the attributes given to her by others whenever they mention her language and her abilities. She understands that her greatest skill can easily bring about her downfall when unaccompanied by palpable results. The magic of language suffices at this point only to express fear, while the clear and present danger of physical punishment alerts the bawd momentarily to the zone where words no longer exert control: "even of they don't want to kill me, they may toss me in a blanket or lash me cruelly."[209] Ironically, Celestina expresses this lack of confidence in the power of words in a typically convincing fashion, as highlighted by her imaginary encounter with Calisto in which repetition and sentence structure adequately convey the point.

The bawd's acute awareness of punishment does more than just express her personal fear. It indicates her understanding that her client can shift the dynamics of power. The true nature of her anxiety can best be gauged in light of Michel Foucault's study *Discipline and Punish*, where the writer discusses the attitudes of society towards discipline, looking closely at three types of punishment prevalent in the early modern period: torture, correction (of the kind preferred by

---

[208] Diráme (...): "Tú, puta vieja, ¿por qué acrecentaste mis pasiones con tus promesas? Alcahueta falsa, para todo el mundo tienes pies, para mí lengua; para todos obra, para mí palabras; para todos remedio, para mí, pena; para todos esfuerzo, para mí te faltó; para todos luz, para mí tiniebla. Pues, vieja traidora, ¿por qué te me ofreciste?" (*Celestina*, IV, 87).

[209] "podría ser que (...) cuando matar no me quisiesen, manteándome o azotándome cruelmente" (*Celestina*, IV, 86).

humanist reformers), and imprisonment.[210] Celestina's own fear, that of finding herself tossed in a blanket or whipped, corresponds best to the first category. According to Foucault, for each of these categories, "the type of punishment illustrates the society's dealings with criminals as 'objects' to be manipulated. In all three, a major goal is to shift the balance of power relations[.]"[211] By punishing the criminal, society changes the dynamics of power and transforms the hitherto mighty delinquent into the weaker party in the relationship. Celestina's fear articulates just such a reversal of roles, and her specific anxiety regarding physical punishment supports Foucault's notion that with "the body as the central target,"[212] a severe undermining of the criminal's power occurs to assert "the power and integrity of the law."[213] The fear expressed by the bawd serves as a reminder that, contrary to the suggestions of her public image, the clear-cut opposition of evil procuress versus innocent victim fails to maintain its alleged consistency.

The bawd's moment of self-doubt does not occupy substantial thematic space, yet its presence creates an ironic effect when set against the unanimous opinions held on her by other characters, who repeatedly speak about her in terms of her public image. Another element which it subjects to problematization is Calisto's zealous admiration of the bawd, as seen in Act VI when he calls her "reina y señora mía" ("my queen and lady"), maintaining an exaggeratedly diffident stance with her: "I want to hear your sweet reply on my knees."[214] Clearly, the procuress does not feel completely reassured by such declarations. The clash of these two modes of perception forces a questioning of the long-maintained presupposition that the procuress enjoys a magical hold on her clients at all times. This presupposition reaffirms itself several times through Celestina's remarkable ability to seduce and manipulate, yet the significant step taken by Rojas consists of pointing out a serious crack in the otherwise firm construction of her public image.

Another twist in the public image of the bawd through her private

---

210 Michel Foucault, *Discipline and Punish: the Birth of the Prison*, translated by Alan Sheridan (New York: Vintage/Random House, 1979).

211 Hubert L. Dreyfus and Paul Rabinow, *Michel Foucault: Beyond Structuralism and Hermeneutics* (Chicago: The University of Chicago Press, 1983) 144.

212 Foucault, *Discipline and Punish*, 24.

213 Dreyfus and Rabinow, *Michel Foucault*, 145.

214 "de rodillas quiero escuchar tu suave respuesta" (*Celestina*, VI, 108, 9).

reflections comes about in one of her dialogues with Sempronio, in which she hovers on the edges of several different postures. Her discursive logic provides more than one type of argument in relation to the nature of her role in the community:

> Praise God, you have seen few virgins in this town who sell their goods, whose first sewing up job was not done by me. As soon as a girl is born, I have her entered in my register, and I do this to keep track of those who get away from me. What did you think, Sempronio, was I supposed to make a living on thin air? Did I inherit money elsewhere? Do I have another house, or a vineyard? Do I know anything other than this job? How would I eat and drink? How would I dress and buy shoes? I was born and raised in this city, and I keep my honorable position as everyone knows, so, am I not well-known? If anyone does not know my name and my address, well, think of them as a foreigner.[215]

Typically expressed in a barrage of repetitions and rhetorical questions, the passage deserves full citation since it brings up, in the guise of a peripheral conversation with Sempronio, a number of significant issues related to the *alcahueta*'s own assessment of her role in society.

This speech challenges the mysterious and evil portrait painted of the bawd by others. It brings together two contradictory sentiments: a strong element of pride running alongside a defensive need for justification. Inevitably, this creates "that complex structure of verbal irony" seen by Stephen Gilman as reflecting the complicated "kinds of *converso* reaction to social circumstance."[216] The bawd remains perfectly aware that many solicit her contributions yet those who seek

[215] "Pocas vírgenes, a Dios gracias, has tú visto en esta cuidad que hayan abierto tienda a vender, de quien yo no haya sido corredora de su primer hilado. En naciendo la mochacha la hago escribir en mi registro, y esto para que yo sepa cuántas se me salen de la red. ¿Qué pensabas, Sempronio? ¿Habíame de mantener del viento? ¿Heredé otra herencia? ¿Tengo otra casa o viña? ¿Conócesme otra hacienda, más de este oficio? ¿De qué como y bebo? ¿De qué visto y calzo? En esta ciudad nacida, en ella criada, manteniendo honra como todo el mundo sabe, ¿conocida, pues, no soy? Quien no supiere mi nombre y mi casa, tenle por estranjero" (*Celestina*, III, 81).

[216] Gilman, *The Spain of Fernando de Rojas*, 153. See also the section entitled "The 'selves' of Authors" in the same book, where Gilman explains that the diverse currents which inform *La Celestina* from social points of view need not be thought of as mutually exclusive; thus the seemingly contradictory mingling of "thinly veiled anger" with "affirmation": "Witches, too, are human beings and deserve something better than Inquisitional 'justice'" (153).

her aid, the likes of Calisto, or the clergy, have recourse to the moral double standard as well as the financial control which at any moment can result in her condemnation. Given the contradictory parameters laid out by the community for Celestina, she hovers between confidence and dread regarding her profession. In the speech to Sempronio, she starts powerfully, boasting control and knowledge; she then switches suddenly to a series of defensive questions which indicate her insecurity and need for affirmation. The final plea for understanding also constitutes a blatant stab at society with the rhetorical question: "am I not well-known?" Significantly, Sempronio passes over this tirade and immediately changes the subject. His silence indicates the inability to provide an adequate answer to the bawd's declarations.

Indeed, the paradox of Celestina as a presence in the community vexes others also, albeit in implicit ways; in Act IV when the old woman arrives at Melibea's doorstep, Lucrecia attempts to inform Melibea's mother of the bawd's identity. The maidservant goes about this by way of the description of public image: "that old woman with a scar on her face, who used to live near the tanneries, by the river." This causes disorientation on the part of Alisa, who complains that she cannot place the old woman, whereupon Lucrecia exclaims: "Christ, ma'am! This old woman is better-known than anyone! I don't know how you can't remember her, she is the one they exposed as a sorceress, the one who sold young girls to abbots and who undid a thousand marriages." Alisa asks if Lucrecia knows the name, to which the maid replies: "Do I know it, ma'am? There isn't a child or an old person in this whole city who wouldn't know it, how could I not know it then?" Melibea's mother inquires as to Lucrecia's refusal to say the name, receiving the maid's reply that she is ashamed to say it.[217]

The maid finally says the word "Celestina" with great difficulty. Her vehement reluctance to name the bawd, set against her relished account of the old woman's fame, indicates a fundamentally unre-

[217] "aquella vieja de la cuchillada, que solía vivir aquí en las tenerías, a la cuesta del río." "¡Jesú, señora!, más conocida es esta vieja que la ruda. No sé cómo no tienes memoria de la que empicotaron por hechicera, que vendía las mozas a los abades y descasaba mil casados." "¿Si le sé, señora? No hay niño ni viejo en toda la ciudad, que no lo sepa, ¿habíale yo de ignorar?" (All citations in this paragraph are from *Celestina*, IV, 88 and 89).

solved attitude towards the go-between. On the level of a myth embedded in collective memory, Lucrecia has no problem evoking the old woman with zest; for Lucrecia, Celestina's reputation has attained pure anecdotal form: her public image no longer requires analysis or problematization and repeats itself in the shape of known commonplaces. Yet the act of naming her within a respectable house poses a personal threat which Lucrecia can only define as shame. The dynamic created by these contradictory gestures, that of describing the old woman yet refusing to name her, presents one representation of a crucial double standard subtly illustrated throughout *La Celestina.* It highlights the feeble attempt to claim innocence by stating that one feels ashamed to say the name, signifying that the utterance of the word would somehow stain the speaker. The logic of this argument is shown by Rojas to be flawed; the proud show of knowledge by all characters regarding the bawd and repeated statements that the old woman is known to all have already implicated all speakers. Lucrecia herself describes the bawd's many activities with great enthusiasm: how Celestina makes perfumes, sells herbs, knows about stones.[218] These activities do not suggest isolation and solitude, but rather imply contact with, and some kind of service to, others. Lucrecia's shame after such a description represents a pathetic struggle to erase the traces of this co-dependence, and even Alisa has to laugh at it at the end of the brief episode.

(iv) *The Paradox of Celestina*

The chain of chaos and violence seen in *La Celestina* has no visible origin, even if at first sight the old woman can be blamed for bringing about so much death and destruction. Upon close analysis, one will appreciate that Calisto's death, Melibea's suicide, the servants' brutal fate and even the bawd's own violent end all represent the effects of shifting, elusive causes which have little to do with the notion of the *alcahueta*'s wrongdoing. Calisto's death occurs through sheer bad luck, while the other gruesome fates are realized primarily due to each character's own (mis)handling of lost love, greed, or justice. Surprisingly, prior to all deaths, the old procuress creates a force

---

[218] *Celestina,* IV, 88.

which imposes order on a society otherwise vulnerable to chaos and lawlessness.[219]

The law and order maintained by Celestina are not of the same stock as municipal legislation or society's moral codes. The chaos and lawlessness curbed by the bawd exist in an area which law and morality have always attempted to control, often in vain: that of sexual dynamics. Celestina functions as the unquestionable authority for the direction of confused feelings and the venting of frenzied physical reactions. Both Calisto and Melibea come to the bawd suffering from a physical condition which only the procuress can identify and direct for them, helping them to channel their energies and allowing for that which she considers to be the natural outcome. Celestina's utility is best appreciated in contrast to Melibea's mother, Alisa, who provides the perfect example of the hopeless inadequacy of the family in dealing with the daughter's turbulent sexual development. As Luce López-Baralt indicates, the good provincial lady is quite misguided if she thinks that Melibea is ignorant of sexual conflict and awakening.[220] Only Celestina possesses the know-how and the vision, albeit perverse, to walk young people through their erotic arousal.

The bawd displays a remarkable awareness of the necessity to vent sexual feelings in the previously mentioned monologue where she articulates her fear of Calisto's wrath. Naturally, the fear stems primarily from her anxiety regarding punishment. A parallel line of thought accompanies this visible fear, though; in her hesitation to go forward, the old bawd considers the various outcomes of her task, two of which consist respectively of Pleberio's anger, should she win over Melibea, and Calisto's ire, should the project fail. She decides that in the long run, it is better to offend Pleberio the father than to enrage Calisto the lover.[221] Celestina rationalizes this decision by stating to herself that failing Calisto would brand her a coward and bring her shame. By considering Pleberio the less insane of the two, the bawd sets up a contrast with the irrational feelings of Calisto which she perceives as much more destructive than Pleberio's anger.

---

219 What follows with regards to the role of Celestina as an agent of law and order is the result of discussions with my colleague, Professor Irene Mizrahi, at Boston College. Professor Mizrahi first sparked my interest in this aspect of *La Celestina* and has subsequently provided many useful insights for the articulation of ideas on chaos and law such as they appear here.

220 López-Baralt, 161.

221 *Celestina* IV, 87.

The thematic focus of the play validates Celestina's argument that Calisto's insane ire would bring about more disastrous results than Pleberio's anger, since the repression of sexual energy constitutes a violation of the law of nature and leads to catastrophe. Celestina's mission precisely is to halt that destruction. Here lies the greatest paradox of the go-between's role: her implementation of this valid law requires that she engage in deceit and hypocrisy, that is, in lawbreaking.[222]

From a conventional and convenient ethical standpoint, her guilt also lies in the fact that she manipulates the law of nature towards mercenary ends, drawing as many people as possible into the scheme. This offense does not resolve the paradox in favor of society, because those implicated in her mission include the clergy, ambassadors, students, and young women in distress – that is, "respectable" members of society. A vicious circularity commands her role as she upholds sexual law and breaks its societal counterpart.

(v) *Celestina: The Reconfiguration of the Triangle*

The Calisto-Celestina-Melibea triangle covers a familiar territory. In many ways, it constitutes the traditional configuration encountered in any text where a go-between exists: an ardent male lover, an initially reluctant female, and a crafty go-between. On this familiar ground Rojas maps out a new series of contours and rejects an easy definition for the triangle, for he subjects the reader to a number of conflicting standpoints regarding the liberation and constraint of mediation. In addition to the challenge to the law, the new geography mapped out by Rojas on this otherwise familiar territory demonstrates the extent to which the bawd articulates the conflict based on the force of human sexuality when society remains undecided as to how to regulate it.

Prior to the full expression of that conflict, Celestina recalls the public image of her Eastern counterparts; this includes the natural recourse to her as a player in the game of love, the role of verbal manipulation in her endeavors, and the multiple but ultimately vacu-

---

[222] In a different but nonetheless relevant context, Stephen Gilman mentions the bawd's skill in "using the truth and richly detailed facsimiles of the truth to deceive"(*The Spain of Fernando de Rojas*, 52).

ous references to God in her speech. In other words, her representation as a bawd relies to a considerable degree on the models proposed by Near-Eastern literature which lay great emphasis on a sophisticated grammar of love and delegate significant responsibility to the old woman in the realm of seduction. However, in a manner comparable to Trotaconventos, Rojas' go-between soon surpasses the limits of the Near-Eastern model and enters a thematic realm uncharted by her Muslim counterparts. The elements analyzed above, ranging from discourse to auto-perception, attest to the full development of the *alcahueta* as an individualized character who transcends the limits of the stereotype and who calls urgent attention to the ambiguities intrinsic in mediation. Rojas effectively makes a novelistic character out of his go-between by centering her representation upon irony and conflict, as we have seen in the analysis of her discourse. This in turn confirms the notion that *La Celestina* contributes to the development of a literary genre by subjecting character to a special depth of scrutiny.

It was mentioned earlier that the principal directive idea in Rojas' work concerns the tremendous power of sexuality over human destiny. Rojas stresses repeatedly the fundamental similarities between men and animals in terms of the complete surrender to sexual desire. As his main protagonist and the one who best understands the brutality of sexual energy, Celestina draws attention to the tragic meaning of the work by shifting the focus from the sociological presuppositions of her make-up to the nature of her own predicament. She faces the task of regulating and distributing sexual energy in a society whose linguistic and legal codes can only approach the sex drive in terms of prohibition, illness, dishonor, and scapegoating, while at once nurturing the drive in unhealthily tantalizing ways by sustaining the existence of brothels. By facilitating the union of lovers – whose physical suffering and frenzy is mentioned time and again in the work – Celestina aims to fulfill that which in her view is a natural requirement whose realization would halt further rage and even potential insanity.

Her own views on the human condition are as frenzied and vehement as the complaints of Calisto and Melibea in the absence of sexual intimacy, and the reader need not speculate on the scientific legitimacy of her assertions on human sexuality. That would constitute a redundant pursuit in the context of the literary creation of Celestina; what matters is Celestina's difficult position as a figure for whom the Christian preoccupation with honor and abstinence is a misrecognition of the natural order of things. Her only way of implementing that which she considers natural law is a transgressive and marginal approach, for such negative postures are the only ones which the community around her will recognize as the means to the realization of sexual desire. In other words, given the automatic association of sex with wrongdoing in her society, her sole valid option in fulfilling the sexual desire of others is to present the issue to them on terms which they best understand: these terms are most adequately expressed when their transmitter, Celestina, reveals all the signs of danger and marginality in her very person, so that the receivers of her offerings will have the reassurance of indulging in a transgressive act. Were Celestina to strip the act of its transgressive associations, she would confront her interlocutors with a new and utterly unknown world in which sexual desire would not be a sin at all and for which one need not make all types of base financial arrangements. Celestina's community, as Rojas sees it, is simply not ready for such a take on human desire; from the author's disenchanted and *converso* viewpoint, that society is so deeply entrenched in simultaneous dread and greed toward sexuality that it can only indulge in it if presented as a function of avarice, transgression, and blame. An old woman, no longer fertile, living on the edges of town, dabbling in magic and sewing up hymens, dangerously non-Christian (and in fact Near-Eastern) in image and demeanor, is the best agent for the provision of sexuality as an illicit service. Mediation is at once an immoral and necessary task which places some control over the afflicted sexuality of the community. That is to say, she mediates in society on the latter's own terms.

Neither Juan Ruiz nor Fernando de Rojas attempt to let the go-between off the hook, so to speak. Their works must not be read as apologies for the *alcahueta*. They draw attention instead to the ways in which the character relates to an entire community around herself. They reveal the fact that this community simultaneously disdains and desires the continuation of that which the Establishment has labeled a secret immorality. Rojas and Ruiz unravel the mechanisms by which the procuress, as an agent and an outsider, attempts to secure her own intermediary position within such a contradictory system. No other tradition or genre delves in such detail and from a substantially poetic point of view into the potential of the go-between for the expression of ideas on her own functions and her convictions on the nature of human desire. At the same time, the important elements of mediation underscored by these two Spanish bawds could not be appreciated without a comprehensive critique of the numerous go-betweens from Latin, Romance, and Near-Eastern literatures, all of whom inform the representation of the *alcahueta*. It is thus fitting to end this chapter by relocating the medieval Spanish component in the broader context of mediation in literatures analyzed previously. Many of the questions raised by Romance and Near-Eastern concepts of mediation appear to receive some response in the Spanish *alcahueta*, underscoring the intricate and vital nature of the bonds which link each tradition's idea of mediation to its counterparts.

CONCLUSION: TOWARDS A THEORY OF SEDUCTION

The preceding detailed study of mediation in key Latin, Romance, and Near-Eastern texts has led to a number of diverse and far-reaching conclusions on the typology of intermediary activity and its role in the elaboration of a poetics of profane love. In spite of the many superficial resemblances between agents who take on the task of mediation across literary traditions, different genres project the go-between into their texts in distinct ways. These divergences, as has been shown, reveal each genre and tradition's particular engagement with several thematic concerns.

Even though a given work provides an ultimately particular vision of the go-between, a frame of reference which would allow observations of a theoretical nature on the figure does emerge from comparative study. The principal axis of this frame is constructed by the invisible yet commanding pull which imposes the status of stock character on the go-between, compelling the reader to consider her/him as an agent working in isolation. The interactive nature of seduction is underplayed in favor of the reiteration of a series of preassumed ethical notions regarding the comic or sinful aspects of the task. At first sight, most texts appear to suggest a reading strategy through which the go-between would emerge as a detached figure and therefore be labeled "guilty" or "not guilty" in ethical terms, as though performing a good or bad deed entirely of her or his own will and in an isolated universe. Only upon close reading can it be appreciated that texts do account for the fact that that mediation concerns all parties and that it is a poetic structure as much as a moral one.

As we have seen, society and politics – that is, two factors that warrant ethical considerations – play important roles in the portrayal of the go-between, but they do not exceed the limits of significant variables that only partially explain her characterization. The compounding moral accusations placed on the go-between represent, above all else, the attempt to subdue the uncomfortable within comfortable confines. The uncomfortable in mediation has to do with the threateningly intimate and intricate network of allegiances that bares the fragility of clear appellations such as "victim," "aggressor," "crafty," and "sorceress" in the world of seduction and amorous pursuit. Such terms imply set boundaries and quantifiable degrees of agency, tying in with misogyny and the disdain of old age to construct a seemingly lucid idea of mediation. Our readings have shown that, in fact, all texts provide enough clues to undo the image of their own apparent comfort when faced with intermediary activity.

Once the comfortable is cast away, it becomes clear that in medieval texts mediation appears to pose a serious threat to the semblance of unity projected by love. The threat continues to exist as long as the mediator avoids an expression of her or his own self, resorting instead to deferred and deflected stereotypical tropes that on close inspection fail to fit into the intrinsic logic of seduction, of which they are supposedly a significant component. It is only through a fortified sense of the mediator's self – as with Celestina – that such a system is debunked and replaced with functional definitions of third-party action.

Medieval texts thematize mediation in remarkably varied ways, causing it to give rise to a series of configurations and themes that can only surface once the stereotypical attributes of the activity are problematized via criticism. The poetic themes into which medieval texts blend mediation concern absence, distance, the deciphering of signs, and the crucial roles of all these for the perpetuation of *eros*. If *eros* exists only when absence is guaranteed, then the figure responsible for mediation recalls and even nurtures the existence of a gap, reminding the lovers that fulfillment is absent as long as mediation has to take place. At the same time, this figure threatens to terminate *eros* because her very task consists of bridging the gap and bringing the lovers together.

The internally divided logic of this function is further intensified by the utility of mediation for deciphering signs and learning to speak of love. Barthes' notion that love requires the act of "being talked about" fits third party activity since mediation creates that very interlocutor. It permits the expression of fears, desires, frustrations, and even everyday details that the presence of the object of desire would prohibit. To mediate a love affair is to fulfill at once the requirements of *eros* (absence) and speech (presence) in addition to posing a threat to *eros* by promising the successful end of seduction. Mediation prohibits lovers from venturing alone into the amorous system, and we have seen that each text grapples with this simultaneously binding and liberating role in a unique way. The position of the third party as a potential interpreter of signs creates a threat to the hegemony of seduction as an indecipherable system. Yet it also presents the problem of seduction with one of its only solutions, that of utterance. This double function simultaneously defines and perturbs the lovers' quest. It causes the seductive process to face a series of perplexing antilogies because it affords it a relational perception that offers a seemingly precise conceptual grasp on the evil art of seduction.

The Continually Elusive Conceptual Frame

But the curious theoretical premise outlined above is charged with several other connotations which propel mediation into multiple conceptual realms at once and complicate its role. For one thing, intermediary activity connotes an impurity of transaction. In everyday contemporary language the achievement of one's aim through a "middleman" or an "agent" betrays the dissatisfaction that somehow the purity of the transaction has been compromised. Given that the third party absorbs some of the profit of every financial transaction, the (false) ideal of an absolutely fair and just contract becomes subject to threat in the presence of mediation. In the world of purchase and sale, to achieve one's aim without a third party implies a more profitable, pure, and simple deal. It intensifies the conviction that the mediated affair is lessened in profit while the unmediated one yields more to the two parties involved. The texts studied here carry this conviction into the portrayal of the go-between to varying degrees: it is rarely if ever articulated, but the impression of usury in seduction does govern the portrayal of mediation in illicit love. Courtly love's adamant refusal to admit or acknowledge mediation attests to the link between this act and the radical hazard it poses to the glory and perfection of a secret and pure love. Not only does mediation recall prostitution – a fact reiterated frequently in medieval texts – but also it threatens outwardly to diminish the experience of seduction for the lovers by taking a cut, as it were, from the experience.

Another under-expressed aspect of mediation has to do with its potential to conjure a surrogate identity. The go-between appears to enter the pre-circumscribed space of lover or mother at many junctures, slipping in and out of these locations in accordance with the nature of her or his task. The temporary assumption of the identities of parent and lover affects the poetics of love by endowing it with a pedagogical element. To address the mediator with the passion of a lover or the lament of an offspring causes the subject of discourse to enact positions that will be necessary for success in seduction. It will be recalled that Rāmīn experienced intimacy with the nurse in *Vīs and Rāmīn* prior to his encounter with Vīs and that the appellation "mother" is a frequent prologue to the solicitation of important knowledge from the old go-between in many other texts. This pedagogical role is assumed under surrogate guise and enacted by a third party who cannot fulfill the undertaken status in any formal or consistent manner. The go-between's stereotypical condition of displacement as an old woman or a panderer subjects the content of her lesson to an undercurrent of incredulity on the part of others. Even if a lesson is learned successfully from the mediator, the latter's momentary usurping of a lover or mother's spot creates a wrinkle of suspicion in her portrayal.

The go-between's confinement to stereotypical spaces causes many of the important factors which we have just discussed to exist on a dormant level. It is only upon the scrutiny of the third party's dialogical position that the paradoxes and ambiguities of her or his role come to life. In the previous chapters, one consideration has been the degree of success and failure in each go-between's task of seduction. It is now possible to appreciate that regardless of actual success or failure, the mediator endows the lovers with some of the power to compose an amorous system. The third party is an aid in the game of love as evidenced by her or his spatial position between pursuer and pursued and as a screen onto which the messages and signs of seduction are cast. These signs range from misplaced projections of guilt and anger to direct pleas for help, with numerous other possibilities in between. In all cases, the screen provided by the mediator functions as a place for the construction of amorous language. It allows the lovers to engage in the perverse but necessary manipulation and dislocation of language for the sake of seduction. We have seen that each literary text uses this screen in its own way: elegy and Plautine theater, for example, debunk its declared function and replace it with another without ever acknowledging that they do so, while erotological treatises and traditions of women's deceits filter several key strategies and signs through it.

The literary history of the medieval go-between is the chronicle of an elusive subject that causes interference, bad influence, and sabotage alongside aid, assistance, and consolation. Ultimately, this seemingly paradoxical presence defines and reflects the rhetoric of seduction. The portrayal of mediation reveals the ways in which medieval texts posit the problems associated with language. Mediation brings with it the act of speaking of love: the trajectories and results of this act inscribe the texts' perception of language as well as the implications of dialogical networks. As we have seen, third-party activity gives rise to the articulation of diverse types of discourse commanded by anger, misogyny, guilt, pedagogy, and surrogate identity, to name a few. Even when the emotions that they express are ultimately displaced, these types of discourse communicate the textual awareness of the problems associated with the production of meaning via dialogue. This awareness, peculiar to some extent to each text and markedly diverse in nature, discloses valuable information on the modality of medieval texts in their dealings with carnal love. That is to say, the treatment of the intermediary highlights some of the issues that medieval works are compelled to explore in their handling of discourse.

The discourse that is produced around intermediary activity foregrounds some of the key elements in the poetics of profane love. These include the function of such devices as deceit, performative speech, and inspirational and pedagogical language. Even when she is ineffectual or wrongly attributed with mediatory power, the go-between provides a template for reflection and experimentation with such devices in the world of seduction. The process of dialogue with or about the mediator incites the progress of seductive language, for it involves the apparatus that is indispensable to seduction itself. Performative utterances, deceit, preoccupation with money, pedagogical stances, anger, and loyalty are among the many elements that texture the discourse of mediation or the utterances about it. These also happen to be significant elements of discourse in seduction and endemic to the dialogue between lovers; the mediator, then, potentially creates those circumstances that are necessary for the development of seductive language and the artifice that must uphold it. For example, when Tibullus blames a nonexistent *lena* for separating him from his beloved, his misplaced shift of blame fulfills entirely the function of the artifice that is so necessary for profane love. It infuses his language with deceit (for after all, the *lena* is not to blame), it endows his discourse with an intangible performative quality (for he acts by cursing and does not act where it counts), and it allows him to express a fundamentally obscure jealousy that upon close reading eludes any conceptual understanding. Or, when Fénice turns to

Thessala for help, she effectively translates a morally questionable act (rendering her husband impotent and eloping with a lover) into an act of pure, glorious love. The puzzling logic of this gesture is contained by the go-between who performs the translation: by extension, the recourse to the go-between guarantees that seduction remain an essentially mysterious artifice. All the mediators studied in the previous chapters help construct the enigmatic blend of deceit, pedagogy, loyalty, and performance that constitutes an important component of the artifice of seduction. The comparative literary study of the go-between shows that interaction with a third party is at all times fraught with a curious mixture of anxiety and relief: this mixture reflects, to some extent, the impossibility of defining seduction and reveals the sophisticated level of awareness of this problem in medieval texts.

In chapter 22 of the first part of *Don Quijote*, a chain of galley slaves crosses paths with the Manchegan knight and his squire. Don Quijote, keen as ever on righting wrongs and freeing the unjustly imprisoned, questions some of the prisoners about their crimes. The fourth person to whom he directs his inquiry turns out to have been a go-between "with a touch of sorcerer about him."[1] Don Quijote reacts by stating that only sorcery has damaged the man's profession, for the job of a simple go-between is not a crime but rather a most admirable profession. He goes on to explain that the task is a necessary one in a "well-ordered state, and only to be exercised by persons of good birth."[2] Don Quijote thus confuses *alcahuete* – also defined as "pimp" – with the unmercenary maid and loyal friend of courtly genres.[3] In so doing, Cervantes' hero creates a humorous effect since he remains unaware of the slippage between *alcahuete* and virtuous intermediary. The discussion of third-party activity by this beloved eccentric of literature affords yet another provocative glimpse into the remarkably varied thematization of the topic in literature. Mediation is spoken of by a character whose judgment is suspect and whose specialty consists of confusing lexical fields. Nonetheless, an ethical imperative fuels the comic momentum of Don Quijote's utterance whose "innocent" meaning clashes with the "corrupt"

---

[1] Miguel de Cervantes, *Don Quixote*, the Ormsby translation, edited by Joseph R. Jones and Kenneth Douglas (New York: W. W. Norton, 1981) 153.

[2] Cervantes, *Don Quixote*, 154.

[3] This is also explained in the editor's note (*Don Quixote*, 154).

nature of the galley slave. The comic aspect of the knight's statement serves to highlight his warped sense of reality, but it also provides an emblematic declaration on the convergence of moral and poetic registers in the literary representation of the go-between. That is, it relies for effect on the universally acknowledged corruption of the go-between while infusing the character with a suggestive utility. The signifier "go-between" thus constructs, once again, an axis for an unsteady yet compelling frame of reference in the discussion on love.

Inscribed within a novel whose dialogue with a multitude of medieval and Renaissance traditions and genres is well known, this case recalls the extent to which analysis from a wide range of perspectives is necessary for the critique of mediation in literature. Theoretical and historical inquiry from diverse schools can only continue to shed light on the topic, especially given that the literary manifestation of intermediary activity occurs in so many different forms. This study has established that mediation – even when stifled or presented as a stereotypical activity – is a site for the convergence of numerous consequential themes in medieval texts, playing an important role in shaping each text's encounter with literary and extra-literary questions. In this light the topic lends itself to further meaningful investigation, for it is without doubt one of the most fascinating devices employed in the literary representation of profane love in the Middle Ages.

BIBLIOGRAPHY

ABBOTT, NABIA. "A Ninth-Century Fragment of the 'Thousand Nights': New Light of the Early History of the *Arabian Nights*." *Journal of Near Eastern Studies* (1949) 129-164.

AHMED, LEILA. *Women and Gender in Islam.* New Haven: Yale University Press, 1992.

AKKURT, CIGDEM T. "Social and Spatial Hierarchy of Women in the Architecture of the Topkapi Harem." In *Traditional Dwellings and Settlements: Working Paper Series,* XLV, 33-67. Berkeley: Center for Environmental Design Research, 1992.

ĀL-AHMAD, SHAMS. *Jawāhar al-Asmār.* Teheran: Asadi, 1973.

ALFONSO, PEDRO. *Disciplina clericalis.* Edited and translated by Ángel González Palencia. Madrid: Consejo Superior de Investigaciones Científicas, 1948.

ALLEN, A. W. "Sincerity and the Roman Elegists." *Classical Philology* 45 (1950) 145-160.

ALLEN, PETER L. *The Art of Love: Amatory Fiction from Ovid to the* Romance of the Rose. Philadelphia: University of Pennsylvania Press, 1992.

LPULEIUS, LUCIUS. *Metamorphoses.* Edited by J. Arthur Hanson. Cambridge: Harvard University Press, 1989.

The Arabian Nights. Translated by Husain Haddawy. New York: W. W. Norton and Company, 1990.

ARMISTEAD, SAMUEL G., AND JAMES T. MONROE. "Celestina's Muslim Sisters." *Celestinesca* 13, 2 (1989) 3-27.

ARRIZABALAGA, JON. "The Ideal Medical Practitioner in Counter-Reformation Castile: The Perception of the Converso Physician Henrique Jorge Henriques (c. 1555-1622)." In *Medicine and Medical Ethics in Medieval and Early Modern Spain: An Intercultural Approach,* edited by Samuel S. Kottek and Luis García Ballester, 61-91. Jerusalem: The Magnes Press, 1996.

ASSIS, YOM TOV. "The Judeo-Arabic Tradition in Christian Spain." In *The Jews of Medieval Islam: Community, Society, and Identity,* edited by Daniel Frank, 111-124. Leiden: E. J. Brill, 1995.

BACHER, H. *Zwei Jüdisch-Persische Dichter.* Strasbourg: K. J. Trubner, 1907.

BADEL, PIERRE-YVES. Le Roman de la Rose *au XIVe siècle: Étude de la réception de l'oeuvre.* Geneva: Librarie Droz, 1980.

AL-BAGHDĀDI, ALI. *Les fleurs éclatantes dans les baisers d'accolement.* Translated by René R. Khawam. Paris: Éditions Phébus, 1989.

Bakhtiār Nāma. Edited by Mohammad Roshan. Teheran: 1969.

Bakhtiār Nāmeh, or, The Royal Foundling. Philadelphia: Edward Parker, 1813.

The Bakhtyar Nama, a Persian Romance. Translated by Sir William Ouseley. Privately printed: 1883.

BĀMDĀD, BADROLMULUK. *Zān-e Irānī.* Teheran: Amīr Kabīr, 1966.

BARSBY, JOHN. *Ovid: Amores.* Oxford: Oxford University Press, 1973.

BARTHES, ROLAND. *A Lover's Discourse: Fragments.* Translated by Richard Howard. New York: Hill and Wang, 1978.

BATANY, JEAN. *Approches du* Roman de la rose. Paris: Bordas, 1973.

BEAUDRILLARD, JEAN. *De la séduction.* Paris: Folio, 1979.

BÉDIER, JOSEPH. *Les Fabliaux: Études de littérature populaire et d'histoire littéraire du moyen âge.* Paris: Champion, 1925.

BELL, JOSEPH NORMENT. *Love Theory in Later Hanbalite Islam.* Albany: State University of New York Press, 1979.

BENTON, J. F. "Trotula, Women's Problems, and Professionalization of Medicine in the Middle Ages." *Bulletin of the History of Medicine* 59 (1985) 30-53.

BOASE, ROGER. "Arab Influences on European Love-Poetry." In *The Legacy of Muslim Spain.* Edited by Salma Khadra Juyyusi, 457-482. Leiden: E. J. Brill, 1992.

BONILLA Y SAN MARTÍN, ADOLFO. "Antecedentes del tipo celestinesco en la literatura latina." *Revue Hispanique* 15 (1906) 372-386.

BRANCA, VITTORE. *Boccaccio: the Man and His Works.* Translated by Richard Monges. New York: New York University Press, 1976.

BRÜGEL, J. C. "Love, Lust and Longing: Eroticism in Early Islam." In *Society and the Sexes in Medieval Islam,* edited by Afaf Lutfi al-Sayyid-Marsot, 81-117. Los Angeles: Gustave E. von Grunebaum Center for Near Eastern Studies, UCLA, 1977.

BRUNDAGE, JAMES A. "Sex and Canon Law." In *Handbook of Medieval Sexuality,* edited by Vern L. Bullough and James A. Brundage, 33-51. New York: Garland Publishers, 1996.

—. *Law, Sex, and Christian Society in Medieval Europe.* University of Chicago Press: 1987.

Burkard, Richard. "Courtly Love and Hideous Love: Gentility Followed by Rape in *El libro de buen amor.*" *The Journal of the Association for the Interdisciplinary Study of the Arts* 1:2 (1996) 21-31.

BURTON, SIR RICHARD. *A Plain and Literal Translation of the Arabian Nights' Entertainments, now Entitled the Book of the Thousand Nights and a Night.* Printed by the Burton Club for Private Subscribers: 1885.

CADDEN, JOAN. *Meanings of Sex Difference in the Middle Ages: Medicine, Science, and Culture.* Cambridge: Cambridge University Press, 1993.

Calila e Dimna. Edited by J. M. Cacho Blecua y M. J. Lacarra. Madrid: Castalia, 1987.

Cantigas de Santa María. Edited by Walter Mettman. 3 vols. Madrid: Editorial Castalia, 1986-1989.

CARO BAROJA, JULIO. *Vidas mágicas e Inquisición.* Madrid: Taurus, 1967.

CARRUTHERS, MARY. "The Wife of Bath and the Painting of Lions." *Publications of the Modern Language Association of America* 94 (1979) 209-222.

CARSON, ANNE. *Eros the Bittersweet.* Princeton: Princeton University Press, 1986.

CASTRO GUISASOLA, F. *Observaciones sobre las fuentes literarias de* La Celestina. Madrid: Instituto de Miguel de Cervantes, 1973.

CASTRO, AMÉRICO. *España en su historia: cristianos, moros y judíos.* Barcelona: Editorial Crítica, 1983.

—. *Realidad histórica de España.* México: Porrúa, 1954.

CHAUCER, GEOFFREY. *The Canterbury Tales.* New York: Modern Library, 1994.

CHEJNE, ANWAR. *Islam and the West: the Moriscos, a Cultural and Social History.* Albany: State University of New York Press, 1983.

CHRAIBI, ABOUBAKR. *Contes nouveaux des* 1001 Nuits: *étude du manuscrit Reinhardt.* Paris: Librairie d'Amérique et D'Orient, 1996.

CIRAC ESTOPAÑÁN, SEBASTIÁN. *Los procesos de hechicerías en la Inquisición de Castilla la Nueva (tribunales de Toledo y Cuenca).* Madrid: Diana, 1942.

CIROT, GEORGES. "L'épisode de Doña Endrina dans le *Libro de buen amor.*" *Bulletin Hispanique* XLV (1943) 139-156.

CLINE, RUTH H. "Heart and Eyes." *Romance Philology* 25 (1971-1972) 263-297.

COHEN, ESTHER, AND ELLIOT HOROWITZ. "In Search of the Sacred: Jews, Christians, and Rituals of Marriage in the Later Middle Ages." *Journal of Medieval and Renaissance Studies* 20 (1990) 225-249.

COOK, J. M. "The Rise of the Achaemenids and Establishment of their Empire." In *Cambridge History of Iran,* edited by W. B. Fisher and others, 200-292. Cambridge: Cambridge University Press, 1985.

CRIADO DE VAL, M. "Melibea y Celestina ante el juicio de Don Quijote." *Anales Cervantinos* IV (1954) 187-198.

DAGENAIS, JOHN. *The Ethics of Reading in Manuscript Culture: Glossing the* Libro de buen amor. Princeton: Princeton University Press, 1994.

De amore: Andreas Capellanus on Love. Edited and tranlated by P. G. Walsh. London: Duckworth, 1982.

DEYERMOND, ALAN. "Sexual Initiation in the Woman's-Voice Court Lyric." In *Courtly Literature: Culture and Context,* edited by Keith Busby and Erik Kooper, 125-158. Amsterdam and Philadelphia: J. Benjamins Publishing Company, 1990.

DINSHAW, CAROLYN. *Chaucer's Sexual Politics.* Madison: The University of Wisconsin Press, 1989.

DIXON, LAURINDA S. "The Curse of Chastity: The Marginalization of Women in Medieval Art and Medicine." In *Matrons and Marginal Women in Medieval Society,* edited by Robert R. Edwards and Vickie Ziegler, 49-74. Rochester: Boydell Press, 1995.

DOW, BLANCHE H. *The Varying Attitudes towards Women in French Literature of the Fifteeenth Century.* New York: Publications of the Institute of French Studies, 1936.

DREYFUS, HUBERT L., and Paul Rabinow. *Michel Foucault: Beyond Structuralism and Herneneutics.* Chicago: The University of Chicago Press, 1983.

DUBY, GEORGES, AND MICHELLE PERROT, EDS. *Histoire mondiale de la femme.* Paris: Nouvelle Librairie de France, 1974.

—, and others. *Amour et sexualité en Occident.* Paris: Éditions du Seuil, 1991.

—. *Mâle Moyen Age, de l'amour et autres essais.* Paris: Flammarion, 1988.

Éneas, roman du XIIe siècle. Edited by J. J. Salverda de Grave. Paris: Champion, 1925-1929.

Eneas: A Twelfth Century French Romance. Translated by John A. Yunck. New York: Columbia University Press, 1974.

FARAL, EDMOND. *Recherches sur les sources latines des contes et romans courtois du moyen âge.* Paris: Champion, 1913.

FLEMING, JOHN V. *Classical Imitation and Interpretation in Chaucer's* Troilus. Lincoln: University of Nebraska Press, 1990.

FORBES, THOMAS. *The Midwife and the Witch.* New Haven: Yale University Press, 1966.

FORSTER, E. M. *Aspects of the Novel and Related Writings.* London: Edward Arnold, 1974.

FOUCAULT, MICHEL. *Discipline and Punish: the Birth of the Prison.* Translated by Alan Sheridan. New York: Vintage/Random House, 1979.

FRAPPIER, JEAN. *Chrétien de Troyes, the Man and His Work.* Translated by Raymond J. Cormier. Ohio: Ohio University Press,1982.

FRENK, MARGIT. *Corpus de la antigua lírica popular hispánica (siglos XV a XVII).* Madrid: Castalia, 1987.

—. *Corpus de la antigua lírica popular hispánica. Suplemento.* Madrid: Castalia, 1992.

—. *Estudios sobre lírica antigua.* Madrid: Editorial Castalia, 1978.

—. *Las jarchas mozárabes y los comienzos de la lírica románica.* México: El Colegio de México, 1985.

—. *Lírica hispánica de tipo popular.* México: Universidad Nacional Autónoma de México, 1966.

FRIEDMAN, EDWARD H. "Rhetoric at Work: Celestina, Melibea, and the Persuasive Arts." In *Fernando de Rojas and* Celestina*: Approaching the Fifth Centenary,* edited by Ivy A. Corfis and Joseph T. Snow, 359-379. Madison: Hispanic Seminary of Medieval Studies, 1993.

GALEF, DAVID. *The Supporting Cast: A Study of Flat and Minor Characters.* Pennsylvania: The Pennsylvania State University Press, 1993.

GALLAIS, PIERRE. *Genèse du roman occidental: essais sur* Tristan et Iseut *et son modèle persan.* Paris: Éditions Tête de Feuilles et Éditions du Sirac, 1974.

Games of Venus: An Anthology of Greek and Roman Erotic Verse from Sappho to Ovid. Introduced, translated and annotated by Peter Bing and Rip Cohen. New York: Routledge, 1991.

GARCÍA-ARENAL, MERCEDES, AND BÉATRICE LEROY. *Moros y judíos en Navarra en la Baja Edad Media.* Madrid: Libros Hiperión, 1984.

GHAZOUL, FERIAL J. *Nocturnal Poetics: The Arabian Nights in Comparative Context.* Cairo, The American University in Cairo Press, 1996).

GIFFORD, D. J. "The Place of Verbal Fascination in *La Celestina.*" In *Medieval and Renaissance Studies on Spain and Portugal in Honour of P. E. Russell,* edited by F. W. Hodcroft, D. G. Pattison, R. D. F. Pring-Mill, R. W. Truman, 30-37. Oxford: The Society for the Study of Medieval Language and Literature, 1981.

GILMAN, STEPHEN. *The Art of* La Celestina. Madison: University of Wisconsin Press, 1956.

—. *The Spain of Fernando de Rojas: the Intellectual and Social Landscape of* La Celestina. Princeton: Princeton University Press, 1972.

GINZBERG, J. *Legends of the Jews.* Philadelphia: Jewish Publication Society, 1925.

Gliglois: A French Arthurian Romance of the Thirteenth Century. Edited by Charles H. Livingstone. Cambridge: Harvard University Press, 1932.

The Glory of the Perfumed Garden: the Missing Flowers. Translated by "H.E.J." London: Neville Spearman, 1975.

The Goliard Poets: Medieval Latin Songs and Satires. Translated by George F. Whicher. Cambridge: Cambridge University Press, 1949.

GONZÁLEZ ROLÁN, TOMÁS. "Rasgos de la alcahuetería amorosa en la literatura latina." In *La Celestina y su contorno social: Actas del I Congreso Internacional sobre* La Celestina, edited by Manuel Criado deVal, 276-289. Barcelona: Borras, 1977.

GORGANI, FAKHR AL-DIN. *Vīs o Ramin.* Edited by Mohammad Jaffar Mahjoub. Teheran: The Ibn Sina Library, 1959.

GREILSAMMER, MYRIAM. "The Midwife, the Priest, and the Physician: the Subjugation of Midwives in the Low Countries at the end of the Middle Ages." *Journal of Medieval and Renaissance Studies* 21 (1991) 285-324.

GRIFFIN, JASPER. "Augustan Poetry and the Life of Luxury." *Journal of Roman Studies* 66 (1976) 87-104.

GROUSSET, R., L. MASSIGNON, AND H. MASSÉ. *L'âme de l'Iran.* Paris: Albin Michel, 1951.

GRUNEBAUM, GUSTAVE E. von. *Medieval Islam: A Study in Cultural Orientation.* Chicago: The University of Chicago Press, 1953.

GUILLÉN, CLAUDIO. *The Challenge of Comparative Literature.* Translated by Cola Franzen. Cambridge: Harvard University Press, 1993.

GUNN, ALAN M. F. *The Mirror of Love: A Reinterpretation of the "Romance of the Rose."* Texas: Texas Tech Press, 1952.

GUZMÁN, JORGE. *Una constante didáctico-moral del* Libro de buen amor. Iowa: State University of Iowa Studies in Language and Literature XIV, 1963.

GYBBON-MONYPENNY, G. B. "The Two Versions of the *Libro de buen amor*: The Extent and Nature of the Author's Revisions." *Bulletin of Hispanic Studies* 38 (1962) 205-221.

Handbook of Medieval Sexuality. Edited by Vern L. Bullough and James A. Brundage. New York: Garland Publishers, 1996.

HANDY, OTIS. "The Rhetorical and Psychological Defloration of Melibea." *Celestinesca* 7.1 (1983) 17-27.

AL-HAWRANI, ʿABD AL-RAHĪM. *Les ruses des femmes.* Translated by René Khawam. Paris: Phébus, 1993.

HÉLIN, MAURICE. *A History of Medieval Latin Literature.* Translated by Jean Chapman Snow. New York: W. Salloch, 1949.

HERRERO, JAVIER. "Celestina: The Aging Prostitute as Witch." In *Aging in Literature,* edited by Laurel Porter and Laurence M. Porter, 31-47. Michigan: International Book Publishers, 1984.

HEXTER, RALPH. *Ovid and Medieval Schooling*. Munich: Bei der Arbeo-Gesellschaft, 1986.

History of Persian Literature. Edited by Yunus Jaffery. Delhi: Triveni Publishers, 1981.

HODGSON, MARSHALL G. S. *The Venture of Islam*. Chicago: The University of Chicago Press, 1974.

HOFFMAN, RICHARD L. *Ovid and the Canterbury Tales*. Philadelphia: University of Pennsylvania, 1966.

HOWARD, DONALD. *The Three Temptations*. Princeton: Princeton University Press: 1966.

HUMPHREYS, R. STEPHEN. *Islamic History: A Framework for Inquiry*. London: I. B. Taurus, 1991.

IBN ARABI, MUHYIDDIN. *Fusūs al-hikām*. Cairo: Isa al-Bābī, 1946.

IBN HAZM, ALI IBN AHMAD. *El collar de la paloma: tratado sobre el amor y los amantes*. Translated by Emilio García Gómez. Madrid: Alianza, 1985.

IBN SINA, ABŪ-ALĪ. *Qānūn dar Tibb*. Teheran: Soroush Editions, 1987.

AL-ISFAHĀNĪ, ABU I FARAJ. *Kitāb al-Aghānī*. Teheran: Scientific and Cultural Publications, 1989.

JACQUART, DANIELLE, AND CLAUDE THOMASSET. *Sexuality and Medicine in the Middle Ages*. Translated by Matthew Adamson. Princeton: Princeton University Press, 1988.

JĀMĪ, ABDUL-RAHMĀN. *Yūsuf va Zuleikhā*. Teheran: Amīr Kabīr, 1961.

—. *Youssouf et Zouleikha*. Translated by Auguste Bricteux. Paris: Librairie Orientaliste Paul Geuthner, 1927.

JUÁREZ BLANQUER, AURORA. "Madre y cantiga de amigo." *Estudios románicos* 1 (1978) 295-311.

JUSSERAND, J. J. *A Literary History of the English People*. London: G. P. Putnam's Sons, 1895.

KAHANE, HENRY AND RENÉE KAHANE. "L'énigme du nom de Cligès." *Romania* 82 (1961) 113-21.

KELLER, J. E. "*Cantiga 135*: The Blessed Virgin as a Matchmaker." In *Florilegium Hispanicum: Medieval and Golden Age Studies Presented to Dorothy Clotelle Clarke*, edited by John S. Geary, 103-117. Madison: Hispanic Seminary of Medieval Studies, 1983.

KELLY, DOUGLAS. *Chrétien de Troyes: An Analytic Bibliography*. London: Grant and Cutler, 1976.

KENNEDY, DUNCAN F. *The Arts of Love: Five Studies in the Discourse of Roman Love Elegy*. Cambridge: Cambridge University Press, 1993.

KHADRA JAYYUSI, SALMA, ED. *The Legacy of Muslim Spain*. Leiden: E. J. Brill, 1992.

KING, HELEN. "Sowing the Field: Greek and Roman Sexology." In *Sexual Knowledge, Sexual Science: The History of Attitudes to Sexuality*, edited by Roy Porter and Mikulas Teich, 29-47. Cambridge: Cambridge University Press, 1994.

KINKADE, RICHARD P. "A Thirteenth-Centry Precursor of the *Libro de Buen Amor*: the *Art d'Amors*." *La Corónica* 24: 2 (1996) 123-139.

KIRBY, THOMAS A. *Chaucer's* Troilus: *A Study in Courtly Love*. Massachusetts: Peter Smith, 1958.

KNOX, PETER E. *Ovid's* Metamorphoses *and the Traditions of Augustan Poetry*. Cambridge: The Cambridge Philological Society, 1986.

KONSTAN, DAVID. *Roman Comedy*. Ithaca: Cornell University Press, 1983.

KRAMER, S. N. *The Sumerians: Their History, Culture and Character*. Chicago: The University of Chicago Press, 1963.

KUGEL, JAMES L. *In Potiphar's House: The Interpretive Life of Biblical Texts*. Cambridge: Harvard University Press, 1990.

La "comédie latine en France" au XIIe siècle. Edited by Gustave Cohen. Paris: Les Belles Lettres, 1931.

LACARRA, MARÍA EUGENIA. "La evolución de la prostitución en la Castilla del siglo XV y la mancebía de Salamanca en tiempos de Fernando de Rojas." In *Fernando de Rojas and* Celestina: *Approaching the Fifth Centenary*, edited by Ivy A. Corfis and Joseph T. Snow, 33-78. Madison: Hispanic Seminary of Medieval Studies, 1993.

LACARRA, MARÍA JESÚS. *Cuentística medieval en España: los orígenes*. Zaragoza: Universidad de Zaragoza, 1979.

LAGARDÈRE, VINCENT. *Histoire et société en Occident musulman au Moyen Âge: analyse du* Mi'yar *d'Al-Wansarisi.* Madrid: Casa de Velázquez, 1995.

LÁZARO CARRETER, FERNANDO. "Los amores de don Melón y doña Endrina." *Arbor* 62 (1951) 210-236.

LE CHAPELAIN, ANDRÉ. *Traité de l'amour courtois.* Edited and translated by Claude Buridant. Paris: Klincksieck, 1974.

LE CLERC, GUILLAUME. *The Romance of Fergus.* Edited by Wilson Frescoln. Philadelphia: W.H. Allen, 1983.

LECOY, FÉLIX. *Recherches sur le* Libro de buen amor. (Paris: Librairie Droz, 1938.

LEE, A. C. *The* Decameron, *its Sources and Analogues.* New York: Haskell House, 1909.

LEGOUIS, ÉMILE. *Geoffrey Chaucer.* London: J. M. Dent and Sons, 1928.

LEVERETT, FREDERICK PERCIVAL. *Latin Lexicon.* Philadelphia: The Peter Reilly Company, 1931.

LEWIS, BERNARD. *The Political Language of Islam.* Chicago: University of Chicago Press, 1988.

LEWIS, C. S. "What Chaucer Really Did to *Il Filostrato.*" In*Essays and Studies by Members of the English Association*, edited by Sir Herbert John Clifford Grierson, 56-76. Oxford: Clarendon Press, 1931.

Libro de los engannos y asayamientos de las mugeres. Edited by Emilio Vuolo. Messina: Peloritans, 1971.

Libro del caballero Zifar. Edited by Joaquín González Muela. Madrid: Castalia, 1982.

LIDA DE MALKIEL, MARÍA ROSA. "Nuevas notas para la interpretación del *Libro de buen amor.*" In *Estudios de literatura española y comparada.* Buenos Aires: Editorial Universitaria de Buenos Aires, 1966.

—. *La originalidad artística de La Celestina.* Buenos Aires: Editorial universitaria, 1962.

LILJA, SAARA. *The Roman Elegists' Attitude to Women.* New York: Garland, 1978.

LÓPEZ-BARALT, LUCE. *Un Kāma Sūtra español.* Madrid: Ediciones Siruela, 1992.

LORENZO GRADÍN, PILAR. *La canción de mujer en la lírica medieval.* Santiago de Compostela: Universidad de Santiago,1990.

LORRIS, GUILLAUME DE, AND JEAN DE MEUN. *Le Roman de la Rose.* Edited by Ernest Langlois. Paris: Société des Anciens Textes Français, 1912.

Los más bellos cuentos de las mil y una noches. Translated by Juan Vernet. Barcelona: Editorial Labor, 1965.

MACOVSKI, MICHAEL S. *Dialogue and Literature: Apostrophe, Auditors, & the Collapse of Romantic Discourse.* Oxford: Oxford University Press, 1994.

MAHDI, MUHSIN, ED. *The Thousand and One Nights (Kitab Alf Laylā wa-Laylā).* Leiden: E. J. Brill, 1984.

MALTBY, ROBERT. *Latin Love Elegy.* Bristol: Bristol Classical Press, 1980.

MÁRQUEZ VILLANUEVA, FRANCISCO. "Las lecturas del deán de Cádiz en una 'cantiga de mal dizer'." In *Studies on the "Cantigas de Santa María", Art, Music and Poetry*, Actas del Seminario Internacional sobre las Cantigas de Santa María, edited by I. J. Kotz and J. E. Keller, 329-354. Madison: Hispanic Seminar on Medieval Studies, 1987.

—. "Para el encuadre del tema celestinesco: el tratado de alcahuetería de Nafzāwī." In *Proyección histórica de España en sus tres culturas: Castilla y León, América y el Mediterrá-*

neo II, edited by Eufemio Lorenzo Sanz, 445-459. Junta de Castilla y León: Consejería de Cultura y Turismo, 1993.

—. *Orígenes y sociología del tema celestinesco.* Barcelona: Antropos, 1993.

MARSAN, RAMELINE E. *Itinéraire espagnole du conte médiéval.* Paris: Librairie Klincksieck, 1974.

MARTIN, PRISCILLA. *Chaucer's Women: Nuns, Wives, and Amazons.* Iowa City: University of Iowa Press, 1990.

MASON, H. J. "Fabula Graecanica: Apuleius and his Greek Sources." In *Aspects of Apuleius'* Golden Ass, edited by B. L. Hijmans Jr. and R. Th. van der Paardt, 1-17. Groningen: Bouma's Boekhuis, 1978.

MATTHEWS, WILLIAM. "The Wife of Bath and All of her Sect." *Viator* 5 (1974) 413-443.

MAZO KARRAS, RUTH. "Sex, Money, and Prostitution in Medieval English Culture." In *Desire and Discipline: Sex and Sexuality in the Premodern West,* edited by Jacqueline Murray and Konrad Eisenbichler, 201-216. Toronto: University of Toronto Press, 1996.

MCVAUGH, MICHAEL R. "Royal Surgeons and the Value of Medical Learning: The Crown of Aragon, 1300-1350." In *Practical Medicine from Salerno to the Black Death,* edited by Luis García Ballester, 211-236. Cambridge: Cambridge University Press, 1994.

MEEK, THEOPHILE J. "Mespotamian Legal Documents." In *Ancient Near-Eastern Texts Relating to the Old Testament,* edited by James B. Pritchard, 167-170. Princeton: Princeton University Press, 1955.

MENÉNDEZ Y PELAYO, MARCELINO. *Orígenes de la novela.* Santander: Ardus, 1943.

MENÉNDEZ PIDAL, RAMÓN. *Estudios literarios.* Madrid: Espasa Calpe, 1957.

—. *Poesía árabe y poesía europea.* Buenos Aires: Espasa Calpe argentina, 1941.

MERNISSI, FATIMA. *Beyond the Veil: Male-Female Dynamics in Modern Muslim Society.* Indiana: Indiana University Press, 1987.

—. *Sexe-Idéologie-Islam.* Rabat: Les Éditions maghrebines, 1985.

METTMANN, WALTER. *La historia de la donzella Teodor.* Mainz: Akademie der Wissenchaften und der Literatur, 1962.

MICHA, ALEXANDRE, ED. *Les romans de Chrétien de Troyes.* Paris: Librairie Honoré Champion, 1982.

MIQUEL, ANDRÉ, AND PERCY KEMP. *Majnūn et Laylā: l'amour fou.* Paris: La Bibliothèque arabe Sinbad, 1984.

MONSON, DONALD A. "*Auctoritas* and Intertextuality in Andreas Capellanus' *De Amore.*" In *Poetics of Love in the Middle Ages: Texts and Contexts,* edited by Moshe Lazar and Norris J. Lacy, 69-79. Virginia: George Mason University Press, 1989.

MONTERO CARTELLE, ENRIQUE, ED. *Constantini Liber de coitu. El tratado de andrología de Constantino el Africano.* Santiago de Compostela: Universidad de Santiago, 1983.

MOORE, R. I. *The Formation of a Persecuting Society: Power and Deviance in Western Europe, 950-1250.* Oxford: Blackwell, 1987.

MORAWSKI, JOSEPH DE. *Pamphile et Galatée par Jehan Bras-de-Fer de Dammartin-en-Goële, poème français inédit du XIVe siècle.* Paris: Champion, 1915.

MORGAN, DAVID. *Medieval Persia: 1040-1797.* London: Longman, 1988.

MORGAN, ERICA. "Rhetorical Technique in the Persuasion of Melibea." *Celestinesca* 3.2 (1979) 7-18.

MURRAY, ALEXANDER. *Reason and Society in the Middle Ages.* Oxford: Oxford University Press, 1978.

MUSA, MARK, AND PETER BONDANELLA. *The Decameron: A New Translation.* New York: W. W. Norton & Company, 1977.

MUSCATINE, CHARLES. *The Old French Fabliaux.* New Haven: Yale University Press, 1986.

MYERS, OLIVER T. "Symmetry of Form in the *Libro de buen amor.*" *Philological Quarterly* 51 (1972) 74-84.

AL-NAFZĀWĪ, UMAR IBN MUHAMMAD. *The Glory of the Perfumed Garden: The Missing Flowers.* London: Neville Spearman, 1986.

NEFF, THEODORE LEE. *La satire des femmes dans la poésie lyrique française au moyen âge.* Paris: Giard et Brière, 1900.

NIRENBERG, DAVID. *Communities of Violence: Persecution of Minorities in The Middle Ages.* Princeton: Princeton University Press, 1996.

NIZĀMĪ GANJAVĪ. *Kulīyyāt-e Khamsa-ye Hakīm Nizāmī Ganjavī.* Teheran: Amīr Kabīr, 1962.

NOLAN, BARBARA. *Chaucer and the Tradition of the 'Roman Antique'.* Cambridge: Cambridge University Press, 1992.

NOOMEN, WILLEM, AND NICO VAN BOOGAARD. *Nouveau recueil complet des fabliaux.* 9 vols. Pays Bas: Van Gorcum, 1983-1993.

NYKROG, PER. *Les Fabliaux: Étude d'histoire littéraire et de stylistique médiévale.* Copenhagen: E. Munksgaard, 1957.

ORLANDI, GIOVANNI. "Classical Latin Satire and the Medieval Elegiac Comedy." In *Latin Poetry and the Classical Tradition: Essays in Medieval and Renaissance Literature,* edited by Peter Godman and Oswyn Murray, 97-115. Oxford: Clarendon Press, 1990.

OTIS, LEAH LYDIA. *Prostitution in Medieval Society: The History of an Urban Institution in Languedoc.* Chicago: University of Chicago Press, 1985.

OULMONT, CHARLES. *Les débats du clerc et du chevalier dans la littérature du Moyen Age.* Paris: Champion, 1911.

OVID. *Metamorphoses.* Edited by Frank Justus Miller. Cambridge: Harvard University Press, 1976.

—. *Heroides and Amores.* Edited by E. H. Warmington. Cambridge: Harvard University Press, 1914.

—. *Ars amatoria.* Edited by F. W. Lenz. Torino: Corpus scriptorum Latinorum Paravianum, 1969.

PAPANGHELIS, THEODORE D. *Propertius: a Hellenistic poet on Love and Death.* Cambridge: Cambridge University Press, 1987.

PASTORE STOCCHI, M. "Un antecedente latino-medievale di Pietro di Vinciolo." *Studi sul Boccaccio* I (1963) 349-362.

PAYER, PIERRE J. *Sex and the Penitentials: The Development of a Sexual Code 550-1150.* Toronto: University of Toronto Press, 1984.

PEPIN, RONALD E. *Literature of Satire in the Twelfth Century.* New York: Mellen House, Studies in Medieval Literature, vol. 2, 1988.

PHILLIPS, GAIL. *The Imagery of* El libro de buen amor. Madison: Hispanic Seminary of Medieval Studies, 1983.

PICCOLOMINI, AENEAS SILVIUS (PIUS II). *The Goodli History of the Ladye Lucres.* Edited by E. J. Morrall. Oxford: Oxford University Press, 1996.

PICCUS, JULES. "Consejos y consejeros en el *Libro del cauallero Zifar.*" *Nueva Revista de Filología Hispánica* 16 (1962).

PINAULT, DAVID. *Story-telling Techniques in the* Arabian Nights. Leiden: E. J. Brill, 1992.

PLATTER, CHARLES. "The Artificial Whore: George Buchanan's *Apologia pro Lena.*" In *Sex and Gender in Medieval and Renaissance Texts: The Latin Tradition.* Edited by Barbara K. Gold, Paul Allen Miller, and Charles Platter, 207-222. Albany: State University of New York, 1997.

PLAUTI, TITI MACCI. *Mostellaria* Edited by Frank R. Merrill. London: Macmillan, 1972.

Plautus in Five Volumes. Edited by Paul Nixon. London: The Loeb Classical Library, 1928 and 1932.

Poetics of Love in the Middle Ages: Texts and Contexts. Edited by Moshe Lazar and Norris J. Lacy. Virginia: George Mason University Press, 1989.

POLAK, LUCIE. "*Tristan* and *Vīs and Ramin*," *Romania* 95 (1974) 216-234.

PONCHONT, MAX. *Tibulle et les auteurs du Corpus Tibulliamnum.* Paris: Les Belles-Lettres, 1924.

Primeras jornadas: estudios de Frontera Alcalá la Real y el Arcipreste de Hita. Edited by Francisco Toro Caballos y José Rodríguez Molina. Jaén, 1996.

PROPERTIUS, SEXTUS AURELIUS. *Elegies I-IV.* Edited by W. A. Camps. Cambridge: Cambridge University Press, 1965.

PUYOL Y ALONSO, JULIO. *El Arcipreste de Hita.* Madrid: Sucesora de M. Minuesa de los Ríos, 1906.

QUERUEL, DANIELLE, ED. *Amour et chevalerie dans les romans de Chrétien de Troyes: actes du colloque de Troyes (27-29 Mars 1992).* Paris: Diffusion Les Belles lettres, 1995.

READ, MALCOLM K. "Fernando de Rojas' Vision of the Birth and Death of Language." *Modern Language Notes* XCIII (1978) 163-175.

READ, MALCOLM. *The Birth and Death of Language: Spanish Literature and Linguistics (1300-1700).* Madrid: Porrúa Turanzas, 1983.

REYNOLDS, L. D. *Scribes and Scholars: A Guide to the Transmission of Greek and Latin Literature.* New York: Oxford University Press, 1991.

RICO, FRANCISCO. "Sobre el origen de la autobiografía en el *Libro de buen amor.*" *Anuario de estudios medievales* 4 (1967) 301-325.

RIFFATERRE, MICHAEL. "L'intertexte inconnu." *Littérature* 41 (1981) 5-7.

ROBATHAN, D. M. *The Pseudo-Ovidian* De Vetula. Amsterdam: A. M. Hakkert, 1968.

ROBERT, J. N. *Les plaisirs à Rome.* Paris: Belles Lettres, 1983.

ROBERTSON, D. W. JR. *A Preface to Geoffrey Chaucer.* Princeton University Press: 1962.

RODRÍGUEZ PUÉRTOLAS, JULIO. *Juan Ruiz, Arcipreste de Hita.* Madrid: EDAF, 1978.

ROJAS, FERNANDO DE. *La Celestina, tragicomedia de Calisto y Melibea.* Edited by Dorothy S. Severin. Madrid: Alianza Editorial, 1990.

ROSENTHAL, FRANZ. "Sources for the Role of Sex in Medieval Muslim Society." in *Society and the Sexes in Medieval Islam,* edited by Afaf Lutfi al-Sayyid-Marsot, 3-22. Los Angeles: Gustave E. von Grunebaum Center for Near Eastern Studies, UCLA, 1977.

ROUHI, LEYLA. "'...y otros treynta officios:' The Definition of a Medieval Woman's Work in *La Celestina.*" *Celestinesca* (1999), forthcoming.

—. "Trotaconventos, Doña Garoça, and the Dynamics of Dialectical Reasoning." *Bulletin of Hispanic Studies,* LXXVI (1999), forthcoming.

RUIZ, JUAN. *Libro de buen amor.* Edited by A. Blecua. Barcelona: Planeta, 1983.

RŪMĪ, JALĀL AL-DĪN. *Masnavī-ye Ma'navī.* Edited by R. A. Nicholson. Teheran: Amīr Kabīr, 1984.

RUSSELL, PETER E. "La magia como tema integral de la *Tragicomedia de Calisto y Melibea.*" *Studia philologica: Homenaje a Dámaso Alonso, III,* 337-354. Madrid: Gredos, 1963.

SAINTE-MAURE, BENOÎT DE. *Le roman de Troie.* Paris: Firmin-Didot, 1904-1912.

SALOMON, MICHAEL. *The Mirror of Coitus: A Translation and Edition of the Fifteenth-Century "Speculum al foderi."* Madison: Hispanic Seminar on Medieval Studies, 1990.

SÁNCHEZ CASTAÑER, FRANCISCO. "Antecedentes celestinescos en las Cantigas de Santa María." *Mediterráneo, Guión de literatura* 1, 4 (1943) 33-90.

SÁNCHEZ ORTEGA, MARÍA HELENA. "Sorcery and Eroticism in Love Magic." In *Cultural Encounters: the Impact of the Inquisition in Spain and the New World,* edited by Anne J. Cruz and Mary Elizabeth Perry, 58-93. Los Angeles: University of California Press, 1991.

SCHAUBER, ELLEN, AND ELLEN SPOLSKY, "The Consolation of Alison: The Speech Acts of the Wife of Bath." *Centrum* 5 (1977) 20-34.

SCHLAM, CARL C. "Sex and Sanctity: the Relationship of Male and Female in the *Metamorphoses*." In *Aspects of Apuleius'* Golden Ass, edited by B. L. Hijmans Jr. and R. Th. van der Paardt, 95-105. Groningen: Bouma's Boekhuis, 1978.

—. *The* Metamorphoses *of Apuleius*. Chapel Hill: The University of North Carolina Press, 1992.

SCHLECHTA-WESSEHERD, OTTOKAR DE. *Jussuf und Suleicha*. Vienna: Druck und verlag von C. Gerold's sohn, 1889.

The Sea of Precious Virtues – Bahr al-Favā'id: a Medieval Islamic Mirror for Princes. Translated by Julie Scott Meisami. Salt Lake City: The University of Utah Press, 1991.

SEEBASS-LINGGI, CLAUDIA. *Lecture d'Érec: traces épiques et troubadouresques dans le conte de Chrétien de Troyes*. New York: Peter Lang, 1996.

SEIBERT, ILSE. *Woman in Ancient Near East*. Translated by Marianne Herzfeld. London: George Prior Publishers, 1975.

SEVERIN, DOROTHY SHERMAN. *Tragicomedy and Novelistic Discourse in* Celestina. Cambridge: Cambridge University Press, 1989.

—. "Celestina as a Comic Figure." In *Fernando de Rojas and* Celestina. Celestina: *Approaching the Fifth Centenary*, edited by Ivy A. Corfis and Joseph T. Snow, 165-181. Madison: Hispanic Seminary of Medieval Studies, 1993.

SHAARAWI, HUDA. *Harem Years: Memoirs of an Egyptian Feminist (1879-1924)*. Translated by Margot Badran. New York: The Feminist Press at the City University of New York, 1986.

SHACKLETON BAILEY, D. R. *Propertiana*. Cambridge: Cambridge University Press, 1956.

SHAHRI, JAFAR. *Tārikh-e Ejtemā'iye Teherān-e Qadīm*. Teheran: Ismailian Publishers, 1990.

SHIPLEY, GEORGE. "Authority and Experience in *La Celestina*." *Bulletin of Hispanic Studies* 62 (1985) 95-111.

—. "El natural de la raposa: un proverbio estratégico de *La Celestina*," *Nueva Revista de Filología Hispánica* XXIII (1974) 35-64.

SHOSHAN, BOAZ. "High Culture and Popular Culture in Medieval Islam." In *Studia Islamica* LXXIII (1991) 67-109.

SNOW, JOSEPH T. La Celestina *by Fernando de Rojas: an Annotated Bibliography of World Interest 1930-1985*. Madison: Hispanic Seminary of Medieval Studies, 1985.

—. La Celestina *by Fernando de Rojas: an Annotated Bibliography of World Interest 1899-1999*, forthcoming.

SPONSLER, LUCY A. *Women in Medieval Spanish Epic & Lyric Traditions*. Lexington: The University Press of Kentucky, 1975.

STEARNS SCHENK, MARY JANE. *The Fabliaux: Tales of Wit and Deception*. Indiana: Purdue University Monographs in Romance Languages 24, 1987.

SULLIVAN, J. P. *Propertius: A Critical Introduction*. Cambridge: Cambridge University Press, 1976.

TAINE, H. A. *History of English Literature*. London: Chatto and Windus, 1876.

TATUM, JAMES. *Apuleius and* The Golden Ass. Ithaca: Cornell University Press, 1979.

THOMAS, KEITH. *Religion and the Decline of Magic*. New York: Scribner, 1971.

AL-TIFĀCHĪ, AHMAD. *Les Délices des coeurs*. Translated by René R. Khawam. Paris: Phébus, 1981.

TORO GARLAND, FERNANDO DE. "*La Celestina* y *Las mil y una noches*." *Revista de Literatura* 29 (1966) 5-33.

TROYES, CHRÉTIEN DE. *Yvain: (Le Chevalier au Lion)*. Edited by T. B. W. Reid. Manchester: Manchester University Press, 1967.

TUTTLE HANSEN, ELAINE. *Chaucer and the Fictions of Gender*. Berkeley: University of California Press, 1992.

URBINA, EDUARDO. "Now you see it, now you don't: The Antithesis *corteza/meollo* in the *Libro de buen amor*." In *Florilegium Hispanicum: Medieval and Golden Age Studies Pre-*

sented to Dorothy Clotelle Clarke, edited by John S. Geary, 139-150. Madison: Hispanic Seminary of Medieval Studies, 1983.

V semana de estudios medievales, Nájera 1994. Logroño: Instituto de Estudios riojanos, 1995.

VADET, JEAN-CLAUDE. *L'esprit courtois en Orient: les cinq premiers siècles de l'Hégire*. Paris: Maisonneuve et Larousse, 1968.

VALBUENA, OLGA LUCÍA. "Sorceresses, Love Magic, and the Inquisition of Linguistic Sorcery in *Celestina*." *Publications of the Modern Language Association of America* 109, 2 (March 1994) 207-225.

VANOYEKE, VIOLAINE. *La prostitution en Grèce et à Rome*. Paris: Les Belles Lettres, 1990.

VASVARI, LOUISE O. "Festive Phallic Discourse in the *Libro del Arcipreste*." *La Corónica* 22:2 (Spring 1994) 89-117.

—. "Why is Doña Endrina a Widow? Traditional Culture and Textuality in the *Libro de buen amor*." In *Upon my Husband's Death: Widows in the Literature and Histories of Medieval Europe*, edited by Louise Mirrer, 259-287. Ann Arbor: University of Michigan, 1992.

VI simposio internacional de mudejarismo. Teruel: Centro de Estudios Mudéjares, 1995.

WACK, MARY FRANCES. "The *Liber de heros morbo* of Johannes Afflacius and Its Implications for Medieval Love Conventions." *Speculum* 62/2 (1987) 324-344.

—. *Lovesickness in the Middle Ages*. Philadelphia: University of Pennsylvania Press, 1990.

WALKER, ROGER M. "'Con miedo de la muerte la miel non es sabrosa': Love, Sin and Death in the *Libro de buen amor*." In *Libro de buen amor Studies*, edited by G. B. Gybbon-Moneypenny, 231-252. London: Tamesis, 1970.

WALLACE, DAVID. *Giovanni Boccaccio: Decameron*. Cambridge: Cambridge University Press, 1991.

WALSH, JOHN K. "The names of the Bawd in the 'Libro de buen amor.'" In *Florilegium Hispanicum: Medieval and Golden Age Studies Presented to Dorothy Clotelle Clark*, edited by John S. Geary, 151-164. Madison: Hispanic Seminary of Medieval Studies, 1983.

AL-WASSA'. *El libro del brocado*. Edited by Teresa Garulo. Clásicos Alfaguara, Madrid: 1990.

WHEELER, ARTHUR LESLIE. "Erotic Teaching in Roman Elegy and the Greek Sources, Part I." *Classical Philology* 5 (1910) 440-450; "Part II" *Classical Philology* 6 (1911) 57-77.

WILLIAMS, GORDON. "Some Aspects of Roman Marriage Ceremonies and Ideals." *Journal of Roman Studies* 48 (1958) 16-30.

—. *Change and Decline: Roman Literature in the Early Empire*. Berkeley: University of California Press, 1978.

WINDEATT, B. A., ed. *Boccaccio's* Il Filostrato *and Geoffrey* Chaucer's Troilus and Criseyde. New York: Longman, 1984.

WISEMAN, T. P. *Catullus and His World*. Cambridge: Cambridge University Press, 1985.

WOLTERBEEK, MARC. *Comic Tales of the Middle Ages, an Anthology and Commentary*. Connecticut: Greenwood Press, 1991.

Women in the Ancient World: The Arethusa Papers. Edited by J. Peradotto and J. P. Sullivan. Albany: State Univeristy of New York Press, 1984.

WRIGHT, STEVEN ALLEN. "Literary Influence in Medieval Literature: Chaucer and the *Roman de la Rose*." Ph.D. Diss., Indiana University, 1986.

ZAHAREAS, ANTHONY N. *The Art of Juan Ruiz, Archpriest of Hita*. Madrid: Estudios de Literatura Española, 1965.

ZUMTHOR, PAUL. "Intertextualité et mouvance." *Littérature* 41 (1981) 8-16.

—. "Notes en marge du traité de l'amour de André le Chapelain." *Zeitschrift für Romanische Philologie* 63 (1943) 178-191.

—. *Langue, texte, énigme*. Paris: Éditions du Seuil, 1975.

INDEX

Entries are filed letter-by-letter. Book titles and non-English words are in italics. Boldface locators indicate extensive treatment of a topic.

www.ingramcontent.com/pod-product-compliance
Lightning Source LLC
LaVergne TN
LVHW080847300926
849162LV00003B/352
* 9 7 8 9 0 0 4 1 1 2 6 8 1 *